A Myrtle Among Reeds

A Guide to the
History and Nature of Jewish Prayer

DAVID PRASHKER

THE ARGAMAN PRESS

The Argaman Press

ISBN:0615917666
ISBN-13:9780615917665

DEDICATION

To Elliott, Eliot and Sam, three high school students who helped me lead services over many years, and who taught me more about the realities and the significance of Jewish life than any of the many Rabbis I have known and worked and studied with, Orthodox, Conservative or Reform.

CONTENTS

"Was du geschlagen, Zu Gott wird es dich tragen – whatever has cost you a struggle will lead you to God."

Gustav Mahler, 2nd Symphony

"I heard my soul singing behind a leaf; I plucked the leaf, but then I heard it singing behind a veil. I tore the veil, but then I heard it singing behind a wall. I broke the wall, and I heard my soul singing against me. I built up the wall, mended the curtain, but I could not put back the leaf. I held it in my hand and I heard my soul singing mightily against me. This is what it is like to study without a friend."

Leonard Cohen: The Book Of Mercy

Two simple allegorical responses to those who demand proof of the existence of God.

One: Fill a glass with water. Pour in a handful of salt. Wait till the salt has been absorbed completely, until you are certain it pervades every drop of water, until it has become invisible. Now take out the salt."

Two: Ask an atheist if he believes that the stars are ever-present in the sky. Take him outside when the sky is at its brightest. Ask him to point to any of the constellations.

From the sayings of the Datsmay (Reb David Tsvi Meir ben Ya'akov)

PREFACE

In April 1990 I took up the post of Housemaster at Polack's, the Jewish boarding house at Clifton College in Bristol, England. It was a teaching post for which my experience and background hadn't really equipped me. As well as teaching an academic subject in the school - in my case English, for which I was qualified - it required the pastoral supervision of several score of teenage boys and girls, the boys living in my house alongside my wife and children; plus the leadership of daily synagogue and all other aspects of their Jewish lives. I had no training for this, either as a Rabbi or a teacher of Jewish Studies. My only visits to synagogue in the previous twenty years had been as a tourist. I entered with the taste of pork on my lips, not entirely certain about the status of my faith, and a failed Zionist – I had left Israel disillusioned five years previously. My Biblical Hebrew, abandoned after my orthodox *Bar Mitzvah*, was at best rusty; my knowledge of modern Ivrit, the reinvented language of contemporary Israel, amounted only to the spoken. I had brought with me neither skull cap nor prayer shawl, for I simply hadn't remembered from my childhood that these garments would be needed. And yet, there I was, the world's worst yet most committed Jew, employed not quite as the Rabbi though certainly as the Rav, the father-figure to a generation of teenage boys and girls, many of whom felt exactly as I did about synagogue - and didn't lack the forwardness to stand up and express it. But where they could choose neither to learn nor to participate, my duties and responsibilities placed me on a learning curve that would have taxed the angel at Penuel.

I was raised in a traditional Jewish home, one that was entirely comfortable with its high level of hypocrisy. On Saturdays we avoided synagogue while going to support our favourite soccer team religiously; but Sundays my mother had a WIZO meeting, my father a bridge tournament to raise funds for Soviet Jewry, and I was at B'nai B'rith, the Jewish youth movement. At home we distinguished milk from meat, down to the very drying-up cloth, but away from home we were accomplished at distinguishing langoustes from mere langoustines, and were amongst the earliest masters of the esoteric art of eating pork spare ribs with chopsticks. In preparation for my *Bar Mitzvah* I'd been thrown out of three Orthodox Sunday Schools, because my father wasn't having his son wear *tsitsit* or lay *tefillin*, but no way was he sending me to those *goyim* in the Reform movement either. After my *Bar Mitzvah* I swore never again to set foot inside a *shul* or have anything to do with Judaism - and proved it by becoming, at sixteen the Chair of my local B'nai B'rith chapter, at eighteen a volunteer in the Yom Kippur War, at twenty a campaigner for Soviet Jewry, at twenty-five a kibbutznik on the Lebanese border, and by the time I was thirty the author of four novels, all of course on Jewish themes. And then I came to Polack's, as Housemaster and spiritual leader.

Five and a half years in Israel had made me fluent in modern Ivrit; and because the modern was founded on the classical when it was reinvented at the beginning of the 20th century, it didn't take long to learn the basic prayers verbatim, first to read, gradually to chant. By the end of five years there wasn't a service that I couldn't lead, even allowing for complex variations to the ritual, a full moon falling on the Sabbath of a leap year, a new moon on the interim morning of a pilgrim festival. Why, I could *daven* every inch of Yom Kippur without so much as swallowing, all the way from *Kol Nidre* to *Ne'ilah*! And all the rest could be evinced from books - history, culture, laws. Ten years after I arrived, naïve and ignorant, at Polack's, the learning curve had not yet flattened out - nor will it ever - but the steepness of the curve had started flattening. To teach others, I first had to teach myself, and the evidence of GCSE and A level results, the quality of Jewish life at Polack's, the success of DAVAR, the Jewish Institute in Bristol which I co-founded in 1994, provided testimony. It had taken ten years, but I felt that I knew, by no means everything, but everything that was necessary to the job. That is to say, I knew "what", and "how" and "when". It had never once occurred to me to question "why".

Daily morning service, plus Friday evenings and the whole of shabbat morning, every festival that fell in term-time, Yom ha-Sho'ah, Independence Day, Grace before as well as after meals - after a while it's very easy for prayer to become little more than a habit, a routine like washing one's teeth, a mechanical function in which one mouths the words, but chewing, never savouring – rather like school food. The one who prays without his heart in it becomes a function of the liturgy, a part of the furniture of the synagogue, inexorable but inanimate. Ten years after I came to Polack's, I began to feel this happening to me. And I didn't like it. Judaism speaks of *kavanah*, the intention behind prayer, and I was aware that my intention was increasingly to get through the service without losing my temper with those who constantly chattered and fidgeted and interrupted. And I didn't like it.

Apparently, I had reached the end of that particular phase of learning, and the time had come to stagnate or develop. When I began, I had needed to learn the letters of the alphabet, then whole words, then the tunes that accompanied the words, and then the correct order and especially the variations of the words in given circumstances. Whether following the parallel English translation, or simply from understanding the Hebrew, I had also come to grasp the meanings of the words. But what of the meanings of the meanings? Where did the words come from? Who put them there, and why, and when? I found myself needing to understand the nature of my habit, in the way a caffeine addict will explore a dozen brands of tea, and want to know where the leaves were grown, how composted, where packaged. So with these prayers. Why did we stand or sit, why sing or speak or chant, why silently, why in this order, why on these days; why, in short, did we repeat day after day this strange and anachronistic ritual that seemed to occupy no sensible place at all in the rational, technological world that we inhabited between prayer services, but which nonetheless gave to our lives a spiritual dimension that was miraculously deeper and more personal even than listening to Mahler or to Leonard Cohen? But why, why? Why these silly superstitions like kissing a dropped prayer book or covering the Torah scroll while blessing the one who has been called up to read from it? Why compulsory silences at certain times? Why so much anarchic but tolerated coming and going, and then, at certain times, an absolute injunction against entering or exiting the synagogue? Why keep the head covered in synagogue when every other religion removes its hat? Why the variations in dogma (and in dogmatism) between communities? Why? Where was it written? Did God tell us to do these things at Sinai? And if not God, then on whose authority? I had become deeply curious, and deeply puzzled too. Doubts as to the purpose and validity of all this liturgy and ritual, doubts harboured secretly for years and years, unballasted themselves and floated to the surface.

As if this wasn't enough, my research threw up a question, bigger in its implications than any I had yet asked. When Israel was conquered by the Romans, and the Temple destroyed, the people enslaved or despatched into exile, the surviving Rabbis set up a "substitute", to hold the Jewish nation together "in the interim", until we returned to Israel, and reclaimed our sovereignty. So Talmudic Judaism was invented, and we survived and thrived for 2,000 years. But in May 1948 that interim ended, the substitute was no longer needed, the prayers and ceremonies were surely rendered obsolete. Why, then, are we still fielding the substitute? Why are we not engaged in creating a new Judaism, for the new conditions. Why are we still asking God for what we already have – and in many cases have rejected?

I could have gone to the Rabbis, of course, whether the contemporary *amora'im* and *tana'im* or the greater sages of the past, but they would have given me their answers, and I needed mine. So I began to keep a notebook, working through the prayers one by one, seeking their source, their intention, their raison d'être in a world that now has Israel; learning about their authors, trying to understand how the words had changed over time, and how they might now change, as we answer the challenge of a restored Israel. This piously irreverent book - at once an act of faith and a response to that challenge - is the consequence.

CHAPTER ONE: PRELIMINARIES

Hashkamat Ha Boker - Upon Waking

Modeh Ani

'Modeh ani lephanecha, melech chay ve-kayam, she-hechezarta bi nishmatay be-chemlah, rabah emunatecha."

I do not propose to set the Hebrew text - if only because it would occupy too much space. Those who can't read Hebrew would find it mystifying at best, patronising at worst. Those who can read Hebrew are warmly encouraged to follow me through their own copy of the prayer book – I'm working with the Revised Singer and the new Art Scroll, both "orthodox" *siddurim*, and with *Mishkan T'filah*, the new Reform Prayer Book. But this is not a denominational critique; this is an exegesis of the traditional prayers by a Jew who regards denominations as a way of dividing Jews, when we should be seeking paths of unity.

I will, however, present many of the prayers in transliteration: to give a point of reference to my observations; to provide a support for those who wish to learn the Hebrew; to convey the musicality of what was always intended to be voiced, not read in silence. No phonetic system can ever be perfect, and particularly with Biblical Hebrew, which is spoken in a hundred different modern and mediaeval accents, none of which are accurate to the original. My own dialect is the modern Israeli, based on the Sephardi, but infused with Polish Ashkenazi from my childhood. Those who are dissatisfied are reminded of the words of the second Rabban Gamliel, Shimon, who said: "All my life I grew up among scholars and I discovered that nothing is more fitting to a man than silence." Hamlet, as I recall, said much the same, albeit in slightly different words.

'Modeh ani lephanecha, melech chay ve-kayam, she-hechezarta bi nishmatay be-chemlah, rabah emunatecha."

"I stand gratefully before you, God who lives, whose existence I acknowledge, for restoring me to my soul, and with compassion. Your faith in me is boundless."

With this, and many other prayers, I shall offer my own translation, something perhaps more modern than the conventions of the traditional versions, something perhaps larger, not in the spiritual sense, but in the circle of containment for the multiplicity of meanings in the Hebrew. So, here, for example, most translations thank God "for restoring my soul to me" - but only because there is nothing in the English language, other than this gloss, to explain the *dvaita*, the duality of the restoration. So, also, with the closing phrase, normally rendered as "Your faithfulness to me". But what is faith, if not an expression of loyalty to an untenable idea?

Those who wish to question the validity of my translations are invited to return to the sources, and to examine the meanings for themselves. They will find, I think, that there are no inaccuracies in my renditions, only space for disagreement over my interpretations. Good. This is how it should be. The history of Jewish thought and prayer is the history of passionate disagreement, a dialectic of definition (the lack of an absolute conclusion suggests I ought to say "a dialectic of indefinition"), a dynamic founded precisely upon contention. Was it not the very struggle with the Man of Penuel that first created Israel? Hillel versus Shammai. Pharisee versus Sadducee. Babylon versus Jerusalem. *Hasid* versus *Mitnaged.* Orthodox versus Reform. We argue because we care. This too is an expression of our faith, and of our faithfulness.

"Modeh ani lephanecha, melech chay ve-kayam, she-hechezarta bi nishmatay be-chemlah, rabah emunatecha."

"I stand gratefully before you, God who lives, whose existence I acknowledge, for restoring to me my soul, and with compassion. Your faith in me is boundless."

With these words every Jew should begin each morning, reciting even while he[1] still lies in his bed (as God isn't actually mentioned in the prayer by name, it is permissible to pray while dormant), before he speaks a single word, liturgical or vernacular, before he thinks a single thought, secular or unsecular, before the daily world has replaced dream in his consciousness.

Why grateful? And what for? Implicit in the prayer is the linking of sleep with death, the soul with consciousness. The body sleeps, but the soul departs. Where to? Gehenna? Is Gehenna then the place in which we dream, and thereby cleanse and purge ourselves each night, to come back sinless in the morning and begin again? What an astonishing notion: daily

[1] For Reform Jews, gender is a major issue, women having an equal status in prayer with men; if I have chosen to retain the masculine throughout, it is only because women in orthodox Judaism are excused the time-bound obligations of prayer

redemption, a perpetual *Yom Kippur*, requiring no Messiah but only God's infinite compassion - infinite in time as well as scale. And if the *Lilim*, the night demons, should attack us, if Lilith herself, the night-demoness whom the *Talmudic* Rabbis say was Adam's first helpmeet before Eve, if Lilith should turn dream into nightmare, then how much more purgative the sleep, how much greater the compassion. Sleep, then, as spiritual therapy. Lord, favour me with cat-naps in the day-time too.

Gratitude is the point here – many prayers are not really prayers at all, but forms of thanksgiving. Sleep hasn't murdered me. In sleep I haven't died. To wake up with my faculties intact is to experience the personal miracle. The daily *Pesach* after the nightly *Yom Kippur*. Sinai after slavery. With a strong hand and an outstretched arm, God brings us from the darkness that has plagued us, equally with nightmares and sweet dreams, from the underworld, the netherworld, the realm of limbo. And yet. And yet. Didn't God also guard us in our sleep? Are we inferring, are we accusing, a period of Divine absence? No, of course not. He was there – it's we who were temporarily absent, unaware of Him. Even in our sleep He guarded us. And shouldn't we also praise Him for this? The answer to this quandary, I know, lies where modern orthodoxy doesn't wish to find it. To thank God for bringing us out of darkness into light, is to thank a male deity, the sun-god of the Priestly Blessing, the one who turns His face to shine upon us. The guardian of the night is Yah, the triple-goddess of the new, the full, the waning moon, whose queen is Lilith and whose serving-maids the *Lilim*; Delilah in her Danite incarnation. Lilith, deposed from the double-throne by the patriarchal Rabbis, reduced to ghostly status, a mere spirit, albeit Holy Ghost, Divine Numen, the Radiance of Heaven, the *Shechinah*: once androgynous, now strictly feminine, indeed the principle of femininity itself: the Queen, the Sabbath Bride. *Va-anachnu nevarech Yah* - and we will praise Yah. But not yet, not now. In the closing lines of the *Ashrey*, and in *Hallel*. At the appropriate moment.

I have translated "*melech*" as God, not King - the original, Moloch, was both. But one metaphor for the Universal Pulse is quite sufficient. And as to "*chay ve-kayam*". It's David's epithet, of course, sung by every Jewish child for centuries: "*David, Melech Yisrael, chay, chay ve-kayam*". But I prefer to draw out the full meaning, however prolix. A God who isn't supernatural so much as super-metaphysical - who transcends time and space, but who inhabits, who *is*, the physical substance of which creation is compounded, the pre-atom of the Big Bang. What I like is the mutuality, the notion that God restores my soul because He has faith in me - greater faith, I venture, than mine in Him, or even mine in me.

The *Modeh* is in Hebrew, an abbreviated version of the *Elohay Neshama*, written, probably, in the 17th century, first printed as an addendum to the *Seder ha-Yom* of 1695; but like so many prayers it has its Yiddish rendering, and of all Yiddish songs, the version of the *Modeh* sung by the French *kletzmerist* Moshe Leiser is the most moving I have ever heard - perhaps because it's also the most plaintive. Leiser sings the *Modeh* itself as the chorus, in a Yiddish accent. He also adds, interpolates, these verses:

"Oi Gott, oi Gott mitt tsoren, keek vus is mitt dein kind; eyn der fremd gevoren, shveyre yuren, länder vieleh, ich gedenk nischt mir di tefillah.

"Oi keek, oi keek, ich bin evek dich suchen oyf prayte veygen; ich bin noch ying, umer fahren; es kennen fremde menschen mir vernahren."

"O God, O God of sorrows, look what has become of your child. In a foreign land, difficult years, so many countries, I can no longer remember my prayers.

"Look! Just look! I've gone off in search of you, along crooked paths. I am still young, inexperienced. Strangers could lead me astray."

And then the gratitude, the Hebrew words sung with a Yiddish intonation:

"*Moydeh ani, oi moydeh ani*!"

The song of the assimilating Jew. The Lord's song in a strange land. Still sung today, but as nostalgia for an exile we no longer inhabit, even though many continue to name as dispersal – the Diaspora- what is now really ex-patriacy.

What was it ibn-Gvirol wrote, in Malaga around 1050, about his illness in fact, not about the *Modeh*, though it might as well have been? "Consider my song as my redemption, and let my dreams ransom me from death." Yes, we need such songs, new songs, for our redemption from two thousand years of exile, to celebrate our restoration in the *yishuv*, the land of Israel.

Reyshit Chachma - The Source of Wisdom

Judaism may be a spiritual religion, but it doesn't hide from the acts of the body. Every human incident owes its origins to God, who created Mankind for a purpose, however obscure and indecipherable. So even the first human act upon arising from one's bed, the act of ablution, is consecrated with a prayer; though for delicacy the prayer is named for its aftermath, the washing of the hands.

"*Reyshit chachma yirat Adonay; sechel tov le-chol oseyhem. Tehilato omedet la-ad. Torah tsivah lanu Moshe morashah kehilat Ya'akov. Shema, beni, musar avicha, ve-al titosh torat imecha. Torah, tehi emunati, ve-El Shaddai be-ezrati. Baruch shem kavod malchuto le-olam va-ed.*"

The attached ritual is abstruse and shamanistic, akin to enacting magic. Take the vessel of water in the right hand (Mosaic and Rabbinic laws make no allowances for taps and faucets; but we could easily add taps and faucets), pass it to the left hand and pour water over the right. Then with the right hand pour water over the left. This is repeated three times. No soap is mentioned, though this doesn't preclude its use (all allusions to soap inevitably end up in the demoniacal laboratories of Auschwitz, where soap was made from human skin, boiled down) but perhaps the ritual is less about cleanliness than about libation, a mimetic reminder of the duty of sacrifice – the word, in Latin, means "to make holy". Nor does the attached blessing in any way inform the ritual, though clearly these words constitute as good a set of phrases for the starting of a Jewish day as any other that might be considered. And if we wanted to bring this prayer into contemporary meaningfulness, we have only to consider the extraordinary watering of the Negev desert, to make it fertile, and the draining of the Hula and the Jezreel swamps, to make them habitable. Blessed Art Thou O Lord Our God, Who Has Given Me Clean Water For My Hands, And For My Harvest, And Who Has Preserved My Skin In Good Health.

The words as they stand at present are, in English: "The source of wisdom is the fear of God. May all deeds be informed by common sense. May His praise endure forever. May the *Torah* in which Moses instructed us be the heritage of the congregation of Jacob. May you take heed, my son, of the morals of your father; may you not reject the teaching of your mother. May the *Torah* be my faith, and *El Shaddai*, Almighty God, my helper. Blessed be His glorious name, and may His kingdom last for ever and for ever."

The opening three phrases come from Psalm 111:7, the first of innumerable bridges thus built between the *Talmud* and the *Tanach* - the "Old" Testament as non-Jews would dismiss it. To Moses, sacrifice was everything; the Tent and the Tabernacle which would become the Temple were the spiritual heart of Judaism, with the Cohen – originally Moses' own brother Aaron - its High Priest. To the Prophets, God was sated and wanted no more sacrifices; only obedience. To the *Talmudists* the Law was everything, the Rabbi its authorised teacher and interpreter, the *yeshiva* and the synagogue its twofold home, the act of obedience transformed into, confirmed by, the continuous acts of observance. So did Judaism evolve.

But each phase of evolution depends on its precursors, while constant retrospection validates the new. Traditions may only be bettered when they have first been mastered – as the paintings of Matisse or the symphonies of Shostakovich likewise confirm. These bridges become bulwarks and buttress stones and barbicans. Even those facets which *Talmudic* Judaism rejects may serve as testimony and witness to the legitimacy of rejection, and of replacement. So the Biblical Psalms inform the *Talmudic* liturgy. So the *piyyut* of the middle ages is rooted in the *shirim* of the period of the Judges. So the source remains constant, and is available for renewal.

The set of phrases from "May you take heed" to "my helper" do not appear in the Art Scroll, but are in the Revised Singer. I am at a loss to identify them. I can say of them only that they reflect the fifth commandment of the ten, to honour your father and your mother, and the first commandment of the *Shema*, that you teach your children diligently, and that *El Shaddai*, "God of my Breast", was Abraham's name for God (this isn't the place, I know, to argue this particular controversy, but *El Shaddai* almost certainly meant "the multi-breasted god", which was precisely how the ancient Canaanites and others of the region visualised the mother goddess). Represented by his initial letter *sheen* (ש), His is the name we make when we spread the phylacteries around our fingers, His is the name we make when we raise our fingers in the ritual bath, His is the name the *Cohanim* make when they utter the *Yevarechecha*, the priestly blessing, His is the name inscribed on the cover of the *mezuzah*. It shouldn't be ignored either, that the role of the mother in teaching the children is exactly equal to that of the father; and not surprising, since this is how they were created.

The final phrase, "*Baruch shem kavod, malchuto le-olam va-ed*", recited in a whisper save only on *Yom Kippur*, belongs not to Man but to the angels, for this is the line they interject when the *Shema* is recited in heaven. Yes, but do they too, the angels, do they also perform the curious triple-ablution of the hands?

The *Shema* echoes and reverberates, fragments and reunifies, through every act of worship. Rightly, for it is the credo, the central testament of faith in Judaism. Like the One Thousand and One Nights, in which there's a tale for every night, and amongst them one tale which is itself the tale of the One Thousand and One Nights; like the legend of that dark and stormy night on which three robbers sat in a cave, and the story that one of them told was of a dark and stormy night on which three robbers sat in a cave; so the *Shema* is a structure that contains and recontains itself, over and over, eternally self-referential. Thus it commands the placing of *mezuzot* on the lintels of the doors; and inside each *mezuzah* is a parchment copy of the *Shema*. Thus it commands us to teach our children diligently. Teach what? Why the *Torah* of course, whose pivotal declaration of belief is precisely the *Shema*. Thus it commands us to bind our forearm and forehead with phylacteries - *tefillin*; and inside each phylactery, a parchment copy of the *Shema.*

Infinity is a mirror, reflected in a mirror.

Where the Chinese and the Russians make their self-containing dolls of alabaster, the Jews make theirs with words that transmit deeds into deeds that affirm words - with prayers.

✡

Levishat Tsitsit - Putting on the Fringed Vest

The third act of the morning is the donning of the *tsitsit* - something I confess I've never done. The commandment to wear *tsitsit* is contained in Numbers 15:38, in the third paragraph of the *Shema* (once again the self-referential commandment, eating its own tail):

"Speak to the children of Israel and tell them that they are to put *tsitsit* on the corners of their garments throughout their generations; and on the corners of the *tsitsit* a thread of purple. So these shall be your *tsitsit*, and when you look at them they will remind you of the laws of God, so you will perform them, and not follow [the desires of] your hearts and eyes which lead you into error."

The verse is probably as interesting to anthropologists as it is to theologians. It implies the common wearing of a four-cornered garment, a rectangle of cloth with a hole cut in the centre for the head. Where the four corners hung loose, the commandment required the tying of purple fringes. Garments with more or less than four corners did not require *tsitsit.* The style however is Greek, not Canaanite - one of many occasions when the text seems to hint at retrospective validation, that process by which later practices were posited in the mouth of Moses, to give them the special weight of *halachah* possessed by every ordinance of Sinai. The garment commonly worn today is a simple linen undershirt, known as the *tallit katan* or small prayer shawl. But this garment isn't obligatory. Only the *tsitsit* are obligatory. Any four-cornered garment may be sewn with fringes.

Why these fringes? A matter of symbolism, not ornamentation. The key passage is "when you look at them they will remind you of the laws of God, so you will perform them." The fringes are irrelevant, a mere memorandum, no more significant than a note left on the fridge. What matters is the remembering.

He who wears the *tallit katan*, the ritual undergarment, doesn't also wear the regular *tallit* - the prayer shawl - for prayer. Even holiness has its restrictions.

The literary critic in me can't resist observing the change from "they" in the first sentence, to "you" in the second. "They" implies only the generation of Moses, who received the commandment; "you" implies all generations, the recipients of the commandment and the inheritors of the legacy. In this way does the eternal become eternal, the universal universal.

This matter of the fringed vest continues to cause me doubts: even the merely symbolic must have some root. My suspicion is that the fringes were either something entirely different, or had some ancient value that was lost, either by consequence of the destruction of the Temple, or deliberately, when the Rabbis assumed unto themselves the authority of the *Cohanim*. What is the *tsitsit*? A tassel of embroidered linen in the shape of a pomegranate, hanging down like a pompon on a Persian coat. So it is explained - the simile notwithstanding - and so it has been worn for centuries. But Exodus 28:36 gives the High Priest a single *tsits*, and here it isn't a linen tuft at all, but a solid plate, a strip of metallic gold, shining on his forehead, with the words "*Kadesh l'Adonay* - sacred to God", engraved on it: a holy Mark of Cain. How do we get from this to the fringed vest? Or should each of us wear such gold plates, whether actually or symbolically, and not on the corners of our garments?

There are further references in the Scriptures. Psalm 132:18 gives *tsits* as a crown flourishing, by inference on the head of the Messiah. Job 14:2 has a similar meaning, a flower on this occasion doing the flourishing, whereas in Isaiah 28:4 it serves the opposite meaning, of a flower fading. Jeremiah 49:9 uses *tsits* to mean a wing, as in those a bird will fly with, and Ezekiel 9:3 has *tsits* as the forelock. What each of these has in common is a something fine and thin and dangling at the end - a wisp of hair, a corona of petals, the peaks of a crown, a tassel of embroidered linen. But none of them engraved, as the High Priest's forehead-plate was once engraved, right there where the head-piece of the *tefillin* is now laid. And none of them pomegranate pompons on the corners of a vest.

The thread of purple lace (there are three distinct shades of purple in the Bible, of which this is *techelet*, the bluest) also recalls the High Priest's headgear, for just two verses further on in Exodus 28, the same thread is sewn upon the mitre, and the mitre placed above the head of the *tefillin*, "that Aaron may bear the iniquity of the holy things, which the children of Israel shall hallow in all their holy gifts; and it shall always be upon his forehead, that they may be accepted before the Lord."

A Mark of Cain indeed! But how can the holy things be iniquitous?

Nevertheless, the evolution of the ritual garments is clear. The *tsitsit* has been modified, whether by Moses or the Rabbis, in order to place the crown of Aaron on the head of Israel. Symbolically, by wearing it upon our clothing. The *tsitsit* is the *tefillin* and the *tefillin* is the *tsitsit*, crown and thread, thread and crown. So each of us is rendered *kadesh l'Adonay*, sacred to God, holy.

The *Torah* tells us all to wear *tsitsit.* It does not specify the when, only the wearing. But since the purpose is to see them, and in the seeing to be reminded of the commandments, the Rabbis agreed that *tsitsit* need not be worn at night, since no one can see in sleep and therefore the point is moot. This became the tradition, though it isn't a law. However, in Judaism, traditions are inviolable, and so it acquired the status of a law. Since night is an element of time, this law must, of necessity, be categorised with all the other laws that speak of time; and since women are not obligated by commandments of time, women do not need to wear *tsitsit.* This too has become, by the same process, a law. Such is the marvellous methodology of *halachah.* The *Torah* tells us all to wear *tsitsit.* It doesn't specify the when, only the wearing. But because men do not need to wear *tsitsit* at night, women may never wear them. One of several occasions on which the fence around the law serves also as a *mechitsah.* One of the many *mechitsot* that could easily be torn down, or perhaps, as the orthodox like to do, made acceptable by declaring them an *eruv* - an urban area enclosed by a wire boundary that symbolically extends the private domain of Jewish households into public areas, permitting activities within it that are normally forbidden in public on the Sabbath. I shall no doubt say this more than once in this text, but the law of the *eruv* provides an orthodox base for many potential answers to the challenges of modernity and restoration in Israel, the position of women especially. A fence around the *Torah*, and then an *eruv*, metaphorical rather than physical, established by the fence.

The ritual for donning the *tallit katan* is almost as complex as that of washing the hands. First hold the garment in readiness, then inspect the *tsitsit* - if they're damaged, the garment is *pasul* and can't be worn. Having put on the *tallit*, each of the four *tsitsit* is taken in the hand (it isn't specified which hand), pressed to the lips, and kissed. Only then is the blessing recited. Only then are other clothes put on, with less care, inevitably.

Two prayers accompany the ritual. The first is a simple *berachah*, a benediction, acknowledging the commandment.

"Baruch atah Adonay eloheynu melech ha-olam, asher kidshanu be-mitzvotav, ve-tsivanu al mitzvat tsitsit."

"Blessed are you, O Lord our God, King of the Universe, who has sanctified us with His laws, and commanded us to keep the law of *tsitsit.*"

The second is apparently an extension of the first, a statement of humility, accepting the will of God, the requirement to keep all the commandments. But flawed. Flawed.

"*Yehi ratson mi-lephanecha, Adonay elohay ve-elohey avotay, she-teheh chashuvah mitzvat tsitsit lephanecha, ke-ilu kiyamtiha be-chol perateyha ve-dikdukeyha ve-chavnoteyha, vetaryag [613] mitzvot ha-teluyim ba. Amen selah.*"

"May it be your will, my God and God of my forefathers, that you regard my fulfilment of the commandment to wear *tsitsit* with the same worthiness that would accrue if I had fulfilled it in all its details, implications and intentions, along with the six hundred and thirteen commandments that depend on it."

Would...if! Would...if I had done it properly! Then even in donning the *tsitsit* there is an acknowledgement that they are not correct, that this is not the garment that we should be donning, this is not the *tsitsit* God intended, that some breach in the commandments has occurred. No wonder I'm so uncomfortable about wearing them.

But it isn't in fact in this that I find my spirit resolutely irresolute. God, I'm told, has given me free will, but it's expected that I shall exercise it only to resign my free will in favour of strict adherence to the fixed and immutable commandments (the Yezhov terror was propounded on precisely this same principle). No, this is a definition of servitude, not liberty - and perhaps that's why the word *avodah* means both worship and slavery. When I dress, I put on no *tsitsit.* So I approach God as I, as Man; and He may choose of His own free will to reject me, if He wishes, if it be His will.

So much ritual, ceremony, tradition, and the day not yet begun! We have already offered up several prayers, but we haven't yet begun to pray - or not in the sense that a Christian or a Moslem would understand the term, the formal structure of communal liturgy. All we have done is act within the world, and render certain actions holy, by adding our words to the Word. We've risen from our beds, visited the lavatory and washed, put on the ritual undergarment - but even within these banalities we have exposed the sacred. In Judaism there is a prayer for every feasible occasion. Or practically. A specific blessing when you put your clothes on - though only if they're new. A blessing before the orange juice (*Baruch atah Adonay eloheynu melech ha-olam* - this is the way all blessings begin - Blessed are you O Lord our God, King of the Universe - Creator of countless living beings with all their needs, for all the means that You have created to sustain the life of each of them, blessed be the ever-living one). Another before the cereal (*boreh miney mezonot*). A third for the fried egg on toast (*she-ha-kol niheyeh bidvaro* for the eggs, *motseh lechem min ha-arets* for the toast). Another for the fragrance of the flowers on the breakfast table (*boreh isvot ha-samim*). Still one more for the thunder roaring outside (*she-kocho u-gevurato maleh olam*), and a separate blessing when the lightning flashes (*oseh ma'aseh bereyshit*). Yet another if perchance you hear good news on the morning radio (*ha-tov ve-ha-meytiv*). The very same one if, as is more likely, you hear bad news on the morning radio (the principle of *Adonay natan Adonay lakach*, the Lord gives and the Lord takes away, applies; but so also does the principle of "justifying the judgement" which ought to rule out the practice of petitionary prayers). A special blessing for setting out for synagogue (too long to record in full here, it includes the ever-optimistic "deliver us from every enemy, ambush and danger on the road, and from all afflictions that trouble the world"). And two *berachot* of the highest order when you meet, in the entrance to the *shul*, a person distinguished in worldly learning (*she-natan mey-chachmato le-vassar va-dam*), and his friend who is a *chacham* in the *Torah* (*she-chalak mey-chachmato li-reyav*). This is by no means the complete list (in Shmuel Agnon's novel "The Bridal Canopy" the full list takes Rabbi Yudel more than five hundred pages just to get to lunch). If the rainstorm dries out to a rainbow, there is a blessing for that (*zocher ha-brit, ve-ne'eman bi-vrito, ve-kayam be-ma'amaro*). If you live near the ocean, or pass beautiful trees, or catch sight of an animal or a malformed person, if the trees are blossoming for the first time, if the woods are fragrant with early bluebells, if a shooting star should pass across the sky, if you're in the high mountains, in vast deserts, by the shores of the great ocean. If the day is the first of the new moon, a fast day, a slow day, the intermediate day of a pilgrim festival…and if you've drunk strong liquor, *baruch atah Adonay, melech ha-olam, she-ha-kol niheyeh bidvaro*, blessed are you O Lord our God, King of the Universe, by whose word all things exist…strangely the same gratitude for whisky as for eggs. Most Jewish prayer, as I have already commented, is simply a sacral way of saying thank you.

And anything may be either sacred or profane; or become both. Action may become prayer, prayer action. Our words, and the Word of God. A deed performed consciously or unconsciously, with negligence or the deepest intensity of inwardness. Even prayer may be uttered blithely. The true harmony of the self depends upon this balance of the inner and the outer life.

✡

Chapter Two: The Origins and Nature of Jewish Prayer

Ahavah Rabbah - Great Love

The ancientness of prayer, in something like the form that we think of it today, is attested in the *Torah*. In Genesis 20:17, in a strangely insufficient story that seems to reflect some ancient legend of the Mother Goddess, Abraham "prayed to God - *yitpalel el-ha-elohim*" for the restoration of fertility to the family of Avi-Melech. What words he used is not given, nor is it stated whether he stood, knelt or prostrated himself, though we can assume the latter. But in Genesis 18:22, after God had proclaimed the wickedness of Sodom and Gomorrah, "the men [who were angels] turned" from the place - an interesting phrase in the light of the Jewish concept of "*histir panav*" - and fled, while Abraham "stood before the Lord"; the mood of the Hebrew - "*odeynu omed*" - conveying something equally of defiance and of indignation, as though, like me with the *tsitsit*, this was an action that required a Man on his two feet, and not a servant on his belly. "And Abraham drew near and said, 'Will You also destroy the righteous with the wicked?'" This isn't prayer, this is litigation, a motion for breach of contract filed in the heavenly court. Because a covenant, even a covenant between Man and God, must be a relationship of relative equality, else it isn't a covenant at all but, like so many contracts of employment, a legal definition of vassalage. When Abraham speaks to God, he doesn't whine or whinge or wail, he doesn't plead or seek to propitiate with an opening stratagem of sacrifice or flattery; he stands before the bench, and states his case. And where he is demonstrably in the right, God acquiesces. "*Yesh din ve-yesh dayan* - there is a God, and there is Justice."

The books of Leviticus and Deuteronomy purport to a similar antiquity, in that they too form part of the *Torah* given by God to Moses on Mount Sinai. Yet the practices they describe belong to that period, up to a thousand years later, when sedentary Jews inhabited walled cities and worshipped at the Temple in Jerusalem, whereas the Mosaic refugees were desert wanderers who attended their nomad deity in a linen tent. Still, prayer is prayer. Leviticus 5:5 stipulates the practice of *Vidu'i* - confessional prayers to accompany the bringing of a sin-offering. Deuteronomy 26:5-15 provides the oldest formal liturgy, tantamount to a credo, a public recitation to accompany the triennial tithes and the annual first fruits: "And you shall speak and say before the Lord your God..." - a full fifteen verses avowing the duties incumbent upon the signatories to a formal covenant.

Probably of the same period, though the Bible theoretically separates them by a millennium, the Levites regarded the Psaltery as equivalent to a daily prayer book, and read, *inter alia*, the *Shema* and the Ten Commandments to the Temple congregation on a regular, possibly even a daily basis, as well as reciting the *Yevarechecha*, the Priestly Blessing (Numbers 6:22-27). But sacrifice remained the centrepiece of Temple *avodah*, and prayer is a Rabbinic not a Mosaic ordinance (*Berachot* 21a), which is to say that it was the Rabbis who fixed the times, the contents, the order, even the number of the services, where none had existed while there was still a Temple. So says Maimonides, who is never wrong. But Maimonides omits to put a name or date on this, allowing us to presume the *Talmudic* Rabbis, when in fact it was Ezra the Scribe, with the 120 men of the Great Assembly, around 485 BCE, when the Babylonian exiles were returning.

Before the *Talmudic* period, when Temple sacrifice was the focus of the cult, prayer tended to be flexible and spontaneous, without a fixed liturgy. *Berachot* 11b and 12a call those prayers recited in the Temple "*ahavah rabbah* - great love", a reference to the injunction in the *Shema* that "you shall love the Lord your God with all your heart and soul and might" - and suggest they included the repetition of the Ten Commandments, all three paragraphs of the *Shema*, the first three and the seventeenth blessings of the *Amidah*, the *Yevarechecha*, a set of three blessings known as "*Emet ve-Yatsiv*", and of course the full Psaltery. These were fixed in the sense of being established texts, but unfixed in that they had no formal set place in the sacrificial service.

There are Psalms (5, 27, 54, 56) which make explicit reference to the act of prayer, usually as an accompaniment to sacrifice (Amos 5:23 finds God complaining of this custom). There are actual prayers in Ezra 9:5-15, Nehemiah 1:4-11, Daniel 6:11 (in this latter, interestingly, he faces not east but specifically Jerusalem), Daniel 9:3-19, 1 Chronicles 29:10-22 (this is chronologically the oldest). 1 Chronicles 15 and 25 refer to the Levite choir and orchestra, comprising both men and women, who led or accompanied the Psaltery. 1 Kings 8:22-53 is Solomon's prayer at the dedication of the Temple. There are other references to specific prayers, or the record of actual prayers, such as Isaiah 56:7, Jeremiah 32:16-35 and Job 42:1-6. Nehemiah 4 gives a full account of a communal prayer service entirely separate from the sacrifices. Deuteronomy 21:7-8 gives the liturgical formula to be used when the person responsible for a murder can't be found - "Be merciful to Your people, Israel, whom You have redeemed, and do not charge Your people Israel for blood of which they are innocent..." Deuteronomy 6:20-25 provides the earliest *seder* for the feast of Passover.

More formal and specifically prayerful prayers are found in the

Apocryphal texts. 1 Maccabees 4:30-33, 38-40 and 54-55; 2 Maccabees 3:19-20; Judith 8:31 and 13:4-7, the Testament of Simeon 2:13 and the Testament of Judah 19:2, Baruch 1:11, Tobit 4:19. 2 Enoch, 2 Baruch and 4 Ezra contain prayers that belong to the Christian era. Baruch's prayer is found in 1:13-3:38. There are further prayers in Aristeas 256, Wisdom 9:1-18 and 15:3, Ben Sira 51 and 24:23-27.

Prayer, then, doesn't belong to the synagogue, but was transferred to the synagogue from the Temple, and then developed – important this, because it precedes the "substitute" and is therefore not at risk if the "substitute" is terminated. This origin the Rabbis affirm. *Mishnah* (*Tamid* 5:1) speaks of the daily recitation in the Temple of an introductory benediction, with the Ten Commandments, the *Shema* (all three paragraphs), the *Yevarechecha* (of course) and the appropriate disposition of the one hundred and fifty Psalms (one hundred and fifty-one, if you include the apocryphal Psalm, found in the Septuagint, on the slaying of Goliath by the boy David).

The literature of the Essenes, the so-called "Dead Sea Scrolls", likewise contains numerous testimonies to the full development of prayer in latter Second Temple times. The Essene "Rule of the Community" refers to the *Shema*, the "Benedictions" (almost certainly the *Amidah*), and *Birkat Mazon* (the grace after meals), as regular aspects of their services. The Angel Liturgy, which accompanied Sabbath sacrifices, is particularly interesting because the prayers are addressed to the angels and not to God - proof perhaps of the Zoroastrian influences in Israel at the time, for it was from Persia that the angelology entered Judaism, at the end of the First Exile. There are innumerable apocryphal *hoda'ot* - hymns of praise - as well as prayers for *Yom Kippur* and *Yom ha-Bikurim* - the proper name for *Shavu'ot*. There are daily prayers for both morning and evening, for purification ceremonies and for weddings. The "*Divrey ha-Me'orot* - Words of the Luminaries" contains texts for prayers on the fourth day, Wednesday, which the Essenes appear to have regarded as a special day, almost a half-*shabbat*; owing, according to official Jewish explanations, to its being the middle day of the week - the truth is that the fourth was the day on which the sun moon and stars, which is to say the planetary deities and the stellar angels, were created; further evidence again of the influence of Zoroastrianism. There are also texts which parallel the *Amidah*, *Tachanun* and *Vidu'i*, and in the Psalms Scroll the role of King David is given a status that makes his entire history appear to echo mythologically the tale of Orpheus.

The final set of evidence for the institutional establishment of prayer before the Second Temple fell and the Rabbis at Yavneh elaborated prayer as a substitute for sacrifice, lies in the Christian scriptures, notably the "Lord's Prayer" itself, every word of it a quotation from or an allusion to the scriptures, but which is described quite explicitly (Matthew 6:14-15) as a "replacement" for the erstwhile liturgy. Luke 1:68-79 and 2:25 are also pertinent.

Each of these sources makes clear that the Ten Commandments formed a centrepiece of such formal liturgy as there was. What other reading from the *Torah* could be more appropriate? But even before the Roman destruction of the Temple, the Ten Commandments had been removed from the liturgy, because of "trouble stirred up by sectarians" according to *Berachot* 12a. Tantalising image! Was there some dispute as to the terms of the Ten? Were there moves, perhaps, to remove the prohibition against adultery, or to reduce the reward for honouring one's parents? Or did some esoteric cult wish to introduce new legislation, some contemporary piece of political correctness? We shall never know. Rabba bar Hana in the early 4th century, and Aremar of Nehardea a generation later, tried to reintroduce it, but both were over-ruled. To this day, Thou Shalt Not Recite The Ten Commandments In The Synagogue. Not as prayer anyway – it's still conventional to rise when they're read from the *Torah* on their given week. And in most synagogues they are engraved upon or above the *Aron ha-Kodesh*, thus rendering them unavoidable. Not praying them doesn't, presumably, exempt us from adhering to them.

Temple v Synagogue

The development of the religion we call Judaism - as opposed to its predecessor, Hebrewism, for want of a better word - depends on two distinct, complementary but unequal traditions, the Temple and the Synagogue. Mosaic Law presumes the eventuality of the Temple as the central focus of Hebrew worship, regulated by *Cohanim* and *Leviyim*, the two orders of priests, and to this day the Orthodox, but not the Reform who have elected to abandon the enterprise, continue to pray for the restoration of the Temple. But the truth is that, for all but five hundred years of our nearly four thousand year history, the centrality of the Temple has been entirely symbolic, and nothing more denotes it than its absence, its non-existence. Mosaic Law established it, somewhere between 1800 and 1200 BCE; Solomon built it around 900, but the civil war following his death deprived it of centrality, or at least of predominance. Nebuchadnezzar destroyed it in 586 - the year in which, properly speaking, the religion of Judaism was born - and then the two traditions began their competition.

What became the synagogue had its origins in Babylon, during the fifty year exile after 586 BCE. Exactly as Yochanan ben Zakkai would ordain in 70 CE, after the destruction of the Second Temple, some substitute was needed to keep the people together and the religion alive. The answer was a primitive form of Zionism, summed up in the Exile's Psalm, Psalm 137: "By the rivers of Babylon, there we sat down and wept when we remembered Zion…If I forget you O Jerusalem, let my right arm lose its cunning; if I do not remember you, let my tongue cleave to the roof of my mouth; if I do not make Jerusalem my highest joy."

Zionism or Judaism - the two at that time were indistinguishable, and with the restoration of Israel, so they should be again today. But Judaism since that time has always functioned as an act of expediency and pragmatism, a second-best in the absence of the authentic, in the way a football team, deprived by illness and suspension of its finest players, will field a team of adequate reserves. Now that the illness has been cured and the period of suspension is complete, can we take up the challenge to create a new Judaism for a new Jewish nation based on Israel and ex-patriacy rather than exile and diaspora?

Though the word is Greek, the origin of the synagogue is the establishment in exile of the *Beit ha-Knesset.* At the outset this simply meant a place of assembly, but it quickly became a forum for prayer and study, and prayer itself quickly changed from the private petitions that accompanied sacrifice to a form of congregational worship. But it should never be forgotten: prayer based in the synagogue came into being only because Temple and sacrifice had been rendered impossible. Synagogue and prayer began as makeshift, second-best, substitutions. And so they will always remain.

When the exiles returned to Israel, when they built their Second Temple, they also retained the new customs and traditions they had developed in Babylon. Symbiosis, let alone amalgamation, was never achieved - the battle between the Sadducees and Pharisees provides the most obvious evidence of this, but so does the whole history of the religion's evolution. From the outset, Judaism was neither an absolute nor a definitive philosophy, but rather a structure that contained the conflicts between different interpretations of the intentions of God. Synthesis, and resynthesis - never symbiosis. Argument and disagreement are intrinsic and implicit, not by-products. This dialectic promotes the dynamism without which Judaism would never have survived the Diaspora, let the alone the pogroms and the Holocaust. Orthodox and Reform Jews, *Hasidim* and *Mitnagdim*, like the respective supporters of Hillel and Shammai, should take comfort from this.

Of all of Ezra's institutions, the most significant was the paralleling of

Temple practice in the *Beit ha-Knesset*, the making of prayer into an echo of sacrifice by requiring thrice-daily services of worship, at *Shacharit* to conjoin the sacrifices to Sirius, the dawn or morning-star; in mid-afternoon, to complement the *Minchah* offering; and in the evening, at the going down of the sun (which isn't quite the same, of course, as the rising of the moon, though it was the moon that was really intended), when there were no sacrifices, but merely the cleaning of the altar by burning off the remnants of the previous holocaust.

The triple-service is mentioned in the Bible - Psalm 55:18 for example, as well as Daniel 6:11. Psalm 5 is specifically a morning prayer, Psalm 4 an evening prayer. But Ezra's inspiration is said to have been three quite different references: Genesis 19:27, which finds Abraham praying in the morning, Genesis 24:63, where Isaac prays at dusk, and Genesis 28:10, where Jacob prays at night. Beautiful construct! It belongs to the *aggadic* tradition and can be found in *Berachot* 26b; but even there it's set aside by the *Talmudic* Rabbis, in favour of the sacrificial explanation. In Second Temple times, worship meant sacrifice, and prayer accompanied and strengthened sacrifice but wasn't equal with it; since the destruction of the Temple, prayer has replaced sacrifice. That there is no diminution is explained in *Yoma* 86b, by reference to Hosea 14:3. God, apparently, never really wanted our sacrifices anyway, but only the symbolic proof of our trust and faith and loyalty. As with Isaac, so the ram - an affront, a waste, an unnecessary cruelty, an offence against God's creation. Where the story of the *Akeda* replaced human sacrifice with animal sacrifice, so in the act of prayer we may also redeem the ram (a concept that Christians especially might like to think about). "We will render," said Hosea, "instead of bulls, the offerings of our lips." This is immensely significant. *Midrashic* legend tells of Moses pressing burning coals against his lips when still a child - the explanation for his stammering but also an allegory of Hosea's meaning. The same is true of Isaiah, whose calling to the mantle of prophesy involved (Isaiah 6) one of the *seraphim* taking a live coal from the altar and touching it to Isaiah's lips. "Instead of bulls, the offerings of our lips." Prayers and holocausts! If God can create the universe with words, what more appropriate form than this in which to worship Him? If we are all creations of the Word, what deeper symbiosis than the act of poetry-in-prayer? Perhaps this is what the Australian aboriginals mean when they say that their ancestors, in the Dream Time, sang the world into existence. In the beginning was the Word.

For five hundred years then, after the return from exile, synagogue and Temple existed, not always comfortably, side by side, the Temple officially predominant, the synagogue perpetually gaining ground. But the obligation to pray never took hold until *Talmudic* times, when the Temple was no more and the Rabbis held sole and complete authority. Yet even then the fixing of three daily services of prayer (*Berachot* 21a) reflected Temple practice - the morning and afternoon services obligatory, because these were the times of sacrifice; the evening service voluntary, at the time of the cleaning of the Temple and the removal of the remains of sacrifice.

According to Psalm 119:164: "Seven times a day do I praise you because of your righteous judgements" - seeming to imply that the number of acts of worship in the Temple was actually seven, equivalent to the holy number of God. But no other Biblical or *Talmudic* evidence supports this. It may be interesting to note, nonetheless, that in a mediaeval monastery the number of daily offices was also seven: Matins, Lauds, Prime, Sext, None, Vespers and Compline. It may well be that the Psalm reflects the fact that the duties of the Temple priests involved more than just the acts of sacrifice.

The fixing of the three daily services is commonly attributed to Daniel 6:11 where, King Darius having signed the decree forbidding any man from petitioning his God, Daniel immediately "went into his house, and his windows being open in his chamber toward Jerusalem, he kneeled upon his knees three times a day, and prayed, and gave thanks before his God, as he had previously."

But this fixes nothing. It merely confirms Daniel's determination to maintain a custom that must already have existed. But for how long had it existed? The story of Daniel is set in the court of king Nebuchadnezzar, in Babylon, immediately after the exile - which would indicate that thrice-daily services had been in place since the period of the First Temple. Alas, the text of Daniel is now known to have been, not a record of actual events, but an allegorical fable, set down in Maccabean times, when Greek tyranny was at its height, but saying so directly was injudicious.

Rabbi Joshua ben Levi, (*Berachot* 26b), notes that the evening service which we call *Ma'ariv* should properly be called "*arvit*", after the night-time burning on the altar of the fats and organs left over from the daily offerings. A prayer service to accompany the scouring and the washing-up - how quaint!

One other variant is worth the mentioning. The afternoon service is named *Minchah*, and *Minchah* is understood to mean "a gift" - it is used as early as Cain's rejected "offering" in Genesis 4. But the root is obscure, and in Hebrew obscurities may always be challenged. Onkelos, who translated the *Torah* into Aramaic in the 2nd century CE, regarded *Minchah* as an error for "*menach*", meaning "rest" (the names Noah and Menachem both derive from it). Onkelos recalls that in Genesis 3:8, Adam and Eve heard the voice of God walking in the garden "*le-ru'ach ha-yom* - in the cool of the day", and presumed that this referred to the phenomenon, common throughout the

Mediterranean, by which a change in temperature attracts gusting winds in the middle afternoon, inducing the need to seek sheltered rest. A prayer service for the siesta then - why not?

The final change was due to Rabban Gamliel II, at the time of the Roman destruction, when the synagogue replaced the Temple and the religion urgently needed to establish forms and structures to survive (see, for example, *Mishneh Berachot* 4:3-4). It was then that the *Amidah* found its final order; then that the *nusach*, the official text, was made statutory. It was then that the *Pirkei Avot* - the Ethics of the Fathers - were written, a collection of wise saws, drawn from the *Mishnah*, that established for all time the credentials of the Rabbis. The opening phrase of that seminal work - so important it's studied on Sabbath afternoons for three months of the year - consolidates the synagogue's authority: "Moses received the *Torah* at Sinai and handed it down to Joshua, Joshua to the Elders, the Elders to the Prophets, and the Prophets handed it down to the men of the Great Assembly." The men of the Great Assembly were Ezra and his founding Rabbis. Strange that this line of authority over the Law of God fails even to make mention of the *Cohanim* and *Leviyim*, the Temple Priests.

✡

Tefillah - Prayer

In *Ta'anit* (2a), a section of *Mishnah* that deals mostly with fasts, I read that prayer isn't a list of requests but a process of introspection, a clarifying, refining process of discovering what one is, what one should be, and how to achieve the transformation.

I like this. It suggests the same intensity of inwardness that I hope to find in a novel by Patrick White or a symphony of Jean Sibelius. It suggests that studying the sunset, or indeed the nature of prayer, may itself be a way of praying. It suggests that one prays, not *to* something, not *for* something, but *within* something: the soul, the self.

And if it's like this, then why does prayer require God at all, except in the same way that a composer needs an orchestra, an essayist a reader?

The Hebrew word for prayer is "*tefillah*", from a root which means "to judge, to clarify, to decide". The verb "to pray" is a reflexive as well as a reflective. Prayer is the soul's yearning to define what truly matters and to ignore the trivialities that often masquerade as essential.

These are not my words. They sound remarkably like a paraphrase of *Ta'anit*, but in fact they come from the *Siddur Avodat Ha Lev*, the prayer book of 20th century Reform Jews in the United States.

The three main modes of Jewish prayer are petition, benediction, and thanksgiving. A logical enough process, though they are by no means equal in importance. To petition is to ask for something. To bestow a benediction is akin to special pleading, the courtesies attached to asking for a favour from a king. Thanksgiving, as everyparent teaches everychild, is simply courtesy.

Petition is achieved by supplication. Biblical references inform us of the modes and postures of supplication. Standing (1 Samuel 1:26). Kneeling (Daniel 6:11; Ezra 9:5). Prostrate (Joshua 7:6). Head bowed (Genesis 24:26; Nehemiah 8:6). Hands stretched out or lifted upwards (1 Kings 8:22, Psalm 28:2). Face between knees (1 Kings 18:42). Seated (2 Samuel 7:18). Today we have abandoned all but standing and sitting, though kneeling and the prostrate position are both reverted to momentarily during the *Aleynu* of *Yom Kippur.*

The most common form of prayer in Judaism is the *berachah* or benediction ("Blessed are you…"). It's also the most extraordinary. It's a prayer which denotes a blessing, but it doesn't solicit a blessing upon the one who prays. On the contrary, it offers the blessing upwards, from Man to God.

The direction of prayer, of course, is inwards, and upwards, but the body has to face in some direction too. The matter is open to dispute - facing east, or facing Jerusalem? Daniel 6:11 faces Jerusalem. In Europe, when a synagogue is built, or even when a room is converted to contain a synagogue, the Ark is placed on the wall that faces east. Is this true of Los Angeles, of Adelaide, of Pietermaritzburg, of Baghdad? The answer is yes. However a tale in the *Mishnah* records the priests who drew the water reaching the east-facing gate and turning round to face the Temple in order to face God - suggesting that it's neither east nor even Jerusalem that is the axis, but the Temple itself. Ezekiel 8:16 however records precisely the opposing custom:

"And he brought me into the inner court of the Lord's house, and there, at the Temple of the Lord, between the porch and the altar, were some twenty-five men with their backs towards the Temple of the Lord and their faces towards the east; and they worshipped the sun towards the east."

The importance of this passage is that it was intended critically - what was being described was common practice, but also anathema, and in the following verse would be described as an "abomination". And yet the practice wasn't outlawed.

The argument continues in the Babylonian *Talmud*, where the most marvellous compromise is reached - one may face any direction one chooses, since God is everywhere. I wonder then, why an Orthodox Jew may not pray in a cathedral, or a mosque, or a mandir, or a field, or a mountain-top, or even a Reform synagogue, all these being houses of the One God Who Is Everywhere? The blind Rabbi Shesheth, a Babylonian *amora* of the late 3rd century CE, insisted that it mattered not a jot which way one faced. His argument coheres with mine. When one prays, the direction one should face is neither Templewards nor eastwards nor upwards nor Jerusalemwards - but inwards.

But of course there is a definitive answer to this question – any answer given by Maimonides is definitive. In the *Hillel Tefillah* (5:3), he states that one should face Israel, not the east, to pray, while worshippers in Israel should face Jerusalem, and worshippers in Jerusalem should face the Temple Mount. And in a variation of my own conclusion - hugely satisfying to discover this - "those who do not know which way to face should simply direct their prayers to heaven."

The language of prayer is predominantly Hebrew. This may seem obvious, but in fact the *Talmudists* and *Tosafists* and mediaeval *Payyatanim* who wrote the prayers weren't themselves Hebrew speakers, but natives of Aramaic, or its successor Arabic, or else they were Latinists and speakers of European tongues, or possibly Yiddish, or Ladino. Just as the monks who illuminated manuscripts in the Middle Ages in Latin, so too the *yeshiva* Jews, and especially the Diasporal Jews - all of them men who speak to God in a language that isn't to them as it is to Him, a language they do not indigenously understand. The same, of course, was probably true of Moses.

But in what language should we pray? In Second Temple times all manner of languages were used, including Greek and Aramaic. In Alexandria, Hebrew was so far lost that the *Tanach* had to be translated into Greek (the famous Septuagint) - and thank God it was, for it was through this Septuagint version that it spread across the world, travelling first into Latin, and thence into each and every language (more than a hundred and forty of them today), until it became what it was always meant to be, a truly universal book. In Judea, from the mid-6th century BCE, Aramaic replaced Hebrew as the daily tongue to such an extent that special prayers in Hebrew had to be appended – if Jesus knew his scriptures well, he also knew them in a foreign language, for he too would have spoken Aramaic. Two thousand years later the same dispute goes on, over French or English versions. What matters isn't who is right or who is wrong; what matters is that there are still people in the synagogues to pray in any language, that people still care enough to argue it.

Each prayer book varies slightly from the others, right down to what's included and what excluded, and in what order. The order is especially important, for it's the proper meaning of *siddur*, which we mistranslate as prayer-book. Nothing is fixed or definite, not even the tradition that nothing should be fixed and definite. Brodie improved Herzl, who revised Singer, all the way back through the *Shulchan Aruch* to Rav Amram Ga'on in the 9th century, who is credited with having devised the very first prayer book. I am working predominantly from the Art Scroll, because it's the one I happen to keep on my study shelf (in *shul* we use the Revised Singer), and because it's the most detailed in its instructions for the liturgy. But it isn't absolute. Nothing in Judaism is ever absolute. Not even Truth. Not even, perhaps, God.

Development of the *Siddur*

It was never intended that we should have prayer-books, because it was never intended that we should have prayer services. But once established, a statutory liturgy requires writing-down. Nonetheless the *Talmudic* Rabbis were intensely conscious of their impiety in committing anything unnecessary to parchment, especially the *Talmud*, the Oral Law. An impiety because, by definition, an Oral Law is one that hasn't been, cannot be, and shouldn't be written down; a tautology and an absurdity as well - for a written Oral Law is surely a contradiction in terms. But the vicissitudes of History compelled it, as they now uncompel it.

Just as there was resistance to writing down the Oral Law, so there was a reluctance to write down the words of the prayers, and until the 8th century of the Christian era the prohibition held its ground. Prayer was always something learned by heart, or else composed spontaneously. The change to a written liturgy, fixed for universal use, was one of the ways in which Judaism ceded its individuality and moved towards the totalitarian; a great irony this, since in all other ways the spread of literacy which written Laws and written prayers demands has nourished and nurtured democracy.

Writing down was not simply frowned upon; it was explicitly forbidden. In the *Tosepha* to *Shabbat* 13:4, for example: "writers of blessings are like those who burn the *Torah*." I find this phrase alarming. To write a blessing is the same as perpetrating the *Sho'ah*? I beg to disagree. Blessed Are you, O Lord Our God, King of the Universe, Who Created Many Great Things But Also Many Foolish Ones, Many Great Rabbis But Also Many Foolish Ones, And Gave Even Dilettantes Like Myself The Licence To Dissent.

Nevertheless, while writing down their commentaries and explications of the Written Law might just be justifiable, the founding Rabbis wouldn't condone or countenance the writing down of prayers or blessings. So for centuries, even when the form was fixed, it was fixed in memory and not on parchment. A bardic tradition amongst the Jews. How marvellous!

But by the 8th century even this had succumbed - or perhaps the text had grown too large. Yehudai ben Nachman Ga'on, the spiritual leader of the Jews of Babylon and head of the Sura academy, noted in his "*Halachot Pesuchot*" (Yehudai was blind, and dictated his philosophies to his secretary) the existence of unofficial prayer books, and formally permitted a written text - a *Siddur* - to be used on *Yom Kippur*.

His successor, Natronai bar Hilai, wrote a *responsum* of such inordinate length on this subject to the Jews of Lucena, near Barcelona, in Spain, defending the *Talmudic* tradition that a man should offer up a hundred benedictions every day, and organised his "*me'ah berachot*" in such a formal way, that the *responsum* itself came to form the nucleus of a prayer book.

But it was Natronai's successor, Amram ben Sheshna, who published the first full and formal *siddur*, which is to say the first systematic catalogue of prayers, including all the blessings, *halachic* explanations of the liturgy and the rules that govern synagogue activity. The "*Machzor d'Rav Amram*" is regarded as the first prayer book as such; it became so widely used and known, it was quoted extensively in *Rashi*, *Tosephot*, Caro and others.

Even Amram's work is overshadowed, however, by that of Sa'adiah ben Joseph Ga'on, the last and greatest of the Sura academicians. In 921 a conflict of intense bitterness erupted over dates and times, which Sa'adiah resolved by fixing the Jewish calendar once and for all; a resolution which also, by inference, ended the claim to final authority over Judaism of the community in Palestine. Sa'adiah translated the *Torah* into Arabic, wrote commentaries as well as *piyyutim* - religious poetry - and compiled lexicons of *halachah* and grammar. He was also a powerful opponent of the Kara'ites, a recently formed sect of anti-*Talmud*, anti-Rabbinic Jews, who insisted on individuality and self-definition in a more democratic Judaism - a position taken by swathes of Jews today, though none, as far as I know, has yet declared him or herself a Kara'ite. Such was Sa'adiah's invective against them, such was the tenacity of the public polemic, the sect became so far marginalised as never really to be a force again - until, perhaps, today.

Sa'adiah's major contribution was the "*Sepher ha-Emunot ve-ha-De'ot*", a philosophical work in theory, though in practice it was the first full and complete prayer book in Jewish history. Written in Arabic, it's as much an anthology of the prayers of which he did approve as it is an attack on those which, in his opinion, "had no root in tradition" or which "spoil the intention" of the one who prays. I imagine Sa'adiah as an arrogant, dogmatic man, absolutely certain that in all things he knew best, and quite prepared to say so. He stated quite baldly that his reason for compiling the *Sepher* was "the neglect, addition and omission" that he witnessed in a life of frequent travelling. Sa'adiah knew what was correct in synagogue, and what was incorrect; once his book became known, the term "correct" and the name "Sa'adiah" became synonymous and even interchangeable, and to all intents and purposes they have remained so ever since. Sa'adiah's prayer book is the source and starting-point for every Jewish prayer book in existence. But it remains merely the opinion of one man, and not an ordinance of God; which is to say, it may be altered.

After Sa'adiah, Maimonides, that inexorable human deity. Contained within his "*Mishneh Torah*", the compendious encyclopaedia of Judaism that bears his name, is a fragment, a very substantial fragment, called the "*Seder Tefillot Kol ha-Shana* - a book of prayers for the whole year" - which includes a rejection of *piyyut* such as that written by Sa'adiah, because he regarded prayer as a communal activity, much as Rabban Gamliel had done before him, and private petition at best an interruption, at worst a Kara'ite heresy. Great irony here, that the principal refutant of the Kara'ites, Sa'adiah, should be accused of Kara'ite tendencies by its second greatest refutant, in a book whose personal and individualistic precepts were at loggerheads with convention, and sought to alter them!

The last of the great mediaeval *siddurim* was that of Simcha ben Samuel, one of *Rashi*'s closest disciples. He came from Vitry in northern France, and named his prayer-book for his town - the "*Machzor Vitry*". Where Amram and Natronai and Sa'adiah reflected the *Mizrachi* practices of Babylon, and Maimonides the Sephardic practices of North Africa, the "*Machzor Vitry*" reflects closely the third of the great Jewish communities outside Palestine, the Ashkenazi practices in Norman Europe, particularly those of Rhineland Germany, France and England. (Today, Ashkenazi prayer-books tend to reflect the Palestinian, Sephardic the Babylonian; this isn't entirely true, but as a broad generalisation it suffices.)

The "*Machzor Vitry*" contains much that is lifted wholesale from the "*Seder Rav Amram Ga'on*" and the "*Siddur Rashi*", but it also gives much that's new: *ma'avirim* and *hoshanot*, the Passover *Haggadah*, the prayers for *Simchat Torah.* And with these it provides the key primary source of explanation for mediaeval metamorphoses in the *Kaddish* and the prayer *Nishmat Kol Chay.*

Key figures in the development of the mediaeval Ashkenazi liturgy were the family of Kalonymos ben Meshullam - particularly Kalonymos the Elder, Moses his son, and Kalonymos the Younger with his brother

Yekutiel, who contributed prodigious quantities of poetry to the liturgy. The family dominated the community in the Rhineland for the best part of four hundred years, counting rabbis, preachers, teachers, poets, moralists, theologians and most of the pre-eminent community leaders from the 9th to the 13th century in their numbers. They traced their origins through Italy to Alexandria, claiming Onkelos himself amongst their ancestors. Eleazar ben Yehudah ben Kalonymos of Wurms wrote the "*Roke'ah*", a polemic on the subject of authentic Jewish prayer and - an entirely connected subject in his view - the distinguished pedigree of his family, circa 1220. Samuel ben Kalonymos he-Hasid founded the *Hasidei Ashkenaz* and, with his son Judah, wrote the "*Sepher Hasidim*", the key text establishing that tradition. Judah ben Kalonymos ben Meir of Speyer was the author of a *Talmudic* lexicon of truly gargantuan proportions, entitled "*Seder Yichussey Tanna'im ve-Amora'im*". Having survived the pogroms unleashed by Bernard of Clairvaux, the founder of the Benedictine Order, in the early years of the 12th century (pogroms officially though quite erroneously remembered as "the Second Crusade"), the family appears to have died out in Provence somewhere in the late 13th century.

First the Crusades, then the expulsions, then further Crusades and further expulsions, finally the Inquisition, the Ghettos, the Pale of Settlement, all left their indelible marks, until Jewry became more localised in Europe upon western Russia and the lands of Poland. The *Siddur* in use today, in England and America and in much of northern Europe, is essentially the Polish evolution of the mediaeval *machzorim.*

✡

Strange as it may seem, given the amount of time that Jews are meant to spend in synagogue, whether engaged in, or disengaged from, the act of prayer, the early Rabbis who laid all this liturgy down weren't really very interested in prayer. Just as the prophets insisted on sacrifice, but made it clear that God wanted the obedience to the law of sacrifice rather than the sacrifice itself, and obedience to all laws even more, so the early Rabbis placed their emphasis on study as the first principle of "good" Judaism – which is why we call a synagogue a *shul*, when *shul* is really *schule*, the German word for school. I find this mildly reassuring - when it comes to studying, I am as observant as a *Hasid* and as fastidious as a *yeshiva bucher*; never miss a weekday let alone a *shabbat* or a high holy day. Whereas in prayer the trend is laxity.

At the very opening of the "*Pirkei Avot* – the Ethics of the Fathers", Simon the Just tells us that the world depends on three activities: *Torah*,

Temple Service and Good Deeds. By *Torah* he means "obedience", but he recognises that *Torah* requires study, for who can possibly obey what he doesn't really understand; and if he isn't taught, then how will he know how, let alone what, to obey? Temple service passed into prayer service with the fall of Jerusalem, but it remains second to *Torah* (and second-best even to itself). And as to good deeds, Rabban Yochanan ben Zakkai himself declared that the means of atonement for sins hadn't been lost with the destruction of the Temple, but passed to the practise of good deeds. Good deeds - *tikkun olam* and *derech erets* - not the prayer-service. The disputation between the Rabbis on this issue is described in *Sanhedrin* 74a, but Rabbi Akiva's declaration that "study leads to deeds" seems to have clinched the matter. So the *Beit ha-Midrash* became more crucial than the *Beit ha-Knesset* - and has remained so for two thousand years. For a people whose central icon is a concise library of books, it's hardly surprising that study ultimately triumphs over prayer.

"He who turns his ear away from learning *Torah*, even his prayer shall be an abomination."

Methinks sometimes the Rabbis do protest too much!

✡

In the closing pages of his wonderful historical-fictional reconstruction of the life of Josephus, Lion Feuchtwanger puts the following words into the mouth of Yochanan ben Zakkai, the Rabbi who persuaded Titus and Vespasian to permit the seminary at Yavneh that produced the Palestinian Talmud. It's the 9th of Av in the year 3830 (the 28th of Augustus in the Roman year 823), and the Temple in Jerusalem is burning. Receiving the news in Yavneh, ben Zakkai tears his garments in the custom of mourning, strews ashes on his head, and summons his colleagues to a meeting.

"Until today," he announces, "the High Council [the Sanhedrin] of Jerusalem has had the power to interpret the Word of God, to lay down when times begin, when the moon is new, when it is full, what is right and what is wrong, what is holy and unholy; the power to bind and to unloose. From today, the Council of Yavneh has this authority.

"Our first task is to establish the boundaries of the Holy Scripture. The Temple is no more, the Scripture is all our Kingdom now. Its books are our provinces, its sentences our cities and villages. Until now the Word of God has been intermingled with the words of men. Our essential task is to decide to the last comma what pertains to the Scripture and what does not.

"Our second task is to perpetuate the commentaries of the sages for future generations. Until now a curse has been laid on the handing on of these holy commentaries in any form except by word of mouth. We annul that curse. We are resolved to transcribe the 613 commandments on good parchment, to show where they begin and where they cease, to hedge them about and shore them up, so that Israel may be able to take its stand upon them for ever.

"The seventy-one of us gathered here are all that is left of God's kingdom. Purify your hearts, that you may be a kingdom more enduring than Rome."

Who knows whether ben Zakkai spoke these words, or even similar words. But they distil the essence of what really happened - if not his words, then certainly his achievement. They define the moment when the Oral Law formally replaced the Written Law, when prayer formally replaced sacrifice, when the Rabbis formally replaced the priests and prophets - and they establish the terms of Judaism to this day.

Chapter Three: Dressing for Prayer

Atiphat Tallit - The Donning of the Prayer Shawl

So it is time to enter the synagogue. Where a Moslem would pause at the threshold and discard his shoes, there do I deposit my intellect, my empirical, objective mind, close the gate upon the outer world, and enter inwards. This, the House of Prayer by any name to any god, this is the grandest form of ritual theatre known to Man, and like all theatre it requires, no, not an act of faith - the opposite - the willing suspension of disbelief.

Synagogue communities these days are mostly the habitats of old men or Lubavitch *Hasidim*, the Jewish equivalent of Jehovah's Witnesses; except on major festivals and Saturdays, when men gather to discuss business during the silent *Amidah* and women show off their new frocks between sorties to check there are no flies on the chopped liver and no children's hands purloining the *gefilte* fish intended for the *Kiddush*. At my *shul* it's different - never less than fifty of us every morning, though how many of these schoolchildren would attend if it weren't compulsory is a question better left unasked. For me, it's an extraordinary privilege, to have my own *shul* without the requirement of *smicha*, Rabbinic ordination.

The *shul* reflects but doesn't repeat the Temple, contains it in memorial but not in practice. Where the Holy of Holies stood, the Ark now stands. Where the *Menorah*, the seven-branched candlestick, now the *Ner Tamid*, the Eternal Lamp, an electric light bulb if the truth be told, dependent on a miracle that's entirely subject to human competence. There are important differences too: where the Cohen faced the congregation, serving as the medium through which God addressed Man, now the prayer leader occupies the central space amid the congregation, but facing the Ark, serving as the medium through which Man addresses God (Reform retains the Temple mode). Nor does the prayer leader need to be a Rabbi. Any adult male will do - adulthood defined as thirteen, the age of *Bar Mitzvah*. Any adult male will do. Even me. (Reform, and even some Conservative synagogues, allow women too!). Why are women generally excluded? Now there's a question for another book!

✡

Barchi Naphshi - Bless my soul

"Barchi naphshi et Adonay, Adonay elohay gadalta me'od, hod ve-hadar lavashta, oteh or ka-salmah, noteh shamayim ka-yeri-yah."

"Bless my soul, O Lord, O Lord my God who is very great, who has donned majesty and splendour, cloaked in light as with a garment, stretching out the heavens like a curtain."

No one can take part in a theatrical activity without first putting on the costume that denotes the part we're here to play. Like the *tallit katan*, the ritual undergarment, the *tallit* for prayer is four-cornered with *tsitsit.* To put it on is to wrap around your shoulders a cloak of light, to draw to yourself in an embrace the whole stretched fabric of the universe, all two hundred and forty-eight organs, all three hundred and sixty-five sinews, denoting the six hundred and thirteen commandments, represented in the six hundred fringes, the five knots, the eight threads of the *tallit.* So may God protect you, in silk, and majesty.

These images of light and majesty have their origins in Psalm 104, where God is pictured as covering himself with light "as with a garment", and stretching out the heavens "like a curtain" - a conventional masculine sky-god if ever there was one, counterpart and counterpoint to mother-goddess Yah who inhabits the early Psalms.

No less than five prayers accompany the donning of the *tallit.* The first (*barchi naphshi*) that verse from Psalm 104, which binds each human soul in harmony with God's creation, making of him one organ, one sinew, of the cosmic corpus. The second (*le-shem yichud*) formalises this, a declaration of God's unity, and of Man's unity with God. The third (*hareyni)* details it, enumerating the organs and sinews and commandments, equating them harmoniously; and then spreads it further, till it covers this world and the world beyond. The fourth (*le-hitateph ba-tsitsit*), recited while holding the *tallit* ready to put on, blesses God and acknowledges the commandment to put on the *tallit.* The fifth (*mah yakar*), spoken while wrapping the *tallit* round the head and body - an experience spiritually akin to re-entering the womb - completes the process, returning again to the Psalms, nourishing the son in the life-source of the father, a moment less of religion than of poetry. Or simply one of those moments in which the two are frankly indistinguishable. Psalm 36:8-11, to be precise, imagining God as an eagle with his wings full-spread, echoing the phrase from Deuteronomy 32:11 in the third prayer. At the tips of the eagle's immense wing-span, let us not forget, those powerful feathers are the ones that Jeremiah described as *tsitsit.*

"Baruch atah Adonay eloheynu melech ha-olam, asher kidshanu be-mitzvotav, ve-tsivanu lehitateph ba-tsitsit."

"Blessed are you O Lord our God, King of the Universe, who sanctified us with His commandments, and commanded us to wrap ourselves in *tsitsit*".

✡

Hanachat Tefillin - The Laying of Tefillin

After the costume, so to speak, the make-up and the props - still one more ritual before the formal structure of the liturgy may be addressed, and this, as noted, I have never done: the laying of *tefillin.* (In *Talmudic* times, and later in some communities, men donned the *tallit* and *tefillin* at home, and then set out for *shul.*)

Two small black boxes, capsules really, set on a black plinth, from two of whose corners leather thongs hang down, their ends knotted, but overflowing the knots, the one to be wrapped around the skull, the other around one arm. The head tefillin is called the "*Shel Rosh*", the arm *tefillin* the "*Shel Yad*", and the thong that is wrapped around the fingers the "*Retsu'ah*". I am no expert on the history of tanning, but it seems to me a fair bet that the fleeing slaves of Egypt are unlikely to have been equipped with either leather for the thongs or whatever material it was that made the plinths. If the *tsitsit* seem to be a Rabbinic variation on some earlier priestly symbolism, the *tefillin* cannot surely belong to any but the Rabbinic era. But where on earth did the idea come from?

The answer, for the *Shel Rosh* at least, may well lie in the ceremonies for the consecration of a priest in Temple times, and for the coronation of the priest-king as well – may lie, indeed, with the *tsitsit.* As described previously. Exodus 28:36 and 39:30 speak of a "plate of the holy crown of pure gold" and "upon it this writing, akin to the engraving of a signet, 'Holy To The Lord'". The plate - probably in the shape of a flower - was fastened to the mitre with a blue lace and the mitre placed upon the head. Where exactly on the head is not stated, but Leviticus 8:9 resolves it: "And he put the mitre on his head; also on the mitre, even on his forehead, did he put the golden plate, the holy crown." The dedication then, worn like an inversion of the Mark of Cain, where the *Shel Rosh* are now laid, upon the forehead.

In Deuteronomy 6:8 we are instructed to bind the commandments - by which the Rabbis understood a scribed copy of the *Shema* - "as a sign upon your hand and as frontlets between your eyes." The phrase occurs elsewhere, and all four passages containing the phrase are stored inside the boxes. In Deuteronomy 11:18, "Place these words of mine upon your heart and soul, bind them as a sign…", which is clear enough, for the "words" of God are self-evidently the *Torah*. But Exodus 13:9 precedes the giving of the Law at Sinai, even though it is itself contained in the text there given. The passage finds the children of Israel still slaves in Egypt, the Pharaoh hardened to nine plagues, and now a tenth previsaged, the Passover plague itself, the sacrifice of the beloved first-born son. First God institutes the Feast of Unleavened Bread, in the month of *Aviv* which is to be - the Rabbis later moved it despite the immutability of Divine Law - the first month of the year.[2] "For seven days you shall eat unleavened bread…and it shall be as a sign upon your hand and as a memorial between your eyes." So the frontlets are a memorial as well as a sign. (So we eat unleavened bread because we were instructed to, and not because there was no time to bake the bread!)

But then, in verses 13-16, the sacrifice of the first-born – yes, the final plague was also a holiness - and the *Pidyon ha-Ben*, the redemption of the first-born, are detailed, and these too "shall be as a sign…" A sign of what? That "by strength of hand the Lord brought us out of Egypt." The first of the Ten Commandments. And what, in Hebrew, is a memorial? Why - *Yad va-Shem* - hand and name. The two principal powers of God. His hand. His name.

This is where Nachmanides, the 13th century Rabbinical apologist, sought his explanation of the *tefillin*. He understood the symbolic intention of the *tefillin*, but he couldn't easily fathom from where in the Biblical text the Rabbis deduced that the *tefillin* should be square boxes with leather thongs attached and copies of the *Shema* inside? He doesn't find an answer, but guesses, speculates poetically, though he calls it theologics. It was necessary to use leather, because leather is the strongest bond. It was necessary to wrap the *tefillin* around the head, to denote the total dedication of our minds and intellects to God. And upon the forearm, because it's the strongest muscle, and with a strong hand and an outstretched arm did God defeat the

---

[2] This is not the place for detailed commentary on scripture. It is nevertheless interesting to wonder if the calendar was different in Moses' time. Verse 4 fixes Passover in the month of *Aviv*, which means the month of spring. But a Jewish lunar calendar of 354 days should cause a precession of months across the year, taking the festivals with it, in the way that Islam does. Since *Talmudic* times we have added two days to each month, to better align our lunar with the solar calendar, and have repeated the month of *Adar* as a leap month, seven times in every nineteen years, in order to maintain the spring alignment and the lunar-solar synchronicity. But was this already the case in Moses' time?

Pharaoh. And not just either forearm, but placed upon the weaker forearm by the stronger, for the same reason. Nachmanides provides an explanation for every facet of the ritual. The leather thongs are wrapped seven times around the upper arm, because seven is the holy number of God. Three times around the palm, because there are three Patriarchs; and in the shape of the letter *sheen* (ש), and around the middle fingers so they too make a *sheen*, because *sheen* is the initial letter of *El Shaddai*, "God of my Breast", Abraham's name for the Divine, and the initial letter of the *Shema* itself. The same *sheen* that appears on the boxes of the *tefillin*, as on the *mezuzah*, both of which contain copies of the *Shema*. But this, like so much Rabbinic exposition, is retroactive validation, the imposing of a logical explanation where the truth is: we don't know.

The *Yad* in Hebrew may be any part of the arm, from the shoulder all the way to those *tsitsit*, dare I call them, those fringes that hang down at the end of every palm. The human feathers, petals, peaks. The fingers which, by curious coincidence of the English language, form both a simile and an anagram for fringes. But the *tefillin shel yad* are laid specifically on the bicep, to convey that note of strength Nachmanides describes.

Law and tradition are once again in conflict. All four of the phrases contained in the *tefillin* convey an idea of eternality, of something that should be done at all times and forever. What is a sign is perpetually a sign; what is borne on the head and arm should be a constant memorial. Yet the Rabbis stated that *tefillin* should not be worn at night, on Sabbath, or on Festivals. This connoted it as a time-bound law, and so women were first not obligated, then excused, and finally excluded altogether. Yet through the generations the pious have worn *tefillin* as they have worn *tsitsit*, in prayer and away from it. This can't be easy, because who can maintain intellectual and bodily purity at all times? So custom restricted the *tefillin* to the morning service only, and of course to men. In Judaism, customs become law by the second generation, a process not of *halachah*, but of osmosis. But can eternity really be time-bound, and occasional?

Yad va-Shem – "Hand and Name" - is the name given to the central Holocaust Memorial in Jerusalem, precisely to convey this eternality, the intention that it should be a monument for ever. Given that the *tefillin* are intended as a "sign and a memorial" - in other words that their value is symbolic - and given that it's no longer considered necessary to wear them at all times, provided that the sign and the memorial remain, in spirit, on our arms and in our minds, why then is it necessary to wear *tefillin* at all?

The Rabbis answer this by saying (*Berachot* 14b) that a man who does not wear *tefillin* is "like one who bears false witness against himself" - a phrase which sounds remarkably like moral blackmail. Rabbi Yonah explains that it's because the act of binding the thongs is symbolic of Man's complete submission to God. "To utter the prayers without *tefillin* subtly implies a lack of sufficient submission."

Subtly? There's nothing subtle in my refusal. It's direct, overt defiance. I refuse the *tefillin*. I am a Jew, not a Moslem. I am a man, not a slave. With a strong hand God brought me out of Egypt, out of the House of Bondage. For what purpose? To make me his slave in Sinai, or his freeman in Israel? The end of submission is Auschwitz.

✡

Le-Shem Yichud

For the laying of the *tefillin*, seven prayers - an incremental increase of spiritual intensity as formal prayer draws closer.

The first is "*Le-Shem Yichud*", the same declaration of God's unity and Man's unity with God that accompanied the donning of the *tallit*; omissible if *tallit* and *tefillin* are worn together.

"Le-shem yichud kudsha berich hu u-shechinteh, bi-dechilu u-rechimu le-yached shem Adonay be-yichudah shelim, be-shem kol Yisra'el."

"For the sake of the unification of the Holy One, Blessed be He, and His Presence, in fear and love, to unify the Name in perfect unity, in the name of all Israel."

The second is "*Hineyni Mechaven*", a lengthy didactic exegesis of the four phrases which command the laying of *tefillin* and are contained as parchment in the capsules, and an expression of hope that the performance of the ritual will have a beneficial impact. "May some of the spiritual influence of the commandment of *tefillin* be extended to me so that I have a long life, a flow of holiness and holy thoughts, free from sin and iniquity..." White magic. The imputation of healing power to an inanimate object. The point at which Judaism reverts to its pagan roots and breaks its own divine prohibition of superstition.

For the third phrase ritual squires prayer - or is it prayer which duennas ritual? Standing, the arm-box is placed on the bicep of the weaker arm, and held in place whilst the prayer acknowledging the ritual is recited:

"Baruch atah Adonay eloheynu melech ha-olam, asher kidshanu be-mitzvotav, ve-

tsivanu le-hani'ach tefillin."

The thong is then tightened, wrapped seven times around the arm. Samson told Delilah that "If they bind me with seven green withs that were never dried, then I shall be as weak as any other man" (Judges 16:8); but Samson was wilfully deceiving her; there is no diminution of strength from the act of binding. Not yet around the fingers please, however. Without pause the head-box is put on, above the hairline, between the eyes (stage directions Beckettian in their precision). Again the prayer acknowledging the ritual is recited, slightly modified:

"*Baruch atah Adonay eloheynu melech ha-olam, asher kidshanu be-mitzvotav, ve-tsivanu al mitzvat tefillin.*"

and only then is the thong tightened. Acceptance of servitude precedes the act of binding. Isaac must go willingly to the altar on Moriah. The animal intended for the slaughter likewise, whether beast or human. *Arbeit*, in the Orwellian sense that Work is Slavery and Labour the punishment imposed on Adam for the sin of Eden, *Arbeit*, which word in Hebrew, *avodah*, yields both Work, Slavery and Worship, *Macht Frei.*

The fourth phrase is the most extraordinary. At the very moment of surrender, Man becomes as the angels, for the prayer that accompanies the tightening of the head-thong is the angels' *addendum* to the *Shema*, already recited once each morning with the washing of the hands - "*baruch shem kavod, malchuto le-olam va-ed.*"

The fifth is "*U-mey-chachmat'cha*", the favours asked, the requests made, that are so rare in Jewish prayer because - and here again the battle between free will and pre-determinism raises its head - God on the sixth day handed over to Man autonomous dominion, and then rested; from that point on, it's no longer His place to interfere or intervene in human history. Yes, but what parent doesn't seek to influence their child? And what child doesn't reach out at times for the safety-line of the umbilical cord? Grant me wisdom, Lord. Grant me understanding. Be kind to me. Cut down my enemies. Give me oil for my candle. Spread a little goodness round the world. None of these are much to ask. But this - "Open your hand and satisfy the cravings of every living thing"? Just because it's a line out of Psalms (145:16) doesn't excuse it, doesn't make it any the less greedy, any the less impertinent.

"*U-mey-chachmat'cha El Elyon, ta-atsil alay, u-mi-biynatcha teviyneyni, u-ve-chasdecha tagdil alay, u-gevuratcha tatsmit oyevay ve-kamay. Ve-shemen ha-tov tarik al shivah keney ha-menorah, le-hashpi'a tuvcha li-vriyotecha. Poteyach et yadecha u-masbiyah le-chol chay ratson.*"

"From Your wisdom, O supreme God, may You imbue me, from Your understanding give me understanding, with Your kindness be magnanimous with me, with Your power cut down my foes and rivals. May You pour oil of quality on the seven branches of the *Menorah*, to cause Your good to flow to all Your creatures. May You open Your hand and satisfy the cravings of every living thing."

There are prayers that I, as a human, cannot accept, and therefore cannot pray. This, surely, is one that God, being God, cannot accept either.

The sixth phrase, accompanying the wrapping of the *Retsu'ah*, is the loveliest, the most poetic. Ever since Hosea and the "Song of Songs", somewhere around the 8th or 9th century before the common era, the covenants between God and Creation and between God and Man have been allegorised as a marriage. In Hosea, adultery had caused the marriage to fail. In "Songs" it's the nuptial rites that are celebrated. In wrapping the leather strap of the *tefillin* around the middle finger of the weaker hand, Man betroths himself to God exactly as a bride does to her groom. *Lecha dodi likrat kalah.* Come, my beloved, greet the bride. As we welcome the *Shechinah* - the Holy Spirit, the Divine Presence - on Sabbath eve, so now does the binding of the *tefillin* make union of Man and God. It's my one regret at not laying *tefillin* (though two creatures may still be bound in common law, without a clergy marriage). Instead I take the *tsitsit* of my *tallit*, and wrap them round my middle finger, just as is done when the scroll is raised on *shabbat* for the reading of the Law. It's not the same. It's a marriage but it isn't a binding. It's a marriage, that's to say, of equality, not submission. A very modern marriage. And symbolically, for me at least, enough.

"*Ve-eyrastich li le-olam ve-eyrastich li be-tsedek u-ve-mishpat u-ve-chesed u-ve-rachamim. Ve-eyrastich li be-emunah, ve-yada'at et Adonay.*"

"I will betroth you to me forever, and I will betroth you to me with righteousness, justice, kindness and mercy. I will betroth you to me with fidelity, and you shall know the Lord."

We should never overlook the status of a woman in her marriage in the ancient world. A form of vassaldom. *Lecha dodi likrat kalah.* Come, my beloved, greet the bride. But the bride has a ring through her nose, denoting chatteldom, exactly like the young calf that you bought at market on your wedding morning. Thus also Man to God, ringed with *tefillin*.

Custom requires that all four phrases commanding the *tefillin* be recited while wearing them. Two are in the *Shema*, which occurs later in the communal prayers. The other two, the Exodus references - which are also the sources of the Passover rituals, the *pidyon ha-ben*, the Temple sacrifices and the covenant of the Land - provide the seventh phase of laying the *tefillin*, and are recited now. For reasons unclear they are treated as two, separate verses, though they are recited consecutively, as they appear in the original, in verses 1-10 of Exodus 13, then verses 11-16.

The *tefillin*, then, are worn only at the morning service, which thereby forbids women to wear them. They are worn only by men, never by boys, and so they are one of the two main religious symbols of *Bar Mitzvah* - the other is the right to be called to the reading of the Law. They are worn only on weekdays, and not then either if it's a festival. They are put on after the *tallit*, because "that which occurs more often takes precedence over that which occurs less often" (*Zevachim* 89a). The arm *tefillin* is put on before the head *tefillin*, because the *Shema* tells us to love God with our heart first, then our soul, then our might; and on the bicep, because it's the part of the forearm closest to the heart. The ritual is slow, elaborate and complex. Precise details are given as to how much length of strap should remain in the hand after the wrapping of the arm, the position of the knot, the part of the knuckle around which, the point of the wrist at which, the shape of the knot, the angle of the plinth, the exact point in the procedure at which particular words of particular prayers should be recited - everything but whether the angels lay *tefillin* when they dance upon the pin-head. And everything in just as much detail at the end of the service, when the *tefillin* have to be removed again. A person who does not lay *tefillin* is in breach of eight positive commandments. A person who does lay *tefillin* is guaranteed a long life, according to Isaiah 38:16, which informs us that "the Lord is with them, they shall live." Like a Japanese tea ceremony or the marriage rites of Asherah, the laying of *tefillin* is almost a complete religious service in itself. After all these elaborate processes, does God really require a whole service of prayer as well?

Chapter Four: *Berachot ha-Shachar* - Morning Blessings

Kavanah - Intention

8.15am. The boys, invariably, are late; the girls, with more excuse, are even later (the boys live in the house, adjacent to the synagogue; the girls a street away). They arrive in dribs and drabs, only to be sent away again to gather in their comrades. We have a *minyan* soon enough, but don't start until all who can be expected have arrived. Fifty or so by 8:20, seventy if we're lucky by 8:25. If the service were voluntary there would never be a *minyan*; because it's compulsory the ambience is damaged. What we perform is a religious ritual, when it ought to be a spiritual rite. Four or five lay *tefillin*, two dozen at most join in the prayers with serious attention; the remainder sit or stand, hands in pockets, chattering, compelled by me to silence in the holiest parts, sporadically involved, positively enthusiastic in the parts they like (*Oseh Shalom* rarely gets less than three reprises, and never a silent voice). It's a form of compromise that works, as is the service itself, an abbreviated *Shacharit* that nonetheless includes all the most important elements, *davened* from the orthodox prayer book, with the girls seated apart, but not behind a *mechitsah*. In an age when more Jews define their Jewishness ethnically and culturally than religiously, it's more than most would do, less than all should do, and much, much better than not doing anything at all.

Maimonides speaks of "*kavanah*", the intensity of inwardness required for satisfactory devotion. I look around this synagogue and wonder what hope there is for this amongst this crowd. *Kavanah* would be a fine thing, and "*ru'ach*" - ambience - as well, if only we could achieve it. At various points I will interrupt the service to insist on silence, and if I'm lucky I will briefly obtain some. But silence isn't *kavanah*. Silence is little more than reluctant respect and resigned presence. Maimonides writes that: "One should pray as if one were standing in the Divine Presence." I don't understand his employment of the term "as if".

✡

Minyan - Quorum

Why do we require a *minyan*? The answer is: we don't, but there's a special merit in praying with the *edah*, the community, because "God stands in the congregation of God" (Psalm 82:1). This is understood to mean (*Berachot*

6a) that where a congregation meets to pray, God will be present. But will God not be present if there's less than a full congregation? Surely God is everywhere, at all times? Why, then, do we require a *minyan*? We might as well ask: "Why do we require a synagogue"? The answer, there too, is that we don't, but if a community is to assemble for the purposes of prayer it needs a venue, and a synagogue, by definition, is precisely that - a meeting-place for the community. But may less than a *minyan* pray, in any space they find? Yes, to both parts.

How many of the *edah* constitutes a *minyan*? The answer is ten, but the source isn't obvious. It might be rooted in Numbers 14:27, where the concept of congregation is stated unequivocally, allied to the ten spies who came back deeply unimpressed by their reconnoitres in the land of milk and honey; only God lambasts this congregation and declares it evil. Genesis 18:32 finds Abraham asking God to spare Gomorrah for the sake of ten righteous men; but this isn't regarded as the source of the *minyan* either, because it was a number Abraham failed to find. Ruth 4:2 is more acceptable; there Bo'az takes ten elders of the city into the gate to pronounce on his Levirate claim to marry Ruth. Ruth who will grandmother King David and ancestress the Messiah. It has long seemed to me that twelve is a more logical number – one for each of the tribes, and because of the tribes, also the number who served each day as assistants, *mishmarot*, in the Temple. But no. The answer is as plain as the fingers on your two hands. The correct number for a *minyan* must be ten.

It is, however, considered deeply iniquitous to count a *minyan* on the fingers of your two hands - a superstition left over from the census of King David. Instead a poetic formula is used, a ten-word verse from Psalm 28:9: "*Hoshi'a et amecha u-varech et nachalatecha u-re'im ve-nase'im ad ha-olam* - Save your people and bless your inheritance, feed them and ennoble them forever." Silly superstition really. Judaism is full of this kind of atavistic nonsense.

Where a *minyan* cannot be convened, the prayers that cannot be said are *Kaddish*, the repetition of the *Amidah* and the responsive *Barechu*. All other prayers may be recited. Indeed, there is no law prohibiting a man, or woman, from praying all but these three exceptions entirely alone.

The law of the *minyan* requires ten to worship, but only three to judge, two to serve as witnesses and two to study. Given the exceptions to the law of *minyan*, given that God, like Moses, judges single-handed, given that one witness is deemed sufficient in the case of a husband who has been reported dead, which areas of study constitute transgression when I undertake them on my own? I'm merely pointing out the inconsistencies.

✡

Mah Tovu

"Mah tovu ohaleycha Ya'akov, mishknotecha Yisra'el. Va-ani be-rov chasdecha avo veytecha eshtachaveh el heychol kodshecha be-yirotecha. Adonay ahavti me'on beytecha, u-mekom mishkan kevodecha. Va-ani eshtachaveh ve-echra'ah evracha liphney Adonay osi. Va-ani tefillati lecha Adonay, et ratson elohim be-rov chasdecha aneyni be-emet yishecha."

"How lovely are your tents, O Jacob, and your dwelling-places, O Israel. As for me, through Your abundant kindness I will enter Your house, I will prostrate myself before Your holy sanctuary in awe of You. O Lord, I love the house where You dwell, and the place where Your glory resides. I will prostrate myself and bow down, I will kneel before the Lord who made me. As for me, may my prayer to You, Lord, be at an opportune time. O God, in Your abundant kindness, answer me with the truth of Your salvation."

"*Mah Tovu*" is one of those strange amalgams that are commonplace in Jewish prayer - a precursor of the techniques of Joyce and Eliot - a chain of phrases plagiarised from elsewhere in the liturgy, often contrapuntal, always straining towards harmony like the vaults of a cathedral on their flying buttresses. Phrases that bear no relation one to the other in their own contexts, but which come together to form a new context that is perfectly harmonious unto itself.

The chant is full of paradoxes. "How lovely are your tents, O Jacob" ought to come from Genesis, but is in fact from Numbers (24:5), and not only from Numbers but from the story of Balaam, a non-Jew inspired by the piety of Israel. We sing the praises of the synagogue by remembering the praises of a non-Jew for the desert shrine, as though we should be able to inspire ourselves through our capacity to inspire others. Then, entering the wrong house - nowhere in the *Torah*, nowhere in the entire Jewish Bible, is a *Beit Ha-Knesset*, a synagogue, referred to - we vow to prostrate ourselves in the ancient manner; but yet don't do so. And then we make the vow a second time; and for a second time don't do so. But modern Judaism is marked by broken vows like this. At the end of Passover and *Yom Kippur* we vow to be "Next Year In Jerusalem", knowing we intend to stay in Golders Green. And in the *Amidah* we ask for the in-gathering of the exiles from the four corners of the earth while preferring the Diaspora for ourselves, and for the restoration of a Temple in Jerusalem that is politically as well as religiously unbuildable. These paradoxes arrest and undermine me from the outset. If we can accept this about these prayers, then what faith can we have in any other vows? In the vow of covenant itself? Either we should keep our vows, or else not make them. Either we should mean our prayers, or else rewrite them. I vow not to lay *tefillin* nor to wear *tsitsit* nor to keep strictly *kosher* nor to guard the *shabbat* laws. These are vows I know that I can keep, unhypocritically. These are the vows that help me to define my Jewishness. These are the paradoxes that do not arrest or undermine my faith.

The other verses that constitute "*Mah Tovu*" are all from Psalms - 5:8, 26:8, 69:14 and 95:6, the latter modified from its original plural to the singular here. In Sephardi communities - the communities of Jews from Spain and North Africa – "*Mah Tovu*" isn't sung, but Psalm 5:8 is recited on entering the synagogue, and Psalm 5:9 on leaving it. So many differences between the two traditions - Sephardim will have to forgive me if I focus on the Ashkenazi in this account.

The inspiration of Balaam led him to recite a blessing over the Children of Israel. At one point the authors of the *Talmud* apparently intended to include that blessing as a part of the *Shema*, and if they left it out it was no other reason than its terrible verbosity.

Adon Olam

Shlomo ben Yehudah ibn-Gvirol of Saragossa, born around 1020, died at the age of only 37, leaving behind some of the most glorious poetry in the Hebrew language. Philosophically a neo-Platonist, spiritually a mystic, his body was crippled from early age by terrible disease - so much so that illness becomes an allegory in his poems.

> Forgive, my God, and overlook my sins
> Though none can fathom their number or their depth
> Remember, for my sake, your kindness, Lord
> Pay no heed to sins of dust and earth.
>
> Even if the decree has gone out against my life
> Annul it, my God, make it of no effect
> Consider my illness as my redemption
> And let my pain ransom me from death

Ibn-Gvirol began writing at the age of just 16, and found a patron in

Yekutiel ben Isaac ibn Hassan. But the Jews of his day disliked him and mistrusted him. His "*Machor Chayim*" found too much favour among non-Jews, and worse, it was written in Latin, not Hebrew. The few books that survived him were all in Latin, so that their authorship became unknown until Solomon Munk discovered the Hebrew originals in the 19th century: what is now known is the ethical code "*Tikkun Middot ha-Nefesh*", the elegy "*Bi-Yemei Yekutiel Asher Nigmaru*", and especially the "*Keter Malchut* - the Crown of Glory", which added a new dimension to the Hebrew canon: the pious song addressed inwards to the soul in its intellectual aspiration to discover God.

To most Jews the name Shlomo ibn-Gvirol means little more than an eponymous street in Tel Aviv. But every Jew knows his "*Adon Olam*", and every Jew has at the very least five melodies to sing it to: sometimes in its slow, rhapsodic form, sometimes mournfully, sometimes as a round, even to the tune of "Yellow Submarine", which fits it perfectly. We sing it only on the Sabbath, at the conclusion of the morning service, though it stands here in its historic place, in the morning service immediately after "*Mah Tovu*". As an expression, a definition of the metaphor God - the so-called "ontological argument" isn't one Jews bother too much about; no point, after all, debating the meaning of a metaphor - it is sublime. As a song of praise in honour of God, it's the perfect demonstration of what the Christians call a hymn.

Adon olam asher malach be-terem kol yetsir nivra
Le-et na'asah ve-hephtso kol azay melech shemo nikra

Ve-acharey kichlot ha-kol levado yimloch nora
ve-hu hayah ve-hu hoveh ve-hu yiheyeh be-tipharah

Ve-hu echad ve-eyn sheyni le-hamshil lo le-hachbirah
Beli reyshit beli tachlit ve-lo ha'oz ve-hamisrah

Ve-hu eli ve-chay go'ali ve-tsur chevli be-et tsara
Ve-hu nisi u-manos li menat kosi be-yom ekra

Be-yado aphkid ruchi be-et iyshan ve-a'irah
Ve-im ruchi geviyati Adonay li ve-lo irah

Master of the universe, who reigned before any form was created
At the time of Creation He was proclaimed King

After everything has ceased to be He, the Awesome One, will rule alone

He who was, is, and shall remain in splendour

He is unique, unseconded, there is none to compare with Him as His equal
Without beginning or conclusion, He is the power and the dominion

He is my God, my living redeemer, rock of my pain in time of stress
He is my banner, my refuge, the portion in my cup when I call out

Into His hand I entrust my spirit when I sleep and when I wake
My spirit and my body shall remain as one, God is with me, I have no fear

Of course, it may be erroneous to attribute the hymn to ibn-Gvirol at all. There are suggestions that it was written earlier, in Babylon. But tradition places it in ibn-Gvirol's hand, and who are we to doubt or question a tradition? What is certain is that the hymn was in use from the 14th century, for it appears in its 12-verse form in manuscripts from Germany, and in its 16-verse form among the Sephardim, on both occasions in the morning service, though in fact the closing couplet seems to suggest that its inclusion at the conclusion of the night-time prayers would be far more apposite. In many communities it's sung as part of *Kol Nidre* on *Yom Kippur*; in Morocco it's both a wedding song and a death-bed confession. For those with access to a copy, the 18-volume Encyclopaedia Judaica (actually there are 19 volumes, when you count the index, but we still call it the 18-volume) has printed scores for the hymn that include a mediaeval setting from Djerba in North Africa, an eight-voice acapella from the Venice Ghetto, and the adaptation of a 19th century Bavarian folk song. Avatars of the universal!

But who and what precisely is this metaphorical divinity whom ibn-Gvirol characterises? The timeless, infinite and omnipotent, yet always invisible Creator, whom men anointed Cosmic King because in our littleness we require a monarch to bow down before. "Master of the Universe", "the Awesome One", "He who was, is, and shall remain", "unique, unseconded", "my banner", "my refuge". No, there's nothing anthropomorphic here, nothing of the old man with a white beard sitting on His throne in heaven, scribing His judgements of our lives into a book. This is more Brahman than Brahma - pure urge, kinesis, energy: the Cosmic Unity. This is what the ancients intended by *El* and *Elohim* - the word *El* suggests "force" or "power". The constant generating and regenerating power of the Universe. The pulse of Life itself. How can you subject this to an ontological debate? No wonder the ancients spoke of "fearing" God, and not, as we do in our intellectual paltriness, of "believing in" Him. Who could disbelieve in Life? And who, after singing such a potent celebration, such a joyful attestation of his power, and of our part in it - who could fear

Him, or not fear Him?

✡

Yigdal

How very different the *Yigdal*, which follows, and which, like *Adon Olam*, is there for historical reasons though it's only ever sung at the conclusion of the Friday evening prayers. Where *Adon Olam* was all poetry and subjective faith, *Yigdal* represents an intellectual statement of the attributes of God, of rational belief. This isn't even a metaphorical God. It's a paradigm to explain a metaphor.

Yigdal elohim chay ve-yishtabach nimtsa ve-eyn et el metsiyuto
Echad ve-eyn yachid ke-yichudo nelam ve-gam eyn sof le-achduto
Eyn lo demut ha-guph ve-eyno guph lo na'aroch elav kedushato
Kadmon le-chol davar asher nivra rishon ve-eyn reyshit le-reyshito
Hino adon olam le-chol notsar yoreh gedulato u-malchuto
Shepha nevu'ato netano el anshey segulato ve-tipharto
Lo kam be-Yisra'el ke-Moshe od navi u-mabit et temunato
Torat emet natan le'amo el al yad neviyo ne'eman beyto
Lo yachaliph ha-el ve-lo yamir dato le-olamim le-zulato
Tsophey ve-yodeya setareynu mabit le-sof davar be-kadmato
Gomel le-ish chesed ke-miphalo noten le-rasha ra ke-rishato
Yishlach le-kets yamim meshichenu liphdot mechakey kets yeshu'ato
Metim yechayey el be-rov chasdo baruch adey ad shem tehilato

Exalted be the living God, and praised, He exists, unbound by time
He is One, there is none like Him, inscrutable and infinite in His unity
He has no body nor likeness of a body, his Holiness is beyond compare
He preceded all Creation, He was first and nothing precedes His precedence
He is master of the universe to every creature to whom He shows his majesty
He has granted His flow of prophecy to his treasured and splendorous people
In Israel none like Moses will arise again, a prophet of such clear vision
God gave His people the true *Torah* through His most trusted prophet
He will never amend nor exchange His law for any other, for all eternity
He sees and knows our hidden secrets, He understands everything at once
He rewards with kindness according to the deed, and evil in equal measure
At the end of days He will send his Messiah to redeem those longing for salvation

He will revive the dead in His abundant kindness, blessed forever is His name.

The source of *Yigdal* is Moshe ben Maimon, *Maimonides* as he's usually known, or the *Rambam* - student of Averroes and by a long way the most versatile and significant of Jewish mediaevals. Greater even than *Rashi.* Maimon came a century after ibn-Gvirol, but from the same Islamic world which revered Jewry as the inspirer of Mohammed, and gave them a golden age in North Africa and Spain even while the barbarians of the First Crusade were slaughtering Jews in Europe wherever they could find them - on the Rhine particularly. Born in Cordova in 1135, he lived most of his life in Morocco and Egypt, serving as personal physician to the Caliph and as the voice of ecclesiastical authority to the Jews. In the "*Mishneh Torah*" he created the first encyclopaedic codification of Jewish Law, and in the "Guide for the Perplexed" he synthesised it, giving Rabbinic judgement on almost every issue of *halachah.* He was taken to Israel after his death, and buried at Tiberias, the dream-city of a Roman Emperor, by the Sea of Galilee.

It was in his commentary on the *Mishnah*, that section of the *Talmud* in which the Rabbis commented on the Sinaic Laws, that Maimon enumerated his "Thirteen Principles of Faith", which he regarded it as heresy for any Jew to reject, and of which "*Yigdal*" is a summary in rhymed and metric verse. The original, which also gives rise to a song based on the repetition of the title alone, was called "*Ani Ma'ameen* - I Believe".

"I believe with complete faith that the Creator, blessed be His name, creates and guides all creatures, and that He alone made, makes and will make everything.

"I believe with complete faith that the Creator, blessed be His name, is unique, and there is no uniqueness like His in any way, and that He alone is our God, who was, who is, and who always will be.

"I believe with complete faith that the Creator, blessed be His name, is not physical and is not affected by physical phenomena, and that nothing may be compared to Him."

No problem thus far, provided that "*emunah shlemah*" is rendered as "complete", or if you prefer "whole-hearted", and not as "perfect" faith. No man should ever claim to have achieved perfection.

"I believe with complete faith that the Creator, blessed be His name, is the very first and the very last.

"I believe with complete faith that to the Creator, blessed be His name, and to Him alone, is it proper to pray, and that it is not proper to pray to any other.

"I believe with complete faith that all the words of the prophets are true."

Yes, now, here, I begin to waver. "All" the words of the prophets? Even those which seem to contradict themselves, let alone each other? And how do you define truth? I believe with complete faith that the words of the prophets were uttered in complete sincerity, and that they convey universal truths. There, does that go far enough?

"I believe with complete faith that the prophecy of Moses our teacher, peace be with him, was genuine, and that he was the father of the prophets - both those who preceded him and those who followed him."

Father of those who preceded him! Now there's a Borgesian concept if ever there was one.

"I believe with complete faith that the entire *Torah* now in our hands is the same one that was given to Moses our teacher, peace be with him."

Still, I managed to hold out as far as number seven. Alas, no further. I haven't spent four decades compiling my "BibleNet" and writing "City Of Peace" in order to recant now, upon hearing the Articles of Faith let alone seeing the Instruments of Torture that await the heretic. No, I have to discur. "The entire *Torah* now in our hands"? What, even the parts that reflect Second Temple practices of nearly a thousand years later? Even the God-given alternations? Even the parts that couldn't have been written down in Hebrew because neither Hebrew nor the art of writing down had been invented yet? Even the Oral Law, defined by men a millennium later? Time for someone to write a 21st century version of *Yigdal.*

"I believe with complete faith that this *Torah* will not be exchanged nor will there be another *Torah* from the Creator, blessed be His name."

"I believe with complete faith that the Creator, blessed be His name, knows all these deeds of human beings and their thoughts, as it is said: 'He fashions their hearts all together; He comprehends all their deeds.'"

No, a line from the Psalms (33:15) isn't enough to overthrow this fundamental principle - Judaism is not a cult of pre-determinism. Everything is undermined by this single phrase - forgiveness and redemption, free will, the autonomy granted on the sixth day. If to be a Jew requires the renunciation of free will and an acceptance of the superstition of Fate…no, we cannot claim free will and then declare events in our lives to be *beshert*, determined in heaven, written in the Book of Life like a playscript, and ourselves mere actors. One or the other, but not both. Either we wear the leather thongs and submit ourselves to following the script like automatons, justifying the judgement at every stage and not petitioning for change, or we have the dignity to stand as conscious, thinking human beings, making the bad decisions of our lives and dealing with the consequences. And anyway it makes a mockery. Did God know in advance that Moses would strike the rock at Meribah, that Jonah would take ship for Tarshish, that David would put Ur-Yah in the vanguard of his army, that Nebuchadnezzar and Antiochus Epiphanes and Titus would ransack Jerusalem, that He himself would appear to Job in the whirlwind, that Hitler would become Chancellor? It mocks. It mocks. If everything is predetermined, then that car that knocked your child down in the street was sent by God, just as much as the doctor who happened to be on the scene, and saved your child's life; and we should thank the car driver for fulfilling God's will as much as we should thank the doctor. Pre-determinism and free will are polar opposites. Judaism fools itself when it tries to claim both.

"I believe with complete faith that the Creator, blessed be His name, rewards with good those who keep His commandments, and punishes those who violate them."

The evidence of History is not, alas, strong in support of this. This, of course, is the central dilemma of the twentieth century Jew, never more lucidly expressed than in the writings, and ultimately in the death, of Primo Levi. It's Job's questions, and in the epoch of the *Sho'ah* it's all our question: was this God's punishment, or the birth-pangs of the Messiah?

"I believe with complete faith in the coming of the Messiah, and even though he may delay, nevertheless I anticipate every day that he will come."

The Santa Claus school of Judaism. And what if I don't believe in the coming of the Messiah, what if I reject the notion altogether as the puerile fantasising of desperate and superstitious Jewry - does this make me no longer a Jew? Maimonides says it does.

"I believe with complete faith that there will be a resuscitation of the dead whenever the wish emanates from the Creator, blessed be His name and exalted be its naming, forever and for all eternity."

The very rendering of "*techiyat*" as "resuscitation", instead of the customary "resurrection", demonstrates the way that even the immutable ground may shift. The translation is from the Art Scroll, not from me. The change is theological, not linguistic. In some of the texts of the Reform movement the concept of revival of the dead has been expurgated altogether.

And did Maimon, the greatest physician of his day, really believe there was a power of medicine greater, more miraculous than his own? And if he did, how could he go on practicing his trade, without pessimism, without dejection, without despair?

"From Moses to Moses, there was none like Moses." So say the sages. But how many marks out of thirteen would Moses of Sinai score on Moses of Cordova's examination of faith? Checks for 1, 4 and 5, humble reservations over 7, checks again for 9, 10 and 11, but that tallies only to an exact half, and all the rest would either be wrong or meaningless to him. Thus do immutable religions change and change.

And as for me, the inheritor of the legacies of both Moseses - the same score, but checks and crosses in quite different places. I, for example, accept the invisibility of God where Moses would have credited him with physical being; I refute the terms of His so-called Justice, which Moses himself defined. But what I reject most is the reduction of spiritual life to a set of rules, with the prospect of expulsion from the club if the rules are not adhered to; Thou Shalt Wear *Tsitsit* is really no different from my golf club, which won't let me play without a collared shirt, or my office manager, who insists on ties: does the clothing really impinge upon my *kavanah*? No, this isn't religion, but ideology; and if the 20th century has taught us anything, it's surely the dangerousness of dogmatic ideology. And anyway, it's impertinent of Maimonides to make universal doctrine out of personal prejudice and interpretation. This isn't how one speaks the inner dialogue.

The source of *Yigdal* is the Thirteen Principles of Faith. But the source is not the stream. The authorship of *Yigdal* itself is disputed between the rival claims of Daniel ben Judah and Immanuel ben Solomon, both of them Roman Jews of the early 14th century. Ben Judah was a *dayan* - a Rabbinical Judge - of the Roman Beit Din; nothing else is known of him except the legend that he spent eight years refining it, completing the work in 1404. Ben Solomon, by contrast, is a well recorded figure, a wandering teacher and the author of the "*Machbarot*", a collection of poems both light-hearted and intensely serious, but whose real significance lies in their having introduced the sonnet into Hebrew. Ben Solomon went by the *nom de plume* of Manoello Giudeo when he published his Italian verse, and is the favoured candidate in the rivalrous dispute, primarily because of the technique of the poem, its metrical construction and its use - *Adon Olam* does the same - of a single continuous rhyme through each of its fourteen phrases (fourteen, despite there being only thirteen principles of faith - the last phrase is repeated in the Ashkenazi version; in the Sephardi a line is added by the poet, stating that "these are the thirteen basic tenets of Jewish faith and Law).

Immanuel, of course, has to be the favourite candidate, if for no other reason than his friendship with Dante Alighieri, the author of the Divine Comedy - we Jews are nothing if not historic name-droppers. Dante was extraordinary in many ways, but none more so than for the total absence of anti-Semitism in his work. There are no Jews amongst the heretics, the counterfeiters, the murderers, the general sinners, not even amongst the usurers whom he encountered on his journey through the Inferno. In Paradiso 5:80-81 he even says: "Be like men and not like foolish sheep, so that the Jew who dwells among you will not mock you." Immanuel of Rome was almost certainly the only Jew that Dante ever met. After Dante's death Immanuel and another of Dante's close friends, Bosone da Gubbio, marked the event by an exchange of obituary sonnets; and when Immanuel himself died, da Gubbio had a similar exchange of sonnets with Cino da Pistoia, in which Dante and Immanuel are united in a single phrase. Immanuel's own "*Machbarot ha-Tofet ve-ha-Eden*", the last of the twenty-eight sections of his "*Machbarot*", is a Dantesque description of a journey to the world-to-come, in which he's guided, not by Virgil, but by one Daniel, who might well be his rival claimant Daniel ben Judah, but whom scholars regard as Dante himself, thinly disguised.

First Blessings

"*Baruch atah Adonay eloheynu melech ha-olam asher kidshanu be-mitzvotav ve-tsivanu al netilat yadayim.*"

"Blessed are you O Lord Our God, King of the Universe, who sanctified us with His commandments, and commanded us to wash our hands."

"*Baruch atah Adonay eloheynu melech ha-olam asher yatsar et ha-adam be-chachma u-vara vo nekavim nekavim chalulim chalulim. Galu'i ve-yadu'a liphney chiseh chevodecha she-im yipateyach echad me-hem o-yisater echad me-hem, i-ephshar lehitkayam ve-la'amod lephaneycha. Baruch atah Adonay rophe chol bassar u-maphli la'asot.*"

"Blessed are you O Lord Our God, King of the Universe, who fashioned Man in his wisdom and created in him many openings and orifices. It is obvious and known before Your Throne of Glory that if but one of them were to be ruptured or blocked up, then it would be impossible to survive and stand before You. Blessed are You, O Lord, who heals all flesh and does such wondrous deeds."

To argue with the theology isn't simply the right of every Jew, but actually his duty and his responsibility. So Abraham disputed with God at Gomorrah. So Job argued with the whirlwind, until it finally appeased him. So Jonah disputed Justice in the shade of a ruined gourd. The Socratic method borrowed by the *yeshivot* - the rabbinical seminaries - relies on exposition and debate, the syllogising and synthesising of contradictory proofs and disproofs. There could be no Hillel without Shammai. The process by which we deduce law from the *Torah*, defined by Rabbi Yishmael, was hotly disputed by both Rabbi Joshua and Rabbi Akiva. Nothing, ultimately, is certain, not even law, not even uncertainty.

But here I wish to state a disagreement that isn't theological but organisational. The two introductory blessings which appear now (*Netilat Yadayim* and *Maphli La'asot*) shouldn't appear now, in *shul*, when we are wrapped in holiness. The first, also, should be the second. Thus, upon awakening, the "*Modeh Ani*", then, surely, "*Maphli La'asot*", the prayer for relieving oneself, then "*Netilat Yadayim*", the blessing for the washing of the hands, and finally the "*Reyshit Chachma*" when one is clean. Action must be linked to prayer, prayer to action. I'm asking, not for a modification of belief nor a change of *halachah*, but simply for logic in spirituality.

There is a splendidly Swiftian quality about the lavatory prayer, the recognition that the profane and the sacred are both God's creation, that however high we may exalt the spirit, so just as low will the body earth us, much in the way that Jacob dreamed his ladder at Bethel (the ancients, incidentally, used the term "Jacob's Ladder" for the Milky Way). Without mockery, without irreverence, it sets the noble in an authentic context, to wonder what Moses did for a latrine during his forty days on the mountain, to imagine a Prophet with constipation or diarrhoea. And indeed, isn't the whole point of King David that here was a serial lecher who also wrote psalms, a man who erected permanent cathedrals of song and prayer precisely because of the permanency of his own erections. Blessed are you, O Lord our God, who also introduced lust and defecation into the world, alongside mercy, justice and compassion.

✡

Berachot ha-Torah - The *Torah* Blessings

"*Baruch atah Adonay eloheynu melech ha-olam asher kidshanu be-mitzvotav ve-tsivanu la'asok be-divrey Torah. Ve-ha'arev na Adonay eloheynu et divrey Toratecha be-phinu u-ve-phi amcha beyt Yisra'el. Ve-niheyeh anachnu ve-tse'etsa'eynu ve-tse'ets'a'ey amcha beyt Yisra'el kulanu yodeya shemecha ve-lomdey Toratecha lishmah. Baruch atah Adonay ha-melamed Torah le-amo Yisra'el.*"

"Blessed are you O Lord Our God, King of the Universe, who has sanctified us with His commandments and commanded us to engross ourselves in the words of the *Torah.* Please, Lord, our God, sweeten the words of your *Torah* in our mouths and in the mouths of your people, the family of Israel. May we and our offspring and the offspring of Your people, the family of Israel - all of us - know Your name and study Your *Torah* for its own sake. Blessed are You, O Lord, who teaches *Torah* to His people Israel."

"Baruch atah Adonay eloheynu melech ha-olam asher bachar banu mi-kol ha-amim ve-natan lanu et Torato. Baruch atah Adonay noten ha-Torah."

"Blessed are you O Lord Our God, King of the Universe, who selected us from all the nations and gave us His *Torah.* Blessed are You O Lord, giver of the *Torah.*"

Another moment of contradiction. We're told that it's forbidden to study or to recite passages of *Torah* until the *Torah* blessings have been made. And yet we've already recited from the *Torah* several times in the prayers to date, and we still haven't made the blessings. Why then are they here, and not earlier? Is it because here we'll not only recite but study, because here we'll deal not only with the *Torah* but also with the *Talmud*? Is there, again, a usurpation of authority by the Rabbis, a bestowing upon themselves of unwarranted pre-eminence?

The recital and study of *Torah* is fundamental to Judaism, for its own sake and as part of prayer. To pray is to bless, of course, but more so when you make a blessing first. Yet there are oddities even here. In these first two blessings, two short songs of praise for the giving of the *Torah* in the first place, and specifically for giving it to Israel, we ask God to "sweeten" it, a phrase which by definition infers sourness in the original, for there can be no need to add sugar to what is already palatable. Why is the *Torah* sour? Because it's hard, the sages answer. Hard in the sense of difficult, and so requiring study. Hard in the sense of harsh, and so requiring either tolerance or submission. Hard, by both definitions, in the sense of rigorous.

These blessings deal with our duties towards the Law, which include teaching and studying and not mere blind obedience. (Given what has been said previously on this subject, I'm inclined to repeat that sentence: these blessings deal with our duties towards the Law, which include teaching and studying and not mere blind obedience. The keywords here are "mere" and "blind".) Hence the *Mishnah* tractates that will follow. But first there are important ordinances. There is the notion - fundamental to the formula of every prayer - that God has "sanctified us with His commandments". "*Lehakdish*" in Hebrew means "to set apart", and something which is holy is so because it's differentiated from the rest. We are holy not because we keep the laws but because we're differentiated from those who do not keep them, Jews as well as non-Jews. So there are levels of purity, but there are also burdens of purity. There is the notion that God "has chosen us from among the nations", which defines Judaism as first an ethnic, and only then a religious identity; but more importantly it states the nature of the burden of purity. Chosen doesn't mean elite or superior, as the anti-Semites have for so long chosen to interpret it. The rest of the world is bound only by the seven Laws of Noah, the Jews by the whole *Torah*. Holiness is an aspect of rigour.

The second of the two blessings, "*Noten ha-Torah*", is also the blessing that will be said by the *oleh*, he who is called to the Reading of the Law. Nehemiah (8:1-6), describing the return of the exiles to Jerusalem, tells how Ezra the Scribe brought a *Torah* scroll out to the Water Gate on the first day of the seventh month (*Rosh ha-Shana*, according to Leviticus 23:24), and read it to them from morning until noon, standing on a wooden pulpit. "And he opened the scroll in the sight of the people, and when he opened it all the people stood up. And Ezra blessed the Lord, the great God, and all the people answered *Amen*, *Amen*, and bowed their heads, and worshipped the Lord with their faces to the ground." The first recital of the *Torah* in the holy city since the destruction of the Temple. From such events are customs born.

✡

Yevarechecha: the Priestly Blessing

"*Yevarechecha Adonay ve-yishmerecha. Ya-er Adonay panav eleycha vi-chunecha. Yisa Adonay panav eleycha ve-yasem lecha shalom.*"

"May the Lord bless you and keep you. May He turn his face to shine on you and be gracious to you. May He lift up his countenance to you and bring you peace."

We who bless are also blessed. The relationship between Man and God is dialectical, a covenant signed by two parties, a dialogue, even if the closing chapters of Leviticus, so dark with threats of violence, do make it seem like the feudal relationship between a noble and his serf. We bless God, and through his Priests - not the Rabbis, who lack authority - we in turn are blessed (originally, according to *Bamidbar Rabbah* 11:2, God made the blessing Himself, but passed the authority to the Patriarchs, and after them gave it to the *Cohanim*). It's everyone's favourite prayer, a regular in Christian churches too, for the words in their case, for both the words and the melody in ours, and for the "*ken yehi ratson*" with which we punctuate each line (I note this only because Reform synagogues continue to say "*amen*". The distinction is straightforward: when a prayer is addressed to God, we say "amen", a statement that we believe in the legitimacy of the prayer; but the *Yevarechecha* is a blessing addressed to us by God, and so we respond with an acknowledgement – "if it be your will"). Yet this prayer too is an oddity in a monotheistic cult that abhors idolatry - for it's patently the blessing of a sun-god.

Where *Yigdal* is a sonnet, *Yevarechecha* is a *haiku*, fifteen words built pyramidically in lines of three, then five, then seven words. To understand its overt meaning isn't difficult, but there's also a pyramid of subtleties beneath the surface too. In the *Targum*, the translation of the *Torah* made either by Onkelos or by Aquila, a 2nd century proselyte living in post-exile Israel, it's made clear that the first line is intended as a blessing for success in one's daily occupations and for protection in circumstances of difficulty and danger; that the second line relates to *Torah* study, and is a request for enlightenment of the intellectual kind; that the third verse is an act of supplication, asking God to listen to us when we call to Him; and that the final phrase is a supplementary prayer for peace at all times and in all places.

If this was the official interpretation in the 2nd century CE, then it seems churlish to dispute it now. And yet it makes no sense at all. For centuries, when the Temple stood, the Priestly Blessing was a daily feature of the service, immediately after the morning and afternoon offerings (*Tamid* 7:2 and Maimonides' *Hillel Tefillah* 14:14). Onkelos' interpretations imply a supplication upwards, from Man to God. But unlike every other prayer, in whatever form, the *Yevarechecha* was a blessing downwards, from God to Man, transmitted through His intermediaries the Priests. Where the blessing appears in the original *Torah* (Numbers 6:24-26), it's followed by this qualifying phrase, precisely to ensure that there was no misunderstanding of the role or power of the Cohen in the blessing: "Thus they shall put My name before the children of Israel, and I will bless them."

Perhaps the answer to the Onkelos mystery lies in the wider usage of the *Yevarechecha*. Even while there was still a Temple, even before there were synagogues, it was common to recite the Priestly Blessing at every gathering of the *Anshei Ma'amad*, the twenty-four tribal officers who conducted all aspects of religion locally and took their annual turn as clerics at the Temple in Jerusalem (*Sotah* 7:6, *Ta'anit* 4:1). A holy act that is repeated too often loses its holiness, in that it ceases to be the difference and becomes the sameness. So the sacred is reduced to the profane. So the mysterious becomes the banal. So it's possible to reinterpret the universal into the personal. So it's easy to make the extraordinary ordinary.

The notion of God "turning his face to you" and "shining on you" is doubly significant. What happens if He doesn't, if he chooses to "*histir panav*", to turn His face away from you, to offer a blind eye? What if He acts as described in Leviticus 17:10, "And whatsoever man there be of the house of Israel, or of the strangers that sojourn among them, that eateth any manner of blood, I will set My face against that soul ("*ve natati phanay ba nephesh*") that eateth blood, and will cut him off from among his people"? In this notion lies the Jewish explanation of the existence of evil in the world. It isn't a dualism like the Christian or the Hindu or the Zoroastrian, where an adversary (Satan) or a fallen angel (Lucifer) or a destructive power (Shiva) operates in intended opposition to the preserving God. Evil is what happens when God turns his face aside. The absence of a blessing is a curse.

In modern Israel, and in Sephardic communities, the full *Yevarechecha* is recited daily, complete with "*duchening*" - the ascent onto the platform before the Ark. In the Diaspora, the recitation of the *Yevarechecha* at this moment of *Shacharit* is little more than formal and ceremonial, a footnote in the historical text. It's merely part of the flow of service, and doesn't even require a congregational response. In the additional service for Sabbath it's given a fuller treatment, the ceremony formally introduced with an explanatory verse, each phrase chanted, each phrase greeted with the response "*ken yehi ratson* - if it be Your will". But the full and formal and proper recitation is reserved for *duchening*, which takes place before the prayer for peace at the end of the *Amidah*, on all the Biblical festivals - the three pilgrim festivals, plus *Rosh ha-Shana* and *Yom Kippur*. This is because the *Yevarechecha* should only be recited "in joy", and for centuries the atmosphere of the Diaspora precluded it. Is there any reason, then, for not reviving this loveliest of ceremonies today?

The rite which we wrongly call *duchening* should properly be known as "*nesi'at kapayim*", the "lifting up of the hands", and it has as its source two phrases. The first is in Leviticus (9:22): "And Aaron lifted up his hands to the people and blessed them"; the second, in *Talmud Shabbat* 118a, speaks of the *Cohanim* "going up to the *duchen*", originally the platform in front of the Holy of Holies in the Temple. It's a lovely ceremony and well worth describing in full. After the *Kedushah* in the repetition of the *Amidah*, the *Cohanim* and *Leviyim* depart the praying area of the synagogue, in order that the *Leviyim* may wash the hands of the *Cohanim*, in preparation for the rite.

Immediately before the blessing "*Retsey*", those members of the congregation who are the descendants of the Temple priests remove their shoes - the laces, if they have any, are untied before the washing of the hands - re-enter the praying area, and are called to ascend the modern equivalent of the *duchen*, the platform before the Ark (if there's only one *Cohen* present, the call is omitted; if there's no *Cohen* present, the whole ceremony is omitted). They ascend with their heads wrapped in their prayer shawls, facing the Ark. At the conclusion of *Modim*, the Thanksgiving Blessing, the prayer leader calls out "*Cohanim*" and the priests raise their hands, spreading their fingers in conjoined pairs to form the letter *sheen*, and recite the "*Yehi Ratson*" blessing that precedes the *Yevarechecha*, timing it so that the two prayers end together, and a single "*amen*" from the congregation harmonises them.

The Priestly Blessing itself is performed responsively, the prayer leader calling out each word individually, in the form of a chant, but quietly, because his role is prompter, not chief protagonist. The congregation through this merely stands, facing the *Cohanim* but not looking at them, recipients of the blessing, heads bowed and eyes cast downwards in the traditional posture of humility. Any person standing behind the Priest is outside the aura of the prayer, and so is excluded from the blessing. It is permissible to move.

In some communities the congregation actually turns its back on the *Cohanim*, a bizarre response which seems to imply a denial of the Priestly Blessing. The source for a rejection of this practice is no less an authority than *Rashi*, Rabbi Solomon ben Isaac of Troyes, the leading mediaeval commentator on both the Bible and the Talmud. *Rashi* noted that in *Talmud Chagigah* 16a, it states that "their eyes become dimmed" if they look at the *Cohanim* during the blessing, and explained that this was because the Divine Radiance literally emanated from the fingertips of the *Cohanim* when they pronounced the *Shem ha-Mephorash*, the secret, hidden name of God - the so-called Tetragrammaton, YHVH - within the Holy of Holies of the Temple. *Rashi* specifically proscribed the practice of turning the back, not on the grounds of discourtesy, but because the danger to the eyes simply isn't present when the Priestly Blessing is recited outside the Temple. *Adonay* is said in place of the *Shem ha-Mephorash*, and the power of God, apparently, isn't converted into pseudonyms.

Superstition and ratiocination dwelling side-by-side! The same is true of the ancillary prayers attached to the *Yevarechecha*. An entire liturgy of prayers were written to accompany the Priestly Blessing, but the *Talmudic* Rabbis themselves couldn't make up their minds whether they should be said, or read, or utterly ignored (*Sotah* 40a) The question raised was: are we being rude to recite other prayers while God is blessing us through His priests, or are we being properly obedient, by reciting verses that acknowledge and show gratitude to Him for his blessing? The official conclusion is attributed to Rabbi Chanina bar Papa, a Palestinian *amora* of the early 4th century who belonged to the famous circle of Rabbi Jonathan that included Abbahu, Isaac Nappacha, Ammi and others. Chanina was held to be the greatest preacher of his day, and so holy that even the *Lilim*, the night spirits, feared him, because he distributed alms at night, sometimes even while his body was in bed asleep. So holy was he, indeed, that when the Angel of Death came to take him, he asked for an extra thirty days of life in order to complete his studies, and not only did the Angel of Death agree to his request, but arranged for a pillar of fire to come down when he departed for the world to come. Chanina joined the debate about the *Yevarechecha* at a late stage, but his contribution sealed the matter. "Can you imagine a servant who is not attentive to what is being said to him?" he asked, with what one imagines was a comprehensive shrugging of the shoulders. The ancillary prayers were dropped.

But not the personal prayers. It's considered not only legitimate but positively virtuous to introduce a personal request or meditation after each verse of the Priestly Blessing, and two are provided in the liturgy for this purpose. The first is "*Ribbono Shel Olam* - Lord of the Universe", and it's based on the statement of an anonymous *Talmudic* sage in *Berachot* 55b, that if a man has had a dream, and is uncertain whether it was foretelling good or evil, he should stand before the *Cohanim* when they make the blessing and say "…", after which the prayer is detailed, exactly as it's still said today:

"Master of the Universe, I am Yours and my dreams are Yours. I have had a dream and I do not know what it foretells. May it be Your will, O Lord my God and God of my fathers, that all my dreams regarding myself and regarding all Israel be good ones - those I have dreamed about myself, those I have dreamed about others, and those that others have dreamed about me. If they are good, strengthen them, fortify them, make them endure in me and in them like the dreams of the righteous Joseph. But if they require healing, heal them like Hezekiah, king of Judah, from his sickness; like Miriam the prophetess from her sorrows, like Naaman from his eczema, like the waters of Marah through the hand of Moses our teacher, and like the waters of Jericho through the hand of Elisha. And just as You transformed the curse of the wicked from a curse to a blessing, so may You transform all of my dreams regarding myself and regarding all of Israel for goodness. May You protect me, may You be gracious to me, may you accept me, *amen*."

A God who lives everywhere, both in reality and in virtual reality! The invocation of the miracles of God as healing agents through the transformative act of dreaming! And dreams themselves as acts of healing! Did Freud not know this prayer? Surely, if he had, he would have considered it worthy of an essay, a monogram, a volume?

The second, logically entitled "*Yehi Ratson* - If It Be Your Will" - was composed in the 17th century, but by whom isn't recorded. It constitutes a *Kabbalistic* code-poem, a complex formulation in which a 22-letter name of God, one which may be scanned with the eyes but never spoken, one which is derived from the words of the Priestly Blessing itself, is incorporated into the text. Between superstition and ratiocination, the middle path - mysticism! Forgive me if I don't transpose it here.

✡

Elu Devarim

So to the *Mishnah*, and surely it's no coincidence that a Rabbinical passage should be placed immediately after the Priestly Blessing (I've phrased it this way, rather than saying "should be preceded by", because it's precisely the afterness that's significant), as though to emphasise that that jealous sibling rivalry is still alive today - though there are, of course, both *Leviyim* and *Cohanim* among the Rabbanim, just as there were once Rabbanim in the priesthood. But also because study is as important as, some would say – as we will see shortly - more important than prayer.

Mishnah means study, not in the Hebrew but in the Aramaic, from the root "*tanna*" which also gives the word "*tanna'im*", the early exponents of the dual sciences of hermeneutics and exegesis - the interpretation of the Scriptures for the purpose of deducing the detail of God's intention in the laws He gave to Moses. In short, the Oral Law. These *tanna'im* were the Rabbis of Babylon and Palestine, during the first two centuries of the Christian era, which is to say from around the year nought, when Hillel and Shammai were the acme of Jewish wisdom, until the final compilation of the *Mishnah* late in the 2nd century, under the guiding hand of Judah ha-Nasi. The objective of *Mishnah* was to make a written copy of the Oral Law, to put flesh on the skeleton of *Torah*, so that men and women who could no longer worship by sacrifice in the Temple would nonetheless understand what was required of them if they were to live in as full an obedience to the Law as the loss of Israel and especially the Temple allowed: the defining of the substitution. The detail was everything. *Torah* says: "You Shall Not Kill" - but is this a universal generalisation, or is it relative to circumstances: what about killing animals for food, or men in war, in self-defence? Whether as an academic discipline in the *yeshivot*, or as a matter of making real judgements on real cases in the *Beit Din*, the Rabbinic court, the *tanna'im* laid down in the *Mishnah* the first detailed commentary on the Laws of Moses.

The *Mishnah* contains the nucleus for all the *halachah* - legal - and *aggadah* - non-legal - commentaries preserved in the *Talmud*. It is divided into six sections, known as Orders: *Zera'im* (Seeds), *Mo'ed* (Seasons), *Nashim* (matrimonial law), *Nezikin* (civil law), *Kodashim* (aspects of holiness) and *Tohorot* (ritual purity). But Judah ha-Nasi's redaction wasn't definitive. No final text of the *Mishnah* was published until the Spanish edition of 1485, of which only a handful of pages survived the expulsion seven years later; the Naples text of 1492 is now regarded as the first complete edition. But that was eleven hundred years after Judah ha-Nasi, during which time the *tanna'im* and *amora'im* continued to revise and emend and update the text continuously - every time indeed that they found a clearer interpretation, a new alternative hypothesis, a further example out of actual case law, another piece of casuistry, a seeming contradiction or simply a cleverer way of saying it. This last statement is immensely significant. It took the Rabbis two hundred years to conclude that they did not know the final answers, to recognize that what they had put in place was not only a substitution for the authentic, but an uncertain, a provisional substitution, still open to review, revision, improvement, clarification. As it still is today

Mishnah then is the commentary on the Law. *Gemara*, the task of the *tanna'im*'s successors, the *amora'im*, in the centuries following Judah ha-Nasi, was the commentary on the *Mishnah*, and the two together - give or take a handful of other minor texts - comprise the whole of the *Talmud*. *Gemara* means completion, but that doesn't infer that commentary has ceased. Commentary on the *Gemara* is known as *Tosepha*, and though its greatest exponents were *Rashi* and Maimonides in the Middle Ages, the process continues to this day. In a very real sense, the study of *Mishnah* as part of prayer may be said to contribute to it.

As far as our morning service is concerned, the first excerpt we encounter is from Tractate *Pe'ah* 1:1, the second tractate in the order *Zera'im*. Where the original *Talmud* is in Aramaic, the version in the *Siddur* has been translated into Hebrew. Hebrew ceased to be a daily or a written language in the 580s BCE, when Nebuchadrezzar (sic) of Babylon took the tribe of Judah into captivity and replaced them in Israel with the Aramaic-speaking Samaritans. But Hebrew has always remained the language of poetry and prayer. The subject of *Pe'ah* is the laws relating to the gleaning in the fields (Leviticus 19:9-10).

"These are the precepts that have no fixed measure: the corner of a field, the first fruit offering, the pilgrimage, acts of kindness, *Torah* study."

No fixed measure. Yes - I like this. As limitless as God Himself, the extent of charity we give, the scale of sacrifice we may render, the number of times we may visit the Temple, the fervour of our humanity. And of course *Torah* study. When the totalitarian impulse is removed and men are left to make their own way through the wilderness to Sinai - the personal wilderness, the personal Sinai - it is a most philanthropic and civilised philosophy that we propound. Indeed, I suspect that the greatness of Judaism way well lie right there in that tiny space, too small for pin-heads let alone for angels or men to dance in, that separates the religion from the philosophy, and that this may also explain why so many of the great achievements of Jews in the past two hundred years have taken place in the secular world, by men and women who had left behind the religion, but taken with the core of the philosophy.

As the *Mishnah* comments on the *Torah* (here *Pe'ah* on *Yevarechecha*), so the *Gemara* comments on the *Mishnah* (here *Shobbas* 127a on *Pe'ah* 1:1).

"These are the precepts whose fruit a person enjoys in this world but whose principle remains intact for him in the world to come. They are: the honour due to father and mother, acts of kindness, early attendance at the house of study in the morning and the evening, hospitality to guests, visiting the sick, providing for a bride, escorting the dead, absorption in prayer, bringing peace between man and his fellow man - and the study of *Torah* is equivalent to them all."

First the Rabbis denote that the reward for keeping these commandments will be equal in this world and in the world to come, a necessary scholium since "the world to come" had never really been conventional Judaism before this time. That is to say, there is no world to come in the *Tanach*, the "Old Testament", but only "dust to dust, ashes to ashes", only "the Lord gives and the Lord takes away", diversely repeated and unequivocal.

Then the Rabbis built their famous "fence around the *Torah*", defining among other things the five precepts of no fixed measure, until the individual was once again subsumed within the given universal structure. Which acts of kindness? Any, you would think, if they're of "no fixed measure". But the Rabbis disagree. "The honour due to parents, early attendance at the house of study morning and evening, hospitality to guests, visiting the sick, providing for a bride, escorting the dead, absorption in prayer, bringing peace between man and man - and the study of *Torah* is equivalent to them all."

This is immensely comforting to the book-worm, but in truth outrageous. To study this passage that I'm studying now, in the privacy and solitude of my study as I'm doing now, or in the *yeshiva* with a friend and a master as the *Pirkei Avot* advises, is equivalent to making tea for visitors, or sitting at a sick man's bedside and eating all his grapes? Honouring one's parents, which is one of the Ten Commandments, and which carries with it both an implied threat of punishment and a promise of reward - "that your days may be long upon this earth which the Lord your God has given you" - has the same status as getting to *shul* in time for *Ma'ariv*? No, this is the Rabbis making a hedge around the fence, and a brick wall around the hedge, and an *eruv* of the brick wall, and a ghetto of the *eruv*, and ultimately a shield of electrified barbed wire against which the heretics may be thrown.

But all of this is just an argument between men and men. What matters is the peace between Man and God. And this is now restored.

✡

Elohay Neshama

"My God, the soul You placed in me is pure. You created it, You fashioned it, You breathed it into me, You safeguard it within me, and eventually You will take it from me, and restore it to me in time to come. As long as the soul is within me, I gratefully thank You, Lord my God and God of my forefathers, Master of all works, Lord of all souls. Blessed are You, Lord, who restores souls to dead bodies."

If only that were really so. And if only it weren't in complete contradiction to "*Adonay natan, Adonay lakach*"; yet again we see Judaism trying to eat its *matzah* with its *chamets*.

I am interested in the transitions between prayer and prayer, which show "prayer" to be a generic term too vaguely universal to be entirely satisfactory. Changes of tone, of ambience, even of direction (sometimes we pray inwardly to God, at other times outwardly to each other), the constant shifts from heart to mind to soul, even to body, and then revert again. Blessing becomes meditation, meditation becomes tractate, tractate becomes supplication, supplication becomes hymn, hymn becomes ritual, ritual becomes silence. We talk to God, we talk to ourselves through God, we speak the words with which God addresses us, directly or indirectly, through His intermediaries the patriarchs or prophets or priests. We chant, we recite, we listen…and He never responds.

Talking to God is prayer. Hearing God answer is schizophrenia.

But the eschatological is always there, the Messianic, the Gehennic. Judaism has always been an evolutionary cult, changing, growing, developing, never remaining static despite its theoretical immutability. One of its great traditions is that new customs may be established whenever a new community is formed, or for the benefit of a community in a specific cause and place and circumstance and time of need (this custom was itself originally an example of this); and that new customs may be absorbed into the firmament of Judaism, assimilated as part of that tradition, which remains, for all that, still, eternally, immutable. So the space is open to acknowledge that the Sho'ah happened, and was survived, that the State of Israel has come into existence, and is strong. So there is no longer any need to field the substitute.

What was given by God to Moses on Mt Sinai is written law - *mitzvah*. What was interpreted by the Rabbis and written down in the Talmud is Oral Law – *chok;* though there are also *chokim* in the *Torah*, which distinguishes *chokim* from *mishpatim*, gathering the two as *mitzvot*. The *mitzvot* are binding, the Rabbinic *chokim* are subject to constant scrutiny, revision, reinterpretation, and are only binding insofar as custom and tradition are binding. But this leaves a bad taste in the mouth. How often will the Rabbis use immutability as an excuse for conservatism, but then argue custom and tradition as a pretext for a change when it's convenient? If they can introduce the resurrection of the dead as a first principle, if they can create an entire angelology complete with Satan the Adversary, if they can allow a child's mother, in the uncertainty of his father, to define a child's Jewishness, then surely they could also unchain women from tyrannical or recalcitrant husbands, or accept as Jewish the child of a Jewish father whose mother is not Jewish – like Bilhah and Zilpah's sons, and Joseph's? Would it not, after all, be an act of kindness, which as we've just prayed is one of the five precepts that have no fixed measure? "How goodly are thy tents, O Jacob, your dwelling place, O Israel. As for me, through your abundant kindness, I will enter your house..." It was enough for Balaam, a non-Jew. Yet apparently it isn't enough for many of those born Jewish.

The Fourteen Blessings

"A person," according to the *Talmud* (*Menachot* 43b), "is required to recite one hundred *berachot* [benedictions] every day." Fourteen of them are recited now, the *Shacharit* Blessings as they're traditionally known.

"Baruch atah Adonay eloheynu melech ha-olam, asher natan la-sechvi vinah le-havchin beyn yom u-veyn laylah."

"Blessed are You O Lord Our God, King of the Universe (each one of the blessings begins with this phrase), who gave the cock the intelligence to distinguish day from night."

The comic first, which praises God for giving to the cock the intelligence to distinguish day from night, and whose comedy is so disarming to the orthodox in contemporary America that they've chosen to mistranslate "*la-sechvi*" as "the heart" in preference to "the cock" (actually I'm being very slightly unkind; Job 36:36 also uses the term "*la-sechvi*" and there it clearly does refer to the heart; "the naked, thinking heart" as John Donne called it; Judaism has long believed that the heart and not the mind is the nexus of human thought).

"Baruch atah Adonay eloheynu melech ha-olam, she-lo asani nachri."

"Blessed are You…for not making me a non-Jew."

The problematic second. Throughout the centuries the text has read "*she-lo-asani nachri*", which is then misconveyed as "heathen", a denotion of religion, instead of "stranger", a denotion of ethnicity. The Singer prayer book continues to use "*nachri*", but the American Art Scroll has amended "*nachri*" to "*goy*", which means "nations" in the sense of "gentiles", and thereby affords both the religious and the ethnic. This clarifies without taking sides (what is the point of building a fence around the *Torah* if you refuse ever to come off it?), but it also tolerates certain pejorative inflexions. To say "*Goy*" is akin to saying "*Yok*", a retort to "*Yid*" at the same pitch of derogation; wouldn't it be more mature to thank God for the positive of making us Jews, rather than the double-negative of not making us non-Jews?

In the case of converts to Judaism, neither "*nachri*" nor "*goy*" is used, but rather "*ger*", for a man, "*giyoret*" for a woman, meaning proselyte; this at least demonstrates some maturity. But it is also disingenuous. In its frequent Biblical usage, especially in Leviticus, a "*ger*" was not a convert, because such a concept simply didn't yet exist ; a "*ger*" was a non-Israelite dwelling among, or working for the Israelites, and the phrase "*ka ger ka ezrach*" was established as a fundamental principle of life in Canaan: laws that applied to the Israelites must also apply to non-Israelites, unless they required membership of the tribe to carry them out. Thus, for example, a "*ger*" living in your house or town could not be asked to break the Sabbath laws on your behalf. "*Ka ger ka ezrach*" implicitly prohibits the "*shobbas goy*".

"*Baruch atah Adonay eloheynu melech ha-olam, she-lo asani aved.*"

"Blessed are You…for not making me a slave."

The heroic third - heroic, because those Jews imprisoned in the *Arbeitungslager* who still managed to say their prayers did not expunge this verse.

"*Baruch atah Adonay eloheynu melech ha-olam, she-lo asani ishah.*"

"Blessed are You…for not making me a woman."

The apparently misogynistic fourth - I say apparently because the attitude of the *Talmudic* Rabbis to women was always reverential, and if women were exempted from certain acts of prayer it wasn't originally a matter of exclusion but of absolution, an "act of kindness". In *Niddah* 45b, for example: "The Holy One, blessed be He, gave a greater measure of understanding to woman than to man." Or *Yevamot* 62b: "A man should honour his wife even more than his own self." Though it's true that this latter adds as an expedient to its counsel, "for the sake of peace in his home". Nonetheless, it has come to be regarded as misogynistic, and in many parts of the modern Jewish world this prayer has now been expunged. Can we not regard it as argument in time and circumstance that this is one prayer that should be removed, replacing the slur by removing the language?

"*Baruch atah Adonay eloheynu melech ha-olam, she-asani kirtsono.*"

"Blessed are You…for making me according to His will."

At this point there generally ensues a space of silence in which the doubly patronising fifth may occasionally be heard, the voice of a woman permitted on this rare occasion in the synagogue, but please inaudibly, behind the screen - the voice thanking God for making her "according to His will". This extends my list of oddities, because of course woman isn't now as God intended her, and the will of God has had to be subjected to probate; what God did in fact will is unclear, but equality is manifest in Genesis 1:27, and childbirth wasn't part of it, until it was added as a punishment at the time of the expulsion from Eden.

Obviously men do not say the fifth blessing; it's there for women as their alternative to "*she-lo asani ishah*". Would it not be better, again arguing the right to change custom when time and circumstance ordain it as appropriate, to allow the women's blessing to be recited by men also, restoring our equality, and with it the removal of the misogynistic slur by dint of granting the women's blessing precedence?

And then the readily acceptable blessings. The sixth (*pokeyach ivrim*) for opening the eyes of the blind. The seventh (*malbish arumim*) for clothing the naked (the same blessing is used when putting on a brand-new garment). The paradoxical eighth (*matir asurim*) – paradoxical because it's recited while wearing the *tefillin* - for freeing the bound. The ninth (*zokeph kephuphim*) for raising up the bowed. The tenth (*rokah ha-arets al ha-mayim*) for making the continents. The eleventh (*she-asah li kol tsarki*) for supplying our wants – a blessing from which the poor and needy are not excused. The twelfth (*ha-meychin mitsadey gaver*) for making our steps firm. The thirteenth (*ozer Yisra'el bi-gevurah*) for making Israel strong. The fourteenth (*oter Yisra'el be-tipharah*) for crowning her with glory - especially at Dir Yassin, and at Sabra and Shatilla, and at Taba, and in Chevron, moments of our brightest modern lighthood to the nations; but at least the intention is a good one. The fifteenth (*ha-noten la-yayeph ko'ach*) for strengthening the weary.

And yes, I know that makes fifteen. And indeed, the Art Scroll calls these the Fifteen Blessings, which must be regarded as a most radical liberalism and modernisation. Singer prefers the traditional Fourteen, with the women's prayer parenthesised, and those that follow moved each one rung up the ladder of patriarchal sanctimony. The resolution of the difference lies in the fact that the women's blessing was added only after the *ga'onic* period, which is to say in the early middle ages, and it's a moot point whether it's regarded as the women's substitution for the men's "*she-lo asani ishah*", or as a parenthesis, or as an addition. Rabbi Aaron Soloveitchik, one of the great contemporary *amora'im*, has put the case for the women's blessing being a diplomatic declaration of women's innately superior status, noting that the Hebrew word for compassion – "*rachum*" - is etymologically connected to "*rechem*", the womb. I suspect, however, that this is more a sop to feminism than a sincerely expressed *Responsum*.

The origin of the Fourteen is the *Talmudic* tractate *Berachot* (60b), which takes a mystical view of the blessings, regarding them as a kind of spiritual code or allegory, subject to interpretation. Thus the routine actions of the day are elevated and extolled. In the first blessing we awaken. In the second we recognise both our nakedness and, in the case of men, the sign of our Jewishness, and doing as Adam and Abraham, we dress. In the third we put our free will to good use, deciding how to live this day. And so on. The morse isn't easy to decode, but the Rabbis insist that the actions included are sitting up and stretching, getting out of bed, standing on the floor, putting on one's shoes, setting out to one's destination, fastening one's clothing, and putting on a hat.

Judaism is full of this kind of trashy quasi-science, anything from *Gematria* and the Tree of Life to these sorts of readings-into-text, and latterly such stupendous nonsense as the Bible Codes. *Arizal*, for example (Isaac ben Solomon Luria Ashkenazi, also known as "The Ari), in connection with the Fourteen Blessings, observes that the word "*tsaddik*", the Ba'al Shem Tov's *hasidic* equivalent of a Bodhisattva, is made up of letters with the numerical values 90, 4, 10 and 100. He therefore concludes that a righteous Jew - a *tsaddik* - should say the *Kedushah* four times daily, keep the Ten Commandments, say *amen* to each of the hundred daily blessings, and recite a further ninety of his own. For those of you who like to count, by the time you have completed this section of the *Shacharit* service, a pious Jew should already have passed the quarter mark, twenty-five.

It is disputed whether there are not, in fact, sixteen blessings (Ned Temko, the former editor of the Jewish Chronicle, once commented to me wryly that it's precisely these heated disputations about the type of pin-head on which the angels danced that give Judaism its inner dynamism, and that they are therefore to be encouraged. An *Arizal amen* to that.). This is because the Fourteen (or Fifteen) are immediately followed by another, much longer benediction, "*Ma'avir Sheyna*", for God "who removes sleep from my eyes and slumber from my eyelids". Is this appended, or is it subsequential? To me the answer is - it should be moved entirely, for it's self-evidently misplaced. Either it should come second, after cock-crow, or at the very start of day, with "*Modeh Ani*". Am I being overly fastidious in once again wanting my prayers, and my God, who supposedly made order out of chaos when He created the universe, to conform to logic?

There might very well have been sixteen, in fact. In the original blueprint for this set of benedictions, a blessing "for not having made me a boor", which is to say an ignoramus (or possibly an agnostic – for this is the precise translation of "ignoramus" into Greek), was included. The argument was simple, if patronising – boorish, actually; it suggested that an ignorant man couldn't possibly know the *Torah*, and was therefore bound to sin. But the Rabbis rejected this, and a thousand years later *Rashi* explained why. An ignorant man is still required to keep the commandments. Ignorance is never a mitigating circumstance. One should attempt to keep even those laws of whose existence one is unaware.

But this doesn't apply either to women, or to slaves, or to non-Jews, for whom there can be exemption. Non-Jews because they're only expected to keep the seven Noachic laws. Slaves because they're bound to their masters before God and ought also to be non-Jews. Women because the only laws which apply unequivocally are those not bound by time – except that there are exceptions: reciting or hearing *Kiddush* and *Havdalah*, eating *matzah* on the first night of Passover, listening to the reading of the *megillah* on *Purim*, lighting the candles on *Chanukah* and *shabbat*, drinking four cups of wine at the Passover *Seder*, and rejoicing in the festivals being the time-bound laws from which women are not exempt.

In place of this proposed but rejected blessing, the Rabbis inserted what is now the third of the fourteen benedictions, "*she-lo asani aved*", the blessing in gratitude for not having been made a slave.

✡

Ma'avir Sheyna

Those who regard "*Ma'avir Sheyna*" as separate from the Fourteen Blessings, thereby resolving that dispute, are still not satisfied however. If it's not to be appended to the prayers that come before it, is it nonetheless to be prefixed to the prayers that follow it? Should it stand alone, or is it in fact a preface to the first of the two "*Yehi Ratson*" prayers that come next? These seeming trivialities matter, in the way that disputes over musical scores matter. In prayer, a silence too long or too short can be completely devastating (think of the close of the final movement of Mahler's 4th). The soul quavers, and likewise the heart crotchets and the mind semi-breves. A switch from *legato* to *andante* could shatter Paradise.

"Blessed are you O Lord Our God, king of the universe, who removes sleep from my eyes and slumber from my eyelids. And may it be Your will, O Lord Our God and God of our forefathers, that You accustom us to studying the *Torah* and bind us to Your commandments. Lead us not into error, transgression or sin, nor into temptation or scorn. Do not allow the Evil Inclination to dominate us. Keep us far from a bad person and a bad companion. Bind us to our Inclination towards Good and to good deeds and compel our Evil Inclination to be subservient to You. Grant us today and every day grace, kindness and mercy in Your eyes and in the eyes of all who see us, and bestow lovingkindness upon us. Blessed are You O Lord Our God who bestows lovingkindness on his people Israel."

The text of "*Ma'avir Sheyna*" is fascinating, a succession of entreaties to protect us from the power of evil, with evil known by many names and many forms: the power of error, the power of transgression, the power of sin, the power of temptation, the power of scorn, and most of all the dualistic *Yetser ha-Ra* - the Evil Inclination - and *Yetser ha-Tov* - the Inclination towards Good. The apotheosis of such abstract concepts seems

Hellenistic, yet to the Greeks it was always the positive virtues that were deified, not the negative vices as in this case. The Evil Inclination, opposed by the *Yetser ha-Tov*, the Inclination towards Good, is the ultimate proof that free-will trumps pre-determinism in the Jewish world-view.

There are resonances of the Lord's Prayer, the one that Jesus of Genasseret allegedly wrote, in the enumerated calls to God. It is all present, phrase by phrase. The hallowing of the name, the heavenly kingship, the daily forgiving of sin - our own sin, and our forgiving of other people's sins. The very phrases Jesus uses - "for Yours is the kingdom", "for ever and ever" - are core Jewish liturgy, with which he as a Rabbi would have been familiar; indeed, most of the phrases he used are quotations from the scriptures, anthologised in precisely the same style of the day that his fellow Rabbis favoured. But there is nothing in the Christian doxology that quite replicates the profound Idea that underlies this prayer, this concept of *Yetser ha-Tov* and *Yetser ha-Ra*, which I regard as one of *Talmudic* Judaism's most sophisticated contributions to both philosophy and psychology, but which - and this needs bold, italic and underline - simply isn't tenable in the face of scientism and pre-determination, is irreconcilable with that fatalistic paradigm of a Man whose deeds are known from the outset. Either God does indeed know, and we are automatons, or we are autonomous, driven by the contrary Inclinations, making choices at every moment of our own free will, guided by *Torah*, goaded by the threat of punishment and the promise of reward. Either one or the other. The theologians can't have it both ways.

"*Ma'avir Sheyna*", almost more than any other, seems to be a prayer directed to ourselves, an inner dialogue, a disputation of the mediaeval sort, in which the ears of Faust are simultaneously bent both ways. But in the prayer it's the voice of the Inclination Towards Good that's heard, a gentle voice, a courtier's voice, petitioning its sovereign with p's and q's. There is a covenant after all, that You will be our God, look after us, protect us, bring rain in its season, guarantee justice, mercy and compassion. So it isn't really a favour that's being asked at all, it isn't a request beyond the terms agreed. There exists a covenant, a contract, and each side is obligated to fulfil it. In the highest court of the Universe the voice of Good insists: I will have my bond. Keep the Adversary from my door.

And then a courtier's bow, a step backwards, the descent of the dais away from the throne. A final gesture of humility - a final glance to see if the king has turned His face to shine on you, or else turned it away - before departing from the Royal Presence. "Blessed are You, Our Lord, who is very kind and gracious to his people Israel."

The paradox of a covenant which declares equal in the sight of the Law, One who is a King, one who is His lowest vassal. Equal in the court of universal Justice.

✡

Yehi Ratson

The "*Yehi Ratson*" which follows echoes the "*Ma'avir Sheyna*", but variously. Just as the Ten Commandments are divided, five between Man and God, five between Man and Man, so here. "*Ma'avir Sheyna*" asked for protection against the Inclination Towards Evil which is inside us but allegorised as *ha-Satan*, the Adversary which is outside us (in its original form *ha-Satan* was simply the name given to the accuser in a court of law; c.f. Psalm 109:6, Zachariah 3:1). "*Yehi Ratson*", by contrast, asks for protection against actual men, those who have succumbed to the Evil Inclination and would afflict us contagiously, those of us who are bound by the commandments as well as those of us who are not. Experience shows that, when praying for protection from evil, it's as well to pray against the bad Jews as against the bad non-Jews.

"May it be Your will, O Lord my God and God of my forefathers, that You rescue me today and every day from arrogant men and from arrogance, from a bad man and a bad companion, from a bad neighbour, from any mishap, from a violent adversary, from a harsh trial and a harsh opponent, whether he be a signatory to the covenant or not a signatory to the covenant."

As so often in Jewish prayer, "*Yehi Ratson*" makes reference not just to the specific god of he who prays, but to the Universal God of all who pray, now and in the time of our forefathers, meaning, though on this occasion not naming them, Abraham, Isaac and Jacob. Whatever else it may be, Judaism is always atavistic, a form of ancestor worship really, though our founding fathers were not gods, not even sons of God like the Greek Titans, not even Prophets; our patriarchs were ordinary men, venal, mediocre, subject to error and vanity, but capable of instances of greatness. That the God who is our God was also their God establishes a link and a constancy across time, just as the fact that every Jew in the world recites the same prayers in the same order (more or less), and at the same of time of day (even if the longitudinal shifts of time-zone make this unsimultaneous), establishes a link and a constancy across space. So we too are universal, in the image and the likeness of our God.

That "*Yehi Ratson*" should follow the Fourteen Blessings may be appropriate after all. "Deliverance from arrogance" after the misogyny of the fifth verse and the blemished light-unto-the-nations of the fourteenth! But that it should follow "*Ma'avir Sheyna*" is difficult to understand, since the two prayers seem to echo each other in their content as well as their intent. The answer is probably that "*Ma'avir Sheyna*" was the original prayer, "*Yehi Ratson*" written as its improvement; but that Judaism, which is excellent at adding, is generally incapable of subtracting, at least when it comes to liturgy. Properly the two should now be said as if one single prayer, but in fact the division is maintained - a matter of honouring the great rather than for any religious reason.

The authorship of "*Yehi Ratson*" merits a digression. Rabbi Judah ha-Nasi was a direct descendant of Hillel, and the son of Rabban Simeon ben Gamliel, born, according to *aggadic* tradition, on the very day that Rabbi Akiva died, tortured and executed by the Romans in Caesarea in 135 CE. For many years Judah had charge of a *yeshiva* in *Beit She'arim*, but spent the last seventeen years of his life at Sephoris on the Sea of Galilee, making it the headquarters of the *Sanhedrin* of which he was *Nasi*, the Prince or President. Given that these were the years that followed the rebellion of Shimon bar Kochba and the final destruction of Jewry in the land of Israel, Judah's good relations with Rome, including personal friendships with two emperors, Septimius Severus and Antoninus Caracalla, were to say the least surprising. Judah briefly revived the use of Hebrew as the first language of the Jews of Israel, and ruled that the *Shema* might only be recited in Hebrew, where previously the Rabbis had condoned its recitation in whatever language.

But his greatest contribution was the redaction of the *Mishnah*, the rabbinic commentary on the Written Law. According to tradition, when Moses received the laws from God at Sinai, they came in two forms, the written and the oral, which is to say a set of 613 commandments, scored on stone for anyone to read and know, and with them, but not written down, the full meaning of those laws, their usage and interpretation, their clarity and application. "All offerings must be salted" doesn't make clear the quantity of salt. "To the foreigner you may lend at interest" doesn't fix a rate nor a time-scale nor establish a penalty clause for failure to repay. "Stolen property must be returned to its owner" fails to provide compensation to an innocent third party. "You shall not boil a kid in its mother's milk" doesn't automatically lead on to the prohibition of ice cream after roast lamb without at least some explanation. The *Torah* establishes the principles but omits the sub-clauses. It was more a manifesto than a White Paper.

The answers to all these questions and a thousand more were also, it was said, given by God to Moses, and passed on by him to Joshua, who informed the elders of the tribes, who passed the baton to the Prophets, who brought it in its fullness to the Rabbis of the Great Assembly, who decided, out of historical necessity when the Temple was destroyed and the bulk of the people taken off into captivity, that now the Oral Law must be written down, or else it and the Jewish people would be lost. For the best part of two hundred years, in Babylon at first and latterly in Israel, the writing down had been in process, but randomly, haphazardly, without structure or logic. Judah collected, arranged and codified the whole gamut of Oral Law - the technical term is redaction. It was this that would later, but much later, acquire for him the sobriquet "*rabbenu ha-kadosh* - our holy teacher".

Chapter Five: Submission and Sacrifice

The Akeda

The story of the binding of Isaac, told in Genesis 22:1-19. How God instructed Abraham to take his son Isaac, and sacrifice him on the altar on the top of Mount Moriah. How Abraham unquestioningly carried out the task, but at the last moment was precluded by the intervention of an angel, who informed him it was just a test, that he had passed, and that he should sacrifice instead the ram that was bleating in the bracken. The termination for all time of human sacrifice, at least as far as Judaism is concerned.

Before re-telling the story, with an introductory verse taken from the *Zichronot*, the memorial prayers recited in the *Amidah* of *Rosh ha-Shana*, we ask God to remember, first us, then the protagonists - a marvellous conceit that I'm minded to work into my fiction at some point. Though it isn't in fact God that we ask, but all the gods, the pantheon that preceded monotheism, "*eloheynu ve-elohey avoteynu*", the great Multiple Plural, the All-In-One.

"Our God and God of our forefathers, remember us favourably and recall us with a mixture of salvation and mercy from the lofty and primeval heavens. Remember on our behalf, O Lord our God, the love of the patriarchs Abraham, Isaac and Jacob, Your servants, and the covenant, the kindness and the oath that You swore to our father Abraham on Mount Moriah, and the *Akeda*, when he bound his son Isaac on the altar, as it is recounted in Your *Torah*."

Follows the complete text of Genesis 22:1-19. I am interested in the mysticism that surrounds what is the most worldly of tales - I mean worldly in the sense of being firmly rooted in the material and phenomenological universe. The *Kabbalists* claim that to reiterate the *Akeda* is, like the making of a *golem* or a magic charm, to amulet one's own children against the knife (historical evidence tends to suggest the amulet isn't efficient). It also serves as a prophylactic against punishment, being regarded as an act of penance in its own right. This is pleasing, if rather silly. One can't imagine too many courts of justice who would accept thirty repetitions of the *Akeda* as an alternative to custodial sentence, let alone regard it as an argument for exculpation, though I'm fully aware that in Catholic jurisprudence a similar number of *Pater Nosters* or *Ave Marias* is regularly accepted.

It's strange that Christianity doesn't dwell more on the tale, which after all describes a father leading his beloved son to the summit of a mountain - the same mountain, the Hill of Skulls, Golgotha, Calvary, Moriah - the son carrying the wood for his own sacrifice, the father allowing the son to be bound. There are even the other two men, who keep them company. There's the name Moriah, which is rendered as Maria in the Latin, Mariamne in the Greek, and which denotes the Temple Mount and Hill of Calvary. There's even an aroma of veronica, among the flowers on the hillside, and a hint of myrrh among the crowds come out to witness this strange new version of the Azazel. Or perhaps the Christians pass the story over (my phrasing is intentional) because in their version the father mistook the son for the paschal lamb, the one that was bleating in the bracken, and failed to re-sheath the knife.

Checking my Singer, I discover to my surprise that the *Akeda* is missing from the service. I go to Rabbi Jeffrey M. Cohen's guide to the synagogue service, looking for an explanation, but all he says is that "few congregations recite Art Scroll's pages 22-24 inclusive" - which is rather an odd way of putting it, almost a guiltily embarrassed way of putting it; to find out what he's referring to you would have to have an Art Scroll, and if you don't, there's no hint that it's the *Akeda* that's omitted. Now I'm seriously intrigued, where before I was merely surprised. Has the *Akeda* been air-brushed, Orwelled, sent to Kolyma? Why the secrecy, let alone the expurgation? Is there something post-Holocaustal happening here? I feel an e-mail to the Office of the Chief Rabbi coming on. (But my e-mail evoked no satisfactory *responsum*, which I take to mean that the Chief doesn't know the answer either - if anybody reading this does know the answer, please pass it on.)

✡

Ribbono Shel Olam - Master of the Universe

Whatever meanings are to be drawn from the tale itself, the supplicatory paragraph appended to the story, headed with the phrase "*Ribbono Shel Olam*", contains them all. It's the cry of Job writ large, and it links back to the matter of the Evil Inclination. "Lord, may You be as Abraham, and not as God." What a terrible condemnation! It's expressed more subtly than my paraphrase, but this is nonetheless the gist. God who sent the Flood, who destroyed Sodom and Gomorrah, who sent Abraham to Moriah; and Abraham who accepted the Covenant which included God's penitential rainbow, who argued God into Justice at Gomorrah, who accepted the ordeal of the knife, and passed the test. We humans may recognise our image in the deity, but we must find our role-models in other men, however frail. What more despondent or despairing prayer to lay before the feet of God - "may You be as Abraham."

And to ensure that He is, a reminder of his pledge to Moses. Covenants are legally empowering, Lord, covenants are legally binding. Covenants cut both ways.

"Master of the Universe, may it be Your will, O Lord...that You remember for our sake the covenant of our forefathers. Just as Abraham our forefather suppressed his mercy for his only son and wished to slaughter him in order to do Your will, so may Your mercy suppress Your anger against us and may Your mercy overwhelm Your other attributes. May You overstep with us the line of Your law and deal with us - O Lord our God - with the attribute of kindness and the attribute of mercy. In Your great goodness may You turn aside Your burning wrath from Your people, Your city, Your land and Your heritage. Fulfil for us, O Lord our God, the word You pledged through Your servant Moses, as it is said: 'I shall remember my covenant with Jacob and my covenant with Isaac and my covenant with Abraham, and the land too I shall remember."

Descriptions of the attributes of God abound throughout the liturgy. Here it's the borders of His realm that are enumerated: "Your people, Your city, Your land, Your heritage." The first three are transparent, but what, pray, is God's heritage?

The essence of the prayer is a calling upon God to remember His covenant. What kind of a relationship, what lamentable history of bad experience, leads us to remind an omniscient and omnipotent deity of His promises? Are we doubting His omniscience? Are we questioning His omnipotence? Have we forgotten already the completeness with which we so recently declared our thirteen principles of faith?

The phrasing throughout is tortuous and torturous, but it elucidates a request of quite stupendous impudence. "Just as Abraham our forefather suppressed his mercy" - ! - "and wished" - ! -"to slaughter" - ! - "so may You suppress Your anger against us and may Your mercy overwhelm Your other attributes." How does mercy suppress anger - and why, anyway, is God quite this angry with us? The Jews of *Angst* live on eternally, terraced in guilt. And why this querying of the quality of His mercy? And then the real *chutspah*: "May You overstep the line of law with us, and deal with us in kindness and with the attribute of mercy." May You overstep the line of law! What is this? A bunch of green-backs in a brown envelope? Incitement to corruption? The misuse of *protectsia*? Come on God, forget what it says in the rule book, forget the exact terms of the covenant (forget the fact that what we're asking you specifically to do is to remember the exact terms of the covenant), and turn a blind eye, just this once, to our transgressions (not that we're prepared to turn any sort of a blind eye to Yours). But no, God is a traffic warden, not a drugs-bust police officer; God isn't susceptible to back-handers and rejects the special pleading. "I shall remember My covenant." Then did it fail, or did it work? And is this the reason why "few congregations recite Art Scroll's pages 22-24 inclusive"?

As if this paragraph weren't odd enough already, the recollection of the Covenant is given, uniquely I think, in reverse order - first Jacob, then Isaac, then Abraham. I presume this is done to give symmetry to the passage, allowing it to end as it began, with Abraham. (It is, besides, a quote out of Leviticus. The order is *Toraic*, not Talmudic - Leviticus 26:42 – and well worth reading that chapter in the context of God's anger: not the utopic first fourteen verses but the dystopia that follows, a litany of the torments that God will inflict "if you will not hearken unto Me, and will not do all these commandments").

This "*Ribbono Shel Olam*" - one of many in the liturgy that begin with the same phrase and therefore bear the same name - has great historical status, both for its authorship (it was written by Yochanan ben Zakkai for inclusion in the *Vidu'i* or "Confession" service of *Yom Kippur*) and for an incident of its use. According to *Talmudic* sources (*Berachot* 7a), when Rabbi Yishmael was serving as High Priest in the Temple, and went into the Holy of Holies on *Yom Kippur*, God asked him for a blessing and it was this verse - one has to admire his tenacity - that he spoke.

Rabbi Yishmael, serving as High Priest! Now there's the cue for a piece of historical research well worth the undertaking. Take each word slowly as a pill dissolved in water, and hear the resonances. In the days of the Second Temple, when the Pharisaic and Sadducaic traditions co-existed, but with little mutual empathy, a Rabbi served as High Priest in the Temple. Legally possible, of course; there is nothing to prevent a Cohen from becoming a Rabbi.

But which Yishmael? The *Talmud* offers no more information - which is itself a valuable piece of information: it infers that everybody would have known; students of American history don't ask "which Lincoln?" or "which Jefferson?", any more than those of English literature ask "which Shakespeare?" - so I'm guessing that it must have been Yishmael ben Phabi II, who was appointed High Priest by Herod Agrippa in 59 CE (the only other plausible candidate was the innocuous Yishmael ben Phabi I whom the Procurator Valerius Gratus appointed High Priest in 15 CE). *Berachot* 7a claims that it was Yishmael ben Elisha, the author of the "*Bera'isa Zevachim*" that we shall encounter shortly; and even more contentiously claims that Yishmael ben Elisha was Yishmael ben Phabi by a pseudonym. The circle of choice for the High Priest was extremely close, and the Phabi family stood at the nucleus. Originally Egyptians, from the important Jewish colony of Alexandria, they moved to Israel under Herod I. Josephus names Yishmael as one of the co-delegates in the embassy to Rome to protest against Agrippa II, when Agrippa refused to allow the priests to put up a defensive wall around the Temple. Nero supported the priests, but detained Yishmael as one of several hostages, and appointed a new High Priest, Joseph ben Simeon, in his place. As a footnote to that piece of history, the sad and failed and traitorous career of Rabbi Joseph, later Flavius Josephus, was itself founded on the captivity of Yishmael, for it was precisely in the hope of securing his release that Joseph was originally sent to Rome.

Several *Talmudic* fragments allude to Rabbi Yishmael (*Pesachim* 57a, for example), and a famous passage of the *Tosepha*, the additional material appended to the *Talmud* after its completion, laments: "Woe is me because of the house of Yishmael ben Phabi, woe is me because of their fists...for the Temple Court cried out: 'Lift up your heads, o ye gates, and let Yishmael the son of Phabi, the disciple of Pinchas, let him enter and serve us as High Priest." (*Tos. Men.* 13:21)

During his brief time in office he was privileged to be one of the very few High Priests in history to preside over the ceremony of the preparation of the ashes of the red heifer - either seven or nine instances are recorded, depending on which source you read. The ceremony of the red heifer is detailed in Numbers 19, and refers to the Laws of Purification found in Leviticus 12-15. It's a ceremony of purgation of the defiled, and so mysterious are its meanings and its esoterica that King Solomon himself is said to have despaired of ever understanding them. When asked by a Roman to explain them, Yochanan ben Zakkai, the founder of the *yeshiva* of Yavneh which did more than any other single act to save Judaism after the destruction of the Second Temple, could only explain the ceremony by means of a pagan analogy:

"Just as a person afflicted by melancholy or possessed of an evil spirit is freed of his disease by taking certain medicaments or by the burning of certain roots, in the same manner the ashes of the red heifer, prepared in the prescribed way and dissolved in water, drive away the unclean spirit of defilement resulting from contact with the dead."

White magic and aromatherapy!

The Roman was satisfied with ben Zakkai's answer, but the Rabbi's disciples were not. Recognising that the master's response had been a "warding off with a broken reed", they demanded a proper explanation.

"By your lives the dead man does not make you impure, any more than the ashes dissolved in water purify you. But the law concerning the red heifer is a decree of the all-holy, whose reasons for issuing that decree it behoves not mortals to question."

In other words, he didn't know either.

But two things are known. The first is that red heifers are very rare, and that perfect red heifers - and only perfect red heifers are suitable for the ceremony - are almost unicorn. The second is that, when Yishmael ben Phabi prepared the ashes of the red heifer for the ceremony, the Pharisees weren't content he'd done it properly, and so he used a second perfect beast, and got it right!

✡

Le'olam Yehei Adam

"Let a man be always God-fearing, privately and publicly."

Yes, this ought to go without saying. But we all grow up to be comfortable with our personal version of hypocrisy.

We have entered fully into the dialogue now. Objectivity no longer matters. To the man of faith, God exists, even if He doesn't. And if God exists, then He exists whether or not men believe in Him. So perhaps we're addressing the void, or the blackness beyond the void, or the nothingness beyond the blackness, but we're still addressing something - nameless, infinite, metaphoric, invisible. A black hole, or God.

"Let a man be always God-fearing, privately and publicly. Let him acknowledge the truth, let him speak the truth in his heart."

Even if there's only the black hole, it's still worthy of the praying.

Acknowledging the truth at all times is, of course, a highly dangerous activity. Amongst the many titles I considered for this book, the one I finally settled on was "A Myrtle Among Reeds", a phrase which recalls Rabbi Abba bar Zabda, a Palestinian *amora* of the 3rd century CE and the leading scholar of his day at the Tiberias *yeshiva*. In a portion of the *Talmud* Abba noted that a Jew who has sinned is still a Jew, in the same way that a myrtle that grows up among reeds is still a myrtle, and still called a myrtle. And even if not as a title for this book, the phrase will unquestionably serve me for an epitaph, though please, God, not just yet.

Because I'm happy to be called a sinner, but not happy to be called an apostate. I'm not opposed to Law as such, but merely indifferent to certain portions of it, in a state of lovers' quarrel with some others, downright indignant and even dissident over not a few. Nor am I a Reform or a Liberal or a Reconstructionist Jew, though that's where I find myself the least uncomfortable. Ultimately I reject all denominations and insist on my rights of membership of the whole people. I am a Jew, without need of adjectives. I do not seek to justify my lapses theologically.

So I have spoken the truth, and from the heart, just as the prayer ordained. I am no less God-fearing because I offer Him my criticisms with my prayers.

But then the self-detriment, always this grovelling, sycophantic self-detriment.

"Master of all worlds. It is not because of our righteous deeds that we lay our supplications before You, but because of Your abundant mercies. What are we? What is our life? What is our piety? What is our righteousness? What is our salvation? What is our strength? What is our might? What can we say before You, Lord our God…?"

Well I shall tell you what we can say before Him. Our life - is ours to live freely, fully, and with dignity, standing upright. Our kindness - that of Jonah before the gourd, of Abraham before Gomorrah. Our righteousness - not to be confused with our contemptible self-righteousness. Our salvation - belief in this world, not the next one, which belief will bring us salvation from deluded fantasies and life-impeding vanities; which will drive us to achieve such levels of humanity that we will qualify for after-life as well, if it turns out that there is one. And our might - why I've already stated that. Our might is our humanity, made in the image and the likeness of almighty God.

"Are not all the heroes as nothing before you?"

The derogation of History.

"The famous as if they had never existed?"

The blotting-out of memory.

"The wise as if devoid of wisdom?"

The subversion of *Tanach* and *Talmud.*

"The perceptive as if devoid of intelligence."

The discrediting of every sage and scholar.

"For most of their deeds are vain, and the days of their lives are empty before You. The pre-eminence of Man over beast is non-existent; for all is vanity."

What does one do with all this garbage? Bury it, or recycle it? Ignore it, or laugh at it? It makes me angry, very angry. And then, out of the anger, a thought intrudes. Perhaps it's only rhetoric and irony? Why didn't I register this from the outset? Perhaps it's Biblical black humour. Perhaps this extraordinary *Kohelet*, this Preacher (the lines of the prayer are all taken from Ecclesiastes 3:19), is really an ancient Samuel Beckett, singing his ironic dirge of time-that-would-have-passed-anyway and actions that fill it up with falsehood and illusion, with his tongue pressed firmly to his cheek. Rhetorical, hyperbolical, an inverted bathos in which all this ridiculous nonsense will be elevated to the sublime in the peroration. Classic Jewish joke, that begins in total darkness, and is subsumed by joy! O, I hope it is!

"Nevertheless we are Your people, sons of Your covenant, the children of Abraham, Your friend, to whom You made a promise at Mount Moriah; we are the offspring of his only son Isaac, who was bound on the altar; we are the congregation of Jacob Your first-born son, whom You named Israel and *Yeshurun* because of Your love for him and Your delight in him."

The joy is specifically identified with God's first-born son, "the congregation of Jacob", by contrast with Abraham's...the text gives "only son", which might not please the heirs of Ishmael very much.

But not Jesus anyway, another "only son" of God; or are the Christians making a similar denial of the "congregation of Jacob"?

Which congregation is here named Israel and *Yeshurun*. *Yeshurun*? Yes, here I must take a pause and offer an explanation - or, rather, undertake a piece of detective-work.

✡

Yeshurun

God's pet-name for Israel isn't widely known. It occurs only four times in the scriptures, three of them in Moses' departing song and blessing before he hands over to his successor Joshua and departs for the summit of Mount Nebo and his death. The piece has all the cryptic, mythological flavour of an oracle, a form of language much more familiar in the writings of Prophets such as Isaiah; perhaps no coincidence then, perhaps even a clue to the accurate dating of both texts, that the fourth reference is from Isaiah, as probably was that terrible dystopia in Leviticus 26.

"For the Lord's portion is His people; Jacob is the lot of His inheritance" - which happens to answer my previous question: what is God's heritage? - "He found him in a desert land and in the waste-howling wilderness, He led him about, He instructed him, He kept him as the apple of His eye. As an eagle stirs her nest, flutters over her young, spreads wide her wings, takes her young and bears them on her wings, so the Lord alone did lead him, and there was no strange god with him. He made him ride on the high places of the earth, that he might eat the increase of the fields, and He made him suck honey out of the rock, and oil out of the flintstone, butter of milch-cows, and milk of sheep with fat of lambs, rams of the breed of Bashan and goats with the fat of kidneys of wheat; and you did drink the pure blood of the grape. But *Yeshurun* grew fat, and kicked - you are waxed fat, you have grown heavy, you are covered with flesh - and he forsook God who had made him, and lightly esteemed the rock of his salvation." (Deuteronomy 32:9-15)

This first is from Moses' song. The second and third are from his valedictory blessing:

"And he was king in *Yeshurun* when the heads of the people and the tribes of Israel were gathered together." (Deuteronomy 33:5)

"There is none like unto the god of *Yeshurun* who rides the heavens to bring you help, and is the excellency of the heavens." (Deuteronomy 33:26)

"Thus says the Lord who made you, who formed you from the womb, and who will help you, 'Fear not, O Jacob, my servant, and you, *Yeshurun*, whom I have chosen." (Isaiah 44:2)

The Septuagint treats *Yeshurun* as an adjective and translates it to mean "beloved", which is pleasing, but surely incorrect - King David is the one whose name means "beloved", and his son Solomon as well, who was known as *Yedid-Yah*, "beloved of Yah", before he took Solomon for his king name. William Gesenius, the 19th century etymologist of Halle who knew more about the lexicography of the Hebrew, Aramaic, Chaldean and other ancient Semitic languages than any man before or since, was completely stumped by *Yeshurun*, noting simply that three of the Biblical references denote *Yeshurun* as a person, but one (Deuteronomy 33:5) as a place, from which he is able to draw no significant conclusion. In the end he treats *Yeshurun* simply as a diminutive of, a variation upon Israel, a poetic synonym.

In terms of definition, the root appears to be "*yashar*", and "*yashar*" means "straight" or "upright", not that Jacob himself ever was, but it's how the "congregation of Jacob" is supposed to be. *Yeshurun* - the upright one. This is the preferred definition of the Rabbis.

Rabbi Nosson Scherman, on the subject of "speaking the truth in our hearts", tells the following anecdote:

Once, while praying and therefore not able to speak, Rav Safra was offered a fair price for something that he wished to sell. The buyer failed to comprehend that Rav Safra's silence wasn't a negotiating position but an act of devotion, and continued to auction himself upwards. But when Rav

Safra finished praying he accepted not the final but the original bid, because in his heart he had already accepted the fairness of it.

A perfect - if in both senses a fabulous - definition of *Yeshurun.*

✡

Lephichach

The "*Ribbono Shel Olam*" is the first in a series of prayers that build towards the first recitation of the *Shema.* "*Le'olam Yehei Adam*" completes it. "*Lephichach*", closed by the *chazan*'s peroration, prepares that recitation and introduces the Temple Service.

"Therefore it is our duty to thank You, to praise and glorify You, to bless, sanctify and offer praises and thanksgivings to Your name. Happy are we! How good is our portion, how pleasant our lot, how beautiful our heritage! Happy are we who, early and late, morning and evening, twice each day proclaim:

"Hear O Israel, the Lord Our God, the Lord is One.

"Blessed be the name of His glorious kingdom for ever and ever."

"*Lephichach*" gives expression to the diversity of Jewish prayer, which is never one thing or another, but always manifold. Thanks, praise, glorification, blessing, sanctification, and still more praise and thanks. The praise and the thanks, like the open curtains of the Ark or the Temple pillars Bo'az and Yachin, standing sentry at both ends.

Speaking of standing sentry, there is something more to say about "*Le'olam Yehei Adam*" that it would be disgraceful to omit. Prayer is a relationship between Man and God, but it's also a relationship between Man and History, and every prayer deserves its context. "*Le'olam*" more than many others.

The words of "*Le'olam*" derive partly from the *Tanach*, partly from the *Talmud*, but the actual construction of the anagram in this form dates from the year 456 CE. In that year, not for the first or the last time in Jewish history, the ruler of Persia, Yezdejard II, issued an edict prohibiting the Jews of Babylon from keeping the *shabbat* or from reciting the *Shema* in public. How to respond? When the Greeks forbade the public reading of the *Torah*, the public reading of the *Haphtorah* was instituted in its place - an easy resolution. But the *Shema*? To be forbidden the recitation of the central credo? A form of words was needed to circumvent this, and so the ironies and rhetorical devices and the seeming paradoxes that I've already depicted in this text came into being with the "*Le'olam*". Camouflage. The transmutations of the chameleon upon the leaf. Knowing the context, how very different do some of those lines now sound.

"At all times let a man revere God, in private as in public."

Licence to say the *Shema* alone, even in silence, and for it still to possess its customary *gravitas*.

"Acknowledge the truth, and speak the truth in his heart."

The eloquence of silence. The inner dialogue that presses on God's ears as loudly as the Word itself.

Yezdejard's edict was, clearly, impossible to enforce. A *Shema* can be recited silently and still reach the ears of God. The *shabbat melachot* on the other hand - the thirty-nine acts specifically prohibited on *shabbat* - allow for precisely the sort of coercion Yezdejard intended, for the *melachot* define all the things a Jew cannot do, and you can only take away a person's right to not do something by requiring them to do it - and make yourself look very silly in the process. All Jews will carry a household item to the city gates, where they will be expected to cut their fingernails, count money and light a candle. To force someone to do what is prohibited on *shabbat* is actually a way of sanctifying the *shabbat*. Yet this is what Yezdejard attempted.

Yezdejard posted sentries in the synagogue during the first quarter of the day, the period of *Shacharit*. By way of a response the Rabbis instructed the Jews to recite the *Shema* at home before attending synagogue, and included it as part of the *kedushah* in the *shabbat Musaph* service, by which time the sentries had departed. On each occasion only the first paragraph is recited, as *Berachot* 13b tells us that this is sufficient in time of emergency (indeed, in times of dire emergency, the first line, even the first word, is quite enough).

After the death of Yezdejard the edict was revoked, but in Judaism custom and practice is never rescinded – itself a custom and practice that it is now a good time to rescind. Instead, the home recital of the first paragraph was moved to this point in the service - where else could it go, but immediately after "*Le'olam*"? - but made non-obligatory, provided the full *Shema* is recited later. To recite it now is thus not a religious but a historic duty. We recite, not the Oneness of God, but the memory of oppression.

Atah Hu

Following it are the two prayers that begin "*atah hu* - You are he who…": "*atah hu ad she-lo*" and "*atah hu Adonay*".

"You are He who existed before the world was created. You still exist now that the world has been created, You are the same in this world, and You will be the same in the world to come. Sanctify Your holy name through those who sanctify Your holy name, and sanctify it throughout Your world. Through Your salvation may our rising to pray be exalted. Blessed are You, O Lord, whose name is sanctified throughout the Universe."

The first phrase of "*Atah Hu*" is congregational, the latter spoken by the *chazan*, and then, somewhat surprisingly since by now any number of them will have been pronounced, the first formal and statutory, the first written-down "*amen*". Why here? *Amen* is a complex word. As a noun "*aman*" suggests a prop or stay or other structure of support. As a verb the inference is trust rather than belief, but the word faith could stand for either. Anciently Judaism, and even more so the Hebrewism which preceded it, may have put its faith in God as an old man does his willow stick or a babe its mother's arms, but it didn't believe in God in the intellectual manner of cognitive apprehension, the way one believes in Big Bang Theory or the Second Law of Thermodynamics. (And besides, to deny the existence of God is logically impossible. If God did not exist, there would be nothing to deny. And yet the act of denial would bring Him into being.) To say *amen* is to declare one's certainty that God will not let us down, which is really just another way of stating the equal dubiousness of our certainty in ourselves.

The prayer was written in reference to those Jews who died as martyrs for their forbidden Judaism, who lived and therefore died it in the pricks of oppression. Rightly or wrongly, substantiated or deluded, true or false, they died for their certainty of themselves, which they called God. No Jew can gainsay that. It is the most fundamental starting point of all our lives, even if we do not believe in God. Our Jewishness will sustain us. However we, as individuals, define it, it will give us a prop, a stay, a willow-stick, a source of strength, a certainty, and that will sustain us.

Amen.

"You are the Lord our God in heaven and on earth, and in the highest Heaven of Heavens. In truth, You are the First and You are the Last, and besides You there is no God. Gather those who hope for You from the four corners of the earth. Let all Mankind realise and know that You alone are God over all the kingdoms of the earth. You made the heavens and the earth, the sea and all that is in them. Who is there among all the works of Your hands, of the heavenly or earthly beings, that can say to You, 'What are You doing?' Heavenly Father, deal kindly with us for the sake of Your great name by which we are called, and fulfil for us, O Lord our God, that which is written: 'At that time I will bring you home, and at that time I will gather you; indeed I will give you renown and praise among all the peoples of the earth, when I bring back your exiles before your very eyes', says the Lord."

The second "*Atah Hu*", "*Atah Hu Adonay*", underscores the first. The liturgy is beginning to repeat itself - but frankly what else is there for it to do? We acknowledge the Creation, we bless praise thank and sanctify. We quote the scriptures (here Deuteronomy 6:4, Isaiah's Alpha and Omega in 44:6 which Jesus adopted, 2 Kings 19:15, Zephaniah 3:20). Repetition is the essence of prayer. Repetition becomes mantra. The music of the mantra is what opens the inner door.

Chapter Six: The Temple Service

In the *yeshivot*, the Rabbis and the would-be Rabbis study the Law, but especially the commentaries on the Law. The *Talmud* is everything; the *Torah* - important, but reduced to a secondary status. Since we no longer have a Temple, what purpose is there in studying its rites and ceremonies and practices? Only those parts of the *Torah* which deal with our actual lives have any significance now. When they speak of the patriarchs and the great sages, they mean Hillel and Akiva and Bar Zakkai, not Abraham and Moses and Ezekiel. The Christians wrote their "New Testament", thinking it a replacement for the "Old", but the truth is that, while it founded a new religion that bears really very little semblance to its *alma mater*, for Jews the *Talmud* is the New Testament, and it too regards the Old as – no, not anachronism: the lore of the ancient Hebrew cult. The lore, but not the Law. The substitute we call Judaism is the religion of the *Talmud*, rooted in the *Torah*, reverential of the *Tanach*.

But *Talmud* cannot exist without *Torah*, and even the defunct practices form part of history and tradition. The Temple is no more, the *Cohanim*, the *Leviyim*, the ritual sacrifices are no more, but one day, we are told, the Messiah will come - not a son of God out of the heavens of mysticism, but a genuine descendant of the House of David, an earthly king to restore an earthly dynasty - and the Temple will be restored. So we need to know. So we have a duty to remember, in order to be able to reinstitute – assuming, that is, that we want to reinstitute. So the information is recorded, and passed on - the appropriate scriptural passages that we come to now, detailing the ceremonies, and the long tractate of *Mishnah* (*Zevachim* 5) that accompanies it. Except that it isn't studied. The Temple Service is present in the prayer book, but it's there passively, not actively. That's to say, there is no pause in the service to take note of it. At most it's glanced at hurriedly, read silently, never recited aloud. Its presence is at best an act of nostalgia, which is less even than an act of memoration; at worst a sop, an act of lip-service by the Pharisees to the Sadducees, a formal bow whilst gloating that the Pharisaic *shul* has now replaced the Sadducaic Temple, and that the latter never will be restored, despite our prayers. A matter of politics, not religion.

But for the Sadducees among us, for those, that is, who pray in the *Amidah* three times a day, four times on *shabbat*, five on Yom Kippur, for the restoration of the Temple, and who do so, we must assume, with serious intent, with *kavanah*, genuinely wanting what they are praying for, sincere in their petition; for those who are therefore waiting for a site to be identified in the newly restored Israel, not necessarily the ancient site because nothing in *Torah* defined the location of the Temple, a site somewhere that can be dedicated to the ancient practices, in our days as in theirs; for those who would reinstate the *Cohanim* and *Leviyim* and presumably make arrangements with El Al or Zim for the ferrying of goats from Brooklyn and Stoke Newington, for these Jews the Temple memories now take over and the presence of the text serves as an open door to studying the future through the past.

These are the parts of the prayer-book that I find the most fascinating, the insight into ancient rituals and ceremonies and practices that allow us to see what our ancestors believed and practiced, before the synagogue replaced the Temple and Law itself was set up like a god, to be worshipped in its double-temple, the *shul* and the *shul*, which is to say the synagogue and the *yeshiva*, paraded it about so men can kiss its hem and women stare at it in wonder from behind a screen, as though this one idol were exempt from the prohibition against idols. But in ancient times, before the transformation of the cult, God didn't want our prayers, nor our obeisance, but only our worship in the ordained form: sacrifice: the act of making holy.

"If God will be with me, and will keep me in this way that I go, and will give me bread to eat, and clothes to wear, so that I can come again to my father's house in peace; if the Lord will be my God, then shall this stone which I have set up as a dolmen be the pillar of God; and of everything you give me, I will surely give back ten per cent to you." (Genesis 28:20-22) The sacrifice isn't the burning of the meat, but the surrendering of something that is dear to you, the act of making holy.

Though the text is merely present, let us explore it anyway.

The Temple

God gave the Ten Commandments to Moses on Mount Sinai, inscribed on tablets of stone (this is not the place to debate whether the giving was a physical transaction or an act of inspiration). Moses placed the tablets in a chest of acacia wood, some four feet long, two and a half feet high and a further two and a half feet wide, known as the Ark of the Covenant, and the Ark was kept in a tent known as the *Mishkan* or Tent of the Testimony (not to be confused with the *Ohel Mo'ed*, the Tent of Meeting, which served a different purpose). The Ark was covered with gold plates and had rings attached, through which poles were run when the Ark was transported. Over the Ark was a plate of gold of the same size, known as the Mercy Seat - in Hebrew the *Kapporet*. Two *cherubim* stood at each end of the *Kapporet*, covering it with their wings – massive statues of winged lions with human heads, something in the manner of the sphinxes of Egypt. The honour of carrying the Ark belonged to the *Leviyim*, and the Ark held centre-stage when the camp of Israel crossed the Wilderness - the Ark in the centre, the sons of Aaron in front, the Gershonites behind, with the other priestly groups, the Merarites on the north side and the Kohathites on the south. These were then surrounded by the tribal groupings, Asher Dan and Naphtali on the north side, Gad Reuben and Simeon on the south, Menasheh Ephraim and Benjamin at the rear, the west side, and Zevulun Judah and Issachar at the front, the east. Whenever it moved, the Israelites sang the words: "*Kumah Adonay ve-yaphutsu oyevecha ve-yanusu mesanecha* - Arise, Lord, and let Your foes be scattered, let those who hate You flee from You" (Numbers 10:35), which are still sung today when the *Torah* is removed from the Ark in synagogue. Whenever the Ark came to rest, the cry was: "*Shuvah Adonay rivevot alphey Yisra'el* - Return, Lord, to the myriads of Israel" (Numbers 10:36), which likewise is still sung today when the *Torah* is returned to the Ark in synagogue. We're told that Moses received the whole *Torah* at Sinai, but if the whole *Torah* was given written down, we're not told where it was kept, and the Ark of the Covenant was clearly far too small for as many stone tablets as would have been required (alphabetic writing, let alone alphabetic-writing-in-Hebrew, hadn't been invented yet; it would have required Egyptian hieroglyphics and literally hundreds of tablets; and that in itself is an as-yet-unstudied subject for potential biblical exegesis). Deuteronomy 31 informs us that the "second Law" - Moses' parting reiteration - was placed "beside the Ark of the Covenant of the Lord" - but that's all we know.

The Tent of the Testimony camped wherever Israel camped during the forty years in the wilderness. After the conquest, Joshua housed it at Shiloh, but from there it went on almost permanent pilgrimage around the principal Hebrew shrines - Bethel, Gilgal, Shiloh, others - and was carried into battle. At the battle of Aphek it was captured by the Philistines, but recovered, after which it was kept at Gibeon until David brought it to Jerusalem, where Solomon built its final resting place - the Temple.

The Temple, modelled on the Tent, was a long building, with an opening on one of its shorter sides. Inside it was divided into three sections, the *Olam* or porch, the *Hekal* or "holy place", where the Israelites worshipped, and the *Devir* or "Holy of Holies", where the Ark of the Covenant now resided. The whole Temple was twenty cubits wide (a cubit is the length of a man's arm, about two and a half feet); the *Olam* was ten cubits long, the *Hekal* forty and the *Devir* twenty. The *Olam* and the *Hekal* were separated by a stone wall, the *Devir* only by a curtain. Even allowing for the considerable thickness of ancient stone walls, we are talking about a building that was smaller than most parish churches, perhaps 180 feet long by 50 feet wide; 11,000 square feet, the size of about five family homes.

The Holy of Holies was an enlarged stone version of the Tent of the Testimony, with massive *cherubim* stretching the whole width and reaching half-way to the ceiling. The word in Hebrew is *keruvim*, and a *keruv* was originally a djinn or genie - an adviser to the gods and an advocate for the faithful: the adversary, so to speak, of the Adversary. Nothing else stood in the Holy of Holies but the Ark of the Covenant.

The *Hekal* contained the incense altar (known variously as the cedar altar and the golden altar), the table of shewbread and the ten candlesticks. The bronze altar, where sacrifices took place, stood in a courtyard beyond the Temple, on the south-east side. It was an enormous stone basin supported by twelve statues of bulls (yes, bulls – fully grown golden calves). In addition, five on either side of the entrance to the courtyard, stood ten wheeled pedestals, each one supporting a bronze basin, which the Priests used to purify themselves before and after the sacrifices, and where the sacrificed animals were washed after slaughter.

The act of sacrifice was central to the cult of the Hebrews. It's the details of those sacrifices which are explored in the section of the morning prayers known as the Temple Service.

✡

Ha-Kiyur - The Laver

"The Lord spoke to Moses saying: 'Make a laver of copper, its base of copper, for washing; place it between the Tent of Meeting and the Altar and fill it with water. Aaron and his sons are to wash their hands and feet from it. When they arrive at the Tent of Meeting, or when they approach the Altar to serve, or when they burn a fire-offering to the Lord, they are to wash with water so they do not die. This is a decree for all time - for Aaron and for his offspring throughout their generations.'"

First, the ritual washing of the hands and feet, still in force in Moslem mosques and Hindu mandirs, reflected in the morning laver on the first page of the *siddur*. The *Kiyur* was one of the ten copper basins in the Temple courtyard; in Moses' time it was kept between the *Ohel Mo'ed* - the "Tent of Meeting" - and the Altar.

The practice of washing the hands of the *Cohanim* is retained today, as we have seen, on the occasions of the recitation of the Priestly Blessing, when the *Leviyim* go out with the *Cohanim* and pour the water for them. But only the hands now, not the feet. There is no requirement to remove the socks and shoes except when stepping upon holy ground. Where the Temple was regarded as holy, the synagogue, though sanctified, is not.

The text (Exodus 30:17-21) states that they will die who fail to perform the laver. This is a divine injunction, not a human one. It is not the Priestly or Rabbinic Court that will put them to death, but God himself, and who can say that God has not so decided, but simply stayed the execution? The punishment is a consequence of stepping on holy ground unpurified, and not of the act of washing *per se*. And if it applies only to the sons of Aaron - the Cohanim - and not to all of us, this is because we may never step on holy ground, clean or unclean, pure or impure.

✡

Terumat ha-Dashan - The Taking of the Ashes

Next, the taking of the ashes, also called the elevation offering. The altar was effectively a stove - the words for "sacrifice" and "altar" and for "cook" and "kitchen" all stem from the same root. Oil would serve as fuel, whether poured or made from the fat of sacrificial animals. At the end of each day, when the rites were complete, some of the ashes would be kept burning, to ensure a fire on the morrow. Then, first thing, a portion of the ashes would be removed, to bellow the fire back from simmering to cooking heat.

The Cohen put on his linen raiment, right down to the linen breeches, and moved the ashes from the pyre to the side of the altar. Then he changed his clothing - this particular *sonderkommando* was dirty and dusty in the extreme - and took the ashes out of the Temple altogether, to a sacred dump, somewhere in the *Gey Ben Hinnom*, the Valley of Gehenna, beneath the Temple Mount. Then new wood was placed upon the fire, to keep it burning, until it was ready for the new day's barbecue.

Because the fire on the altar is referred to three times, each time slightly differently, the Rabbis deduce that there must have been three distinct and separate fires, on three distinct and separate altars. But there is no evidence to support this, either in the text or the archaeology; and the evidence of "*Va-yedaber*", below, is quite clear. The act was described three times because it took place three times, morning, afternoon and evening, always on the same altar, always slightly differently.

The instruction for the emptying of the ash-pan is in Leviticus 6:1-6. "The Lord spoke to Moses saying, 'Instruct Aaron and his sons. These are the instructions for the elevation offering, The elevation offering is that which stays on the Altar pyre till morning; the Altar fire should be kept burning from it. The Cohen should don his linen garment and put linen breeches on his flesh. He is to pick up the ashes of whatever of the elevation offering the fire has consumed and place it next to the Altar. Then he should remove his garments and don other garments; then he should remove the ashes to the outside of the camp, to a place which is pure. The fire on the Altar must be kept burning - it may not be extinguished. The Cohen shall burn wood on it every morning. He is to prepare the elevation offering on it and burn on it the fats of the peace offerings. A permanent fire should remain burning on the Altar - it may not be extinguished.'"

✡

Kurban ha-Tamid - the Perpetual Offering

No doubt about the purpose of the *Tamid* or "perpetual" offering. It's the *Angst* sacrifice, grovelling and penitent. The authorities argue as to whether it should be recited sitting or standing, but surely it's obvious - this of all prayers should be uttered on our knees.

"May it be your will, O Lord our God, and God of our forefathers, that You have mercy on us and pardon us for all our errors, atone us for all our iniquities, forgive all our wilful sins, and that You rebuild the Temple speedily, in our days, so that we may offer to You the Perpetual Offering, that it may atone for us, as You have prescribed for us in Your *Torah* through Moses Your servant, from Your glorious mouth, as it is said..."

What I like is the style and manner of the verse. We are knowing sinners - all of us, myrtles among reeds; all of us, without exception - wilful sinners even. We have done wrong, and we will do wrong again, though our owning-up is genuine. We want to be punished, provided the punishment is fair. We want a set of rules to live and to be guided by - and within the reach of the long leash, a set of rules to rebel against - and a system of rewards and punishments anchors the boat in any weather, provides a womb of safety and security. We need to know why we are alive, and this provides an easy answer - we live to keep the commandments. There is a quality of "fanshen" though, about this process of owning-up and demanding punishment – "fanshen" was the strategy of voluntary confessions that marked the first years of the communist revolution in China. Owning-up was the process by which the guilty and the oppressed became collaborators in their own victimhood.

But it provides an ethical and moral platform, and without an ethical and moral platform – this is the answer you should give if ever you are asked "Who is John Galt?" - there can be no civilisation.

✡

Va-yedaber

"The Lord spoke to Moses saying, 'Command the children of Israel, and tell them that they are to be scrupulous in offering to Me, at their appointed times, My offering, the food for My fires, and My satisfying aroma. Tell them that the fire-offering they are to bring to the Lord should consist of male lambs in their first year, unblemished, two per day, as a perpetual elevation offering. You are to perform one lamb-service in the morning, and the second lamb-service in the afternoon, with a tenth of an *ephah* of fine flour for a meal-offering, mixed with a quarter-hin of crushed olive oil. This is the continual elevation offering that was made at Mount Sinai, for a satisfying aroma, a fire offering to the Lord. Its libation is a quarter-*hin* for each lamb, to be poured onto the Holy Altar, a fermented libation to the Lord. The second lamb-service you are to perform in the afternoon, with the same meal offering and libation as in the morning, as a fire offering for the satisfying aroma to the Lord. He is to slaughter the lamb on the north side of the Altar before the Lord, and Aaron's sons the *Cohanim* are to dash the blood upon the Altar, all around."

The "*Yehi Ratson*" prayer is meaningless without this Biblical allusion (Numbers 28:1-8) that follows on from it. There is the ceremony of sacrifice, and there are its details. God requires three things: the "offering", the "food" for the fire, and the "satisfying aroma". But God himself only receives the last of these. For a half-shekel, paid annually, each Jew has a share in the daily offering, in that his sins are counted amongst the general sins for which the sacrifice atones. That is the "food" for the fire, and it goes into the Temple treasury. As to the offering itself, a tenth of an *ephah* of flour will do little more than batter the sacrificial beast, as the quarter-*kin* of oil will escalope it, so the priests can enjoy the shoulder, the *shechem*, which is their designated portion, and the donor of the beast with his family the remainder, grilled on the communal rotisserie. But God doesn't eat. Like a bull whose nostrils dilate when it's angry, and who can be appeased with sweet aromas of incense, so in the same way what God wants is the gorgeous smell of cooking from the kitchen.

The lambs must be male, unblemished, first-year. We are not in the business of making an insurance claim on dodgy mutton. This is intended as a sacrifice, and anything but the very best male yearling would not properly constitute a sacrifice.

The recipe is quite specific in other matters too. Fine flour, not coarse. Crushed olive oil. A quarter-*kin* of wine in addition to the oil. This is a meal for God, after all, *côte d'agneau suprème*, not some lamb stew.

And twice a day, for lunch and supper. No one will ever understand the nature of the Jewish God or the Jewish people who does not salivate copiously at the thought of eating.

"He is to slaughter it on the north side of the altar…" (Leviticus 1:11). Why the north side? As we shall see in the exposition of *Zevachim* shortly, different offerings had different levels of holiness. The most holy were slaughtered in the courtyard, to the north of the altar.

The opening prayer also called for the restoration of these rites today, returned from exile, in a rebuilt Temple. Do people who pray this really mean this? I jested earlier about taking our goats to Israel on an El Al jet, but really it is no jest, but the reality of restoration. And if no one truly means it, is it not insulting to God to pray for something that we do not want? Should we not remove the prayer, here, and from the *Amidah*?

Yehi Ratson

Like a reprise, the final prayer echoes the first. A hope that we've carried out the ritual properly, so that it can be accepted. The alternative is to suffer the rejection which Cain suffered.

"May it be your will, O Lord our God and God of our forefathers, that this recital be worthy and acceptable, and favourable before You as if we had offered the continual offering in its set time, in its place, and according to its requirement."

Formal recognition that the act of prayer in synagogue may well not be acceptable, precisely because it isn't really what God requires.

Ketoret - Incense

Atah Hu

"It is You, O Lord our God, before whom our forefathers burned the incense-spices in the days when the Holy Temple stood, as You commanded them through Moses Your prophet, as it is written in Your *Torah...*"

The altar for the *Tamid* offering was located in the Temple courtyard, presumably for ventilation. Incense, on the other hand, was burned on the Golden Altar inside the Temple itself. The courtyard altar was large and covered with copper plates; the Golden Altar was smaller and, as its name conveys, embossed with gold.

We are entering, I think, one of the most ancient of all religious practices. It is present in Hindu *puja* with much the same importance, though I'm hard pressed to find any explanations for it. Robert Graves posits that the senior divinity wasn't simply depicted as a bull, but treated like one. When a bull is angry, its nostrils flare up and dilate, it hisses and sighs through them, and only pacifying smells will calm it down. So I've already pointed out with regards the aroma of the *Tamid* offering. So even more so with the herbs and spices that were burned to aromate the Temple, burned in part to dissipate the odours of burning flesh from the *Tamid*, in part too, I imagine, to intoxicate and thereby rouse the worshippers to a suitable state of piety.

✡

Va-yomer

Which herbs, which spices? The second paragraph, citing Exodus 30:7-8 and 34-36, supplies the answer, but in Hebrew that isn't easy to translate. "*Samim*" is rendered as "spices", but in today's parlance "*samim*" means "drugs", and specifically those that aren't generally prescribed by doctors so much as by "medicine men" in back alleys. Four specific spices are mentioned : "*nataph*", "*shechelet*", "*chelbenah*" and "*levonah zachah*". *Nataph* means "a drop", in the sense of something liquid dripping (Job 36:27 is its only other Biblical occurrence); here it's understood to be that odoriferous gum called myrrh, associated with the goddess Mor-Yah in the Canaanite cults of Jerusalem, with Myrrha in the Lebanon. *Shechelet* is regarded by some as the shell of a mussel found in the lakes of India, along with nard; when burned it emits an odour that resembles musk; but *shechelet* is thought by others to be onycha, the rock rose also known as the poppy, whose seeds produce an opium-like substance called laudanum. *Chelbenah* is galbanum, another strong-smelling gum, native to Syria and elsewhere in the Levant. *Levonah zachah* is pure frankincense, so-called in Hebrew because of the perfect whiteness of the raw form.

"The Lord said to Moses, 'Take an equal weight of spices - myrrh, musk and galbanum - and pure frankincense. Make it into incense, a spice-compound, the handiwork of an expert spice-compounder, thoroughly mixed, pure and holy. You are to grind some of it finely and place some of it before the Testimony in the Tent of Meeting, where I shall designate a time to meet you; it shall be a holy of holies for you.'

"It is also written, 'Aaron shall burn the incense spices upon it [the altar] every morning; when he cleans the lamps he is to burn it. And when Aaron ignites the lamps in the afternoon, he is to burn it, as continual incense before the Lord throughout your generations."

Impossible to ignore the Christian mythology here. Two of the three gifts brought by the Magi to Ahura Mazda reincarnate on the threshing-floor of Tammuz were precisely two of the four spices used as incense in the Temple, burned on an altar of the same metal as the third gift, gold. And the name of the mother? Why, the gift of spice again - Myrhha, Mor-Yah, Mary, the goddess of the plant from which it came, the name of Isaac's hill, where he was spared crucifixion.

✡

Tanu Rabbanan - The Teachings of the Rabbis

First the Biblical extracts, now the Rabbinic commentary. This is the normative method of the rabbinic *yeshiva*, the whole purpose of *Talmud*. The first *mishnah* is from *Kereisos* 6a and *Yerushalmi Yoma* 4:5

How was the incense made and used? The Biblical text makes it clear. Take the four species, with other unnamed spices, all of equal weight. Grind some of the mixed compound finely and place it "before the Testimony in the Tent of Meeting" - in other words, in the Holy of Holies, so the air will be conducive to a meeting of men and God. Hallucinogenic then? Or to create an ambience of intoxication? It can't simply have been to protect the nose of God from the unsandalled feet of men.

But the *Talmudic* explanation doesn't concur with the Biblical source. And what's more, the Rabbis have made their usual arithmetical mess over the ritual. Despite the unambivalent clarity of the Biblical passage, they conclude that not four but eleven herbs made up the incense, regarding *samim* as two because it's plural, and then four because it's repeated, which syllogism also proves that the four species must be repeated and so must be eight, plus the frankincense in addition. A similar *gematria* is performed on the mixing of the compound. Three hundred and sixty-eight *maneh* (approximately 20 ounces makes one *maneh*) were in the mixture, 365 being one for each day of the solar year at a reckoning of half a *maneh* every morning and another half each evening, plus three extra *manim* for the special services on *Yom Kippur*. Why reckon on the basis of a solar year, when the lunar calendar was in use? And from where is the quantity of spice deduced as half a *maneh*? (The *maneh* is actually the same word as that from which we derive the manna of the Mosaic desert - really it means a portion).

The Rabbis who decided that there are eleven species, on the basis of the repetition of *samim* and frankincense, now forget that calculation and deduce eleven entirely different species, which they list as: *Tsari*, *Tsipporen*, *Chelbenah* and *Levonah*, each weighing 70 *maneh*; then (despite the injunction in Exodus to "equal weights") *Mor*, *Ketsiyah*, *Shibbolet Nerech*, *Karkom*, each at 16 *maneh*; 12 *maneh* of *Kosht*; 3 of *Kiluphah*; 9 of *Kinnamon*. Supplementary to this the *Talmudic* recipe adds nine *kabin* of *Brit Karshina* (a *kab* is about 40 fluid ounces); three *se'in* and three *kabin* of *Yayin Kaprisin* (a *se'ah* is equal to 6 *kabin*); a quarter *kab* of salt from the Dead Sea; and finally a minute amount of an unspecified *ma'aleh ashan* or "smoke-raising herb". Rabbi Natan the Babylonian augments an equally minute amount of *Kipat ha-Yarden*, but insists that honey must not be used on pain of invalidation of this witch's brew - or ritual mulled wine, as it would seem.

Translating the whole recipe into English, we appear to have:

1400 oz	balsam (often referred to as "balm of Gilead")
1400 oz	onycha (laudanum from the rock rose poppy)
1400 oz	galbanum (gum resin from the Persian ferula)
1400 oz	frankincense (aromatic gum resin)
300 oz	myrrh (sweet cicely)
300 oz	cassia (a type of cinnamon)
300 oz	spikenard (aromatic ointment made from valerian)
300 oz	saffron (made from the stigmas of the autumnal crocus)
240 oz	costus (unclear what this is)
180 oz	cinnamon (inner bark of the cinnamon tree)
60 oz	aromatic bark

mix in a compound and grind to a fine powder; then add:

360 fl oz	Persian lye (!)
820 fl oz	Cyprus wine
10 oz	salt

sprinkle a thimble of what appears to be hashish, plus a similar quantity of crushed date-palm; leave to simmer and burn as incense when ready.

I haven't tried it. Any reader of this book who wishes to do so is invited to inform me of the consequences.

✡

Rabban Shimon

However one reads the concoction, however much it may resemble urine, the one thing that it certainly is not is urine. This is clearly stated by the learned Rabbi Shimon ben Gamliel, not the first Shimon ben Gamliel who was president of the *Sanhedrin* at the time of the destruction of the Temple in 70 CE, and who personally changed an immutable law of *Torah*, allowing a woman to remarry on the basis of only one and not the required two witnesses to her husband's death; but the second Shimon ben Gamliel, the father of Judah ha-Nasi and one of the few members of that most illustrious family - six of whom had served as president of the *Sanhedrin* - to survive the Roman purge that followed the rebellion of Shimon bar Kochba.

"Why is Persian lye used?" this descendant of Hillel wondered with a rhetorical flourish worthy of the Greeks who ran the Roman empire. And answered: "To bleach the onycha, to make it pleasing. Why Cyprus wine? So the onycha can be soaked in it, to make it pungent. Even though urine would be more suitable, urine cannot out of respect be brought into the Temple."

So there you have it, on esteemed Rabbinical authority, that Persian lye is equivalent to bleach, and Cyprus wine to urine. Would that be Cyprus wine from the Turkish north or from the Greek south, I wonder?

The disparity between the instruction given in the *Torah* and the practice described in the *Talmud* is significant, precisely because both obviously reflect the practices of their day. The attempt to deduce one from the other fails, but practice is everything and practice is always in a state of flux. Here again is proof that the Rabbis took upon themselves the authority to modify immutable law. And if they could in this regard, why not in others?

The amount made from the recipe above, as the 368 *manim* made clear, was intended for use throughout the year. What is also clear is that the incense year began at *Yom Kippur*, but would have needed a few days beforehand to prepare the incense. Is there a hint in this of why the New Year (yet another fixed immutable of the *Torah*) was moved to the beginning of the seventh month?

"If he left out any of the spices, he was liable to the death penalty." Stringent to the point of being positively Draconian.

Rabbi Natan the Babylonian - he who adduced the crushed date-palm but warned against the honey - was more fully Natan ben Isaac ha-Cohen ha-Bavli, a 10th century chronicler who lived in Haroun al-Rashid's magnificent Baghdad, and was closely connected with the Exilarch Ukba, the head of the Jewish community in Babylon, whose dispute with the *Ga'on* of Pumbedita, Kohen Tsedek, was one of the two major controversies of 10th century Babylon: an enormous row over a finitesimal triviality, the question of the income of the academy from the region of Khorosan. The other dispute, which Natan also recorded, both of them in his "*Akhbar Baghdad*", an account of the Jewish community in Babylon, was between one David ben Zakkai, his successor, and no less a personage than Sa'adiah Ga'on, the compiler of the first prayer book.

This dispute merits another brief digression. Ukba was removed from office as a consequence of the Khorosan dispute, and his nephew David ben Zakkai eventually appointed to succeed him, against the wishes of the local Jewish aristocracy, but as the only candidate capable of sustaining Pumbedita's equal importance with Sura as a rabbinical centre. David appointed Sa'adiah as *Ga'on*, having become close friends when they jointly defeated the *Ga'on* Aaron ben Me'ir of Palestine in an even sillier controversy over the calendar - in 922 ben Meir announced that Passover that year would fall on a Sunday, but Sa'adiah held to the Babylonian calendar, and insisted it must fall the following Tuesday. Sa'adiah acknowledged David's leadership, and wrote glowingly about his *halachic* judgement, but the two fell out in 930, the aristocrats supporting Sa'adiah in seeking to replace David with his brother Josiah Hassan, David successfully fighting them off by ousting Sa'adiah in favour of Joseph ben Jacob of Sura. From then on it was handbags all the way - a succession of reciprocal bans, accusations, even litigation in the court of the Caliph. David eventually won. Sa'adiah was ousted. But history favours the eternalities of scholarship over the ephemeralities of politics. David may have won the short-term conflict over the status of Pumbedita; it's Sa'adiah who is remembered, for the "*Tafsir*", his translation of the Bible into Arabic, for his philosophical works, for his *halachic* writings especially, which reached the Ashkenazi communities along the Rhine and became their principal source of wisdom for three hundred years; and especially, and this is why I have allowed myself the digression, for his creation of what became the first *siddur.*

But to return to text and service. Was Rabbi Natan explaining a practice that was still continued, or was it simply dispassionate scholarship? And why the injunction against honey? I'm reminded of the story of Saul and Jonathan, after the battle of Gibeah (1 Samuel 14, specifically verses 25-28), where Saul had given instructions on the eve of battle that no food was to be consumed, but Jonathan who knew nothing of the order put his hand into a honeycomb and ate. I'm reminded too of the tale of Samson, who found a swarm of bees and honey in the carcass of a lion (Judges 14:8-9) and transformed it into a riddle. What have these to do with Temple incense? I've no idea – I'm simply looking for connections to explain the otherwise inexplicable. Honey is made by bees of course, and the bee-goddess Deborah has links with the pagan rites and practices of the Canaanites: Rebecca's wet-nurse was named Deborah and she was buried in a beehive-tomb beneath the weeping oak at *Alon Bachot.* Was honey regarded as in some way *treif* - not kosher? Perhaps it was simply a matter of not wishing to over-sweeten the concoction. Or is there a connection with the *chelev*, the fat that would grease the altar when an animal was sacrificed, and which required innumerable paragraphs of law in *Torah*? The root of *chelev* is also the root of *chalav*, milk, and Israel is poetically the land of milk and honey – the only two foods in the world, incidentally, which are eaten raw but taste cooked.

Tanya Rabbi Natan

The fifth paragraph of this section, the "*Tanya*" or "teaching" of Rabbi Natan - the same Rabbi Natan the Babylonian - contains a glorious superstition, the notion that "the sound of the grinding is beneficial to the spices". Even more interesting is what follows.

"If one mixed it in half-quantities, it was fit for use, but as to a third and a quarter, have we not heard the law? Rabbi Yehudah said, 'This is the general rule: In its proper proportion, it is fit for use in half the full amount; but if he left out any one of its spices, he is liable to the death penalty.'"

There's no need for a legal prohibition if the act to be prohibited isn't in widespread use. So the injunction against third and even quarter measures must infer that cheating the recipe was commonplace; presumably the ingredients were expensive and the cheat was able to pocket the profit. Yet there's no evidence of the death penalty ever being carried out.

✡

Tanya Bar Kappara

Bar Kappara, a scholar of the 3rd century CE, the period between the *tanna'im* and the *amora'im*, also took up the oddity of the honey. Amongst the writings left behind at his *yeshiva* in Caesarea was the collection known as the "*Mishneh* of Bar Kappara"; his commentary on Leviticus 2:11 notes that, since "you shall not burn any leaven, nor any honey, in any offering made to the Lord by fire", this must include the incense. And yet he also says that "had they put one *kortov* of fruit-honey into the mix, nobody could have resisted its aroma". The *kortov* - a "pinch" in English - is equivalent to one two hundred and fifty-sixth of a *kab*, or one twentieth of a fluid ounce. But even to that infinitesimal degree it was not permitted.

And still it's not clear why.

Good scholar that I am, my next port of call must be Leviticus 2:11 itself, and here I find that Dr Hertz, the late Chief Rabbi of the British Empire as his *chumash* styles him, does offer an explanation.

"The prohibition," he explains, and attributes his explanation to Maimonides "extended only to their being burnt upon the altar. Leaven was regarded as a symbol of fermentation and corruption; and man's tendency to sin was later viewed as a process of moral fermentation. Honey was deemed in heathen cults a favourite food of the gods, and its prohibition was intended to free the mind of the Israelite from any degrading notion that sacrifices might be the food of God."

Then my guess was right. What Jonathan and Samson ate wasn't just honey, it was ambrosia. Yet what it says about the sacrifice is surely far more interesting. If the sacrifice isn't food for the gods then what is it? Simple: like the blessing that goes upwards and not downwards, it's the giving, not the receiving, that's significant. Which makes the rejection of Cain's sacrifice still more galling. Can we presume that Cain's sacrifice was rejected, not because it was less than Abel's, but because Cain only gave it grudgingly?

And as to short measures, Bar Kappara has actually gone to the trouble of calculating the leftovers in the bottom of the basin, reckoning that it will take between sixty and seventy years to build up half a year's supply; but that once this has happened, in that year the leftovers may be used, topping up by making just a half and not a full year's quantity, the death sentence for depletion being then suspended. This is almost embarrassing. What kind of a mind engages itself in so anorakal a degree of computation?

I failed to give Bar Kappara's explanation of the honey in full - and it's not the same as Hertz's. It's forbidden, he says, because the *Torah* forbids it. But why? Because the smell of honey is sweet, and would make the incense pleasant! Has he somehow missed the point?

✡

Adonay Tseva'ot Imanu

"The Lord of the Heavenly Host is with us
a stronghold for us is the God of Jacob (selah)
Lord of the Heavenly Host
fortunate is he who trusts in You
Save us, Lord, may the king answer on the day we call
You are a shelter for me, from distress You preserve me, with glad song of rescue You envelop me (*selah*). May the offering of Judah and Jerusalem be pleasing to the Lord, as in days of old and former years."

As a break in all this Talmudic exposition, there are now inserted these four phrases from the Psalms (46:8, 84:13, 20:10 and 32:7), and one from the prophet Malachi (3:4), conjoined as a single prayer and recited three times. Why these phrases? Who chose them? When were they introduced into the liturgy? And why, given that this part of the liturgy isn't actually used? These seem to me to be the most fundamental questions, and yet I can find no answers to them anywhere, not even in the "*Shulchan Aruch*", Joseph Caro's 15th century encyclopaedia of Sephardic custom and tradition, nor in Moses Isserles' Ashkenazi equivalent, the "*Mappah*". Indeed, such explanations as are given serve only to raise more questions.

For example: that the phrases are recited three times on the authority of *Arizal*, Isaac ben Solomon Luria Ashkenazi; but Luria was a mystic, a key figure in the development of *Kabbalism* in Safed in the 16th century, a millennium after the writing of the *Talmud*; and *Kabbalah* isn't generally the source of explanation for mainstream Jewish mysteries.

Or for another example: Rabbi Yochanan, in *Yerushalmi Berachot* (5:1), says that the first two phrases from Psalms "should never depart from our mouths", and so the pretext is taken to include them here. But why three times, when two would suffice to make the point? And what led to Rabbi Yochanan's remark? And why these phrases and not others? And why here and not elsewhere? These questions demonstrate the limits within which a book like this must work. This kind of analysis, regarding the history of prayer as history as well as in itself, simply doesn't have a tradition in Jewish tradition; and I don't like the idea of accepting anything as "correct" for which there is no validating authority, whose explanations are themselves in need of explanations.

The two psalmic phrases of which Rabbi Yochanan so approves both refer to "*Adonay Tseva'ot* - Lord, God of Hosts", also known by Christians as *Saba'oth*. The Hosts are the Heavenly Army, the angelic paramilitary so to speak, led by Michael with his sword - a most un-Jewish conception that seems to have been added very late (around the time of Daniel, if not later; though this is a difficult way of dating anything, for Daniel is itself almost certainly a work of fiction written for allegorical purposes several hundred years after the supposed event), and then given retroactive legitimacy in the final stages of the redaction. So much of scripture happened in this way. The rewriting of history which Orwell lambasted is as prevalent in religion as in politics.

I must also observe the error of the word "*selah*", which appears throughout the Psalms and has entered the Christian litany as a form of closure. *Selah*, please take note, is not meant to be pronounced. It isn't a word. It's a primitive form of musical notation, the indication of a break. This is why I've placed it in parenthesis above. *Selah*.

Those Bible Critics - the school of Ferdinand Christian Baur, founded in Tübingen in the 1820s - who like to analogue the scriptures in columns headed J and E and D and P, might do well to look into the prayer book too. These phrases - the Psalmic as well as the Malachi - are all J.

Abbayey

In Babylon, in the early decades of the 4th century CE, the head of the Academy in Pumbedita and chief of the *amora'im*, one Abbayey by name, wrote down in the *Talmudic* tractate "*Yoma*" - a section dedicated principally to *Yom Kippur* - the details in order of the Temple Service, as he had learned them from Abba Sha'ul's disciples, Abba Sha'ul himself having learned them from Rabbi Me'ir, who was alive when the Temple was still in use. The routine was as follows:

a) The arrangement of the large pyre - the pyre at the centre of the altar, on which the offerings were burned.

b) The arrangement of the secondary pyre (the pyre near the south-west corner of the altar, from which glowing coals were taken into the Sanctuary to burn the daily incense) for the incense offering. [It was almost certainly this ritual in which Isaiah was participating when he was called by God - Isaiah 6:6]

c) The placement of the two logs - restoking the large pyre.

d) The removal of the ashes from the inner altar - where the outer altar was a staggering thirty-two cubits across, the inner altar was just a single cubit wide. It was made of wood and used only for the incense.

e) The cleaning of five lamps from the *Menorah* - the lamps were always cleaned in the same pattern: first five, then two.

f) The dashing of the blood from the *Tamid* offering - the implication is that slaughter must already have taken place, but Abbayey doesn't say when. I presume that the slaughter and the dashing are to be regarded as a single act, though Art Scroll infers that slaughter precedes the cleaning of the lamps. If that were so, would Abbayey not say so?

g) The cleaning of the last two lamps (I am intrigued to know which. The Temple *Menorah* was a seven-branched candlestick, and each branch was dedicated to a specific day of the week, originally the seven planetary deites having a day each. Logic says that the two ought to have been two from three of yesterday/today/tomorrow. But which? Which?)

h) The offering of incense.

i) The burning of the limbs - of the *Tamid* offering.

j) The meal-offering - the flour on the *Tamid* offering.

k) The pancakes - the full meal-offering included, quite literally, a pancake, though given how Americans make their pancakes today, this may not be descriptively precise; the Temple pancake was thin, more like a French crèpe. It was baked in a low, flat pan called a "*chavtin*", whence the offering was known as the *Chavtin* offering.

l) The pouring of the wine - the official term is libation.

m) The *Musaph* or additional offering - on Sabbaths, festivals and New Moons only.

n) The bowls of frankincense - two bowls were placed with the shewbread every week. The bread was eaten by the *Cohanim*; the incense was burned after the shewbread had been removed.

o) The afternoon *Tamid* offering - the afternoon service is still known as "*Minchah*", which means a "gift offered to a divinity", in other words a "sacrifice".

Abbayey adds, quoting Leviticus 6:5, that "he is to arrange the elevation-offering on it and burn the fats of the peace-offerings on it", which tells us that the morning *Tamid* was a guilt-offering (see my notes earlier), but that in the afternoon the purpose of the sacrifice was different. "*Olah*", referred to in the text, is the process of "going up" to the Temple, for whatever purpose, but normally the making of a sacrifice to propitiate or to petition God; the term is still in use today for a person who is called to the reading of the Law or who goes to live in the land of Israel. The peace-offerings - note the plural - are self-explanatory. But instead of singing the "*Oseh Shalom*" hymn now, which would be logical, we recite instead the lovely prayer of Rabbi Nechuniah ben Hakanah, written in the very last days of the Temple, possibly - the vehemence of the exhortation seems to insist on it - during the last hours of the destruction itself, in 70 CE. The prayer is called "*Ana be-Ko'ach*".

Ana be-Ko'ach

"We beseech you, with the great strength of Your right hand, tie our bundle tight. Accept the wailing of Your people, lift it up, purify it - O Awesome One. Please, Majesty, guard like the pupil of Your eye, those who seek unity with You. Bless them, purify them, show them mercy, reward them with Your eternal righteousness. In strength and holiness, in Your great goodness, guide this Your congregation. You alone do we exalt; turn to Your people which remembers Your harshness. Hear our cry for help, hear our entreaties, You who know every mystery. Blessed be the name of His glorious kingdom, for ever and ever. Amen"

The anguish that drives these lines is palpable, but untranslatable. It isn't terribly good poetry, but perhaps that doesn't matter. It isn't intended as poetry, but as prayer, and as prayer it's exquisite, in the strictest definition of that word; but spiritually, emotionally, not aesthetically. It sears, it scorches, it blasts the heath. It echoes through every prison and pogrom and persecution in Jewish history, all the way from Titus' burning of the Temple, on the 9th of Av in the year 3731 of the Jewish calendar, to the very gates of Maedanek, Teriesenstadt, Oswiecim. "May God remember the souls of the holy and the pure ones who were killed, murdered, slaughtered, burned, drowned and strangled for the sanctification of Your name…may their souls be bound in the Bond of Life." (From the memorial service - *Yizkor*)

The mystics make much *Kabbalah* out of "*Ana be-Ko'ach*". Taking each line acrostically they make the prayer read: *Avig yatats kara satan nagid yachash betar tsatag chakiv tanu'a pazak shako tsayit*, which may very well be meaningful to them, but defeats my researches in any one of several lexicons and dictionaries (Some words are obviously Hebrew. *Kara* means "called"; *nagid* means "story-teller"; *satan* is Satan; but the rest are merely logical linguistic constructs, nude of meaning.) Nevertheless the mystics are undaunted. The prayer, they note, consists of forty-two words, and the initials taken acrostically spell out the secret name of God (the 42-letter secret name, that is; there are others - but if this one can be spelled out, and if we can know that this is the way it can be spelled out, then how can it also be a secret?) The six initials of each line likewise form divine names (note that the names are neither given nor explained). The *Kabbalistic* reading prefers to split the six-word line into three divisions, whether to make iambic poetry or to distinguish better the complex esoteric mystery. So, they say, it should read:

Av gey tats
Kar as tan
Nag day kash
But rats tag
Chak laph zak
Shak uts yat

which would give Madame Sosostris a severe headache and sadly gets us no nearer to understanding what if anything the mystery may mean.

Ribbon ha-Olamim

Yes, this is what it's really all about.

"Master of all worlds, You commanded us to bring the *Tamid* offering at this time, You gave the *Cohanim* their duties, the *Leviyim* their proper place, the rest of Israel its station. But through our sins the Holy Temple is destroyed, the *Tamid* is now *I-Tamid*, and we have neither *Cohanim* nor *Leviyim* nor Israel in their offices."

This is the bald truth of it. We can't observe the commandments we're meant to observe, and so we've constructed this artifice in its place, a makeshift Judaism, a second-best, in an understudy Temple, replacing deeds with words, actions with memories of actions, events with the mere reciting of events. What we do - mark this - *is not authentic.* This is a devastating realisation. We are all myrtles among reeds, however observant we may or may not be of the substitute *chokim.* Our prayers are not authentic. They are not what God wants. They are mere artifice, makeshift, second-best. How then can we expect them to be received, as though it were the real thing? *Ribbon ha-Olamim* has the capacity to close synagogues.

But there is an answer to this problem. A most important answer. In Hosea 14:3.

"Take with you words, and turn to the Lord, and say to him: 'Take away our sins, receive us graciously, accept the sacrifice of our lips in place of our cattle.'"

The sacrifice of our lips - what a beautiful phrase! But not sacrifice in the sense of giving something up; this surely is what Moses meant when he told God he couldn't speak to Pharaoh because he was "*aral sephatayim* – a man of uncircumcised lips" (Exodus 6:12), a man whose words had not been made sacred.

And so we go on praying.

Accept our words, because we cannot offer sacrifices. Strange to find this on the lips of Hosea, who lived in the heyday of the First Temple, when Solomon had barely finished building it - but of course there was division and dissention even then, for Hosea inhabited the northern kingdom, under Jeroboam, while the Temple was in Jerusalem of Judah, the southern kingdom under Rehoboam, and a civil war keeping the two halves of the kingdom separate.

Accept our words, because we cannot offer sacrifices. Yes, but shouldn't we then give only the first-born of our own lips, perfect words without blemish, young words and tender as a yearling, first fruits newly harvested in our own time, rather than the muttonous anachronisms of two thousand years ago? Shouldn't the words of our prayers be fresh and vigorous as poetry? Shouldn't we be writing new prayers, for the modern Jew, post Pale of Settlement, post ghetto, post stadtl, post exile, post Holocaust, post creation of the State of Israel? Shouldn't they rise up to heaven in place of the incense too?

"Therefore may it be Your will, O Lord, our God and God of our forefathers, that the prayers of our lips be worthy, acceptable and favourable before You, as if we had brought the perpetual offering at its set time and we had stood at its station."

✡

U-ve-yom ha-Shabbat

I am exploring here only the *siddur* of the daily *Shacharit* service, not that of the *shabbat*, nor any other circumstance. Where the text offers its alternatives for special days, I am ignoring them. This is simply a matter of methodology to contain the scope of the book.

Still, I can't help but note that interjected here are the sacrifices of *shabbat* - this needs bold italic and underline - sacrifices which, by their very nature and existence, prove that the 39 *melachot*, the 39 acts prohibited on *shabbat*, have completely misunderstood the laws and nature of *shabbat*. In Temple times we cut, we tore, we kept the fires.[3]

Zevachim - Sacrifices

Follows a lengthy exegesis from tractate *Zevachim* ("Sacrifices"), chapter 5, the only chapter in the entire *Mishnah* in which there is no *halachic* dispute whatsoever, and one which is regarded as being amongst the oldest of all Rabbinic exegeses. (The notion that it dates back to Moses himself is absurd. The whole of Oral Law theoretically dates back to Moses; in practise the interpretation remained a freemasonry of the *Cohanim* at least until the time of Ezra and the founding of the Great Assembly).

a) *Ayzehu* - Locations

The location of the offerings first. A distinction is made in levels of holiness. The most holy are the sin, guilt and elevation offerings; the less holy are individual peace and thanksgiving offerings. The most holy - the bull and the he-goat of *Yom Kippur* - were slaughtered in the courtyard to the north of the altar, where their blood was also collected for sprinkling between the poles of the Holy Ark, and on the Golden Altar, and in the direction of the Curtain that divided the Holy of Holies from the rest of the Temple; if any one of the blood-sprinklings was omitted, the atonement

---

[3] For the interest, the 39 *Sabbath* prohibitions are owing, Plowing, Reaping, Binding Sheaves, Threshing, Winnowing, Selecting, Grinding, Sifting, Kneading, Baking, Shearing Wool, Washing Wool, Beating Wool, Dyeing Wool, Spinning, Weaving, Making Two Loops, Weaving Two Threads, Separating Two Threads, Tying, Untying, Sewing Two Stitches, Tearing, Trapping, Slaughtering, Flaying, Salting Meat, Curing Hide, Scraping Hide, Cutting Hide Up, Writing Two Letters, Erasing Two Letters, Building, Tearing A Building Down, Extinguishing A Fire, Kindling A Fire, Hitting With A Hammer, Taking An Object From The Private Domain To The Public, or Transporting An Object In The Public Domain. (*Mishnah Shabbat*, 7:2)

was regarded as unfulfilled. Once sacrificed and offered on the pyre, the cooked meat from the most holy offerings could only be eaten within the Temple Courtyard. The less holy offerings were regarded as "take-away" rather than "eat-in", provided they were consumed within the walls of Jerusalem (in those days a relatively small area). Leftover blood was spilled on the western base of the Outer Altar.

The blood is hugely significant, the taboo against eating it as much as the requirement to sprinkle it. I shall return to the subject of blood another time.

b) *Parim* - Bulls

On *Yom Kippur* a bull and a billy-goat were slaughtered in the above manner. Normally only certain parts of the sacrifice were burned in their entirety, the rest being kept for eating. But a burned offering meant literally that - the holocaust of the entire beast - and this was the case with the *Yom Kippur* offerings (it was also the case if a sacrifice was made to atone for an innocent *halachic* ruling by the Sanhedrin that caused the people unintentionally to sin). The rules are as above.

c) *Chatot* - Sin-offerings

Laws relating to sin-offerings, both of the community and the individual. Communal sin-offerings were made on New Moon and festivals, by means of a billy-goat. The blood on these occasions was sprinkled on the four corners of the altar, the Cohen climbing the ramp up to the altar - a distance of some ten arm-lengths to the altar itself; but the ledge, one arm-length wide, six arm-lengths from the ground, is probably intended, as the altar itself would have been scalding hot from the pyres. The four corners of the altar were horned, not in the Egyptian sense that is often imagined by popular novelists - an image of the horned throne of the Egyptian Pharaoh, who took his authority from the bull-god Horus - but in the sense that the side walls of the altar continued up beyond the flat surface where the pyres were laid, extending a full arm's length to make a kind of unroofed stove; but the extensions were themselves flat, not literally horned. The Cohen would circulate on the ledge, at each corner dipping his right index finger into the bowl of blood and depositing it on the horn (the same procedure used by all Jews on Passover Eve for the plague ritual). The Cohen circulated in an anti-clockwise direction, beginning at the south-east corner. The description of his ascent and perambulation allows us to infer that the ramp must have been on the south side of the altar, stage right from the perspective of the worshippers. Leftover blood was poured on the southern base. The sacrifice was eaten within the "curtains" of the courtyard, by male priests only, on the day of sacrifice only, before midnight (though written law says "before the next day's dawn"). No specific manner of cooking is prescribed. "Curtains" here is taken to mean walls, the original law having referred to the desert sanctuary not the constructed Temple.

The purpose of sacrifice, then, appears to have been twofold and complementary. To enable the sinners to atone. To enable the priests, and in some cases the people, to eat meat. Vegetarians and those who keep kosher should take note of this. How do we justify taking the life of one of God's creatures, simply to satisfy our need for food? The answer lies in *shechitah*, the approved manner of killing. Only a *shochet*, priestly or secular, may take an animal's life, and must do so in the ordained manner. By doing so, the animal is sacrificed - not just by us to God, but importantly by God to us. In *kashrut* lies the divine permission to kill for food.

d) *Ha-Olah* - The Elevation-offering

The elevation-offering was one of the most holy in this complex hierarchy of sacrifices, and so it took place on the north side of the altar, both for the slaughter and for the collecting of the blood. There follows an unintelligible regulation: "Its blood requires two applications which are equivalent to four." How can two ever be equivalent to four? (Or are we back in the mystical gematric realm of the *samim*?) The Rabbis say that the blood spilled at two corners would inevitably seep to the other two corners (does this imply that the surface of the altar wasn't flat, like a pancake pan, nor concave, like a pan for frying eggs, but slightly convex, like an omelette pan?), and that in this way two would become four.

This sacrifice also requires flaying and dismembering - after slaughter, of course. This is because the hide is valuable, both as fur and as leather, and so it was given to the priests rather than the fire. As to dismemberment, there must surely have been a prescribed formula - front legs first, or left flank before right, or cuts only at certain joints and knuckles - but alas, or mercifully, the full and gory details of the rites of butchery are not recorded.

e) *Zivchey* - Offerings

First, the rare event of communal peace-offerings. Communal offerings were normally sin or elevation offerings, but in the additional service for *Shavu'ot* (Pentecost) two sheep were offered up for peace, alongside the normal *Shavu'ot* offering of one kid.

Second, personal guilt-offerings. Six different kinds of guilt are listed for which an offering is required: theft, misuse of sacred objects, violation of a betrothed maidservant, ritual contamination of a *Nazirite*, ritual impurity of a leper (in this case the offering is brought on the eighth day after cure is pronounced), and any circumstance in which it isn't clear whether or not a sin-offering is required. If the sin is then demonstrated, the full offering must be made as well.

Sin and guilt are not of the same order. It's hard to see how one can feel guilt for, say, a theft, if one hasn't actually committed a theft, but the implication is that sins aren't the same as crimes, and "*gezelut*", the word used here, isn't a theft in the sense of stealing, but more a matter of the denial of a loan.

The rules for these two types of offering are similar to those for the *olah*. Slaughter and blood on the north, two equivalent to four, meat eaten within the courtyard, male priests only, braised or grilled, not after midnight.

With all these delineations I find myself wondering what might be today's equivalents if the Temple were indeed restored. I simply can't imagine pilgrims flying in from London and New York with billy-goats and yearling bull-calves. What, then, instead? The donation of stocks and shares? The giving of one-tenth of one's income as *tsedakah*, charity? At the heart of every act of Jewish philanthropy there resides this distant memory of the practices of the Temple.

And what definitions of sin, and guilt, would modern Jews accept and understand, guided by the *Responsa* of Rabbi Adler ben Freud. A contemporary six to match the Biblical: desire of the son for his mother (coupled with a yearning to strangle his father with his phylacteries); failure to telephone *bubbe* on her 70th birthday; ritual impurity contracted by dating a *shiksah*; missing Friday night dinner; not showing with sufficient vehemence how much you loved your mother-in-law's *Rosh ha-Shana* chicken soup; laughing at post-Mia Farrow Woody Allen movies. Now those are types of guilt the Jewish mind can grasp!

f) *Ha-Todah* - The Thanksgiving-offering

Two offerings of lesser holiness are the thanksgiving offering, and the ram sacrificed by a *Nazir*. These can take place anywhere in the courtyard, and again the two sprinklings of blood are equivalent to four. They can be eaten, by anybody, anywhere in Jerusalem, prepared in any manner, provided it's before midnight on the day of slaughter. A priestly portion is kept - usually the breast and right thigh, but in the case of a *Nazir* the whole of the right foreleg - and may be eaten by the Cohen's wife and children and not just the male priest.

What is a *Nazir* (the word is usually translated as Nazirite)? According to Numbers 6:1-21, it's a person who takes vows for a specific period to abstain from all forms of intoxication, from cutting his hair, touching a corpse, indulging in sexual activity, or in any way risking impurity. Either men or women may make such vows, which normally last for a single lunar month. The thanksgiving sacrifice is offered at the end of the lenten period, when the *Nazir* returns from monastic holiness to the profane world. Christians who are unaware that the town of Nazareth wasn't yet built in the time of Jesus might like to ponder on his time with John the Baptist in the essenic wilderness, his forty days and forty nights contesting with the Adversary, and ask if he shouldn't more correctly be named Jesus the Nazirite?

g) *Shelamim* - Peace-offerings

Exactly the same regulations apply to peace-offerings, except that they're even less holy, and so the meat may be eaten for two days and one night, which is to say till the midnight after the day of slaughter. Anything beyond that would have required refrigeration!

h) *Ha-Bechor* - The First-born

And still less holy is the sacrifice of the first-born. (This takes me by surprise; the sacrifice of the first-born is one of the most constant themes in Jewish scripture, from Cain through Ishmael and Isaac, Esau, Zerach, the massacre at Moses' birth and at the Exodus; we tend to think of it as somehow crucial to the whole religion. But apparently it's a trivial thing, at least when compared with other sacrifices). The sacrifice of the first-born includes the tithe of animals and the Pesach offering (yes, even the Paschal Lamb itself, that apotheosis of the sacrificial first-born - a trivial thing, the least of all sacrifices).

These may be slaughtered anywhere in the Courtyard, and the blood isn't even sprinkled on the altar, but on the *Yesod*, the foundation-plinth on which the altar is mounted, and not even on the *Yesod* itself, but in one corner of the ledge or gutter which encircles it, so that the *Yesod* isn't sullied.

As to the eating of the meat. The first-born is reserved for the *Cohanim*; the tithe may be eaten by anyone; both may be eaten anywhere in the city, prepared in any manner, by midnight of the second night. The *Pesach* offering may only be eaten at night, and only until midnight, and only by those (Exodus 12:4) who have specifically registered their share in it before it went for slaughter. The Paschal Lamb may only be eaten roasted.

I can't help but find something extremely comic about all of this. The last especially. Knowing how much the Jewish people love their food, and how much care they take in making it, I have this satiric vision of wedding and *Bar Mitzvah* caterers making their reservations at the Temple butchers several weeks in advance of the *simcha*, the great occasion, and the father of the *Bar Mitzvah* boy, or the grandparents of the bride and groom, negotiating lengthily with whoever has scheduled a sacrifice for the day before, to make sure of the quality of the beast, its pedigree, the kind of grain it's been fed on. And in the meanwhile, the family of the lowest caste of Cohen, taking their portion of the *Nazir* sacrifice, stuffed in pitta bread with olives and chili pepper (did they have chips in Temple times?), to eat at home in front of, whatever was the latter-day equivalent of television.

Chapter Seven: Rabbi Yishmael

After the Temple Service, just as the *Yevarechecha* was followed by a text of *Mishnah* to ensure a Scripture-*Talmud*, Cohen-Rabbi balance, so the account of the Temple Service is followed by an explanation of the methodology of the *yeshiva*, a complex judicial promulgation in the tradition of Socrates. It represents, also, a complete shift from the irrational to the rational, from flesh to mind, from the spiritual to the empirical, from the material to the intellectual; the yin and yang of Judaism that co-existed throughout the Second Temple period, but one half of which was lost (until *Hasidism* partially revived it in the 18th century) when the Second Exile began.

Jewish tradition maintains that there are 613 commandments, all of them written down in the *Torah*. But where are they exactly? There are the famous Ten of course, which Moses smashed and God replaced. But where are the others written down? The answer is that most of them aren't written down at all, or not explicitly. Rather, they're deduced. To deduce them accurately, an agreed set of premises is required, and to achieve this Judaism evolved two schools of exegeses, the "*d'vei*" of Rabbi Akiva and the "*d'vei*" of Rabbi Yishmael ben Elishah – he who was not Yishmael ben Phabi. Akiva's was the system that lost out, rejected in favour of Yishmael for reasons that had less to do with Divine Planning than with Human Politics. Quite simply, Akiva's system was too harsh. His rules were based on the theoretically complementary concepts of "*ribu'i* – inclusion", and "*mi'ut* – exclusion". But he also believed in the interpretation of literally every word of *Torah*; including the conjunctions and the marks of punctuation that aren't written down but can be deduced by logic from the meanings of the phrases; including even the particle "*et*" which is used for no other purpose than to indicate a proper noun in the accusative; including even the superfluous and the parenthetical; a pedantry for which his friend and colleague Rabbi Yishmael once reprimanded him:

"Because you interpret the superfluous '*vav*' [the so-called '*vav* consecutive, the conjunction 'and' used as a stylistic prefix to allow the future tense to stand for the past tense], is this woman to be condemned to death by fire?" (*Sanhedrin* 51b)

Yishmael was particularly scathing about Akiva's theory of "amplification". Hebrew frequently uses a form known as the infinitive absolute, the repetition of a verb, once in its active form, once in its infinitive - for example, in Numbers 15:31: "*Ki davar Adonay bazah ve-et-mitzvato hephar hikaret tikaret ha-nephesh ha-hi avonah vah* - because he has shown contempt for the word of God, and has broken the commandments, he shall be utterly cut off, his sin shall be upon him." Yishmael regarded the phrase as mere tautology for the purposes of emphasis - an issue of literary style. Akiva, by contrast, regarded the second phrase as amplifying the first: he would be utterly cut off in this life - *hikaret* - by losing it; but his sin would also be upon him, when he was judged and recondemned - *tikaret* - in the world to come.

Though it wasn't ultimately adopted, Akiva's system, and his commentary on his system, have been immensely influential down the centuries, and two other specific features of the *d'vei* Akiva are worth the mentioning. Hebrew is written in consonants only, with the vowels understood and no other notation except occasional "*nekudot*", dots that are marked inside, above or below certain letters; this is not the same as the "*nekudot*" introduced in the 9th century CE as an aid to reading. Why the former are there isn't known, but many theories have been posited. *Gematria* - the pseudoscience based on the numerical values of Hebrew letters - has engendered all manner of mystical conclusions, pointing out, for example, that the name of Abraham's servant, Eliezer, has the same numerical value (318) as the number of soldiers who accompanied Abraham when he pursued the defeated kings of Shinar towards Dan (Genesis 14:14). Akiva was also a supporter of the methodology of "*notarikon*", a form of shorthand culpable in engendering that modern charlatanism the Bible Codes. Inevitably, given the nature of Hebrew, some words appear to be the acronyms of other words - the most famous recent example was the year 5754 (1994 in the Christian calendar), which is written in the Hebrew alphabet as "*tashmad*". Using the letters as numbers it's an innocent date; using the letters as letters it spells "destruction". The millennial fever induced by this coincidence was comic, yet also real.

Rabbi Yishmael regarded both *Gematria* and *notarikon* with some disdain, and I can only observe again that history has favoured Yishmael over Akiva, which proves nothing in the name of the Divine, but does leave behind a statement that needs making: had Akiva been favoured over Yishmael, the Judaism we live today *would have been radically different.* This cannot be said of any other character in the entire history of Judaism, not even of Moses. There also remains the possibility that Yishmael was wrong, that Akiva was right, or wrong, and either way that deduced laws may be incorrectly deduced even from a correct system, and therefore require continuous revalidation, updating, even correction. This is another aspect of the same post-substitution challenge: to go back and reconsider if we even had the right substitute.

The premises given in this passage of liturgy are the subject of Rabbi Yishmael's "*bara'isa*", which appear as the preface to the *Mishnah* tractate *Sifra*, and are themselves an extension and elaboration of the set of seven principles of exegeses established by Rabbi Hillel.

The *bara'isas* were left out (expurgated? overlooked? ignored? forgotten?) of the *Mishnah* in the final redaction by Judah ha-Nasi, but nevertheless regarded as having such authority that they are cited repeatedly in the *Gemara*.

Jewish tradition remembers Rabbi Akiva ahead of any other Rabbi, and not for his Rabbinical achievements so much as for his martyrdom. Behind Akiva come Hillel and Shammai, the twin founders of *Talmudic* Judaism, and the Gamliels who were Hillel's descendants. Some remember Yochanan ben Zakkai, some likewise Judah ha-Nasi, but the name of Yishmael ben Elisha is rarely mentioned, though in all probability he was the greatest, in the sense of the most impactful, of them all. A member of the priestly tribe, he was among the children taken as captives to Rome at the time of the destruction of the Temple, and later ransomed from captivity by Rabbi Joshua ben Chananiah, one of Yochanan ben Zakkai's inner circle of illustrious disciples. Yishmael was first taught by Joshua at Kfar Aziz, a *yeshiva* in the Judean desert south of Chevron, then moved to Yavneh where he became one of the leading sages, and was certainly one of those who voted for the deposition of Gamliel and the appointment of Eleazar ben Azariah as *Nasi* in his place.

Yishmael is credited as being the founder of Hermeneutics, which is to say the interpretative study of the scriptures - an ancient form of Bible Criticism really, but one which was spared the wilful pessimism and the grotesque dogmatism of the Minimalists, and one, also and more significantly, which scrupulously avoided heterodoxy even whilst seeking the literal meanings of the texts which they regarded as being written in human medium and not in mystical code. His main work was an attempt to corroborate the large number of Rabbinic decisions already in force by attaching them to the Biblical texts from which they were deduced. He wrote legalistic commentaries on the last four books of the *Torah*, of which nothing remains alas except "*Mechilta* – Measure", his work on Exodus from chapter 12 to its conclusion.

Yishmael believed in "receiving all men joyfully" - a quotation that ought to be inscribed on the gateway of every orthodox synagogue, right above the *mezuzah*. In his commentary on the *sedra* "*Acharey Mot*" (Leviticus 16-18), he insisted that it was acceptable to transgress the prohibition against idolatry in order to save one's life; a justification, if one is needed, of those "*conversos*" in the Catholic middle ages who accepted forced baptism while continuing to practice Judaism in secret. He also insisted that *Torah* study should complement worldly occupation rather than superseding it - a man after my own heart, though apparently the Hasidim of Israel, who refuse to serve in the Israeli army, do not concur.

Tradition has it that this Rabbi Yishmael was one of the Ten Martyrs of the Hadrianic persecution, whose story is retold in the most gloriously epic verse on *Yom Kippur* and *Tisha b'Av*. This, however, cannot be, for in verse 8 of the *piyyut* the martyr is clearly denoted as *Cohen Gadol*, High Priest, as he is again in verse 10, and his martyrdom is told in pairing with that of Shimon ben Gamliel. The latter's death we know; it followed Titus' destruction of the Temple in 70 CE - at which time Yishmael ben Elisha was still a child. As to Yishmael himself - he almost certainly died of old age and natural causes, some time before the tragic rebellion of Bar Kochba.

✡

Shelosh-Esrey ha-Midot - The Thirteen Laws of Hermeneutics

Before beginning an explanation of this erudite and sophisticated exposition of the derivation of the legal process, I am minded to quote in full the words of Rabbi Jeffrey M. Cohen, the Rabbi of the Stanmore and Canons Park Synagogue which one part of my north London family attends. In his "Guide to the Weekday and Sabbath Prayers" - a well-meaning work which sadly does little more than inform you which page of which edition of the prayer-book you're supposed to be on, and enjoins you to undistracted silence - he says the following of Rabbi Yishmael's dissertation:

"This section will be incomprehensible, even in translation, to those uninitiated into *Talmudic* study."

I am grateful for his solicitudes on my behalf, but resent the patronising and superior tone; this is the voice of the elitist, preserving and protecting all esoteric mysteries for the select and chosen few - a perennial fault of all religions, not least Judaism.

"However," he continues, "these 13 Principles of Rabbi Ishamel" - he drops the Y, irrelevantly, unless you are Rabbi Akiva - "are of paramount importance as a key to the way Biblical verses are to be analysed and compared with a view to deriving further laws from them."

In which case I had better don my intellectual armour, mount my white steed, bid farewell to the Lady Dulcinea, draw my pen from its scabbard and ride forth into the enchanted forest, undaunted by fear of the Adversary. Unlike Rabbi Cohen (isn't that the most wonderful juxtaposition!), who says only what I've quoted here, and who then takes his own advice and treads no further, I wish to understand as best I can what I'm told is "paramount".

The *bara'isa* appears as the introduction to *Sifra*, a book of *Midrash* on the Book of Leviticus, probably edited by Chiyya ben Abba in the early years of the 3rd century CE. "*Drash*" means "investigation", and enters Judaism as a method of teaching and studying precisely from these 13 Principles of Rabbi Yishmael. That's to say the 13 Principles are the theory, *Drash* is the application, *Midrash* is the book that consequences. So we can already see why this really is "paramount".

But why is it here, in this section of the morning service? That's simple. First, because it's necessary as a basis for all *halachic* commentary. Second, because it's essential to combine study with prayer. Third, and most pertinent, because it's the Book of Leviticus which contains the Temple Service and every passage of scripture requires its sister-section of *Talmud* to complete it.

Did Maimonides plot his 13 Principles of Faith in deliberate echo of Rabbi Yishmael? We have to suppose he did.

✡

1) *Mi-kal va-chomer* - "from light to heavy"

Also translatable as "from minor to major". If a law applies in one situation, then it must also apply in a parallel situation, both by logic and by rule of precedent. This isn't a principle that requires establishing. But there are issues of leniency and stringency within the parameters of a law, and it's legitimate to apply the law upwards from the minor circumstance to the major one. Thus, for example, if it's unlawful to do a certain thing on a weekday, then it must also be unlawful on *shabbat* and festivals, where the rules are always stricter; and if it's permitted on *shabbat* and festivals, then likewise it must be permissible on weekdays.

Leviticus 21:16-21 sets out certain rules, by which priests, who are not disqualified from Temple service because of their age, are nevertheless disqualified because of bodily blemishes. Applying *mi-kal va-chomer*, the Rabbis conclude that the same must also apply to Levites, but that it must even apply to those Levites who are disqualified by age as well. The age disqualification is regarded as the minor, the physical blemish the major.

The principle is logical, but appears not to be correct - or at least not consistently applied. There are, for instance, specific acts forbidden on fast days - the wearing of leather, the washing of teeth - which are nonetheless permitted on the Sabbath. And in the case of the disqualification, it might seem immaterial that there's a second reason when there's already a first which is sufficient.

These are not "laws" however; they are merely the principles upon which laws may be deduced. What I've unearthed above are an exception and a *reductio ad absurdum*, and while exceptions may prove, or in this case disprove rules, while reductions may well lead to apparent absurdities, they do no more than temper principles. This too is something that may be deduced from the principle *mi-kal va-chomer*.

2) *Mi-gezerah shava* - "sentences are equal"

"Sentences" in the sense of phrases, not judicial punishments. The principle is that similar words in different contexts clarify each other. This is akin to the principle which allowed Andrew Wiles to solve the problem of Fermat's Last Theorem by applying the allegorical proof of Takamura's Conjecture (strange to think that these two sets of learned men worked so far apart, the one at the end of his people's second golden age, a thousand years before the other's had even reached its first golden age, and yet reached the same conclusion by means of the same conclusion).

Again the rule is faulty, but the principle nevertheless valid. Philologically a word changes its meaning by context (in English this is especially true, as I have demonstrated by opening this fragment with the ambivalent noun "sentences"; but it's also true of the less multilingually influenced Hebrew), and the change of meaning implicitly refutes the drawing of equivalent inferences. Slang is the obvious instance of this, but it's true of poetry as well; which is more significant since the Scriptures are so frequently in verse. But it's true of all words, because words carry cultural baggage. "*Gezerah*" itself can mean a phrase or sentence, whence Job 22:28 makes it a full-scale decree, but one ordained by men, whereas Daniel 4:14 and 4:21 construe it as an edict passed in heaven; which two uses [of the very word on which the principle rests] cannot possibly be regarded as equivalent.

And then what happens when *gezerah* is used - because there is also the root "*gezer*" meaning "to cut off", and the root "*gazar*" meaning "to divide", and the "*gizrah*", referred to in Ezekiel, an enclosure or side-chapel in the northern part of Solomon's Temple where Tammuz was worshipped - when *gezerah* is used to mean something entirely different? Is a Temple Courtyard equivalent to an abandoned royal city on the borders of Ephrayim, just because Solomon's masons fixed up both?

What I'm trying to say is simply: *caveat interpretor*. These principles aren't just intellectual and judicial jewjaws, but the means of making living laws. And laws are the substance of people's lives. We must at all times keep in mind the possibility that the laws of God we have deduced may not actually be the ones that God intended.

To give a significant example of *mi-gezerah shava*, the phrase "*be-mo'ado* - in its appointed time" is used on one occasion for the sacrifice of the Paschal Lamb (Numbers 9:2), and on another occasion (Numbers 28:2) for the *Tamid* offering. Since the *Tamid* offering is made on every day including the Sabbath, "*mi-gezerah shavah*" allows the Paschal Lamb also to be offered on the Sabbath. The import of this may not be lost on Christians.

Unlike most of Rabbi Yishmael's Thirteen Principles, it's remarkably easy for any amateur or dilettante to find examples of *mi-gezerah shavah* - all it requires, after all, is a systematic search for repeated words or phrases. Amongst the *yeshivot* of Palestine and Babylon, in the early centuries of the first millennium CE, the practice of seeking out examples became so widespread that the Rabbis felt obliged to pass a subsidiary ruling, restricting the making of laws by *mi-gezerah shavah*. So it became unacceptable to advance a *mi-gezerah shavah* independently; only those handed down from teacher to disciple were allowed (*Pesachim* 66a), and only those where both references were in the *Torah*. It also became required to prove that the repeated words were "*muphneh* - free" - in their context; in other words, that the rule deduced wasn't dependent on the words themselves, but could have been deduced anyway. The *d'vei* of Rabbi Akiva has never accepted these restrictions.

Two other rules belong in the category of *mi-gezera shavah* - the principles of "*hekkesh* – comparison" - and "*smuchim* – juxtaposition". *Hekkesh* is the presence of two laws in the same verse, from which a logical deduction would make what is true of one law equally true of the other. A perfect example of this is Deuteronomy 16:3, which states "you shall eat no leavened bread with it; for seven days you shall eat only unleavened bread with it" - the "it" in question being the Passover sacrifice, the Paschal Lamb. At first glance the double-phrase appears tautological, but in fact it's significantly not so. Women are exempt from time-bound positive commandments, but not from time-bound negative ones. The second phrase appears to exempt women from eating *matzah* at *Pesach*, but in fact the first phrase requires them to do so.

3) *Mi-binyan av mi-katuv echad, u-mi-binyan av mi-shney chetuvim*

"A general principle derived from one verse confirms a general principle derived from a second verse."

This is plain and obvious enough - except for the danger of creating syllogisms, which then affirm each other.

Leviticus 17:13 is the favoured exemplar for this principle. "He shall pour out the blood thereof and cover it with dust." Rabbi Joseph, cited in *Shabbat* 22a, states that, because the pouring of the blood is done by hand, so must the covering of the blood with dust be done by hand. But this exemplar is rejected in *Sepher Keritut* 1:3, on the grounds that these are two cases drawn from the same verse, where the principle is about two cases, drawn each from a different verse.

Better then the illustration drawn from Deuteronomy 23:25, which depends on two verses for its confirmation, the principle in one confirming the principle in the other. According to the establishing phrase in Deuteronomy, a farm labourer is entitled to help himself to ripe grapes from the vine or ripe corn from the stalk as a supplement to his wages. Leviticus 19:10 requires the owner of a vineyard to leave the gleanings for the poor; but the portion taken by the labourer cannot be regarded as part of the gleaning, and so the verse doesn't substantiate the principle. Numbers 15:17-21 requires the owner of a corn field to give what is called *challah*, not the plaited bread eaten by Jews on Sabbaths and festivals, but a portion of the dough, for the benefit of the priests; the portion taken by the labourer clearly isn't this, and so the verse again doesn't substantiate the principle.

However, taking the two verses in isolation, there are clear common factors - the requirement to give up a portion and the fact that both are plants - which thus confirm the principle drawn from Deuteronomy 23:25.

4) *Mi-klal u-phrat* - "from the perfect to the scattered"

In legal terminology: "from the general to the specific". This principle states that, where a scriptural verse develops from the general to the specific, the specific alone applies. Thus, for example, Leviticus 1:2: "If a man should bring an offering from his livestock, he shall bring cattle, and sheep, and goats." The general - an offering - could perfectly well include camels, horses, donkeys, chickens, or any other livestock that he happens to possess, but the specific - cattle, sheep and goats - limits the range of beasts that are permitted to these, and these exclusively. Thus it became Law.

However, the next principle in part reverses this.

5) *U-mi-prat u-chlal* - "from the scattered to the perfect"

In legal terminology: "from the specific to the general". Deuteronomy 22:6 prohibits the taking of eggs from the nest if you also intend to take the dam, and *vice versa* (like seething a kid in its mother's milk, it constitutes an unnecessary cruelty). The principle is specific to a certain type of fowl, but the Law applies generally to all creatures; so you cannot slaughter, say, the calf with the milch-cow either.

The part-reversal can be seen in this example, drawn from Exodus 22:9: "If a man delivers to his neighbour an ass, or an ox, or a sheep, or any beast…" The use of the word "any" makes the difference. Now camels, horses, donkeys, chickens and any other livestock are included; the law applies to all of them.

6) *Kelal u-phrat u-chelal; i atah dan eleh ke-eyn ha-perat*

"From the perfect to the scattered to the perfect, you may only rule in the eye of the perfect."

Not an absolutely exact translation, but sufficient to explain the point. In a case where a scriptural verse begins with a generality, develops a specific, but then opens up a second generality, any inference drawn must unify whatever is similar to both generalities.

One of the examples used for this (*Bava Metzia* 57b) refers to Exodus 22:8, which concerns the treatment of a thief. The first generality deals with the issue of his crime, the second with that of the victim's loss, obviously connected, but just as obviously a separate issue. The specific is the measure of punishment, and the law inferred is that a thief must pay back double the value of the stolen goods, regardless of the scale of his dishonesty (first offence or serial burglar), and regardless of any fault on the part of the victim (window left unlocked etc).

But out of the same verse the Rabbis also infer a second law, from the specifics of the items listed, that moveable objects have intrinsic value and can be repaid double, but that immovable objects (land, legal contracts, loans at interest) do not and so cannot. This under rule 4 simultaneous to the application of rule 6. Yet there are inferences in this passage under rule 5 too - why are these not drawn?

7) *Mi-kelal she-hu tsarich li-pherat, u-mi-perat she-hu tsarich li-chelal*

"The general which requires a specific, and the specific which requires the general [in order to clarify its meaning]."

This is now serious hair-splitting, of the sort that tends to invite satire. Its point is that principles 4 and 5 above do not apply if the statements aren't sufficient in themselves, but require further clarification. Leviticus 3:5 offers an instance of this, referring to the peace-offering:

"And Aaron's sons shall burn it on the altar upon the burnt sacrifice, which is upon the wood, which is on the fire."

The specification of the manner of making the offering ends at "sacrifice"; the remainder relates to a quite separate law about the making of the pyre, but is a clarification, not a specification, insofar as it relates to the particular offering.

Another example is the clarification which Exodus 13:2 gives to Deuteronomy 15:19. In the first, "sanctify unto Me all the first-born", there is room to question whether this includes or excludes children born by Caesarean section; but the Exodus text - "whosoever opens the womb" - resolves the ambiguity.

8) *Kol davar she-hayah bi-chelal ve-yatsa min ha-kelal lelamed, lo le-lamed al atsmo yatsah, elah lelamed al ha-kelal kulo yatsa*

Unusually long-winded and legalistic for the otherwise impressively succinct Rabbi Yishmael. "Anything which, being in a general statement, is singled out for special treatment, whatever is postulated from that special treatment must be applied in all instances embraced by the general rule."

So, for example, a general statement which teaches that a man who steals a coat must pay back double, must also apply to a man who steals a sheep, or a tomato. Similarly, where Leviticus 20:27 states that "a man or woman who makes divinations through a medium shall be put to death by stoning", there is a general rule against all forms of witchcraft of which this is a specific instance highlighted for special treatment; from it the Rabbis deduce that all forms of witchcraft are therefore to be punished by stoning (*Sanhedrin* 67b).

9) *Kol davar she-hayah bi-chelal ve-yatsa liton to'an echad she-hu che-inyan, yatsa lehakel ve-lo lehachamir*

"Anything which, being in a general statement, is used as a point to discuss a similar provision, must lead to a conclusion that is more lenient and not more severe."

This is an immensely significant principle, by any standard or definition of justice. The example given by Art Scroll's Rabbi Nosson Schuman demonstrates this in a case where leniency and severity are paramount. He cites Leviticus 24:21, where the *Torah* makes no specific differentiation between premeditated murder and accidental manslaughter. The principle in rule 5 should apply, with the death penalty pronounced in both cases, because the generality expressed in verse 20 states unequivocally: "breach for breach, eye for eye, tooth for tooth; as he has caused damage to another man, so shall damage be caused to him." But under the principle asserted here a more lenient view must be taken, so the fact of accident can be allowed, and a lower punishment imposed.

Verse 23 of that same section of Leviticus insists that "you shall have one manner of Law, for the stranger and for your own people; I am the Lord your God" - thereby establishing Divine sanction for the death penalty. But the Rabbinical ruling allows a human court to commute or overturn the sentence. Is the *Sanhedrin*, then, an even higher court than heaven? So it might seem.

10) *Kol davar she-hayah bi-chelal ve-yatsa liton to'an acher she-lo che-inyano, yatsa lehakel u-lo-lehachamir*

"Anything which, being in a general statement, is used as an illustration to discuss a provision which is not similar, may lead to conclusions which are both lenient and more severe."

Not "either", note, but "both". Because like is not being compared with like, there is neither a transition from the general to the specific nor from the specific to the general, and so none of the previous principles apply. Thinking of the sacrifices listed earlier, a good case might be the punishment for a female priest (the implication of the text is that there must have been such creatures, for why else specify a male priest in certain circumstances?) who eats an offering reserved for a male priest; her punishment should have no connection with that of a secular member of the congregation who eats a portion of the paschal offering without previously registering. Though both are offending against laws that pertain to the regulations governing offerings, their statuses are different, and so different principles apply - and these may be more lenient or more severe according to the judgement of that specific circumstance; and of course the identical punishment may yet be pronounced, but it will have been reached from different principles, and on its own merits.

In analysing all of this it should never be forgotten that hermeneutics, though used as legal apparatus, is really a branch of literary criticism, for what Rabbi Yishmael is trying to deduce is not the Law itself, but the correct manner of reading the text (I almost wrote "decoding" the text) in order to deduce the correct Law.

The end has no connection with the means, but the end is important too, because a method is prolix in a vacuum. The ultimate objective is the correct interpretation of the Law (and for this reason, if not for any other, it really is quite staggering that these 13 Principles were left out of the *Mishnah*, when surely they should have been regarded as the *sine qua non* of everything that followed). It's a most astonishingly modern and sophisticated code of law that's being enunciated, however pedantically. A far cry from the divine barbarism, but also a powerful development of the divine justice, of Mosaic Law.

11) *Kol davar she-hayah bi-chelal ve-yatsa lidon ba-davar he-chadash, i atah yachol lehachaziro li-chelalo, ad she-yachazirenu ha-katuv li-chelalo be-pherush*

"Anything which, being in a general statement, is used as an illustration in a different case, cannot revert to its status as a general statement, unless the scriptural text specifically reverts it."

To cite something general analogously renders it specific, and it can't be regarded as general again. I find this quite absurd. To cite something general analogously is to make a sweeping universalisation, and surely what should be prohibited is the process, not the consequence.

For an example. The guilt offering of a man who has contracted leprosy (leprosy in the Bible seems to have been a generic term for virtually any dermatological disorder, from eczema to psoriasis) requires the placing of the blood on the ear, the thumb and the toe (Leviticus 14:14). This appears to run counter to the general ruling on guilt offerings, where other rituals, such as the sprinkling of blood on the altar, were also required. But the scriptural text reverts to that law, because the preceding verse has stated that "as the sin offering is the priest's, so is the guilt offering". The rules for general guilt offerings apply, and in addition the specific rule for leprosy is addended.

12) *Davar ha-lamed me-inyano, ve-davar ha-lamed mi-sopho*

"A principle deduced from its context, or from the passage which follows."

The Law in the text states, let us say, "You Shall Not Steal". Using earlier principles the Rabbis note that this verse is preceded by "You Shall Not Kill" and succeeded by "You Shall Not Commit Adultery", and since both of these carry the death penalty, they deduce that so must this. However, elsewhere it's made clear that the only crime of theft for which the death penalty applies is kidnapping, and so they construe that God only intended to refer to kidnapping when he said "You Shall Not Steal". This is a principle deduced from its context.

As to a principle deduced from a passage which follows, Leviticus 14:34 says: "And if, when you come into the land of Canaan, I put the plague of leprosy in a house on one of your estates...", this is understood as only referring to houses built with stones, mortar and timber, because these are the materials specifically mentioned in the next verse.

13) *Ve-chen shney chetuvim ha-mach'chishim zet et zeh, ad she-yavo ha-katuv ha-shlishi ve-yachria beyneyhem*

"Two passages that contradict one another, until a third passage reconciles them."

Two passages that contradict one another! In the *Torah*? This is quite some Rabbinical admission!

Exodus 19:20 (the giving of the Ten Commandments) notes that God came down to the top of the mountain. The reprise of the tale, in Deuteronomy 4:36, states in apparent contradiction that His voice was heard from heaven. Which is correct (the entire career of Rabbi Louis Jacobs and the founding of the *Masorti* movement in the United Kingdom hung on this apparent contradiction). The text of Exodus 20:19 resolves it - God brought heaven down to the mountain, and then spoke.

The last three principles belong together, and they are neatly symmetrical in that they follow their own intrinsic sense and logic, the first being here used to make the second point, the second being inferred in pursuance of the first, the third reconciling them.

Yehi ratson

"May it be Your will, O lord our God and God of our forefathers, that the Holy Temple be rebuilt, speedily in our days, and grant us our share in Your *Torah*, and may we serve You there with reverence as in days of old and former years."

Having substituted the laws of the offerings for the offerings themselves, having created a synagogue service to accompany the substitution, in place of the Temple service that accompanied the actual offerings, we finish by praying for the restoration of the Temple, its offerings, its proper service.

This, too, is entirely logical.

And yet. And yet. Since it's the Rabbis who redacted the Scriptures as well as the *Talmud*, since the synagogue and the *yeshiva* survived the destruction of the Temple (why is Yochanan ben Zakkai, who achieved this, not better known, more revered, properly commemorated?), the Rabbis have a huge unfair advantage over the *Cohanim* in the on-going Pharisee-Sadducee debate. The Rabbis will always be right, because there's no one to gainsay them. The Pharisaic tradition will always supplant the *Cohanic* (yet another case of the Biblical first-born yielding to the second). Only the restoration of the Temple can undo this, and retrieve the balance. But a restoration of the Temple can only be achieved if the authority of the Rabbis is first removed. What purpose, what gain, could there possibly be then, for the Rabbis seriously to advocate and to encourage the actual restoration of the Temple?

Kaddish de-Rabbanan - The Rabbi's *Kaddish*

What we are examining is the Jewish daily prayer book. But in Judaism prayer is never simply prayer. Prayer is a substitution for sacrifice, and so we have the scriptural instructions that ordain the precise details of the sacrifices. But in Judaism scripture is never simply scripture, and so we have the Rabbinic instruction that ordains the precise meanings of the scripture. But in Judaism the Rabbi is never simply the Rabbi, he's also the last voice of authority of almighty God; and so, last of all, we have the Rabbi's *Kaddish*, which offers up to God the highest level of praise available in Jewish prayer, exalting and sanctifying Him for the sacrifices, the prayer services, the scriptures, the expositions, the Talmud, even for the substitutions He has given us. So the circle of prayer forms its own Unity. So God is always God.

After studying any fragment of scripture - from the Oral or the Written Law - the convention is not to continue until after reciting the Rabbis' *Kaddish*, which is the longest of the four versions of this prayer that we shall encounter. (I do not propose to undertake a full and detailed exegesis of its history and nature; the best book by far on the subject is Leon Wieseltier's 1997 "*Kaddish*", published by Vintage Books and Random House, ISBN 0-375-70362-4).

Though it's called the Rabbi's *Kaddish*, this isn't because it's recited by the Rabbi, but because it includes a special verse in honour of the teachers of

Judaism and their students, by which is meant, in its proper sense, the Rabbi: the wise man, the learned sage, the expert in Jewish Law. In other words it's a *Kaddish* addressed to, not by, the Rabbis. In fact, custom and practice ordain that the Rabbi's *Kaddish* should be recited by a mourner, and that it's only recited if there's a *minyan*. If no mourner is present, but there is still a *minyan*, then the *shali'ach tsibbur*, the prayer leader, should recite it - and of course the prayer leader may very well be the Rabbi, and the Rabbi may very well be in mourning, but these are incidental (Rabbi Yishmael would tell us, under rule 5, that these are general, not specific). If a mourner is present in synagogue, and no study of scripture has taken place, then such study should be forced, however briefly, however superficially, because it's a great *mitzvah* for a mourner to say *Kaddish*, and a greater *mitzvah* still to enable a mourner to say that *Kaddish* even if it be as a consequence of a truly cursory glance, an intellectually empty gloss over the tiniest fragment of incidental scripture. Any piece of *aggada* will do, however brief. Even reading this paragraph will do. The object of the exercise isn't the studying but the saying of *Kaddish* - not that a moment's study ever did anyone a jot of harm.

I'm conscious that I become highly irreverent and highly critical at various times in this book. I do not apologise for this. Doubt is the natural complement of faith, as irreverence is of piety. No one should chastise me for my iconoclasm, since it's a particular tenet of Judaism that we are opposed to all forms of idolatry and instructed to smash all idols.

The *Kaddish* is one of several *piyyutim* that I could easily call my favourite. In any of the four versions, spoken, recited, chanted or sung to the special festival melodies. In Steven Spielberg's film of "Schindler's List" there is a terribly poignant moment at Plaszow where the *Kaddish* is sung, slowly and elegiacally, in a thoroughly *Litvak* rendition, the stress always placed trochaically - the middle of three syllables - and the *qamats* - the vocalic notation which Sephardi Jews pronounce like the "u" in "umbrella" - enunciated as an Ashkenazi "oy". Thus:

"*Yiskoydel ve-yiskoydesh...yisboyrach...le-oylam.*"

Most of us are more accustomed to the flatter Polish chant, pronunciation almost Sephardic, and with the stress always on the final syllable. But these variations add rather than distract. Judaism becomes less a language than a set of accents and dialects bound by a common thread, in the same way that Geordie and Oxford and Essex and Wessex, let alone New York, Bombay, Hong Kong and Queensland are all still English.

On most occasions the prayer leader recites the *Kaddish*, and the role of the congregation is simply to respond *amen* after each verse except the second, where the *amen* is the prelude to the interjection: "*Yehey shemey rabboh mevorach le-olam u-le-olmay almayah* - a wonderful triplet of which Rabbi Akiva, presumably, would have had a great deal to affirm. There is also a brief interjection – "*berich hu*" - in the third verse, and the option of communally singing the great *Oseh Shalom* prayer in the final verse. But essentially this is an individual, not a community activity, and over the centuries there has been an enormity of dispute over the allowing of more than one mourner to recite the *Kaddish*. In some communities in the middle ages, every mourner said *Kaddish*, one after the other; in other communities complex hierarchies were established, to give rights of representing all mourners to certain thought more worthy (a bridegroom, for example, in the week of his wedding). There are occasions though when the individual is subsumed within the communal. After the final scriptural reading on *shabbat*, for example, and between the *Shacharit* and *Musaph* services, the half-*Kaddish* is sung, not chanted, and here all the congregation joins in. And on *Yom Kippur*, when the *Kaddish* is rendered in the most exquisitely lovely though mournful melody, it's permitted for anyone to join in and help the euphony, to make their contribution to this junction of poetry with prayer, melody with liturgy.

Alone among Jewish prayers, the *Kaddish* is entirely in Aramaic, though it isn't always easy to distinguish the differences. The use of the final *aleph* - א - where Hebrew would have a final *hey* - ה . The un-*dageeshed tav* - ת – , pronounced *sav*. The final *nun* - ן - denoting masculine plural where Hebrew would use a final *mem* - ם . Grammatically, as in vocabulary, they are almost the same language. Interesting, though, that modern Israelis, and Reform Jews, insist on pronouncing the Aramaic as though it were Hebrew.

The object and purpose of the *Kaddish* is to praise God and to list His attributes, so that it's really quite erroneous to describe it as a prayer. It's also, I think, unique among the liturgy in that it nowhere mentions God by any name at all, neither *Elohim* nor *Adonay* nor the Tetragrammaton nor *El Shaddai*, nor any epithet at all except His attributes. There's no *berachah* either, no benediction, except in that one, brief congregational response "*berich hu*". And yet nothing could be more obviously and exclusively about God, nothing could sanctify Him and His attributes more illustriously. Inter alia He is "magnified, sanctified, blessed, praised, glorified, exalted, extolled, declared mighty, upraised and lauded…beyond all blessings, songs, praises and consolations that may be uttered in the world", and He is called upon, in the paragraph that's particular to this Rabbi's *Kaddish*, to send to all who study the Law, and all who teach it, "peace, grace, kindness, mercy, long life, ample nourishment and salvation" - the common diet of favours asked by Man of his divinities.

It's very much a responsive - I shall have to call it a prayer for want of anything more exact in English. Hearing the opening word – "*yisgadal*" or "*yitgadal*" depending on your dialect - is enough for even the noisiest congregation to become instantly silent, upstanding and earnest; though it's also a matter of dispute whether we should sit or stand; congregations vary. The response must be instant, for there are only four words to the first *amen*. The second *amen* is more demanding still, requiring the repetition of a complex phrase whose last three words trip over each other – "*le-olam u-le-olmay almayah*" - something in the manner of the Moslem, "*la-allah illah allah* - there is no God but *Allah*', which likewise sounds wonderful if got right, and dreadful otherwise. "*Berich hu*" after the third phrase, then a series of simple *amens*. The last verse of all is the most demanding. Before speaking, or preferably singing the phrase, by any one of several tunes, take three steps back. Bow to the left on "*oseh*", to the right on "*hu*", bow forward on "*ve al-kol*", finish the line, stay still and silent a moment, then take three steps forward and resume. There is a conjurational element to this element. With such piety has God been evoked in the preceding lines, with such flattery and sycophancy, He is present now in *shul* in a form more palpable than ever else. And so we do what we must do in the presence of the king - we courtsey.

The trickery of the acrostic also crops up again here. Tractate *Shabbat* (119b) notes that *amen*, treated acrostically, spells "*El Melech Ne'eman* - God the Trustworthy King". No doubt, with access to a dictionary, it could be made to spell out prophecies of doom, the names of Israeli basketball players and even the winning numbers in the Bible Code raffle too. It isn't the falsity of *Gematria* that I resent, but the way in which it's used to hoodwink the uninitiated who want to believe in superstitious magic.

There is a close linguistic link - a real not an imagined mystical one - between the *Kaddish*, the *Kiddush* and the *Kedushah*. All three are acts of sanctification. In order of precedence, theologically, the *Kaddish* always has priority.

Psalm 30

The text of the *Kaddish* as we have it today probably dates from as late as the 7th century CE, though *Talmudic* references show that an earlier version must have been in use in Temple times. That Jesus was familiar with it is highly likely. "Our Father who is in heaven" can be found in the Rabbi's phrase "*avuhon di vishmay*". "Hallowed be Your name" is the opening phrase "*ve yiskadash shemey raboh*". "Your kingdom come" is intended by the "*yehi ratson*" paragraph which precedes the *Kaddish*, and "*yehi ratson*" itself means "Your will be done". "Give us this day our daily bread" is a Christian rendition of the list of favours. "Forgive us our trespasses" is taken from the "*selichot*" prayers later in the service. And so on. "Lead us not into temptation and deliver us from evil" is a quote from Psalm 30, which just happens to be the Psalm that follows the Rabbi's *Kaddish*. Like most of Christ's teachings, his sermons, his prayers and his parables, mainstream orthodox Judaism as practised by the Rabbis of his day can vouch for every word of it.

Mind you, the reciting of Psalm 30 at precisely this point in the service started only as recently as the 17th century. In Temple times it opened the service - as the opening phrase, "For the dedication of the temple of David", quite clearly indicates - and so it would have been one of a dozen or so out of the one hundred and fifty Psalms that every Jew could virtually have been guaranteed to know.

The Psalm was introduced because of a curious development in custom and practice. The *Kaddish* had never been intended as a special function of the rites of mourning, but in the early Middle Ages - probably the 11th or 12th century - this became the convention. First the honour of reciting the Rabbi's *Kaddish* was bestowed upon the mourner; then, with time, it became his right; finally his duty and so his obligation. But there's a second custom, that a mourner always says *Kaddish* twice, the first time as a means of honouring the dead, and the second for his own sake. But the *Kaddish* is only recited after studying Law or Scripture, and so this Psalm was interposed, to allow the second recitation.

Though none of the above explains why it was this Psalm, and not any other piece of scripture. Go take a look at the text in your own time, verses 4 and 12 especially; it will be obvious why this Psalm.

This isn't the place to undertake a detailed analysis of the Psalms. I dissent from the common view that any of the Psalms belonged uniquely to the Jewish liturgy. I regard them as being a cycle, an epic cycle if you will, in which the lives of the three-part divinity are recounted, yes liturgically, but only in the same sense that the *Vedas* and the *Mahabharata* are liturgy. The Psalms attributed to David are really Psalms addressed to David, and not the earthly monarch but the ever-dying ever-reborn Beloved Son, *Adonis Adonay*, Tammuz, the Lord: David's full name, like that of his youngest son who took the king-name Shlomo, was *Yedid-Yah*, the Beloved of the Moon Goddess. Hence the reference in verse 4 to being lowered into the pit or grave (the Hebrew is specific in saying *She'ol*, the Underworld, the kingdom of David's adversary, *Sha'ul*, King Saul), as Joseph was in the Egyptian Osiris-Shet version, as Jesus was in the Ba'al-Anat version whose central locus was the shrine of Anat, *Beit Anatot*, or Bethany, where Jeremiah's father was once a priest. In this form the Psalm reads like a thanksgiving to the Lord of the Underworld for one who has survived a life-threatening experience (I can imagine Dante reciting it as he and Virgil leave the *Inferno* for the *Purgatorio*), and would presumably have been the verbal accompaniment to a thanksgiving-offering. Logical, then, why this Psalm should follow the *Kaddish*.

Orthodox Judaism does not (can not?) accept any of this, and so reads the Psalms as metaphor (and masculinises Yah). The circumstances and the thanksgiving aren't the problem, only the *Gehennic* picture. Theologically Jews don't believe in underworlds, in places of eternal punishment, in *She'ol*, because our monotheistic God cannot be held responsible for Hell, nor identified in any of His attributes with Hades. The *Talmud* (*Nedarim* 22a) simply notes that *Gehenna* is a form of inner torment (the metaphorical interpretation yet again!), something akin to *angst*. "The flames of frustration, anguish and melancholy are the equivalent of the fires of *Gehennom*." So says Rabbi Scherman, looking for rainbows through the windows of the Art Scroll. "Throughout the Book of Psalms," he adds, "most references to 'falling into the lower world' refer to this type of emotional turmoil." Huh! The Jew can accept Psyche, but not *She'ol*. Yet isn't Psyche just our modern theological equivalent, an identical metaphor? We can no more cut open the human head to locate the Psyche than we can cut open the earth and find *She'ol*.

All references to God in the Psalm are *Adonay*. No *Elohim* at all. *Adonay* is the Lord - the beloved son, David.

The Mourner's *Kaddish* which completes this section is the same in all dimensions as the Rabbi's *Kaddish*, save only that one specific paragraph "*al Yisrael*", which refers to the Rabbis. The Jewish custom is to mourn fully for seven days, partially for thirty days (including the seven), then regularly till the end of eleven lunar months. On each day the *Kaddish* should be recited, and in addition *Yizkor*, the memorial prayers for the dead; after the end of mourning, *Kaddish* is recited only on the anniversary of the death. I shall return to the rites of mourning later in this book.

✡

Chapter Eight: *Pesukei D'Zimrah* - Verses of Praise

"I now prepare my mouth to thank, laud and praise my Creator. For the sake of the unification of the Holy One, Blessed be He, and His Presence, through Him who is hidden and inscrutable, I pray in the name of Israel."

A line of *Kabbalah*, optional in the declaration, which serves to prove that everything until now has been preliminary, preparatory, to the extent that it wouldn't be wrong to say the service still hasn't actually begun. We've conducted ritual and ceremony, we've informed ourselves of what we should be doing, and explained why, and why we can't. Now we open the door and enter inwards.

We enter, or should, in silence, and remain in silence until the completion of the *Shemoneh Esreh*. With the exception of certain prescribed a*men*s, we don't even utter the common congregational responses ("*baruch hu u-varuch shemo* – Blessed is He and Blessed is His Name" - after the sounding of any of God's names). But what actually is this silence, since it isn't the silence of making-no-sound? Rather it's the silence of an immense communal effort at unison and harmony. Led by the *chazan* - the prayer leader - all chant the prayers, especially the opening of the *Shema*, the individual's recitation of the Eighteen Blessings, the conclusory *amens*. Silence is thus a concentrated sound, devoid of extraneous noises, from which there can be no distraction. To break that silence - like coughing during the *legato* or going out of the theatre just when Othello is about to confront Desdemona - is to shatter the sound-glass atmosphere of spiritual intensity. If prayer is effective, it hangs the whole world in the balance, and almost any noise can tip the scales. Up till now we've been counting how many angels can dance on the head of a pin. Now, with *Pesukei d'Zimrah*, we too begin dancing.

As if to emphasise that intensity, and in order to focus it, these prayers are recited standing. The two front *tsitsit*, either of the undergarment or the shawl, are clutched in the right hand, and kissed before being released.

Pesukei d'Zimrah is like a movement in a symphony, complete in itself, yet linked to the whole through variations on the same themes and motifs. To demonstrate its integrity, it begins and ends with a *berachah*.

*Pesukei d'Zimrah me*ans, in Aramaic, "Verses of Praise", from the root "*zamar* - to pluck", not in the sense of pruning vines to pick the fruit, but of fretting a harp or lyre to harvest music. "*Kley zemer*" are musical instruments, whence the *Yiddish* "*kletzmer*". So the chain of continuity is locked, from

David, who received the Psalms by inspiration at Jerusalem, and handed them…all the way to the *stadtl*-theatres of Kalisch and the kibbutz campfire at Deganiah.

The Rabbis say that formal prayer isn't possible until the mind and body have been properly composed, for which a phase of meditation is required. *Pesukei d'Zimrah* provides that meditation. To recite it doesn't require a *minyan*; a prayer leader and two respondents will suffice.

✡

Baruch She Amar - Blessed be He who spoke

"Blessed be He who…" 10 blessings, listing some out of the many thousands of the attributes of God. "He who spoke and the world came into being" - the concept known elsewhere as Logos: "In the beginning was the Word, and the Word was with God, and the Word was God." (John1:1)

"He who sustains Creation" - once again the links to Hinduism (the common source is Hittite) reveal themselves. Where the Logos reflects Brahman, the Sustainer is Vishnu.

"He who transforms words into actions."

"He who decrees and then fulfils his decrees."

"He who spreads mercy across the earth."

"He who is merciful to His creation."

"He who rewards generously those who fear Him."

"He who lives for ever and exists beyond eternity."

"He who redeems and rescues."

"He who is praised by the mouths of His people, glorified by the tongues of His pious followers and worshippers, and honoured in the Psalms of David His servant."

And as if this were not sufficient. "We shall praise You with hymns and songs. We shall exalt You, boast You, glorify You, remind people of Your name and proclaim Your kingdom. You are unique, the giver of life to all the Universe, the king who is most bragged about and magnified, now and until eternity."

Practically another *Kaddish*.

The final blessing hardly needs stating, for it's by now a self-evident truth:

"Blessed are you, Our Lord and King, who is showered with innumerable praises."

This isn't prayer. This is devotional love-poetry!

It's legended that these words have no human authorship, but were dropped from heaven and transcribed by the Men of the Great Synagogue, somewhere in the very earliest years of that great institution, the days of Ezra and Nehemiah in the 5th century BCE. If it's true it would have to have been written by the angels, else the references to boasting and bragging would become hubristic!

My younger daughter came home from school with a challenge for me. "Daddy, what's the longest word in the dictionary." I went and looked it up; it turned out not to be that Welsh mountain village that it used to be, but some vast Germanic compilation-word in which a dozen chemicals are strung together like a helix, eighteen, maybe twenty syllables. But my daughter rejected the answer. "Smiles," she insisted. "Smiles is the longest word in the dictionary, because there's a mile between the beginning and the end."

I tried the question on my Year 11 English set at school. They rejected smiles as contemptuously as she had rejected my helix. "A mile's nothing. How about 'motorway', that's several hundred miles." Which led us, at last, to "time" and "space" themselves, to "infinity" and "eternity" - and proof by numbers that time (a mere four letters) is a smaller entity than space, while infinity and eternity are palpably identical. This sort of metaphysics, I thought, is far more fun than real metaphysics. This sort of Gematria I can cope with - even the discovery that God is less than time and space, less than infinity or eternity or mercy or compassion. But only in English. Not in Hebrew. Only in English.

✡

Hodu L'Adonay - Praise the Lord

The Book of Chronicles repeats the account of the first kings of Israel - David, Solomon, the Divided Kingdom - which can be found in the two books of Samuel and the two books of Kings; with the key difference that Chronicles was written for the northern kingdom of Israel and Samuel and Kings for the southern kingdom of Judah. It's less obviously favourable to the establishment in Jerusalem, and there are significant factual differences - for example, Chronicles has David's sons serving as Temple Priests, where Kings has them as government ministers; a distinction that's more than just political, because David's sons were neither *Cohanim* nor *Leviyim* and should not therefore have been eligible to serve as priests.

Such differences, and there are many, are vital to both historians and theologians; there's so little evidence of the period to work with that contradictory testimony can often be the most useful, because the truth can be found in the synthesis. It's also vital to those who would study the literature, for Chronicles occasionally offers variations on the Psalms of a kind that's reminiscent of the folio and quarto editions of Shakespeare.

1 Chronicles 16: 8-36, the Psalm that follows *Baruch She Amar*, is a perfect illustration of this. In Chronicles the text is regarded as complete and integral, yet you won't find it in the Book of Psalms, as such. What you will find is a fragmentary and approximate correspondence.

1 Chron 16:	8 - 22	is virtually identical to Psalm 105: 1-15
	23 – 33	is virtually identical to Psalm 96: 2-13
	34	mirrors Psalm 106: 1
	35	is similar enough to recognise as Psalm 106: 35
	36	is virtually identical to Psalm 106: 36

Tradition has it that this was the Psalm which David wrote specifically for the celebrations when the Ark was brought from Kiryat Ye'arim of Gibeon to be housed forever in Jerusalem. It's addressed to Asaph, the head of the royal choir and orchestra, and we're told that it was performed in the Tent of Meeting by Asaph with Zechariah, Ye'i'el, Shmiramot, Yechi'el, Matityah, Eli'av, Benayahu and Oved-Edom; Ye'i'el playing psalteries and harp, Beneyahu and another priest named Yachazi'el on trumpets, and Asaph himself clashing the cymbals. Queen Michal disapproved of both the noise and the dancing which accompanied it and appears to have fallen out with David as a consequence.

Afterwards the Psalm was repeated daily by the *Cohanim*, the first fifteen verses with the morning *Tamid* offering, the next fourteen with the afternoon *Tamid*; but the practice was terminated with the inauguration of the Solomonic Temple. It will, however, come back into force, at least in part, when the Messiah comes, because Psalm 96, with its first and last verses reinstated (they're missing here) is the song of welcome which the Rabbis have ordained shall be recited upon his arrival.

There's a curious pause in the midst of verse 26 (Psalm 96:5). It reads: "*Ki kol elohey ha-amim elilim, va-Adonay shamayim asah* - for all the gods of the nations are idols, but *Yahweh* made the heavens."

The pause seems natural enough, grammatically, but the Rabbis comment that the phrase is misinterpretable without an elongated pause, to ensure that the word "*elilim* – idols" doesn't run into "*va-Adonay* - but *Yahweh*", lest anyone think that *Yahweh* was an idol too. To make it doubly certain that the error is avoided, the *chazan* alone should recite this line.

Some translate the penultimate phrase "*min ha-olam ve-ad ha-olam*" to mean "from this world to the world to come", when it clearly means "from eternity to eternity". This process of legitimating retroactively is irritating and annoying. The concept of an afterlife has no place in conventional Judaism, which holds that "*Adonay natan, adonay lakach* - the Lord gives and the Lord takes away", and regards dust to dust to be the way of all flesh. But it's in this manner that new dogma, new orthodoxy, is so easily established.

Phrases echo throughout this text. "*Hishtachavu la-Adonay be-hadrat kodesh* - prostrate yourself before *Yahweh* in His holy place" is sung when returning the Scrolls to the Ark, though in that case the words are found verbatim in Psalm 29. "*Hodu l'Adonay ki tov, ki le-olam chasdo*" is a part of *Hallel*, but on that occasion from Psalm 118. And once this confusion of Psalms is finished, there follows what is really little more than a long series of quotations from a variety of Psalms, led by the *chazan* reciting the *Romemu* which accompanies the taking out of the Scrolls (Psalm 99:5,9).

The sequence then is:

Ve hu rachum (Psalm 78:38) - "He is the merciful one"
Atah Adonay (40:12) - "You, Lord"
Zechor rachamecha (25:6) - "Remember Your mercies"
Tenu oz (68:35-36) - "Render might"
El nekamot (94:1-2) - "God of vengeance"
La-Adonay ha-yeshuah (3:9) - "Salvation is the Lord's"
Adonay tseva'ot (46:8) - "Lord God of Hosts"
Adonay tseva'ot (84:13) - "Lord God of Hosts"
Adonay hoshiah (20:10) - "Lord, save"
Hoshiah et amecha (28:9) - "Save Your people"
Naphsheynu (33:20-22) - "Our souls"
Hareynu Adonay (85:8) - "Show us, Lord"
Kumah ezratah (44:27) - "Arise, help Lord"
Anochi Adonay (81:11) - "I am the Lord"
Ashrey ha-am (144:15) - "Happy is the nation"
Va-ani be-chasdecha (13:6) - "And as for me, in Your kindness"

"*Ashrey ha-am*" will occur again, almost immediately afterwards in fact, in *Pesukei d'Zimrah*.

Rabbi Profiat Duran, a refugee from the massacre of the Jews in Spain in 1391, referred to the compendium from *Romemu* onwards, not as *Pesukei d'Zimrah* but as "*Pesukei d'Rachmi* - Songs of Mercy". This is now accepted as an official subtitle.

Mizmor le-todah

The next Psalmic reference in this section is Psalm 100, one of the shortest of all the Psalms at just five verses. Psalm 100 is a thanksgiving Psalm, which is to say it would have accompanied the thanksgiving sacrifices in the Temple. Here it's sung in full, and standing.

"A Psalm of thanksgiving. Call out to the Lord, everyone on earth. Serve the Lord with gladness, come before Him with joyous song. Know that the Lord is God. It is He who made us and we are His, His people and the sheep of His pasture. Enter His gates with thanksgiving, His courts with praise. Give thanks to Him, bless His name. For the Lord is good, His kindness endures forever, and from generation to generation He is faithful."

Yehi chavod

Then, seated again, a further anthology of phrases, from the Psalms and from elsewhere:

Yehi chavod (Psalm 104:31) – "May the glory"
Yehi shem Adonay (113:2-4) – "May the name of the Lord"
Adonay shimcha (135:13) – "Lord, Your name"
Adonay ba-shamayim (103:19) – "Lord in heaven"
Yismachu ba-shamayim (1 Chron 16:31) – "The heavens rejoice"
Adonay melech (10:16) – "The Lord is King"
Adonay malach (93:1) – "The Lord was King"
Adonay yimloch (Ex 15:18) – "The Lord will be King"
Adonay melech olam (10:16) – "The Lord is King for ever"
Adonay hephir (33:10) – "The Lord annuls"
Rabot machashavot (Prov 19:21) – "Many designs"
Atsat Adonay (33:11) – "The council of God"
Ki hu amar (33:9) – "For He spoke"
Ki vachar (132:13) – "For He chose"
Ki Ya'akov (135:4) – "Because Jacob"
Ki lo yitosh (94:14) – "He will not cast off"
Ve lo rachum (78:38) – "He is merciful"
Adonay hoshi'ah (20:10) – "Lord, save"

T.S. Eliot - but two thousand years before T.S. Eliot! An entire poem, constructed bone by bone from the skeletons of other poems. A heap of broken images. Except that the sum reunifies the parts.

But why these bones? Why this arrangement? Why this compendium?

"*Yehi shem Adonay*", the second allusion in the sequence, is the source of Laurence Binyon's poem of 1914, "For the Fallen", the one recited every Remembrance Sunday in Great Britain: "From the rising of the sun till its going down."

The three short phrases which are combined to make "*Adonay melech, Adonay malach, Adonay yimloch le-olam va'ed*" are formulated in exactly the same way to make one of the great hymns of *Yom Kippur.*

✡

Ashrey

According to Maimonides, who based his teaching on *Shabbat* 118b, *Pesukei d'Zimrah* is really the "Six Psalms", by which he meant the last six Psalms of all, numbers 145 to 150. These are now recited here in full, the first of them introduced with single-line quotations from Psalm 84 (v5) and 144 (v15). Far be it for me to correct the *Rambam*, but in *Shabbat* 118b Rabbi Jose clearly intends the recitation of *Hallel* when he speaks of the "Six Psalms". Clearly intends? He overtly states it: "May my portion be with those who recite the *Hallel* daily." Then is it possible that these were once the *Hallel* hymns, and not the ones we think they are today?

In most *shuls* the pattern is for the whole congregation to sing the two introductory verses, then for the Psalm to be recited in an undertone. At the end a closing line is added, from Psalm 115 (v18), which again is sung. Nothing in the Rabbinical writings explains this formal framing of the text, but it does feel like a sort of protective wall. There is no greater merit from any Psalm than from *Ashrey*, and so perhaps such a wall is needed. It's explained that other verses should be recited before and after it, but surely it's *Baruch She Amar* and *Yishtabach*, which frame the whole of *Pesukei d'Zimrah*, which achieve that objective?

Berachot 32b, endorsed by *Yal II Sam* 146, explains the two introductory verses as a reference to those pious souls who arrive before the start of the main service, in order to participate in the preliminaries. It's they, according to this tractate, who are the happy ones, or the meritorious of praise. Blessed are they who arrive on time!

It's customary to hold the *tefillin shel yad* during the first half, to touch the *tefillin shel rosh* during the second half - the switch being made, entirely logically, after "*poteyach et yadecha* - open your hand', in the middle of verse 12.

Ashrey is structurally an alphabetical acrostic, which is to say that each verse begins with a letter of the alphabet, in sequence from *aleph* to *tav*. Except that there's no verse commencing *nun* - nor any explanation of why not; or only one explanation, inevitably from the mystical canon, which suggests that the *nun* is missing because a famous verse of Amos, chapter five verse two to be precise, begins with a *nun* and prophesies the destruction of Israel: "*Naphlah lo-tosaph kum betulat Yisrael nitsha al-admatah eyn mekimah* - the virgin of Israel is fallen, she shall not rise again; she is forsaken upon her land; there is none to raise her up". This hypothesis was rather discredited however, when a version of Psalm 145 turned up amongst the Dead Sea Scrolls, in which not only was there a *nun* verse, but one whose wording achieved the precise opposite of the Amos quote, being a praise of God: "*Ne'eman Elohim bi-devarav ve-chasid be-chol ma'asav* - God is faithful in His words, and pious in all His works". The Psalm Scroll also appends the refrain "*Baruch Adonay u-varuch shemo le-olam va'ed* - blessed be the Lord and blessed be His name for ever and ever" at the end of each line, which suggests that this Psalm would have been used liturgically in the Second Temple, sung responsively in the same style as "*hodu l'Adonay ki tov*", (Psalm 118.)

Translations into English retain the meaning but forego the structure. I wonder if it would repay the trouble of an acrostical English version?

No, it appears that there is an official explanation for the bookends, though it's hardly satisfactory. When in doubt, conjure the mystical - this seems to be the Rabbinical policy (better than the patronising "there are mysteries of God beyond our human capacity to comprehend"). The two preliminary verses both begin with the word *Ashrey* - happy (or praiseworthy, if you stretch the meaning to its limits). *Talmud* declares that whoever recites this Psalm three times a day (i.e. anyone who attends the morning and afternoon prayers - *Ashrey* isn't recited in the evening, but is recited twice each morning) is guaranteed a place in the world to come, so to recite the Psalm is praiseworthy, and so the word praiseworthy is prefixed.

All very well if it were true. The root word really means "prosperous, wealthy, successful", and is overtly pecuniary; since happiness is usually identified with financial prosperity, *asher* acquires this extended meaning: happiness. In Rabbinic terms, knowing you have a place in the world to come also confers happiness, and if being praiseworthy…

What makes the mistranslation even odder is that Psalm 145 is the only Psalm to have acquired a name as well as a number. An important name too, for from this name comes the name for the whole anthology - *Tehillah* for Psalm 145, *Tehillim* for the Book of Psalms. And the meaning of *tehilla*? Why, "praise", of course.

Actually, much more interesting is the earlier meaning of *asher* in these Psalms. Asher was a son of Leah's handmaid Zilpah, whose tribal territory extended along the Mediterranean coast from Mount Carmel - where Haifa now stands - northwards to the border with modern Lebanon, towards the ancient kingdoms of Sidon and Tyre. The name is a variation of the Egyptian Osher, which the Greeks rendered as Osiris, and it was precisely on the coast of Sidon that Osher came to rest after Isis put him out to sea in his coffin following his murder by Set, in Hebrew *Shet*, the third child of Adam and Eve. In its feminine form, Asherah, she was the goddess of fortune, known by various dialect variations in the scriptures as Ashtorah, Ashtoreth, Asherim (for the trees in her sacred grove), Asherot, and quite probably Sarai and Sarah too (remember the *aleph* in Aramaic interchanging with the Hebrew *hey* in the *Kaddish*?) - all of them versions of Astarte or Ishtar, whom the Greeks identified with Venus and who, in the Purim story, becomes Esther. Her husband was Ba'al, the Lord or Master, and her son, simply known as *Adonay* in Hebrew, was Adonis to the Phoenicians and Greeks, another variant of Osiris, the ever-dying ever-reborn beloved son who was worshipped in Bethlehem and at the north gate of the Temple in Jerusalem as Tammuz. Worship of the trinity was commonplace in ancient Canaan, provably so from its predominance in the rancour and the ranting vilification of the Prophets for a thousand years, and its continuance in the cult of Jesus.

Ashrey, then, should be translated, not as happy, certainly not as praiseworthy, but as fortunate. "*Ashrey yoshvey beytecha* - those who inhabit your house are fortunate". House meaning, of course, Temple. Whose house? Clearly in the original, pre-Hebrew version, a pun was intended. The mystical explanation tries, but fails, to circumvent this.

The closing bookend is important too. "*Va-anachnu nevarech Yah, mey atah ve-ad olam, Hallelu-Yah* - we will bless the Lord from this time and forever, Hallelu-Yah." So it's usually rendered. "The Lord" is the translation of both Ba'al and *Adonay*, but it's specifically an epithet for Adonis. Yah was the sister of Ephron, the Hittite equivalent of Ba'al, who appears in the scriptures as the man from whom Abraham acquired the Cave of Machpelah as a burial-place for Sarah (Asherah). That last verse then should really be translated in the feminine, not the masculine: "We will bless Our

Lady from this time and forever, may She be Praised". Whatever else Psalm 145 itself may be, the bookends belong to a much earlier, pagan cult, though of course the patriarchal Rabbis will try to pretend that Yah is masculine, that it's merely one more of many hundred names of the One God. And of course it is - because in creating the world, in making Man in His own image, Elohim was androgynously male and female.

Hallelu-Yah

Like *Ashrey*, all the five Psalms that follow conclude with *Hallelu-Yah*, so perhaps this is indeed what Rabbi Jose meant by the daily *Hallel*. After all, what we think of as *Hallel* is reserved for pilgrim festivals, *Chanukah* and the New Moon.

"*Hallelu-Yah, halleli naphshi et Adonay.*" Psalm 146. Trust in God, not Man.
"*Hallelu-Yah ki tov.*" Psalm 147. God's continuing participation in Creation.
"*Hallelu-Yah, hallelu et Adonay.*" Psalm 148. God's continuing creation.
"*Hallelu-Yah, shiru l'Adonay.*" Psalm 149. Man fights in the army of God.
"*Hallelu-Yah, hallelu el be-kadsho.*" Psalm 150. Symphonies of praise.

All betray their pagan origins, their roots in a deity that was distinctly plural. None more so than the last, whose "*el*" was the Canaanite bull-god, the Zeus of their pantheon. It can also be no coincidence that a cycle of Psalms should end with six hymns of praise that are specific to the mother goddess. To her, and not to her consort, the male sky God, *Yahweh*.

Baruch Adonay Le-Olam

The sequence of Psalms ends with a blessing, and with a double *amen*. As before, this blessing is constructed line-by-line from other Psalms, to complete the symmetry.

"*Baruch Adonay* (89:53) - Blessed is the Lord forever."
"*Baruch Adonay mi-Tsi'on* (135:21) - Blessed is the Lord of Zion."
"*Baruch Adonay Elohim* (72:18-19) - Blessed is the Lord God."

The proper name for Psalms of Praise of this sort is doxology. It's surely no coincidence, given that these are Hymns of Praise to Yah, the mother goddess, that the word doxology is most at home in Christian hymns of praise to Mother Mary (properly Maria in the Latin, *Mor-Yah* in the Hebrew).

✡

Va-yevarech

The Psalms are attributed to David, who purchased the land on which the Temple would be built, raised the money for its construction, arranged the provision of architects and masons from the non-Hebrew King Hiram of Tyre, did everything except actually build the Temple. This task was forbidden him on the grounds that he'd been a soldier all his life and had too much blood on his hands, and specifically because he'd sent Ur-Yah, the husband of Bat Sheva, to die at the front line so that he could marry the widow. Ironically it was Solomon, his son by Bat Sheva, who succeeded him and completed the task, only to neighbour it with a dozen pagan temples, and to fill it with a thousand foreign gods, so that the Temple was Judaically defiled from the outset.

In 1 Chronicles 29:10-13 we read of David's fund-raising drive on behalf of the Temple, which brought in willing donations from all across Israel (and no doubt, because Jewish fund-raising works this way, a thousand pledges that never came to pecuniary fruition) - huge quantities of gold and silver, brass and iron, even precious stones. The four verses, which are recited standing, are David's hymn of thanks to the congregation of Israel - the last act and also the last hymn of his kingship, according to the Book of Chronicles. Perhaps the world's various UJA Federations and WIZO drives should adopt this prayer alongside *Hatikvah* for their closing celebrations.

It's customary to set a sum of money aside for charity at this moment, though this can only be done in the form of a pledge or promise, since it's very much not the custom to pass the *tsedakah* box around in synagogue (Deuteronomy 23:21-23 requires the prompt fulfilling of such a pledge). From the tale of Jacob's flight from Esau, and his dream of the ladder at Bethel, Jews understand that they are to give one-tenth of all they earn to charity; which is to say to God by means of charity.

In Judaism, nothing is ever quite so simple as it might at first appear. Even *tsedakah*, the act of giving to charity, turns out to be multi-layered. Maimonides is yet again the source, in his *Mishneh Torah*.

The eighth, the lowest level of charity, is when one gives, but grudgingly.

The seventh is when one gives less than one really ought, but willingly.

The sixth is when one gives directly to the needy, as a consequence of being asked.

The fifth is when one gives directly to the needy, without even being asked.

These four levels of charity involve personal contact. But even greater is charity that involves degrees of anonymity.

At the fourth highest level, the person receiving charity knows where it comes from, but the giver doesn't know who it has gone to.

The third highest level is the reverse of this, the giver making a gift to a named recipient, but the recipient ignorant of its source.

The second highest level combines these, the giver gives but doesn't know to whom, the receiver receives but likewise anonymously. Coins in a box, contributions to general appeals, communal trust funds, all fall in this category.

But the highest form of charity is when one gives the means to support a person before they ever fall into need. I find this idea staggering in its humanity. To offer a gift to someone in a manner that doesn't offend their dignity. To extend them a loan, at minimal or zero interest. To help them find employment. To establish them in business so they can make their own way in the world. To enable a scholar to continue his researches. And there are consolidating laws to back this. Exodus 22:24 tells us that "if you lend money to the poor, you shall not be as a usurer" which the Rabbis understand to relate both to the charging of interest and to the pressing for the return of the loan from one who can't repay it. Rabbi Yishmael, applying the principle "*mi-binyan av mi-katuv echad, u-mi-binyan av mi-shney chetuvim*", would note that Leviticus 19:13 endorses and even extends all this. Its statement is concise and unequivocal: "*Lo ta'asok et-reyacha* - you shall not oppress your neighbour."

But there's another aspect to this as well. It's incumbent on a man or woman to do all in their power to avoid needing charity. The sages state that a scholar should undertake manual labour, however menial, rather than depend on charity. There is a great tradition of alms in Judaism, but not of begging.

David's collection for the First Temple is mirrored in the work of Ezra and Nehemiah, who were responsible for the reconstruction of Jerusalem and the building of the Second Temple, completed around 436 BCE. Ezra was a priest and a teacher of law - one of the very earliest Cohen-Rabbis - and Nehemiah was the personal cup-bearer to the king, probably the Medean Artaxerxes, of Persia. Each obtained permission to return to Israel around 450 BCE, some eighty years after the first exiles began to come back from the Babylonian captivity, and found much work still to be done in rebuilding the realm. Ezra completed the Second Temple, Nehemiah the walls of Jerusalem; after which the latter left the former in charge and returned to Persia. Ezra was responsible for several important reforms that truthfully mark the founding of Judaism, of which the most significant, still very much in operation today, was the public reading of the whole Law, in annual cycle, on three days in the week, the Sabbath and the two market days, Monday and Thursday. In his time it was read in the market-place itself; today it's read in synagogue.

Placing the text from Nehemiah (9:6-11) next to the David is therefore entirely logical. Like David, Nehemiah is blessing the Almighty. Like David's, Nehemiah's blessing was a public act, before the whole assembly of Israel. Like David's, Nehemiah's inspiration was an act of sacrifice by the people, who had accepted his injunction to give up their foreign wives and gods and to return to Mosaic practices, including the financially costly *shabbat* prohibition on trade, and the jubilee year of rest for farmland and liberation for household servants.

Nehemiah calls the people to return by reminding them of their history, and of the part their God has played in it. From Abraham's flight out of Ur came the covenant of the Land Eternal. From the sufferings in Egypt came the miracles and the Laws of Sinai. In Nehemiah's book the passage continues, but here, in the prayer, we stop, for we've heard enough. We don't need to be reminded, because we're already engaged in prayer. More important, with the mentioning of the miracle of the Red Sea, to sing the song that Moses sang, when the waters had poured back over the Egyptians, and the Israelites knew that they were safe.

✡

Va-yosha

The text is from Exodus 14:30, though the song itself only begins two verses later, at the start of chapter 15, and continues to verse 18, at which point the liturgy adds a double repetition of the last phrase, before resuming and completing with verse 19.

First, two verses to set the context. "On that day the Lord saved Israel from the hand of Egypt, and Israel saw the Egyptians dead on the seashore. Israel saw the great work that the Lord inflicted upon Egypt and the people feared the Lord, and they had faith in the Lord and in Moses His servant."

This is one of the seminal moments in Hebrew history. The God of the Jewish people is unlike other gods - so we've always claimed, and it's through tales such as this that we endeavour to demonstrate the validity of our claim. Where every other god of ancient times sanctioned and even encouraged human sacrifice, the Hebrew God rejected it - so we know from the *Akeda*. And we have faith in Him because we trust the justice and compassion of this humanity, because it conforms to our own intrinsic humanism (the notion that God is humane is in fact logically absurd, since God made humanity in His image, and not the other way around; the point is that we deify our own ideals of humanity by imputing them to God). But God's humanity in this story is complex and contradictory. If it's His humanity that enables him to hear our cry in Egypt and deliver us from slavery, what of His inhumanity in bringing the ten plagues upon the Egyptians? And then the tale of the miracle at the Red Sea appears to challenge that humanity again, and with it the conclusions of the *Akeda*.

Where every other ancient god was capable of magic, ours could go much further - and perform the utterly miraculous. This is a most unstable rock on which to build a faith, because the miracle here is also murderous. At the Red Sea both our salvation and our enemy's devastation. Yet the text is unequivocal: we witness God performing such a devastating miracle, and this causes us to fear God; because we fear Him, we believe in Him; because we believe in Him, we place our faith and trust in Him - and in His humanity. It's the exact opposite of our humanism that's being called into play, and the clash of the two is almost impossible for the intellectual mind to synthesise. Nor is this something which the Rabbis failed to recognise. One mediaeval Rabbi – I'm following this in Hertz's commentary, but he quotes the observation without indicating the source - explained the reason why we pour away a single drop of wine for each of the ten plagues during the recitation of that part of the *Haggadah* at Passover. It's precisely because our joy at God's miracle is tempered by the terrible suffering of the Egyptians. First the death of the first-born; then the annihilation of their armies at the Red Sea. Our joy stems from the miracle, which has liberated us. Our remorse stems from the act of inhumanity, which has fettered our enemy in grief. There is no resolving this paradox. Yet it's not insignificant that it's the humanism which tempers the act of inhumanity, and not the other way around. It's God's humanity which takes precedence over his inhumanity, and which - this is a desperately dangerous idea, one which Dostoievski manifested in his Grand Inquisitor - even permits and tolerates His inhumanity if it serves a greater good: the paradox of the Jewish partisans in the Second World War, who acted ruthlessly against the Nazis, having no other weapons available to defeat them than the ones that the enemy itself was wielding: guns, knives and bombs: killing to save lives. But in terms of faith, the *Akeda* remains more significant than the miracle of the Red Sea. The phenomenological trumps the miraculous.

✡

Shirah - the Song of Moses at the Red Sea

I will sing unto the Lord, for He is highly exalted
The horse and his rider has He thrown into the sea
The Lord is my strength and song and He is become my salvation
This is my God and I will glorify Him; My father's God and I will exalt Him

The Lord is a man of war, the Lord is His name
Pharaoh's armies and chariots He has thrown into the sea
And his appointed captains are sunk in the Red Sea
The deeps cover them - they went down into the depths like a stone

Your right hand O Lord is glorious in power
Your right hand O Lord dashes the enemy in pieces
In the greatness of Your excellence You overthrow whoever rises against You
You send forth Your wrath and it consumes them like stubble

With the blast of Your nostrils the waters were piled up
The floods stood upright as a heap
The deeps were congealed in the heart of the sea

The enemy said: I will pursue, I will overtake, I will divide the spoil
My lust shall be satisfied upon them
I will draw my sword, my hand shall destroy them

Then You blew Your wind and the sea covered them
They sank like lead into the mighty waters

Who is like You, O Lord, among the mighty?
Who is like You, glorious in holiness,
fearful in praises, performer of miracles?
You stretch out Your right hand and the earth swallows them

In love You have led the people You redeemed
You guided them in strength to Your holy habitation

The nations have heard, and now they tremble
Pangs have taken hold of the people of Philistia
The chiefs of Edom are terrified
The mighty men of Moab have been seized with trembling
All the inhabitants of Canaan have melted away

You bring them in and plant them in the mount of their inheritance
The place, O Lord, which You have made for Your dwelling
The sanctuary, O Lord, which Your hands have established

The Lord shall reign for ever and ever

Moses' song ends at verse 18 with "*Adonay yimloch le-olam va-ed*" - a phrase we've already encountered in the sequence of verses accompanying the Thanksgiving. But this isn't the end of the passage, neither in the *Torah* nor in the prayer service. What is added is first a repetition of the phrase "*Adonay yimloch le-olam va-ed*", to strengthen and endorse it, and then its Aramaic *targum* or translation ("*Adonay malchutey ka'em, le-olam u-le-olmey olmayah*") which alludes dramatically to the *Kaddish*. I presume we can place this addition quite easily in time, and assert that it reflects a diminution in the general understanding of Hebrew at that period. Today, if a Reform synagogue were to do the equivalent - to *targum* the phrase into English, say, or French - it wouldn't receive the same approval.

Verse 19 offers a brief prose account of the destruction of Pharaoh's army as the separated waters rushed back. Verses 20 and 21 find Aaron and Moses' sister Miriam leading a group of prophetesses, with tambourine and drums, in a celebratory dance; we can presume from the reiteration of the first two verses of the *Shirah* that the same song was sung by them again and again, in the manner of a round, to accompany the revelries. But in the prayer service verses 20 and 21 are omitted - perhaps I should say replaced - in favour of two verses from the Prophets. Oh why, oh why should this be?

The official answer is that the phrase in verse 18, which speaks of the Divine Kingship, is a notion which requires still further endorsement, even beyond the repetition and translation which the prayer text gives it. So a phrase to the same intent is now appended, from Psalm 22:29: "For the sovereignty is the Lord's and He rules over nations". And then another - as though in special pleading, by means of corroborating witnesses - from the Prophet Obadiah (1:21): "The saviours will ascend Mount Zion to judge Esau's mountain, and the kingdom will be the Lord's". This places the kingship not simply with God, but specifically on Mount Zion, where it will dominate "Esau's mountain" - a reference to the dual shrines of Ebal and Gerizim, which provided a capital and a Temple for the Samaritans. Obadiah - whose name is really *Oved-Yah*, "worshipper of the goddess of the full moon" - Obadiah is making politics here, not religion, asserting the supremacy of the Jerusalemite theocracy.

And then still a third phrase, this time from Zechariah (14:9) - another whose name reflects the mother of the gods - giving all kingdoms universally to God, at the coming of the Messiah, though this is only implied and not overtly stated. "Then the Lord will be king over all the world; on that day God will be One and His Name will be One", Zechariah tells us - worryingly suggesting that monotheism is the end and goal of polytheism, but that the end hasn't yet been obtained. (And in case anyone fails to recognise Zechariah's literary allusion, the liturgy parenthesises the opening line of the *Shema*, in Deuteronomy 6:4.)

The Rabbis deal with the problem inferred by Zechariah with their customary tenacity. God, they say, is indeed One, now, and for all time, but the world is fragmented, and so we can't perceive the whole of His Unity. When the Messiah comes, we too will be One, and so we will see His Oneness. As to His name, we know only the names He lets us know; but in the time of the Messiah we will also know His true name. Others say, that we know the Name, but not how to pronounce it properly; when the Messiah comes, he will bring the correct pronunciation (*Pesachim* 50a).

Symmetry again. The phrase speaks of the Unity of God, and it reverberates with phrases from both *Torah* and *Ketuvim*, the Law and the Literature, itself being of the *Neviyim*, the Prophets. So the unity of the *Tanach*, the Jewish Bible, is reflected also. (This too I'm quoting from the Rabbis, for the sake of perfect symmetry.)

After the phrase from Zechariah there follows, as noted above, a bracketed reference to Deuteronomy 6:4 ("And in your *Torah* it is written: Hear O Israel, the Lord Our God, the Lord is One"). This was regarded by the Vilna *Ga'on* as an "incorrect scribal intrusion"; hence its appearance now in brackets. Elijah ben Solomon Zalman, to give the *Ga'on* his name back, didn't think it should be included at all, since it should have been obvious that this was the intended allusion, and because it forced a premature recital, and of the opening verse alone, of what is about to be recited in full as the most holy and solemn moment of the entire service thus far. Zalman would certainly not have approved of brackets either - for how can the central creed of Judaism possibly be inscribed as a mere parenthesis, a *scholium*? So the words are not recited, but read in silence.

The *Shirah* is transcribed in most prayer books, complete with the musical notation that's used for *leyning* - the method of chanting used for the Five Books of Moses when they're read in synagogue. In fact there's a special melody for the Song which the cantillation doesn't reflect. And anyway, when the Song appears in the liturgy rather than as a *Torah* reading, it's neither sung nor *leyned*, but recited silently.

In Temple times the Song served as an accompaniment to the *Tamid* offering, but only on *shabbat*. Later it was recited daily throughout Israel, but the communities in Babylon and Alexandria didn't adopt the custom and it died out after the Roman destruction. Instead they preferred the daily singing of *Ha-azinu* (Deuteronomy 32), as indeed did that other scourge of persecuted Jews, Portia of Belmont.

There are still other unresolved enigmas surrounding the *Shirah*. There is, in particular, the anachronistic reference to the inhabitants of Philistia; and not for the first time in the *Torah* (Abraham and Sarah lived briefly in their midst, and Isaac squabbled with them over a well in Genesis 26). Yet the Peoples of the Sea whom the *Tanach* calls *Plishtim* didn't actually begin their colonisation of the Danite coast until the best part of a century after the Israelites had conquered Canaan. There is also the geographical inaccuracy - for the Song at the Red Sea should properly be called the Song at the Reed Sea, meaning the marshy regions of the Nile Delta near where Alexandria now stands, several days' hard camel-riding north and west of the Israeli Riviera on the Red Sea.

✡

Yishtabach

Bookends again. As *Baruch She Amar* opened this section, so *Yishtabach* now closes it - prologue and epilogue. Some communities chant the whole prayer, others only the last verses from "*berachot ve-hoda'ot*". When the service is led by a mourner - and it's a great honour to do so - and when two mourners both wish to lead the service, the second takes over from the first at *Yishtabach*.

Yishtabach is less a prayer than a breathing exercise. The fifteen expressions of praise should be recited without drawing breath, or at the very least "without undue pause".

Fifteen, even without the absurd mysticism of *Kabbalistic gematria*, is a most significant number. Letters in Hebrew also have numerical values, which is to say the same symbols are used for both letters and numbers. The number 15 in Hebrew ought to be written *Yud-Hey*, numerically 10+5, but is actually written *Tet-Vav* (טו), numerically 9+6, because *Yud-Hey* (יה) is also the spelling of *Yah*, the mother goddess, and cannot therefore be written. In a lunar month, by no coincidence, the 15th is the day of the full moon. Many of the major festivals fall on it: in year order *Sukkot* (Tabernacles), *Tu be'Shvat*, *Shushan Purim*, *Pesach* (Passover), and the Festival of *Av.* Fifteen is an unavoidable number in Jewish law and lore. David wrote 15 *Shirey Ma'alot,* the Songs of Ascent for pilgrimage to Mor-Yah and the Temple (Psalms 120-134). Fifteen steps led up to the Sanctuary. Fifteen Prophets constitute the Book of *Neviyim.* To the male part of God, the number 7 is the sacred number. To *Yah,* the female principle now sadly reduced to a mere *Shechinah* or Holy Ghost, the sacred number was 15.

The Fifteen Expressions of Praise are:

shir u-shevacha	hymns and celebrations
hallel ve-zimrah	praise and song
oz u-memshalah	power and dominion
netsach gedulah u-gevurah	eternity, magnitude and strength
tehila ve-tipheret	praise and splendour
kedushah u-malchut	holiness and sovereignty
berachot ve-hoda'ot	blessings and thanksgivings

Translation is difficult, both because Hebrew has a larger vocabulary for the distinctions than does English, and also because language changes over time and we are dealing with forms of language used over a three thousand year period.

Shevacha, for example, is a term used three times in the Book of Daniel (2:23, 4:31, 34). Its root, "*shavach*", suggests a purpose of calming or stilling, implying that this is propitiatory praise - praise of God to still His anger. But this defines the purpose, not the nature of praise. In Ecclesiastes (8:15) it appears as a recommendation of levity, "I commended mirth, because a man has nothing better under the sun than to eat, drink and be merry", and this concept of praise as an outpouring of joy - a concept dear to the heart of Israel ben Eliezer, the *Ba'al Shem Tov,* the founder of the modern *Hasidic* movement - is echoed in Psalm 63:4, "Because Your lovingkindness is greater than my life, so shall I praise You", and even more so in the tiny, two-verse Psalm 117, one of the Hallel Psalms intended as joyous celebration that were sung to accompany King David's bringing of the Ark to Jerusalem. "*Hallelu et-Adonay kol goyim, shabechuhu kol ha-umim* - praise the Lord all you nations, praise Him, all you people." The same is true of Psalm 147:12, "Praise the Lord, O Jerusalem, praise your God, O Zion."

These are the only uses of the word in the entire *Tanach,* but it's this form of praise which is regarded as the central duty of every Jew in the *Aleynu* prayer, which begins by stating precisely this: "*Aleynu le-shabeyach la'adon ha-kol* - it is our duty to praise the Lord of all," a prayer which the Rabbis claim was written by Joshua himself after he led the children of Israel across the Jordan. *Shevacha* then is a form of praise in which not the flattery of God but the sight of his chosen people dancing and enjoying themselves in an appropriately religious manner serves to still any anger against us residual in that most manically depressive of creatures, the Almighty. For this reason I have translated *shevacha* as celebration.

Can we draw from this a hidden inference of Dionysic-like mysteries amongst the early Hebrews? I think we probably can. We've just seen Miriam the prophetess leading her priestesses in ecstatic dance to the accompaniment of song and drum, and Michal was furious with David for taking part in such extravagances while bringing the Ark up to Jerusalem. Similar practices are described elsewhere. King Saul's anointing by Samuel, for example, at the shrine of Bethel (1 Samuel 10: 3-6), where Samuel tells Saul that he'll be met by three men "going up to God", carrying three loaves of bread and a bottle of wine - the normal eucharist of the *Kiddush*, though I'm intrigued as to why these three loaves have never found their way into any of our rites or ceremonies; custom and tradition have restricted the number to two.. "When you come to the city," Samuel tells him, "you will meet a company of Prophets coming down from the high place with a psaltery, a tabret, a pipe and a harp. And the spirit of the Lord will come upon them, and you shall prophesy with them, and shall be turned into another man." There's almost a hint that the verb "to prophesy" is synonymous, not with the predicting of the future nor the delivering of oracles, but with the very act of singing and dancing in religious ecstasy.

Is it then, in the words of *Aleynu*, our duty to praise the Lord in this manner to this day? Those who have attended gospel churches, or a *Hasidic* wedding, or who have participated in the drunken revels in the synagogue on *Simchat Torah*, will understand that it is. Those who have ever participated in a rave or disco will know the nature of the psychological state induced by celebrations of this kind.

Hallel also means praise, and "*tehilla*", which is used two verses further on, is simply a participle to the same noun. The root suggests a great deal more foolishness, even a hint of madness, than does *shevacha*, but the principle is identical - the notion of praising God through celebratory activities such as music and dance. The same exactly is true again of "*zimrah*", which is singing, and "*shir*", which is poetry written to be sung. To praise God isn't a matter of words alone, but of physical celebration. Just as in the sacrifices God wants the gravy, not the meat, so here He wants the palpable sincerity of our joy, and not the mere ritual muttering of words. But put the words and the actions together with the same level of sincerity, of intensity, of *kavanah* - to dance even while you're praying - now there's a form of praise indeed. The Reform and Conservative movements in America have long appreciated this, and developed a significant school of song-writers and *bimah*-performers, including Friday nights and *shabbat* mornings; the orthodox, sadly, refuse this, on the grounds that the practice belonged to the Temple, which is no more. Yet Judaism insists that mourning may not continue beyond eleven months. It seems to me that here is one place where the orthodox could easily accept the challenge of the end of substitution, by ending the inappropriately extended period of mourning, or simply by doing what they pray for every day, the restoration of the Temple.

The *Besht* or *Ba'al Shem Tov*, the Master of the Good Name, one Israel ben Eliezer, was born in Okop, a remote village in the region of Podolia in the Carpathian mountains, somewhere around 1700, and for the first thirty years of his life was as anonymous as Jesus or Buddha or Mohammed before their self-revelations. In the mid-1730s he became famous as a healer, and for the radical ideas about Jewish worship which his disciples promulgated in his name, in particular the concept of "*devekut*" or adhesion, which is really an intensification of the Maimonidean notion of *kavanah.* Elie Wiesel sums up the Beshtian philosophy - no, philosophy's far too grand a word; the *Besht* would have rejected it - the Beshtian attitude: "God himself needs love. Whoever loves God will be loved in turn, loved by man and loved by God. It is in Man that God must be loved, because the love of God goes through the love of Man. Whoever loves God exclusively, namely, excluding Man, reduces his love and his God to the level of abstraction. *Beshtian Hasidism* denies all abstraction." ("Souls on Fire", p35)

We are returned to that discussion of humanism versus the miraculous which absorbed us in the Song of Moses.

"To realise himself, the *Baal Shem*'s *Hasidism* teaches us, Man must first of all remain faithful to his most intimate, truest self; he cannot help others if he negates himself. Any man who loves God whilst hating or despising His creation, will in the end hate God." (*ibid*)

Not God the king of some supernatural realm, but God the Creator of the Natural Universe.

For the *Baal Shem Tov*, that line of Ecclesiastes was the most important. He advocated merriment, he made a holy ritual out of eating, he invited his followers to dance even while they were praying - sometimes literally. God the Father is like any other parent in the world; when His children are unhappy, He will be unhappy, but when He sees them glorifying life by living it to the full and smiling as they do so - then God will *shlep* such *nachas* as will have him hurrying the Messiah to get dressed and go do his duty as the leader of the dance.

"*Tipheret*" – to return to the list of the Fifteen Expressions of Praise - is normally translated as "splendour", but this is minimalistic. Proverbs 28:12 tells us that "*ba-alots tsaddikim rabah tipheret* - when the righteous exult there is great splendour", which at least hints at its wider meaning. In *Kabbalistic* terms *Tipheret* is Beauty, and it provides the central, pivotal branch of the Tree of Life, the only principle of the Universe that is directly connected to every other principle. It's the source of Keats' sadly delusory apophthegm that "Beauty is Truth, Truth Beauty - this is all ye know on earth, and all you need to know." The secret name of God is often referred to as the "*Shem Tipheret*", and Psalm 78:61 uses it as a synonym for the Ark of the Covenant itself. To praise God in the character of *Tipheret* is to make a declaration of commitment to the divine that is tantamount to a covenant renewal.

If the six specific forms of praise are difficult to convey in English, so too are the seven descriptions of might which we are called upon to praise in *Yishtabach.*

"*Oz*" is might in the sense of power, and implies something hard, even cruel - the tyrannical side of power, the destroying God of Moses' Song at the Red Sea. *Oz* is used to describe the fortifications of a city, and gives its name to *Aza*, which we know in English as Gaza. *Oz* is also, by a curiosity of language, a billy-goat, presumably because of the vehement character of that beast; and from it comes the *Azazel*, the sacrificial scapegoat whom the inhabitants of Jerusalem drove over a cliff-edge every *Yom Kippur*, bearing on its back their sins.

"*Memshalah*" is dominion, the role of government, and the word has been revived in modern Israel to describe precisely that - the Cabinet and the Prime Minister who run the country.

"*Netsach*" moves God onto the metaphysical plane, denoting His eternity.

"*Gedulah*" has more to do with size, indeed with magnitude. God is great because the borders of His kingdom extend so far - universally indeed.

"*Gevurah*" is strength in the military sense, but the word has become a part of mystical vocabulary, taking a branch of the *Kabbalistic* Tree of Life alongside *Netsach*, *Tipheret* and *Malchut.*

"*Kedushah*" is holiness, which as I have pointed out before really means separateness. God is great because He inhabits a plane apart, a superior plane, an utopia to which we can at most aspire.

"*Malchut*" is sovereignty, distinguishable from *Memshalah* only by the nature of government. A king is sovereign over all of his domains, but in the case of God the day-to-day dominion was vested in Man as one of the central acts of the Creation (Genesis 1:26). Monarchy versus democracy.

The final couplet draws us, the worshippers, back in. The *berachot* and *hoda'ot*, the blessings and thanksgivings, are our contribution to the majesty of God. To pray is to bring God into existence, regardless of the rational arguments for and against. To bless or to express gratitude is to state and to acknowledge a hierarchical position. So we bless God, and thank him, but in *Yishtabach* we do it standing.

The various epithets are strung together in pairs, with one triplet. The definitions don't explain the pairings, nor is the order self-evident, since the forms of praise are interwoven with the forms of strength, and the forms of strength are also being praised. It isn't known who wrote the prayer, nor when, though the fact that it's discussed in the *Talmud* confirms its antiquity. All we can do is speculate about the intentions of the author, who may have made his order and his pairings for aesthetic reasons, for rhythmic reasons, for philosophical reasons, or simply on a whim. There's no logic to the structure, unless at the spiritual level. I imagine a modern editor wanting to rearrange the order, so the six praises and the seven forms of might could stand integrally, rather than being interwoven. I suspect, though, that the interweaving was intentional.

I find many of the daily prayers intellectually problematic, but with *Yishtabach* I have no such difficulty. "Blessed are you O Lord our God, King exalted through praises, God of thanksgivings, Master of wonders, Who chooses musical songs of praise" - (who could possibly have difficulty with such an attribute as that?) - "King, God, Life-Giver of the World." Yes, this I recognise. The Cosmic Pulse. The universal Omnideity. This is a God who will listen with me to Mahler's 2nd Symphony, conscious that it's intended to "assail the heavens", but who will open the windows to hear it better, and stand to give it rapturous applause, and wait in earnest longing for the tubular bells that sound the last notes of the last crescendo, and cry "Bravo" and pray to Himself for an encore.

And then the half-*Kaddish*, serving as the word "*selah*" did within the Psalms: to mark a full-stop.

✡

Chapter Nine: *Shema*

Bookends. Always bookends. Nothing can be "of itself" in Judaism, but must be hedged around, as the Ark was in the Tent, as the Law is behind its metaphoric Fence, for safety, for protection, for the perennial insecurity of the Jews. So with every major act of worship. So with the *Shema*. Hedged around with introductory and conclusory prayers. A palisade of prayers to safeguard a credo.

Barechu

"*Barechu et-Adonay ha-mevorach* - Bless the Lord the blessed one", sung to a slow *mangina* by the *chazan*, bending the knees at *barechu*, straightening them again at *ha-mevorach*. In theory it should be sung slowly enough to allow the congregation time to recite the compilation-meditation "*Yitbarach*".

"Blessed, praised, glorified and upraised is the Name of the King who rules over kings, the Holy One, Blessed be He" - which both is and is not from the *Kaddish*.

"For He is the first and the last, and besides Him there is no God." (Isaiah 44:6)

"Extol Him who rides the highest heavens - with his name, *Yah* - and exult before Him." (Psalm 68:5) [I give the customary, masculine translation, and shall not rehearse again the argument for *Yah* as feminine]

"His name is exalted beyond every blessing and praise." (Nehemiah 9:5)

"Blessed is the name of His glorious kingdom for all eternity. Blessed be the name of the Lord from this time and forever." (Psalm 113:2)

But I've never heard any congregation recite this. Invariably they wait in unmeditative silence for the formal congregational response: "*Baruch Adonay ha-mevorach le-olam va'ed* - Blessed is the Lord, the blessed one, for ever and ever" - bowing at *baruch*, straightening up at *ha-mevorach*.

The *Barechu* is a summons to prayer, and so it's excluded in the absence of a *minyan*. A summons, but not just to any prayer - to the *Shema*, the sacred testament of faith. All sacred acts require a summoning, according to the *Zohar*, the principal encyclopaedia of Jewish mysticism. The *chazan*, the prayer-leader, he too must be thus summoned. And so, after the congregation has responded, or simultaneously, the *chazan* too recites the response. The democracy of Jewish prayer.

✡

Berachot Kriyat Shema

Even the bookends require bookends, to protect and to sustain them. The *Barechu* summons the congregation to prayer with a blessing, but now the *Shema* itself must be blessed, two-fold before it's uttered, a third time afterwards. The blessings are precise and specific in a way few other blessings imitate. But then, this is no ordinary prayer – indeed, it isn't really a prayer at all, but a declaration of faith. The *Shema* is the central section of *Torah*, in which both the Oneness of God and the rites of prayer itself are co-defined. So sacred is it, one shouldn't even interrupt it by saying *amen*.

And yet, for all its sanctity, the *Shema*, and its blessings, are recited neither standing nor prostrate, but sitting down (though many contemporary communities have now adopted the practice of standing). *Kavanah*, Maimonides argued, isn't relevant to the position of the body but rather to the attitude of the heart, the soul, the will.

✡

Baruch

"*Baruch atah Adonay eloheynu melech ha-olam yotser or u-vorey choshech, oseh shalom u-vorey et ha-kol.*"

The first blessing. Touch the arm-*tefillin*, the *shel yad*, at "*yotser or*", and the head-*tefillin*, the *shel rosh*, at "*u-vorey choshech*". The text takes its cue from Isaiah 45:7, "Blessed are you, Lord our God, King of the Universe, who brings forth light and creates darkness, who makes peace and creates everything."

This is where Judaism and Christianity part company, Jewish monotheism leading to a unistic view of the world, the Christian trinitism allowing a dualistic view. God brings forth light. From where? From the darkness which He also created, and into which it will be refunded, flux and reflux, cycle upon cycle, in the same way as life and death, good and evil. But God is both the light and the darkness. This is why he is "*melech ha-olam* - king of the Universe". Because He contains every aspect, but also because *olam* is really a temporal, not a spatial phenomenon. King of Eternity would be a better translation.

✡

Ha-Me'ir

"He-ma'ir la-arets ve-la-darim aleyha be-rachamim, u-ve-tuvo mechadesh be-chol yom tamid ma'aseh vereyshit. Mah rabu ma'aseycha, Adonay…"

The second, much longer blessing, beginning "He who illuminates the earth and those who dwell on it with compassion, and in His goodness renews daily, perpetually, the work of Creation…"

No intellectual God this. This is illumination, not enlightenment. His attributes are of a subjective kind - mercy, compassion. They deal with our human frailties, rather than building up our strengths. The rational, the empirical, the objective, we can handle these ourselves; except that we flounder in the mess we make of them, and require God precisely in the floundering, a rock to cling to like a shipwrecked sailor.

"Kulam be-chachma asita mala ha-arets kinyanecha. Ha-melech ha-meromam levado me'az ha-meshubach ve-ha-mepho'ar ve-ha-mitnaseh miymot olam. Elohey olam, be-rachamecha ha-rabim rachem aleynu, adon uzeynu, tsur misgabeynu, magen yisheynu, misgav ba-adeynu…"

"You make them all with wisdom, the world is full of Your possessions. The King who was exalted in solitude before creation, who is praised, glorified, and upraised since days of old. Eternal God with Your abundant compassion, be compassionate to us - O master of power, our rocklike stronghold, O shield of our salvation, be a stronghold for us…"

The next section of the blessing contains in its kernel a short acrostic poem, alphabetical as most Jewish liturgical acrostics are. It doesn't transliterate easily - "*El baruch gedol de'al, heychin u-pha'al, zaharey chamah, tov yatsar kavod lishmo, me'orot natan sevivot uzo, pinot tseva'av kedoshim romemey shaday, tamid*…and then continues, non-acrostical, until the end, "*mesaprim kevod el u-kedushato. Titbarach Adonay eloheynu al shevach ma'aseh yadeycha, ve-al me'orey or she-asita, yepha'arucha, selah.*"

Nor does it translate easily, and not only because the sentence runs on. An acrostic is an artificial contrivance, a work, indeed, of the rational, empirical, objective mind functioning schematically, an attempt to impose a human order on the divine disorder - and one which, inevitably, flounders. "Blessed God, great in knowledge, prepared and enacted in the rays of the sun, goodness fashioned in the glory of His name, He put lights around His power; the chiefs of His heavenly army are the exaltation of Shaddai, they recount His glory constantly…with His honour and His sanctity. May You be blessed, Lord our God, beyond the praises of Your handiwork and beyond the bright luminaries that You have made - may they glorify You - *selah*."

Except that neither the counting nor the glory are contained in the acrostic. It's illogical, ungrammatical - objectively. But subjectively we know exactly what we mean.

And what we mean is, of course, the sun-god once again, absorbed into the Omnideity along with *Yah*, His consort. "He who illuminates the earth…prepared and enacted in the rays of the sun…He put lights around his power…the chiefs of His heavenly army…" Like it or not, the Jewish God has not transcended paganism, but merely conquered and subsumed it. The roots are visible.

Especially visible when you refer back to Isaiah 45:7, the passage on which the first benediction is based. The Isaiah text has, in fact, been conspicuously modified. What Isaiah actually said was: "I form the light and I create the darkness, I make peace and I create evil; I the Lord do all these things." This is even more strongly anti-dualistic than I've suggested - some modern commentators see it as a response to the Zoroastrian message then prevalent in Persia and the Middle East, which pitted Ahura Mazda as "I form the light…I make peace" against his arch-enemy and source of Lucifer, Ahriman, who "creates the darkness…and makes evil."

But later Judaism couldn't cope with a God who actually created evil. That He allowed it, by infiltration of the Adversary, when He happened to be looking the other way, even this was hard enough to swallow, but was, in the concept of "*histir panav*". Nevertheless His evil nature (yes, God too has a *yetser ha-ra* and a *yetser ha-tov*; He must do, if we do, for we are created in His image) - which isn't the same as the correlative destruction of Moses' Song at the Red Sea nor goes as far as *She'ol*-Hades – is clearly present in the original Isaiah fragment, but expurgated when the text is reconstituted in the liturgy.

✡

Titbarach

"*Titbarach tsureynu malkeynu ve-go'aleynu, borey kedoshim. Yishtabach shimcha la'ad malkeynu, yotser meshartim, va-asher meshartav kulam omdim be-rum olam, u-mashmi'im be-yirah yachad be-kol divrey elohim chayim u-melech olam. Kulam ahuvim, kulam berurim, kulam giborim, ve-kulam osim be-eymah u-ve-yirah retson konam. Ve-chulam potchim et peehem bi-kedushah u-ve-tahara, be-shirah u-ve-zimrah u-mevarchim u-meshabchim u-mepha'arim u-ma'aritsim u-makdishim u-mamlichim.*"

"May You be blessed, O our Rock, our King and our Redeemer, creator of holy ones; may Your name be praised forever our King, fashioner of the ministering angels; all of whose ministering angels stand at the summit of the Universe and proclaim - with awe, altogether, loudly - the words of the living God and King of the Universe. They are all beloved, they are all flawless, they are all mighty, they all do the will of their maker with dread and reverence. And they all open their mouths in holiness and purity, in song and hymn, and bless, praise, glorify, revere, sanctify and declare His kingship."

Titbarach isn't a human prayer, but the echoing in human mouths of the prayers of the angels. Having praised Him ourselves, we now allow the heavenly host to praise Him too, that very heavenly host of whom we've just now spoken. But it's a passage that confuses and disconcerts me. Are we to praise God on behalf of the angels? (Do we even believe in angels?) And why do the angels need our frail voices?

The four words "*Elohim chayim u-melech olam* - the living God, and King of the Universe" - are an allusion to Jeremiah 10:10. The closing phrase, recited by the *chazan* - "*ve-chulam potchim et peehem bi-kedushah u-ve-tahara, be-shirah u-ve-zimrah u-mevarchim u-meshabchim u-mepha'arim u-ma'aritsim u-makdishim u-mamlichim*", is a Hebrew paraphrase of the seven praises in the Aramaic *Kaddish.*

Et Shem

"*Et shem ha-el ha-melech ha-gadol ha-gibbur ve-ha-nora kadosh hu* - the name of God, the great, the mighty and awesome king, He is holy." First hints of the great standing prayer, the *Shemoneh Esreh*, with this virtual quotation from its opening phrases, and more to follow. It's recited by the congregation (it is in fact an elaboration upon Deuteronomy 10:17, augmented by a hint of Psalm 99:3), after which the *chazan* alone states the perfect unanimity-in-surrender of the angels, a phrase which puts me in mind of Islam, and which seems to turn back to the most ancient ideals of worship, in which the human ego was entirely foresworn in subordination and submission (this is what Islam means) to the divine, through prayer and through prostration. At those times, the king really was a King.

"*Ve-chulam mekablim aleyhem ol malchut shamayim zeh mi-zeh. Ve-notnim reshut zeh la-zeh, le-hakdish le-yotsram be-nachat ru'ach be-saphah verurah u-vi-ne'imah. Kedushah kulam ke-echad onim ve-omrim be-yirah…*"

"Then they [the angels] all accept upon themselves the yoke of heavenly sovereignty from one another, and grant permission to one another to sanctify the one who formed them, with tranquillity, with clear articulation, and with sweetness. All of them as one proclaim His holiness and say with awe…"

And then, on behalf of the angels we pronounce the *Kedushah*: "Holy, holy, holy, Lord of the Hosts of Heaven, the whole earth is filled with glory" - which again echoes the *Shemoneh Esreh*. The phrase is taken from Isaiah (6:3), and is recited aloud, usually with gentle gusto, by the congregation, after which the *chazan* repeats it, and adds one of the oddest, most abstruse of lines: "*Ve-ha-ophanim ve-chayot ha-kodesh be-ra'ash gadol mitnasim le-umat seraphim* - then the *Ophanim* and the *Chayot ha-kodesh* raise themselves towards the *Seraphim*, making a great noise; facing them they give praise, saying..."

Ophanim are, properly speaking, wheels; *chayot ha-kodesh* are holy beasts. More complex are *seraphim* - not to be confused with *teraphim*, the stone idols kept as household gods or placed at the entrances to vineyards and orchards. The root of *seraphim* suggests "burning" though it also means "sucking", "swallowing" and "absorbing", any one of which might be applied to Smaug or Gollum. The English word "serpent" almost certainly derives from the root - *saraph* - in the form in which it appears in Numbers 21:16, as a species of venomous serpent. But Isaiah (14:29 and 30:6) uses it for a flying dragon - from an earlier Sanskrit root, *sarpa* = serpent, *sarpin* = reptile.

None of this really helps however (except in sending us back to re-consider the nature of the serpent in the Garden of Eden, to compare him, say, with the dragon who guarded the Golden Fleece or the one whom Wagner renamed Fafner in the *Niebelungenlied*), though it hints. Isaiah 6 is more relevant.

"In the year that king Uzi-Yahu died I saw the Lord seated on His throne, high and lifted up, and His trail filled the Temple; *seraphim* stood above to minister to Him, each one had six wings; with two He covered His face, with two His feet, and with two He flew…then one of the *seraphim* flew towards me with a live coal in his hands…" (vv 1-6)

This is the Damascene moment, Isaiah's cataleptic fit or haoma-induced hallucinogenic trance, in which his unclean lips are purged by coals of fire - as, in the *Midrash*, were those of the infant Moses - and he becomes God's spokesman. Commentators insist that these *seraphim* are an order of angel - the Hebrew word for angel, *malach*, simply means a messenger - but there's nothing angelic, in the Christmas tree sense, about this creature; on the contrary, a six-winged opponent for King Arthur sounds far more plausible. And of course, in the Holy of Holies in the First Temple, there stood two winged *cherubim*, described by Ezekiel as living creatures, each having four faces, of a lion, an ox, an eagle, and a man; with the stature and hands of a man, the feet of a calf, and four wings, two extended upward, meeting above and sustaining the throne of God, while the other two stretched downward and covered the creatures themselves. No abstract divinity here, as in the empty Holy of Holies of the Second Temple!

But the text here speaks of *seraphim*, not *cherubim*, and requires a different reading. Moses' banner, *Nechushtan*, was a fiery serpent made of brass. To the Egyptians, from whom we can safely assume that Moses learned it, it was the Aesculapius, the symbol of healing and wisdom, which reappears in later Hebrew as *Chochma*, who built the mansion of seven pillars and seven houses which T.E. Lawrence cited as the title of his memoirs: "The Seven Pillars of Wisdom". That *Nechushtan* should be the name of a *seraph* is made still more likely when the calling of Ezekiel is compared. For "I looked, and behold a whirlwind came out of the north..." Ezekiel witnesses four extraordinary creatures - John of Patmos later mistook them for the four beasts of the apocalypse - "*chayot ha-kodesh*" in Isaiah's phrase, and much like the *seraphim*, right down to the fact that all four of them "sparkled like the colour of burnished brass - *notsetsim ke-eyn nechoshet kalal*." *Nechoshet* - the root word for *Nechushtan.*

What though of the *ophanim*? To remain in Egypt for a further moment, the wheel was depicted there in Pharonic times as a quartered circle or mandala, with the head of Horus in the northern quarter, and the heads of Isis, Osiris and Set in the other three. It was a sacred object, and used as a focus of concentration in worship, hence its other name, "the wheel of prayer". But in Persia it was known as "the wheel of fire" and it was depicted as a square cross with angled tips and called a swastika; the "*lahat ha-cherev*" or "flaming sword" of the Garden of Eden.

If we accept these two - the *seraph* and the *ophanim* - then the holy beasts are easy, for in Egyptian mythology all the gods were depicted as beasts, and all had taboo animals attached to them. As *Elohim* is the sky-god Ra in his Hebrew form - hence the residual sun references throughout this passage - we can deduce the *chayot ha-kodesh* as the bull Merwer and the bird Bennu. We can also begin to understand what the Heavenly Host must have consisted of. If *Elohim* is the Sun who dominates the sky, and His consort is the moon, why, what else can the Heavenly Host of angels be but stars? Isaiah 14:12 confirms this, calling the fallen angel "the morning star". Job 38:7 confirms it too, when God speaks out of the same whirlwind in which He will later address Ezekiel and recalls the Creation of the world: "when the morning stars sang together, and all the sons of God shouted for joy." This, as Borges observes, makes the angels two days and two nights older than the rest of us, for the stars were created on the fourth day.

Later Jewish mythology of necessity rejected all this. In place of a pantheon of gods with attendant symbolic animals, it redefined the entire terminology, leaving unexplained where it couldn't come up with satisfactory alternatives. Some gods or demi-gods - Abraham, Samson, David - simply became mortal men, or Heroes anyway - Jewish Titans. The *ophanim* became one of the ten orders of angels which even Maimonides (*Yesodei Ha Torah* 2:7) agreed we lack the vocabulary to define - but still better an unexplained angelology for the Heavenly Host than a set of planetary deities. He called them: *Chayot*, *Ophanim*, *Er-elim*, *Chashmalim*, *Seraphim*, *Malachim*, *Elohim*, *Beney Elohim*, *Keruvim* and *Ishim* - in my reading: Symbolic Beasts, Prayer-Wheels, Images of Brass, Winged Serpents, Messengers, Latter Gods, Contemporary Gods, Compound Creatures (the *cherub*, as we have seen, usually consists of man, ox, lion and eagle), and finally Mankind. These make up the *Tseva'ot* or *Sabbaoth* - the Host of Heaven.

All these creatures then, to return to the phrase in the prayer that triggered this digression, give noisy praise to God, saying - and again the congregation recites the words:

"*Baruch kevod Adonay mimkomo*...Blessed be the Name of the Lord from His place" - words taken from Ezekiel 3:12, an extraordinary coincidence in the light of my analysis, though Ezekiel doesn't pronounce these words himself, but hears them "in a great rushing" - a "*ra'ash gadol*", precisely the same words, for the same sound, as in the Isaiah - right at the point of his vision where the spirit takes him up and carries him away to Tel-Aviv, the spring on the river Kevar where the remnant of Israel has been taken captive. And as he hears that "great rushing" and those sacred words, so also does he hear "the wings of the living creatures (*chayot*) touching one another, and the noise of the wheels (*ophanim*) against them."

So the coincidences cannot be coincidences. So the circle of explanation is complete.

Where do the angels Michael and Gabriel and all the others come from, if angel means something other than a messenger of God? The fact that each angel has a name ending *-el*, and a prefix denoting a role or attribute, allows them to be understood as Canaanite, for *El* was the name of the principal deity whom *Yahweh Elohim* in His unity superseded. Michael in Hebrew is "*mi-cha-El* - who is like God", as Gabriel is "*gavri-El* - God is my strength".

But the concept of these *ubermenschnik* superbeings belongs to the Second Temple period, when Hellenisation was in full swing, and it's the figure of Hermes the Messenger of the Gods who comes to mind - the Romans called him Mercury - especially in the Christian Annunciation. Somewhere along the way the Rabbis tried to graft one strain - the Egyptian - on the other - the Hellenic, but unlike Aaron's Rod, it failed to blossom.

✡

Le-el baruch

Nothing like a good Rabbinical dispute to stir the blood. For centuries this one has continued, far less interesting perhaps than the angelology dispute above, but none the less rigorous for being that. The question in question is: is it "*le-el baruch…le-melech el chay*", or is it "*la-el…la-melech*" - a disagreement over the absence or presence of a (the) definite article? "To blessed God" or "to the blessed God"? It may not seem like much to build a mountain on, but in the annals of Rabbinical dispute, far lesser mole-hills have obliged, believe me.

"To [the] blessed God they shall offer sweet melodies, to the king, the living and enduring God, they shall sing hymns and proclaim praises. For He alone effects mighty deeds, makes new things, is master of wars, sows kindnesses, makes salvations flourish, creates cures, is too awesome for praise, is Lord of wonders. As it is said, Give thanks to Him who makes the great luminaries, for His kindness endures forever."

All of which hyperbolous catalogue of supernatural attributes we might take with a pinch of Dead Sea salt, had God himself not arrogantly confirmed each one of them in his discourse to Job.

We are still speaking - or now reciting silently - on behalf of the angels (no explanation is offered as to why angels can't pray their own prayers - my presumption is that we're not really perproing at all, but conjuring an image of the world to come in order to make our own obsecrations more steadfast). Like us, the angels offer sweet melodies - or no longer "like us". In ancient times prayer was always accompanied by music - cymbal, harp, lyre, psaltery - and notation in the Psalms makes it evident that many were written as libretto for well-known melodies. Why the Rabbis decided to abolish live acoustical accompaniment, let alone the choir and orchestra, is quite beyond me. I mean, I understand what the arguments are: that the Temple has gone, that we pray in perpetual mourning – but also in perpetual hope for its eventual reconstruction – and therefore may not make music. I simply don't understand why anyone would want to do such a thing, especially when the period of mourning is halachically restricted to eleven months, with a commandment to resume life with full *kavanah* thereafter. Reform synagogues, as I observed previously, have revived the art.

Like us, as I was saying, the angels offer sweet melodies, singing hymns and reciting Psalms. Oddly, the litany of their praise isn't like ours. No abstractions like mercy and compassion, but quotidian and utilitarian matters: His mastery of warfare, His apothecarial skills, His artisanship. Why can't we have songs like this? Blessed Art Thou O Lord Our God Who Strengthens Our Bowing Fingers And Teaches Us To Cut Marble, Who Is The Master Of Alfresco And Of Cubism, Who Can Comprehend The Mystery Of Calculus And Formulate The E Into MCsquared. Holy Holy Holy, Lord God Who Teaches Us To Compose Prayers Which Relate Directly To Our Lives, Enrich Our Culture And Our Spirits, And Guide Us More Contentedly Through This Life Now And Not In Some Imaginary Future. *Amen.*

Now there's a prayer for men and angels to conjoin in universal harmony.

Blessed Art Thou O Lord Our God, Who Teaches Us To Take Everything In Life Seriously, Especially Laughter.

Now there's a prayer for men who find my piety or my irreverence overwhelming.

For the final phrases, the *chazan* continues alone, "May You shine a new light on Zion, and may we all speedily merit its light. Blessed are You, O Lord, who fashions the luminaries." The luminaries, or the stars, or the angels.

The phrase that preceded it and which gave rise to the blessing is a quotation from Psalm 136:7. Sa'adiah Ga'on, one of the great men of Babylonian Jewry, objected to the blessing, because to speak of "new light" shining upon Zion, to hope that we "may all speedily merit its light" is Utopian. We shouldn't intrude upon the prayers of angels, by sneaking in a human prayer for Messianic redemption. It's a form of corruption, like paying a parliamentarian to ask questions in the House on your behalf, like sleeping with a Countess in order to gain an audience with the King. And why should we pray for "new light" when we don't yet use the "old one" properly?

✡

What "old light" does Sa'adiah mean? The next verse reveals it. Why, the light of *Torah*, obviously. We can't expect the Messiah to come, if we're not keeping all of God's commandments. The Messiah will come only when the conditions are right for the coming of the Messiah. For the conditions to be right we require the coming of the Messiah. Then the Messiah will come, only when he's already here. This paradox defines the role, and goal, of Man.

"With an abundant love have You loved us, Lord our God, with exceedingly great pity have You pitied us. Our father, our king, for the sake of our forefathers who trusted in You and to whom You taught the decrees of life, may You be equally gracious to us and teach us. Our father, the merciful father, who acts mercifully, have mercy upon us…"

The rare event of a prayer that I'm happy to pray, even while my intellect is still engaged.

"Instil in our hearts the capacity to understand and to elucidate, to listen, to learn, to teach, to safeguard, to perform and to fulfil all the words and teachings of Your *Torah* with love."

And then a phrase which loosely paraphrases David's prayer in Psalm 86:11, "Teach me Your way, O Lord; I will walk in Your truth; unite my heart to fear Your name."

"Enlighten our eyes in Your *Torah*, attach our hearts to Your commandments, and unify our hearts to love and fear Your name, and may we not feel inner shame for all eternity. Because we have trusted in Your great and awesome holy name, may we exult and rejoice in Your salvation. Bring us in peacefulness from the four corners of the earth and lead us with upright pride to our land. For You effect salvations, O God. You have chosen us from among every people and tongue…"

The preparation for the *Shema* is now almost complete. As a final act, in the closing phrases of the *Ahavah*, the four *tsitsit* are gathered between the fourth and fifth fingers of the left hand, where they will remain clutched throughout the recitation. The final phrase of *Ahavah* may now be recited by the *chazan*, the congregation sealing it shut with *amen*.

"And You have brought us close to Your great name forever in truth, to offer praiseful thanks to You, and to proclaim Your oneness with love.

Blessed are You, Lord, who chooses His people Israel with love."

In mediaeval *siddurim*, as already mentioned, the *amen* was treated acrostically, read as "*El Melech Ne'eman* - God the Faithful King", and on this occasion of the preface to the *Shema* the phrase was stated in full. Today a simple *amen* is preferred, but when an individual prays alone, or with less than a full *minyan*, "*el melech ne'eman*" is reinstituted. Either way it forms part of the preface, not part of the *Shema*.

"*El Melech Ne'eman*" affords another mediaeval mysticism. The sages taught, alas erroneously, that there are 248 organs in a human body. It would have construed a lovely symmetry, if it were true, because there also happen to be 248 positive commandments, and much could have been made of it (much, indeed, was made of it), just as the 365 negative commandments correspond to the number of days in the Christian calendar (but, alas again, not the Jewish calendar, which has only 360). The *Shema*, yet again alas, has only 245 words, so that much less can be made *gematrically* - unless three more words could be found to make up the difference. Which of course, with "*el melech ne'eman*", they can.

Perhaps I should also translate the three words. *El* is God - in the form of the Canaanite Bull-god of the sun, but let that pass. *Melech* is king - in the form of Moloch, the Phoenician…perhaps I should let that pass as well. *Ne'eman* means, uncontroversially, "faithful" or "trustworthy". Perhaps this is why Catholicism lost so many of its followers when the decision was made no longer to recite the Mass in Latin.

Shema

Different traditions, always different traditions. In some communities the opening line is recited aloud, the remainder silently; in some the whole of the first paragraph aloud, save only the second line, the line of the angels - and then the remainder silently; in others again, all three paragraphs are recited silently, even the word "*emet*", the first word of the ensuing prayer which is generally tacked on to the last phrase of the *Shema* in order to make the service fluid. Whichever tradition is followed, all agree that the eyes should be covered with the right hand, for at least the opening phrase, as a means of gathering intensity and focusing it upon the act of prayer. *Kavanah* – "intention". The Maimonidean *Aum*.

Finding dates for most prayers is difficult. Even if we can deduce when they were written, we can rarely be sure when they were first prayed. Scriptural passages ditto. The *Shema* is slightly easier, since all three paragraphs belong to the Five Books of Moses, which in some form at least were read by Moses prior to his departure to the summit of Mount Nebo, and that of his people across the Jordan into conquest and occupation. Was the *Torah* then as it is now? Orthodoxy demands that it was, but textual evidence, as well as historical and archaeological, suggests that huge portions of the *Torah* were written up to a millennium later, but accredited back, attributed to Moses in order to validate them retroactively. This is most probably true of Leviticus, whose ordinances for the priesthood and whose architectural map of the Sanctuary reflect the norms of Second Temple times, with huge buttress-stones of influence from the Phoenician in particular. Likewise Deuteronomy, where Moses' second reading of the Law so often contradicts the first.

So much for the dating of its writing. When was it first prayed? This is a crucial question, because it's the principal *Toraic* statement of the Unity of God - the concept of monotheism. There is no evidence to prove that it was publicly recited before Ezra instituted the thrice-weekly public readings, mid-5th century BCE; though one might like to think that it was there at least as early as the covenant-renewal ceremonies of Joshua, even no later than the "rediscovered" *Torah* of King Josiah - sadly, it probably wasn't.

The first paragraph is taken from Deuteronomy 6. Verse 4 is separated from verses 5-21 by a single appended phrase, "*baruch shem kavod, malchuto le-olam va'ed* - blessed be His glorious name, may His kingdom endure for ever", about which two very different stories are told.

According to the first, the patriarch Jacob already knew the *Shema*, several generations before Moses received it from God at Sinai; Jacob in fact recited it, as all Jews should, on his death-bed, and his sons, who were gathered around him, responded with the added phrase (elsewhere in the *Midrashim* this is told vice versa, the sons reciting the *Shema*, Jacob responding with the added phrase).

According to the second version, the angels taught the *Shema* to Moses, who taught it to the children of Israel; the added prayer is whispered because it's the special prayer of the angels and we are unworthy to utter it aloud, except on *Yom Kippur*, when our piety and penitence exalt us to their level.

Either way, the phrase is always whispered in an underbreath.

✡

Shema- The First Paragraph

"*Shema Yisrael Adonay Eloheynu Adonay Echad* - Hear O Israel, the Lord our God, the Lord is One."

Stefan Reif, Director of Geniza Research at Cambridge University, makes the case that this phrase alone was recited in the Second Temple period, with the whispered response by the congregated assembly of sacrificers; that later the whole paragraph, then the two, and only in mediaeval times, when in truth most of the liturgy as we now have it was stipulated, the third paragraph. To be honest, I'm more interested in its meaning than its date - its significance, I should say, and at every level.

There is, in truth, little to say about its meaning, which is remarkably straightforward - a statement, uttered collectively, of the *Monotheos*, incorporating both the Adonis mythology and the ancient multiplicity of deities - a theological sleight of hand of the most extraordinary cleverness. God isn't One because God is Single, Unique, Alone In A Universe Where There Are No Other Gods. The word in Hebrew is Elohim (אלוהים), not simply Elim (אלים), which would be a plural form of *El* (אל), the Canaanite Bull-God, but a universal, multiple plural, Elohim (אלוהים). God is One because He combines in a single, abstract but composite form the whole sum of his Multiple Plurality. The statement "God is One", in other words, is a statement of the apotheosis of inclusivity.

"*Baruch shem kavod malchuto le'olam va'ed* - blessed be the name of his glorious kingdom for all eternity."

A third version of the origins of this phrase. It wasn't Jacob, nor did the angels teach it to Moses on Mt Sinai. As Moses climbed the holy mountain he overheard the angels praying, and it was this phrase in particular that struck him. In his arrogant desire to be like the angels - an arrogance that came to fruition when he tapped the rock at Meribah and brought forth the waters of his own mortality - he decided to take the phrase down with him, and gave it to his people as Prometheus had once done with fire. It's our remorse, our shame, on his behalf, that causes us to say it in a whisper.

"*Ve-ahavta et Adonay eloheycha be-chol-levavecha u-ve-chol-naphshecha u-ve-chol-me'odecha.*"

The *Shema*, from this point, degenerates from *credo* into *fanshen* - a mere formal recitation of the dogma, identifying what is orthodox and effectively swearing an oath of allegiance. It reads like a series of commands, complete with rewards and punishments, of which the first at least is one that simply cannot be required - the Cordelia commandment, deserving the response that Lear got:

"You shall love the Lord your God with all your heart and all your soul and all your might."

As though love can be obtained, even by God, upon demand!

The translation is inadequate. Like most translations it conveys only one sense of the ambiguous original. "*Be-chol levavecha*" does indeed mean "all your heart", but it's only very recently that the heart has been understood as the vascular pump, and not much less recently as the seat of all emotions. In fact, it was always previously the other way around; the head, which generates every folly, being perceived as intuition and emotion, the heart (compare John Donne's "naked, thinking heart") as spirit, wisdom, intellect: the Apollonian. So to love the Lord "with all your heart" doesn't infer passion, nor the love a child owes its parents; or rather it does, but it infers the reason also, and first.

"*Be-chol naphshecha*" is still more complex. Judaism uses *nephesh*, *ru'ach* and *neshama* almost interchangeably, intending both "soul" and "spirit" by each one (as the Esquimaux allegedly have fifty words for snow). "The breath of life" might serve as a satisfactory translation of *ru'ach*. The "pulse", metaphorically, will do for any of the three, though I prefer to save that as a metaphor for the deity itself. The best I can offer is this. *Ru'ach* is the breath of God, infused to set the spark of life. *Neshama* is the breathing spirit, the *ru'ach* once it has been infused, and which will cease when the body ceases. *Nephesh* is the soul, that uniquely individual compound of genes and experiences which make a person him or herself, and which Judaism believes lives on, beyond the body, its *karma* to be evaluated when the Messiah comes. To love the Lord your God "*be-chol naphshecha*", is to do so "with your whole being". Cordelia couldn't have done it.

"*Ve-hayu ha-devarim ha-eleh asher anochi metsavecha ha-yom al-levavecha. Ve-shinantam le-vanecha ve-dibarta bam be-shivtecha be-veytecha u-ve-lechtecha va-derech u-ve-shachvecha u-ve-kumecha. U-keshartam le-ot al-yadecha ve-hayu le-totaphot beyn eynecha u-chetavtam al-mezuzot beytecha u-vi-she'arecha.*"

And then it really does become a list of regulations, a matter of ordinance - the divine edict, the Heavenly Bull. "These are the commandments that I give you this day, to inscribe upon your hearts." (Given the original meaning of heart that I've explained above, I wonder if "inscribe upon your hearts" isn't simply an instruction to "learn by rote"). One can almost imagine the Tsar or Caesar or Kaiser of the heavens, stamping his rubber seal upon the deed! "Teach them to your children. Discuss them, when you are sitting in your house, when you are out walking on the road, when you get up in the morning, when you go to bed at night. Bind them as a sign on your arm. Wear them as phylacteries on your forehead. Write them on the doorposts of your houses, and upon your gates."

And fine, yes - we know now what to do with the commandments. But which commandments does He mean? Just the instructions listed here, or the whole *Torah*? If the passage weren't taken out of context it would be self-evident (and indeed, the 2nd paragraph will make it perfectly apparent). And yet - for centuries the Rabbis have taught that it's only the instructions in the *Shema* itself - love, teaching, discussion, *tefillin*, *tsitsit*, *mezuzot* - which are specifically intended, and not the whole *Torah*. This is why it's only the text of the *Shema* that's placed inside the *tefillin* and the *mezuzah*.

I have already explained the rituals for saying the *Shema*, and the methodology of the *tsitsit* and *tefillin*. I have already pointed out that they're self-referential. Touch the *shel-yad* when you state "bind them…on your arm"; touch the *shel-rosh* at "wear them" and kiss your fingertips because what you've touched is holy. Likewise I've explained the *tefillin* already, at the time of binding them, at the beginning of the service. The *mezuzah* isn't the box containing the *Shema* which is attached to the doorpost, but properly the doorpost itself. Because the doorpost sentries the house, to make it holy is to make the whole house holy. An entire tractate of *Talmud* is devoted to this little piece of iconry, and the surviving atavisms from the days before superstitiousness was theoretically abolished.

One additional item of interest however. The most famous *mezuzah*, the most famous doorpost in Jewish history, was the one on which the Hebrew slaves made a mark on the night of the death of the firstborn, to ward off the angel of death. In Egypt, where houses were invariably painted blue, in theory to ward off djinns but actually to ward off malarial mosquitoes. But we know that the ancient code, like the modern, for the protection of a house, was the painting on the doorpost of a red cross, a bloody version of the Mark of Cain – the letter *tav* in Hebrew, which was an *x* back then. Is the *Pesach* then the origin of that organisation's emblem?

Ve-hayah - The Second Paragraph

"*Ve-hayah im-shamo'a tishme'u el-mitzvotay asher anochi metsaveh et-chem ha-yom le-ahavah et-Adonay eloheychem u-le-avdo be-chol-levavechem u-ve-chol-naphshechem ve-natati metar-artsechem be-ito yoreh li-vehemtecha ve-achalta ve-savata. Hishamru lachem pen-yiphteh levavechem ve-sartem va-avadetem elohim acherim ve-hishtachavitem lahem.*

Ve-charah aph-Adonay ba-chem ve-atsar et-ha-shamayim ve-lo-yiheyeh matar ve-ha-adamah lo titen et-yevulah va-avadetem meherah me-al ha-arets ha-tovah asher Adonay noten lachem. Ve-samtem et-devaray eleh al-levavechem ve-al-naphshechem u-keshartem otam le-ot al-yedechem ve-hayu le-totaphot beyn eynechem ve-limadetem otam et-beneychem le-daber bam be-shivtecha be-veytecha u-ve-lechtecha va-derech u-ve-shachvecha u-ve-kumecha. U-chetavtam al-mezuzot beytecha u-vi-she'arecha. Le-ma'an yirbu yemeychem vi-yemey veneychem al ha-adamah asher nishba Adonay la-avoteychem latet lahem ki-yemey ha-shamayim al-ha-arets."

"And it will come to pass that if you continually hearken to My commandments that I command to you today, to love the Lord your God and to serve Him with all your heart and all your soul - then I will provide rain for your land at the proper time, the early and the late rains, that you may gather in your grain, your wine and your oil. I will provide grass in your field for your cattle and you will eat and be satisfied. But beware lest your heart is seduced and you turn astray and worship other gods and prostrate yourself before them. Then the wrath of the Lord will blaze against you. He will restrain the heavens so there will be no rain and the ground will not yield its produce. And you will swiftly be banished from the good land which the Lord has given you. Place these words of mine upon your heart and upon your soul, bind them for a sign upon your arm and let them be *tefillin* between your eyes. Teach them to your children, discuss them when you sit at home and when you walk on the road, when you get up in the morning and before you go to sleep at night. Write them on the doorposts of your house and upon your gates. In order to prolong your days and the days of your children upon the land which the Lord has sworn to your ancestors to give them, like the days of heaven on earth."

The second paragraph is taken from Deuteronomy 11:13-21, and is an exposition of that Jewish doctrine of reward and punishment which complements so well that other Jewish doctrine of individual responsibility founded on free will. Keep my commandments and I will…more interestingly problematic is the nature of the reward. The laws were written for, and given to, a motley band of refugees, fleeing from slavery and uncertain when if ever they would leave the desert for a better life. Yet the text speaks to a farming community of some establishment, and implies regular markets in walled cities. Likewise the diatribe against polytheism: in the desert there were no other gods, or if they surfaced, like the Golden Calf, they were easily policed and prosecuted; but in Canaan, with its plethora of shrines and henges…evidence on two accounts that dating *Torah* to the mouth of God on the summit of Mount Sinai may be good faith but not necessarily good archaeology.

There is then the question of subjective judgement. "If you do not love the Lord your God, and serve Him, with all your heart and soul and might…" Yes, but how can He tell? How can He tell?

The punishment is appallingly fundamental - the withholding of rain in its proper season. The act of a fertility god, who has no other sanction but to withdraw his favours (or goddess...Her favours?); and not that of a universal omnideity, to whom all resolutions are available. Including justice, of the sort demanded by Abraham at Gomorrah, the "just weights, just balances" of this very book. What sort of justice can there be in this - a general punishment when the commandment is aimed at every individual? It cannot rain selectively, watering a good man's field but skirting round the edges of a bad man's. I may love in the prescribed manner, while you are found wanting; and just because you've sinned, why should your cattle suffer thirst? Despite the best efforts of Abraham, Job and Jonah, Judaism still has no answers to these questions which must include, not merely "how could God allow the Holocaust?", but even "if God allowed the Holocaust in order to punish the bad Jews, why should His mere agents the German people have been made to suffer like Egyptians too?" Tough question!

And if the rain is withheld from my lands because of your sin, can I read that as evidence that God has failed to love me with all His heart and soul and might? And what sanctions do I have when He doesn't keep the full terms of the covenant? What favours am I able to withhold? A covenant cuts both ways. But how can I tell? How can I tell?

In the second half of this paragraph the *tefillin* are once again mentioned - and with mentioning, kissed - as are the commandments to love, teach, discuss, wear *tsitsit* and post *mezuzot.* But now a further reward is offered - if receiving rain in its proper season can be regarded as a reward; the text of Genesis 1-3 seems to infer that it's a right, not a privilege, and so not having one's rights may well be a punishment, but having them cannot surely be regarded as a reward. The additional reward echoes the 5th Commandment, where we're encouraged (!) to honour our parents, that our "days may be long upon the earth which the Lord Your God has given you". Here it's our God whom we must likewise honour, and it's precisely in this that the Rabbis explain why the 5th commandment is the 5th commandment. Listed in two columns, the first five relate Man to God, the second five Man to Man. The 5th commandment forms the bridge.

An interesting digression takes us back to the Temple Service and the act of sacrifice. The text gives us "*ve-charah aph-Adonay ba-chem*" which is properly translated as "then the wrath of the Lord will blaze against you" -

properly because it conveys the real intent of the words, even if not their actual meaning. Properly "*charah*" means "to kindle" or "set aflame", and "*aph*" is the nostrils. The wrath of the Lord blazing against you is thus really the nostrils of the Lord being inflamed against you - that same image of the angry bull placated by the sweet smell of the incense which underscores the pagan sources of the sacrificial cult. I find it immensely ironic that the language used by Moses should reflect not the supplanting of the bull-cult of Horus by the un-iconic *Yahweh*, but rather the absorption of the Golden Calf into the Ten Commandments.

✡

Va-yomer - The Third Paragraph

"*Va-yomer Adonay el-Moshe lemor, 'Daber el-beney Yisra'el ve-amarta aleyhem, ve-asu lahem tsitsit al-kanphey vigdeyhem le-dorotam, ve-natnu al-tsitsit ha-kanaph petil techelet Ve-hayah lachem le-tsitsit u-re'item oto u-zechartem et-kol-mitzvot Adonay, va-asitem otam ve-lo taturu acharey levavechem ve-acharey eyneychem asher-atem zonim achareyhem. Lema'an tizkeru va-asitem et-kol-mitzvotay vi-heyitem kedoshim le-eloheychem. Ani Adonay eloheychem asher hotseyti et'chem me-erets Mitsrayim liheyot lachem le-elohim ani Adonay eloheychem.*'"

"Then the Lord said to Moses, 'Speak to the children of Israel and say to them that they are to put *tsitsit* on the corners of their garments throughout their generations. They are to place on the *tsitsit* of each corner a thread of purple. This shall constitute *tsitsit* for you, that you may see it and remember all the commandments of the Lord and perform them; lest you go in search of the desires of your heart and of your eyes, and go whoring after them. So you may remember all my commandments and be holy to your God. I am the Lord your God, who has brought you out of the land of Egypt to be your God."

Before beginning the third paragraph we are enjoined to gather the *tsitsit* in both hands, where previously only the left hand held them. The word *tsitsit* is repeated three times, and each time the physical *tsitsit* are kissed. So prayer intensifies, *crescendo ad coda*. On "*u-re'item oto* - and you shall see it", the *tsitsit* are travelled across the eyes. On the final word, which isn't the final word because the word "*emet* - truth" is carried over from the ensuing prayer to avoid a breach or hiatus, the *tsitsit* are kissed for one last time.

The third paragraph is taken from Numbers 15:37-41, and is the first iteration of the law concerning *tsitsit*. We are told that the thread on each corner should be of *techelet*, which poses another problem. The fringe itself is made of wool, but *techelet* is a shade of blue known as cerulean purple, and it takes its name from a species of sea-mussel, the *helix ianthina*, whose shell was crushed and treated to produce a dye in the same way as the better known, but now equally extinct, *murex* or *chilazon*, a sea-snail whose rich purple dye is known as "*phoinix*" in Greek, "*kinnahu*" in Hurrian (the ancient language of the Canaanites), and "*argaman*" in the Hebrew - giving names to the ancient lands of Phoenicia and Canaan, which manufactured it.

Why is this a problem? Because the commandment in Numbers belongs to the desert period, when the dye would have been unavailable, even if it had been discovered yet, which it hadn't.

The Rabbis say (I know, I've asked any number of them) that God, being al-knowing, was even able to give Moses that which hadn't yet been invented, because human discovery succeeds divine creation. What God gave Moses wasn't the law, they say, but the provision for the law, in advance of its compatibility. And if He could give Moses a set of Laws written in the Hebrew alphabet which didn't yet exist, why should He not give him Laws whose *raison d'être* didn't yet exist? What God gave Moses wasn't an ephemeral, time-based document, intended for present use and no further, but a universal document that had to be capable of sustaining the future too.

Excellent theology, but lousy jurisprudence. The miraculous appears to have played a joker against the phenomenological. The same argument is used in favour of the divinity of the Turin Shroud.

The closing phrase offers an important insight into the nature of the Jewish God, "who brought you out of the land of Egypt to be your God." This isn't some mere distinguishing feature, to help us to discern *Yahweh* from Ba'al - or more particularly from Hor, at whose holy mountain in the Sinai desert the commandments were given, and whose image, the Golden Calf, was set up in Moses' absence. He is the Lord our God precisely because He brought us out of Egypt, away not just from slavery but from the rule of the Pharaohs who worshipped Hor, and from all the rites and practices which the *Torah* specifically abominates, from incest to injustice. We are constantly reminded, as the laws are given, that we were slaves in Egypt, oppressed and maltreated, subjected to corrupt weights and balances. In this sense, Jewish Law is the most reactionary law ever written, because it was formulated, not as an abstraction, but in the teeth of experience, precisely as a way of righting the wrongs of Egypt, justice as a reaction against injustice, laws such as the jubilee laws precisely to avoid the repetition of oppression.

"And if a stranger sojourns with you in your land, you shall not vex him.

The stranger who dwells among you shall be as the native, and you shall love him as yourself; for you were strangers in the land of Egypt. I am the Lord your God." (Leviticus 19:33-34)

We do it the way we do it, not only because it's right, but also because it breaks the old Egyptian habit, or because the Egyptians failed to do it; or we're prohibited, lest we slip back into their ways. And in case there's any doubting this, it's reiterated in the first of the Ten Commandments: "I am the Lord your God, who brought you out of Egypt, out of the House of Bondage."

Jewish law, then, created to establish a just society, a society of justice for both the ruler and the subject, the host and the stranger – *ka ger ka ezrach*. Someone should go tell this to those who order the destruction of the houses of the Palestinians and put up concrete walls along Israel's borders. Someone should go tell this to those divorcees who refuse to give their wives a *get*.

The language of the third paragraph is very different from the previous two, perhaps not surprisingly given that Numbers almost certainly predates Deuteronomy by several centuries. But it's the ideas contained in the language that I particularly mean. Deuteronomy worried that the people might turn aside and worship other gods - a recognition in itself that monotheism is an alternative to polytheism and not its supplanting (after all, one cannot go worshipping other gods unless other gods exist). The same is implicit in Numbers, where the reference to *Elohim* - the gods - immediately calls up a warning reminder that *Yahweh* is our God. But it isn't the worship of these gods that Numbers is concerned about. "Lest you go in search of the desires of your heart and of your eyes, and go whoring after them." Which may well be what other gods are offering, but still, it's not the same language. The text is about morality, not theology. It speaks as much to a modern, secular world as it does to the *Asherah* worshippers of the primordial desert.

It's also a matter of "heart and eyes", where the second paragraph spoke of "heart and soul" and the first of "heart and soul and might". Anthropologists can learn a great deal, not just from what's written in the documents, but from the way it's written, from the tone, the choice of language, those things that are not said. I have a sense of a far more intellectual appeal being made in Deuteronomy than in Numbers, but also of a far more sinful group of people being upbraided in Numbers than in Deuteronomy. The techniques of literary criticism, applied to sociology.

How is it possible to terminate an avowal of faith, without implying the termination of faith itself? One way is to keep making the same avowal, again and again - and this is what we do, by reciting the *Shema* on any number of prescribed occasions. The *Mishnaic* Rabbi Judah even discerned another occasion in the Book of Jeremiah (10:10), where Jeremiah states: "But the Lord is the true God, He is the living God, and an everlasting king." The phrase that begins this - "*va-Adonay elohim emet*" - echoes the last words of the *Shema*, combined with the first word of the paragraph which follows it. It may not be required to run the closing phrase of the *Shema* into the opening of "*va-yatsiv*", but not to do so would interrupt Jeremiah in a statement of the holiness of the divine, and so for this reason it is run on, and to emphasise it as a statement of importance in its own right, it should also be repeated by the *chazan*.

Adonay eloheychem emet.

✡

Va-Yatsiv

I don't understand the necessity for the prayer "*va-yatsiv*", unless perhaps the *amora'im* of the second and third centuries who fashioned it were feeling the threat of Christianity, feared that the declaration by the *Notsrim* that the Old Covenant had been replaced by a New Covenant would lead some Jews to doubt the continuing authenticity of the *Shema;* for it was specifically the *Shema* that "The Lord's Prayer" was intended to supplant. "*Va-yatsiv*" isn't just a testament of faith, it's the exaltation of testament itself, the apotheosis of avowal. What hyperbole! "It is true, and certain, established and enduring, fair and faithful, beloved and cherished, delightful and pleasant, awesome and powerful, correct and accepted, good and beautiful, forever and forever…" - the "it" in question being the affirmation that God is God, and ours, that "It is true that the God of the Universe is our King, the Rock of Jacob is the shield of our salvation. From generation to generation He endures and His name endures and His throne is well-established, His sovereignty and faithfulness endure forever. His words are living and enduring, faithful and delightful forever…" kiss the *tsitsit* now, and only now, this long after ending both the *Shema* and any lingering doubts; now release them… "for our forefathers and for us, for our children and for our descendants, and for all the generations of Your servant Israel's offspring."

Those pairs of adjectives make fascinating literary criticism. True and certain, established and enduring, fair and faithful, beloved and cherished, delightful and pleasant, awesome and powerful, correct and accepted, good and beautiful. How did the Rabbis decide which to place with which, and in what order? Why the enduring repetition of the verb "endure"? I have no answer, but suspect that any literature or Jewish Studies classroom would find the exercise worthwhile.

The evening *Shema* is not followed by "*va-yatsiv*", but by "*ve-emuna*", likewise an overstatement of the continuing commitment of God to the Old Covenant, through a reminder of His many interferences in human history, usually, though by no means always, for our benefit; and a promise of further interference should it prove necessary in the future. The Rabbis seem to like this double-headedness (another kind of bookend), the morning *Shema* looking back and the evening *Shema* looking forward, so that both ends of eternity are tied. But I would rather ask, since God gave Man dominion on the sixth day of Creation; since God didn't take back the knowledge of good and evil that we scrumpied from the holy orchard, but preferred to temper it, to equivocate it, through the giving of the *Torah*; since God has given us free will; since God allowed and even encouraged the sages to make a second, Written Law by emparchmenting the Oral Law - since all of this denotes our intended and approved autonomy, what business is it of God's to interfere in human history at all? Or ours to request it?

Al ha-rishonim

But even now, after making our testament to the testament, after avowing the validity of avowal, after swearing to keep our promises, there is, it seems, still a loose thread of uncertainty, capable of pulling out the seam. Why else would it be necessary to attest again, "*al ha-rishonim* - on the earlier and on the later generations", that "this affirmation is good and enduring forever"? As though God doubted our *Shema*, or our sincerity in uttering it. "True and faithful, it is an unbreachable decree." Yes, He knows, we've said it. "It is true that you are God…our liberator…our rescuer…there is no God but you." Methinks the Rabbis do protest too much.

No poetry in that last line either. The Moslem equivalent, "there is no God but *Allah*", comes in the most exalted alliteration ever: "*La illah ilah Allah*", which knocks spots off the mere "*eyn elohim zelutecha*" of the Hebrew. We could perfectly grammatically have offered "*eyn el eleh Elohim*", but no matter.

Ezrat

And still the affirmation of affirmation continues, on into the next paragraph, "*Ezrat*". A kind of "This Is Your Life" in that strange 2nd person manner which tells the audience a man's biography by recounting it back to the man who lived it - as if he didn't know, or were the victim of total amnesia. "You were born in Kalischt in Austria, the son of a bottle merchant", or "your father was a Warwickshire schoolteacher", or "it was you who persuaded Vespasian to keep open the seminary at Yavneh". As if you didn't know! And here it's the greatest know-all of them all, God the Omniscient Himself. "You are the helper of our forefathers…Your dwelling is at the zenith of the Universe…You are the master for Your people…You are *alpha* and *omega*." To list the attributes and characteristics isn't simply a way of praising God however. It's a way of describing our own needs, the empty spaces which we depend upon God to fill; and so prayer becomes at once an expression of dream and of inadequacy. To state that God is our shield is to ask Him for protection. To state that He is first and last attaches us to His eternity, and helps to numb the pain of inexorable death. To state that He is all-knowing is to recognise our human limitations. To recall His splitting of the Sea of Reeds is to long and hope for further miracles. Mostly we pray to God, not for what He is or was, but for what He might, and hopefully in our days, be.

Lord, interfere in our history only when we need You, and do not interfere in our history at any other time. Lord who is all-knowing, we trust that You Yourself can work out which time is which time. Lord of sympathy and compassion, recognise that we are a species in confusion; were we not a species in confusion, we would not require God.

But the same problem occurs again, this time the other way around. If God has the attribute of mercy, then by inference there must be something that rouses Him to wrath and anger in the first place; and whatever that circumstance may be, it required a God to create that circumstance (the same God, after all, created the serpent and the tree, created gullibility in the woman and naïve trust in the man and naked guile in the serpent; the same omniscient God must have known what would take place, and at some level must have wanted it to happen in precisely the way it did.) To attribute moral characteristics to the deity is to define something much larger than a dualistic Universe, one in which, if there is only One God, a God who is the Unity of everything existing in the Universe, then that God must also have immoral and amoral characteristics. God is merciful because He's cruel, compassionate because callous, generous because mean, a shield because aggressive, a rock because a marsh, a restorer because a destroyer, a forgiver of sins because He, He and no one else, created all things that exist, including *ha-Satan* and Asmodeus and the *yetser ha-ra*. Yet we never praise the tails when we praise the heads, though both are God.

Actually this isn't entirely true. We do praise the tails, only much less frequently. We say *Kaddish* when a person dies. We say "*dayan ha-emet* – the true judge" in the face of bad news. "*Adonay lakach, Adonay natan, baruch shem Adonay* - the Lord gives, the Lord takes away, blessed be the name of the Lord." We magnify and sanctify and give praise to God, even when He breaks our hearts.

Having said which, here is the full text of "*Ezrat*", more meaningful I trust for the given explanation:

"The helper of our forefathers are You alone, forever, shield and saviour for their descendants in every future generation. At the zenith of the Universe is Your dwelling, and Your justice and Your righteousness extend to the ends of the earth. Praiseworthy is the person who obeys Your commandments and takes to his heart Your teachings and Your words. True, You are a master to Your people and a mighty king who takes up their grievances. True, You are the first and You are the last, and besides You we have no king, redeemer or saviour. From Egypt You redeemed us, Lord our God, and from the House of Slavery You liberated us. All their firstborn You slew, but Your firstborn You redeemed. The Sea of Reeds You split, the wanton sinners You drowned, the dear ones You brought across, and the water covered their foes - not one of them was left. For this, the beloved praised and exalted God, the dear ones offered hymns, songs, praises, blessings and thanksgivings to the king, the living and enduring God - exalted and uplifted, great and awesome, who humbles the arrogant and raises up the lowly, who frees the captive, liberates the humble, and helps the poor, who responds to His people when they cry out to Him."

We have returned yet once more to the philosophical territory of the Sea of Reeds and the *Akeda*; the God who liberated us did so by drowning and bereaving scores of others, by killing an innocent ram and not even for the benefit of food. The inextricability of good and evil, incapable of dualistic separation. And yet we are expected to distinguish. We are expected to extricate. We are expected to act without hypocrisy. We are expected to take our punishment when we err.

But now it should also be clear why "*va-yatsiv*" and "*al ha-rishonim*" and "*ezrat*" are as essential as the *Shema* itself. Though we say both sets of prayers, to say the *Shema* is merely to recite a transcript of the words of God, which lay out the articles of covenant. To speak the three prayers that follow it is to respond in our own words, acknowledging the prefaces and memoranda of association, agreeing the terms and conditions, signing with our own seals.

This entire passage, from "*Ezrat*" to the last word before the *Shemoneh Esreh*, is referred to in the *Talmud* as the "*Ge'ulah*" or "Redemption Blessing". When Jews pray, the individual is raised to include the universal, partly as an act of charity for those who can't pray, partly as an act of binding with the community, partly as an act of humility, setting the smallness of the I within its proper context. But the prayer too is raised to encompass the universal. In *bensching* - the Grace After Meals - we thank God not just for the meal we've eaten, but for the land in which we grew it, the covenant which granted us the land, the God who made the covenant, and all the acts of kindness and generosity, past present and future, which God performs, including this meal.

So, now, in preparing for the individual recitation of the Standing Prayer, we begin by acknowledging the universal.

First the patriarchs, and from there the children of every generation - the universal community, bound in time and space. Then God's home, the zenith of the universe, the summit of the cosmic mountain - the whole of Creation gathered in. Then the individual in this context - any individual, as well as you specifically, the one who prays. And then the recognition that God is time and space, the *alpha* and the *omega* of Isaiah 44:6, the Only One of Psalm 106:11, the Jewish God who performed the Exodus miracles, and in whose name we have offered hymns, songs, praises, blessings and thanksgivings ever since. So we are small in making our personal confession. So too we are very large.

But large - not great. Large is the scale of the universe, of which we provide a mere pore in the skin, a follicle. Great is a matter of ego, of self-exaltation. In case of error, we remind ourselves in the final paragraph, that it's God not we who is "exalted and uplifted, great and awesome, who humbles the arrogant and raises up the lowly." Where exactly is the point of balance? Impossible to say. But if we stoop too low, we will be raised up, and if we climb too high, our wings will be melted - *hubris* and *nemesis*, the Greeks called it. But only if we pray - here is where Greek poetry and Hebrew religion part company. "God responds to His people when they cry out to Him."

God the spirit, not God the doer-of-favours.

Now take three steps back, recite the "praises to the supreme God, the blessed one who is blessed," remember that "Moses and the children of

Israel exclaimed a song to You with great joy and they all said…" just a brief extract from the Song at the Reed Sea, the one which gives praise to God for all redemptive miracles, "Who is like you among the heavenly powers Lord? Who is like you, mighty in holiness, too awesome for praise, performer of miracles?" Then the *chazan* alone, "With a new song the redeemed ones praised Your name at the seashore, all of them in unison gave thanks, acknowledged Your sovereignty and said" but loudly, please, extremely loudly:

"*Adonay yimloch le-olam va'ed* - the Lord shall reign for all eternity"

And then, still loudly, sing joyfully the great hymn "*Tsur Yisra'el* - Rock of Israel."

"*Tsur Yisra'el kumah be-ezrat Yisra'el u-phdey chinumecha Yehudah ve-Yisra'el. Go'aleynu Adonay tseva'ot shemo kedosh Yisra'el. Baruch atah Adonay, ga'al Yisra'el.*"

"Rock of Israel, arise to the aid of Israel and liberate, as You pledged, Judah and Israel. Our redeemer - the Lord of the Heavenly Host is His name - the Holy one of Israel. Blessed are You, Lord, who redeemed Israel."

And then silence, deep silence, the hush of introspection, the silence of a soul in collocution with itself, so silent that the closing benediction remains virtually inaudible, and even the *amen* is uttered inwardly so as not to break the hush. Nothing may interrupt the blessing for redemption and the uttering of the nineteen benedictions.

Husssshhhhhh!

Chapter Ten: *Shemoneh Esreh* - The Eighteen Benedictions

Dating the origins of the Hebrew liturgy, as we've seen, is immensely difficult, but the *Amidah* provides the major exception. The *tanna'im* are quite clear on the matter. The *Shemoneh Esreh* were introduced into the Temple Service, by Ezra and the Men of the Great Assembly, circa 436 BCE. When the Temple was destroyed, the *Shemoneh Esreh* were carried across into the synagogue, circa 70 CE.

The Gamliel text, as the first synagogue *Amidah* is known, wasn't in fact the work of *Rabban* Gamliel at all, but of Shimon ha-Pakuli, who worked on it at Gamliel's behest at Yavneh. Shimon, given the immense significance of the work he undertook, remains the most obscure of all historic figures. Only once in the whole *Talmud* does he even get a mention, and this is simply the observation in *Berachot* 28b that "Shimon ha-Pakuli arranged the Eighteen Benedictions in order on behalf of *Rabban* Gamliel II in Yavneh." *Rashi*, a thousand years later, deduced from the etymology of his name that he must have been a seller of tufts of cotton. I like this - both the mundane occupation and the hobby-nature of his scholarship. I imagine a man, exhausted from the stresses of the commercial world, his hands more accustomed to the soft fibres of unretted cotton than the stiffness of a goose-feather quill, quieting his mind and soul after the children are asleep, or perhaps taking a short sabbatical, fulfilling his obligations to the community and his own desire for knowledge, by working away at the rhythms and scansions of the Eighteen Benedictions. Anonymous, unpaid, an artist of the spirit and the soul - the best sort of artist in the world. Borges described such a man in his exquisite epigram of self-description: "Not to have fallen, like others of my lineage, cut down in battle. To be, in the fruitless night, he who counts the syllables." I like the knowledge that the Jewish prayer book contains prayers written by God, by Moses, by David, by Isaiah, by Judah ha-Nasi and by ibn-Gvirol, by the most esoteric of mediaeval scholars; and then this prayer, the centrepiece of the entire liturgy, written by a man about whom nothing is known save that he made his living in the schmutter trade.

The fourth chapter of the *Mishnah*, known as *Berachot*, written in the 2nd century CE, and probably in the early part of that century, records a typical disagreement among the principal *tanna'im*. *Rabban* Gamliel, the President of the *Sanhedrin* and a champion of organised liturgy, pressed for the Eighteen Benedictions to become the statutory requirement of every prayer service. *Rabban* Joshua, on the other hand, saw no need for the formalisation of thrice-daily, mandatory repetition, but wanted just a brief allusion to the main content, and for the rest an abstract, developable *ex tempore*, which gave prayer a framework but nothing more rigid. The fixed liturgy in conflict with spontaneity and individualism.

Rabbi Akiva, presenting a third perspective, worried that most Jews lacked either the creativity to extemporise or the fluency in Hebrew to recite all Eighteen Benedictions, and offered a compromise: those who could should say the Eighteen Benedictions, while those who could not should use the Joshua abstract. Rabbi Eliezer ben Hyrcanus, to open a fourth line of debate, opposed all fixed forms of prayer, regarding Gamliel as too doctrinaire - but Joshua as lacking substance - and insisted that fixed prayer mitigated against authentic supplication. Despite its rejection by the followers of Akiva, Joshua and Eliezer, *Rabban* Gamliel won the day - not by virtue of being right, not by virtue of being able to argue his case more convincingly than the others, but by the much greater virtue of being rich, powerful, the President, and a direct descendant of *Rabban* Hillel. The best arguments of all in any contest! The triumph of politics, and social status, over theology. (We should only be surprised that he didn't demand a plaque and his name inscribed upon the liturgy! Oh, hang on – he did. It's called the Gamliel text.)

So the formal structure of fixed liturgy - the laying of *tefillin*, the twice-daily *Shema*, all of it including the text of the *Shemoneh Esreh* - became established. All of it, bar one exception. Gamliel was overruled in the matter of the evening prayers, which remain to this day entirely voluntary.

There was disagreement too over the number of the benedictions. The Palestinian version had eighteen, but the Babylonian had nineteen. Impossible to say now where the difference lay, since the text had already changed many times, and would continue to do so for another thousand years. All that can be said is that, today, we still have nineteen benedictions, and we still call the prayer the *Shemoneh Esreh* - the Eighteen.

The *Shemoneh Esreh*, or the *Amidah*, the Standing Prayer. Or simply "*Ha-Tefillah* - the Prayer". Thus do the *Talmudists* refer to it, denoting its centrality, and perhaps hinting at its uniqueness. Unlike any other prayer, it commands total reverence. It's recited standing, facing the Ark, feet together. It's forbidden to talk or even to move one's feet during the recitation. Late arrivers at synagogue will wait outside until it's complete, for the whole prayer, but especially so for the individual's recitation, and for the *Kedushah*.

Why do we stand? Because previously, like the Moslems, like courtiers before kings and emperors, the natural posture for worship was prone and prostrate on the ground. "*Ve ani eshtachaveh*", as we sang in "*Mah Tovu*", the hymn that opened the prayer service - "and I will prostrate myself". So we read, in Genesis 19, how Abraham threw himself face down on the ground before the two angels at Sodom.

Avodah, the act of prayer or sacrifice, means "worship", though it also means "service". However the Eighteen Benedictions are not an act of worship; they're a series of blessings, and therefore don't require prostration. For men to offer such a blessing upwards to the Almighty requires the dignity of standing on our own two feet. To kneel is either to grovel or to beg. To sit is either to rest or to relax informally. No, only standing confers the proper dignity, only standing reflects the fullness of a man. Though it seems to me *tefillin* undermines this.

Another reason is suggested for this prayer being recited standing. Ezekiel (1:7) describes the four divine creatures of his vision, whose "feet were straight"; and so, the Rabbis say, must ours be when we pray. This is laughably preposterous. Ezekiel also says that their feet were hooved "like the soles of a calf's foot", that "they sparkled like the colour of burnished brass", that "each had four faces" and "each had four wings". I should like to see the Rabbis emulating all of this while reciting the *Amidah*!

In Palestine, as Rabbi Akiva had rightly worried, a cantor was required to recite the *Amidah* on behalf of those who couldn't. In Babylon, where all Jews had to know Hebrew or how else would they remain Jews, the prayer was said in silent recitation. And later, which tradition should we follow - the public or the private? Because custom and practice allows addition but not reduction - we now do both.

Maimonides became so upset by those who could recite their personal, silent *Amidah*, but couldn't resist the temptation to disrupt the common prayers with chatter (the *Shulchan Aruch* forbids any talk in synagogue), that he abolished the silent *Amidah* altogether, insisting on a single recitation only, led by the *chazan*. This practice, though clearly incorrect, had the weight of authority of Maimonides' name behind it, and so it became correct without ever ceasing to be incorrect, and still more so when the weight of custom saw it endure in some communities for several hundred years.

To call the individual's recitation the "silent" *Amidah* is actually to pronounce a misnomer. It should be hushed, but audible, in the manner of Hannah, the mother of the Prophet Samuel, who "spoke in her heart, only her lips moved, but her voice could not be heard." (1 Sam 1:13)

The *Amidah* contains all three of the major components of prayer, namely praise, petition (supplication) and thanksgiving. But it's essentially a series of blessings, in this order:

three introductory blessings, in praise of God
three spiritual blessings, relating to individual needs
three personal blessings, one physical, one material and one emotional
six blessings relating to the needs of the whole Jewish community
three concluding blessings, expressing thanks

Why this order? *Megillah* 17b-18a offers a *midrash* that gives a scriptural foundation to both the order and the content of the blessings, claiming a historical or miraculous event as the source of each. (*Midrash* is the art of extending and interpreting *Torah* by commenting on the text, answering unanswered questions in the text, or deducing laws and traditions from the text. There are two basic types of *midrashim*: *halachic midrashim* deal with legal matters; *aggadic midrashim* deal with moral and spiritual issues and tend to read like stories.) By contrast a contemporary *tosephah*, the "*Netiv Binah*" of Rabbi Issachar Jacobson of Tel Aviv, seeks to demonstrate that the order and content follows that of the song of Hannah in 1 Samuel. I don't propose to enter any deeper into this, but will point out that the *Talmud* deduces an entirely simpler logic to the prayer. The opening blessings are precisely that, a praise of God and an acknowledgement of our place in the continuing chain of history. The middle blessings begin with Knowledge, the cornerstone of all material and spiritual development. It makes Repentance, the second blessing, possible, and Repentance leads naturally to Forgiveness, without which the fourth blessing, Redemption, is untenable. This likewise engenders the fifth blessing, Health, and the sixth, Economic Prosperity. For the needs of the community in the second half of the middle section, a similar logic is deduced. The first step must be the Ingathering of the Exiles, the *sine qua non* of nationhood in Israel. The Restoration of Justice and the Destruction of Israel's Enemies allow the Righteous to undertake the Rebuilding of Jerusalem, after which the whole process culminates in the Coming of the Messiah. Ah, if only it were that straightforward!

✡

The Three Introductory Blessings

The First Blessing - *Avot*

First, in silence, the individual praying alone, but within the community, beginning with the prefatory incantation, taken from Psalm 51:17:

"Lord, open my lips, that my mouth may declare your praise."

"Lord, open *my* lips."

Even the inarticulate, the stammerers both literal and spiritual. Even the sick may utter it, sitting down if necessary. Even he who cannot say it may still say it, simply by adding his *amen*.

We have moved inward through the community. We have entered the realm of personal, individual prayer. In this way do men still speak with God.

As the *Amidah* recurs three times daily, so also does it come in three parts: the opening triplet of blessings, the central *Kedushah*, the closing prayers. If a *minyan* is lacking - if less than six of those present in the *minyan* are actively participating - then the *Amidah* may be recited silently, but only the first three blessings may be said aloud.

"Blessed are you, O Lord our God..." Take three steps back before beginning the silent reading, as you would take three steps back before addressing a king. Bend the knees at "*baruch*", bow at "*atah*", straighten at "*Adonay*". (Do not bow overmuch however. *Berachot* 34a warns against excessive humility - a phrase which seems to cast a question-mark over the time-honoured art of *shockeling*). Now speak the praises, as you would praise a king before making supplication:

"...and God of our forefathers, God of Abraham, God of Isaac, God of Jacob, the great, mighty and awesome God, the supreme God, who bestows beneficial kindness and creates everything, who recalls the kindnesses of the Patriarchs and brings a redeemer to their children's children, for His name's sake, with love."

The customary sycophantic litany of courtship, flattering for favours. We have become God's courtesans.

"O King, helper, saviour and shield. Blessed are You, Lord, the shield of Abraham."

This first blessing is known as "*Avot* - Forefathers". The request consequent upon the flattery is for the sending of a redeemer, but in the present not the future tense. The name of God in this paragraph is *El Elyon*, which is the name of the God of Melchi-Tsedek, king of Shalem in Genesis 14:18-20. The God of Gods. How can we be praising that God, for sending a redeemer now, when he isn't our God, when there is no Redeemer now? Because He was the God of Shalem, which became Jerusalem. Because His holy mountain came to host our Temple. Because every man has to be his own redeemer, now, and in the future.

"*Avot* - Forefathers". This isn't the place to give the reasons or the arguments, but simply to note, that modern Reform synagogues, in the name of egalitarianism but not only in the name of egalitarianism, have added the names of the Foremothers to the verse, because God was also the God of Sarah, Rebekkah, Leah and Rachel.

Nor is this the place to comment on the Reform prayer book, but one question I would ask: is it reasonable in the name of a perfectly justifiable egalitarianism to impose, by retroactive validation, a matriarchal system on the ancient world, one that clearly never existed?

The phrase "*zachreynu…chayim* - remember us for life, O king who desires life, and inscribe us in the Book of Life, for Your sake, the God of Life" - is inserted between *Rosh ha-Shana* and *Yom Kippur*, after "*be-ahava* - with love". Once again it bifurcates the unity of Judaism. For every question we have three or more conflicting answers, and each answer turns out to be the curious misphrasing of another question. But in the end we have simply to accept that to envisage a God who is the entire Universe is to envisage a God who, by definition, may be all things to all men. Even contradictory things.

This first paragraph with its resonances of ancestor worship contains the classic Jewish ruse (Moses used it after the incident of the Golden Calf). We've been told in the Ten Commandments that the sins of the fathers may be held against the accounts of the children, even unto the fourth generation; and in return, though it's unstated, we expect the commensurate receipt of the rewards of their virtues too. Why not, in the name of all that's fair? Those rewards are of no use to them, after all, so why should we not gain advantage? *Yichus* triumphs over sin.

Nor is this simply the frivolous idea of a modern cynic. *Yoma* 87a is its source, explaining the ruse of the Golden Calf. God had made clear He would destroy the entire people for their bull-worship, and wouldn't countenance any of Moses' arguments, until he reminded Him (Exodus 32:13) of the merits of his "servants, Abraham, Isaac and Jacob" - at which moment God relented.

Given that the tales of Isaac reveal neither virtues nor vices in that remarkably uneventful life; given that Jacob was a *ganaf* who stole both his brother's birthright and his paternal blessing, stole away, stole most of his father-in-law's wealth, cheated his father-in-law a second time with a dubious contract, stole away again, even stole a blessing from a night-daemon by trapping him as the sun came up - a man, that is to say, honoured rather for the fact of being patriarchal than for his virtues – it's perhaps not surprising that when we make the final blessing, we manage to forget both Isaac and Jacob, and to bless God only in the name of Abraham.

✡

The Second Blessing - *Gevurot*

"You are eternally mighty, Lord; You revive the dead; You have the power to save (You make the wind blow and the rain fall); You sustain the living with kindness, revive the dead with abundant mercy[4], support the fallen, heal the sick, release the confined, and maintain Your faith in those who sleep in the dust. Who is like You, O master of mighty deeds, and who is comparable to You, O king who causes death and restores life and makes salvation sprout (who is like You, Merciful Father, who recalls His creatures mercifully for life). You are faithful in reviving the dead. Blessed are You, Lord, who revives the dead."

The second blessing is known as "*Gevurot*", meaning might or power. But this isn't the Creative power of Genesis 1 or Psalm 29, nor is it that human power which tends to the destructive. This is the power of life and death itself, the giving of life, the healing of sickness, even the resuscitation of the dead. This passage should enable us to define the Jewish God more clearly than ever and also to moderate our expectations of Him. He is not the Creator, but Creation itself. God isn't a noun, but a verb.

The verse states, no less controversially for doing so three times, that God has the power to raise the dead, or at the very least to restore life, which may not be the same thing. Awakening man from his nightly slumber is included, and the rain which revives the earth as well. But the literal resurrection of the dead is problematic, for in Hebrewism it was strictly a matter of dust to dust, and even in the Messianic age it's the soul, not the body, that will queue for judgment.

But Judaism does allow for it. *Sanhedrin* 10:1 and *Rosh ha-Shana* 17a both contain it, and Maimonides makes it one of the Thirteen Principles of Faith. For those who deny the existence of the world to come there's a most curious punishment - forfeiture of their portion in the world to come. Surely the *Talmudists* could have thought up a more meaningful reprobation than this one from the works of Grouch Marx.

Of all phrases in this blessing, the most telling is "*u-mekayem emunato li-shney aphar* - You maintain Your faith in those who sleep in the dust". Why, the twentieth century never ceased to ask, why should we continue to

---

[4] The Reform movement, in another flagrant rewriting of theology - one which, on this occasion, I happen to approve - has omitted this phrase altogether; though elsewhere in the liturgy, by error I presume, their equivalents are not omitted.

believe in God, after the Holocaust, after so many wars droughts famines acts of cruelty? The voice of Job, crying among the lilacs in the wasteland. But this phrase of the *Amidah* doesn't ask that question. It asks a very different question. It asks, why should God continue to believe in Man, after the Holocaust, after so many wars droughts famines acts of cruelty? Yes - God too looks around and wonders, where are the roots that clutch, what branches grow, out of this stony rubbish[5]? But He does not despair, as we do, and think of suicide, or run away to Tarshish (though in the past He has done, at the Flood, at Gomorrah, when Korach raised his rebellion in the wilderness). "*U-mekayem emunato li-shney aphar* - You maintain Your faith in those who sleep in the dust". Which is more than can be said of Man's continuing trust in God.

From Job to Jonah is but a short distance. In the one, a man protests the apparent cynical indifference of God; in the other a man protests against the unfairness of divine justice; both end with a moral lesson, given by God in person, which reiterates the dominion given to Man in Genesis 1:26. No point Job protesting against God - Man's fate is his own to determine, his calamities are of his own making, and he cannot think to understand the agendas of the Almighty. No point Jonah protesting against God – he's the one who ran away by boat to Tarshish, he's the one who called on Nineveh to repent, so he shouldn't complain that it has been reprieved for doing so. In both, the burden is placed on Man, removed from God - once again the humanism of the *Akeda* trumps the miraculous. And yet here we are, thanking God for sustaining with lovingkindness, supporting the fallen, healing the sick, releasing the confined, maintaining the faith of those who sleep in the dust? This is the prayer of Jonah in the belly of the whale, disclaiming personal responsibility. What use our own good deeds, our own charitable actions, what use the trained doctors and lawyers, if these are the exclusive philanthropies of God? Where is the prayer that blesses God for giving us the wherewithal and the resolution to do these things ourselves? And when will God make up his mind whether He intends to go on interfering, or to leave us to our own devices. God, too, cannot have his *chamets* with his *matzah*.

I've placed two phrases of *Gevurot* in brackets at the opening of this chapter. The first, the reference to rain which links to the third paragraph of the *Shema*, is bracketed because it's only said through half the year. Between *Shemini Atseret* (22nd *Tishrey* - usually late September in the solar calendar), when the first prayers for rain are uttered, until the start of *Pesach* in the spring, the phrase is included; but during the dry summer months, when to

[5] From "The Wasteland," by T.S. Eliot

pray for rain would anyway be futile, it's omitted. How sensible, only to pray for what is feasible, only to ask for wind and rain when they're expected anyway.

In Sephardic communities, and in modern Israel, the prayer for dew, "*morid ha-tal*", is used during the months when "*mashiv ha-ru'ach*" is not recited. Dew in the dry summer is extremely useful.

Again, between *Rosh ha-Shana* and *Yom Kippur*, a second phrase is added, whose omission like all interpolations would make the repetition of the *Amidah* improper. "Who is like you, Merciful Father, who recalls His creatures mercifully for life?" A fair question deserving a fair answer. Who is like God? Why, we, Mankind, of course, who were created precisely in His image and His likeness! Every praising of God's attributes, every statement of gratitude for God's blessings, infers the capability of Man to do the same himself. Save only the miraculous. In this lies the concept of *Tikkun Olam* - repairing the world.

✡

The Third Blessing - *Kedushat ha-Shem*

When an individual recites the silent *Amidah*, the *Kedushah* is omitted and the three introductory blessings end with the single phrase: "*Atah kadosh ve-shimcha kadosh u-kedoshim be-chol yom yehalelucha (selah). Baruch atah Adonay, ha-el ha-kadosh*" ("*ha-melech ha-kadosh*" during the Days of Awe between *Rosh ha-Shana* and *Yom Kippur*). But when the *Amidah* is repeated - the repetition is properly called "*chazarat ha-shats*" - the *Kedushah* is included, recited responsively according to a fixed format.

First the congregation, then the *chazan*, this, from Isaiah 6:3:

"We shall sanctify Your name in this world, just as they sanctify it in heaven above, as it is written by Your prophet that the angels will call to one another saying 'Holy holy holy is the Lord, God of the Heavenly Hosts; the whole world is filled with His glory.'"

This from Ezekiel 3:12.

"The angels facing them reply: 'Blessed is the glory of the Lord that goes out from this place.'"

This from Psalm 146:10

"The Lord shall reign forever, the God of Zion, from generation to generation Hallelu-Yah."

Then the *chazan* alone, completing the celebration of God's holiness, fixing it in white.

"From generation to generation we shall relate Your greatness and for infinite eternities we shall proclaim Your holiness. Your praise O God, shall not leave our mouths forever and ever, for You O God are a great and holy king. Blessed are You, O Lord, the holy God."

Thus do men exalt themselves to the level of the angels, to praise and sanctify God on earth exactly as the angels do in heaven. For those who believe, it's a moment of intense personal apotheosis, the most sublime moment of the liturgy. Most who pray even raise themselves onto their toes when uttering the *Kedushah*, as if to liberate themselves from earth and soar. But men, being men and not Icarus, return at once to flattest earth.

The distinctions between those lines recited by the *chazan* and those in responsa by the congregation are delineated in the *Shulchan Aruch*, the virtually definitive compendium of Jewish Law established by Joseph Caro in the early 16th century, in Turkey, and finally published in Venice in 1565 after it had been amended and completed by Moses Isserles. The teaching of *Arizal* (Isaac Luria) contests Caro's designations however, insisting that every line should be uttered congregationally. As always in Judaism, each congregation follows its own customs and traditions, and modern trends like Reform and Reconstructionism are in the end simply new customs, new trends, which in a thousand years will seem no more than accents and dialects, regional variations on the universal language of Hebrew prayer.

The first and last phrases of the *Shema* were added to the *Kedushah* in the 5th century CE, a thousand years after Ezra introduced the prayer, when religious persecution in Persia proscribed the *Shema*, and this was found as a furtive act of defiance and insurrection. (I've already recounted this, the tale of Yezdejard's edict, in connection with "*Le'olam Yehei Adam*", earlier in this book).

This, then, is the text. But *Kedushah* is less about the meanings of the words than the significance of praying them. *Kedushah* is one of the trinity of prayers which denote the holiness of God, and create a space and moment of intense inwardness and silence, through which we, the ones who pray, may attain a similar wholeness. *Kaddish*, *Kiddush* and *Kedushah* - the three sacred moments of Jewish liturgy.

The Central Petitions

The Fourth Blessing: *Binah* - Insight or Wisdom

"*Atah chonen le-adam da'at, u-melamed le-enosh binah. Chanenu me-it'cha de'ah binah ve-haskel. Baruch atah Adonay, chonen ha-da'at.*"

"You graciously endow Man with wisdom, and teach insight to a frail mortal. Endow us graciously with Your knowledge, insight and discernment. Blessed are You, Lord, gracious giver of knowledge."

At the end of *Gevurot*, before the *Kedushah*, I asked, "Where is the prayer that blesses God for giving us the wherewithal and the resolution to do these things ourselves?" It was a naughty question, if not quite a rhetorical one, because of course the answer lies right here, in the very next blessing of the *Amidah*, in our thanks to God for providing us with the most essential human tools without which we couldn't possibly fulfil our obligations, the tools of wisdom, insight and discernment - intelligence, in short.

But it's God, not Man, who is made manifest in this account of His attributes, not manifest in physical form, because He is invisible, immaterial and abstract, but manifest in His influence upon the world through us, His custodians. As His angels are the stars, so He is the sun; but really His angels are not the stars, but only the light emanating from the stars; and not even the physical light, but only the metaphor of light transmitted and interpretable by men; and not even the metaphor, but only...it's in precisely this way that God is made manifest in His attributes.

The first attribute is Wisdom, but I've translated *Binah* as Insight because there's also *Chochma* for Wisdom, and these are not the same in Hebrew; and there's also *Da'at*, which is really Knowledge, and this is something different yet again. To make it still more complex there's also *Sechel*, which I've translated here as Discernment, though it tends to be understood as "common sense". To be more precise, *Chochma* is ratiocinative knowledge, sagaciousness or shrewdness, an ability to make judgements based on logical deduction. *Binah* is really intellection, the cognitive capacity to comprehend, the facility to make deduction by intuition. *Da'at* is understanding, the ability to imbibe and process information, and to regurgitate it as one's own. *Sechel* is common sense, the insights and understandings we gain from personal experience. Bloom's Taxonomy in Biblical Hebrew! *Chochma* is the only one absent from this blessing.

"You graciously endow Man with knowledge (*da'at*) and teach insight (*binah*) to a frail mortal. Endow us graciously with Your knowledge, insight and understanding (*da'at, binah, sechel*). Blessed are you, O Lord, gracious giver of knowledge (*da'at*)."

✡

The Fifth Blessing: *Teshuvah* - Repentance

"Hashiveynu avinu le-Toratecha, ve-karveynu malkeynu la-avodatecha, ve-hachzireynu bi-teshuvah shelemah lephanecha. Baruch atah Adonay, ha-rotseh bi-teshuvah."

"Bring us back, O Our Father, to Your *Torah*, and bring us near, O Our King, to Your service. Cause us to return fully and completely [I prefer this as a translation to the usual "in perfect repentance"] to You. Blessed are You, O Lord, who desires repentance."

Jonah's story, and Nineveh's too, though most people only seem to remember the fish and not the outcome. Repentance. A strange tale about a castor oil plant and justice. Especially repentance, except that the English word is all wrong, with its link to penitentiaries as a place for being punished rather than saying sorry, as though contrition is something that can be imposed from the outside, as though a person can be made to feel guilty. Macbeth's "to know my deed 'twere best not know myself" is a potent cry of guilty anguish from within. His demise doesn't require Macduff. Macbeth creates his own hell and damnation, in the dregs of morality left in the teacup of his soul when the storm ebbs out. Likewise Jonah in the belly of the whale, left alone by God because there's no need to torture him - men like Jonah in their *angst* will perfectly satisfactorily torment themselves.

A repent in biology is a root that creeps and grows, just below the soil's surface, like buttercups or certain variegated ivies (curiously, the plant known as Wandering Jew, or *tradescantia pallida* by its botanical name, is such a plant), replanting and rerooting itself continuously, until it has sucked all the nitrogen from the soil and prevented any other seeds from fertilising. Strange - I always thought that the thing which crept and grew in this manner was the feeling of guilt, not the call to repentance.

But *teshuvah* isn't this. In the Book of Job it's the answer which God eventually fails to provide in the whirlwind (one of the great disappointments of literature this; God's final claiming of the cop-out answer, "there are mysteries too great for you to comprehend". I remember reading this for the first time as a child, not long after the Rabbi had given a similar answer to a similar question and my father had told me, "It's just his way of saying that he doesn't know." And God's answer to Job? No. Surely not? Is this really God's voice in the whirlwind, admitting that He too doesn't know? Or does he simply not have the capacity to explain it in a way that human beings can understand? Try us, God. Try us.)

Mostly *teshuvah* is a return, and implicit in the notion of return is the presumption of having been there once before. A *Ba'al Teshuvah* is thus one who returns to religion after a period of wandering in the land of *Belial* - correctly *Bli-El*, one who follows no gods at all. A convert cannot be a *Ba'al Teshuvah* by definition. *Teshuvah* assumes that the sinner was once God-fearing and law-observing, but erred. *Teshuvah* is about rehabilitation, not punishment ("I take no pleasure in the death of the wicked, says the Lord" - Ezekiel 33:11 - "but that the wicked turn from his way and live"). *Teshuvah* isn't the saying sorry for the sin of erring; *teshuvah* is the act of coming back.

"Bring us back, O Our Father, to Your *Torah*, and bring us near, O Our King, to your service. Cause us to return fully and completely to you. Blessed are You, O Lord, who desires repentance."

"*Ha-rotseh be-teshuvah*." Who desires repentance. Or simply - who wants to come back. The *Ba'al Tsehuvah* is always the Prodigal Son.

Is "*ve-karveynu malkeynu la-avodatecha*" that rare event in Jewish liturgy - a deliberate pun? "*Karav*" does indeed mean "near". "*Avodah*" means slavery, service or worship, and refers to both the Temple and Synagogue modes of paying tribute to the divine. The true mode is sacrifice, and a burnt offering is a "*kurban*", from the same root as "*karveynu*" - a means by which we come near to God; the verb *lehakriv* is used repeatedly in the instructions for the sacrifices given to Aaron in the book of Leviticus. But why "bring us near to your service" when it isn't proximity but symbiosis that we seek? I detect a linguistic joke.

In this prayer, and in the next, but only in these two, we refer to God as "*Avinu* - Our Father". And if he is our father, then the duties of a father laid out in the *Shema* - to teach his children - bind him also. The prayers are for repentance and forgiveness, the core of the Christian message too, and I can't help but note that in the Christian story God appears to have reverted to the primitive, to his moral perspective prior to the destruction of the Five Cities and the *Akeda*. In the Christian tale, Jesus goes to the summit of the mountain, just like Isaac. In the Christian tale, Jesus also serves as the ram. In the Christian tale, God does not restrain his hand from plunging in the knife.

✡

The Sixth Blessing: *Selicha* - Forgiveness

"Selach lanu avinu ki chatanu, mechal lanu malkeynu ki pashanu, ki mochel ve-soleyach atah. Baruch atah Adonay, chanun ha-marbeh lislo'ach."

We are still in the stratosphere of *Yom Kippur*, and with the same logic. First we return, then we say sorry - and in the prayer that follows we will obtain redemption.

"Forgive us, O Our Father, for we have sinned, pardon us, O Our King, for we have transgressed."

Communal breast beating, not mere individual *angst*. Public too, not hidden away in the privacy of the confession-booth, anonymous and confidential. Jewish fanshen. Nor is it necessary to state the nature of the sin. "Father, I have lusted after blonde women, eaten pork, stolen money from a blind man's cup, walked one pace beyond the *eruv* on *shabbat*, paid my employees less than a living wage." Irrelevant. Immaterial. The detail is nothing. The confession is nothing. What matters is that mankind outside Eden, by his very nature, is inexorably bound to sin, but willing to acknowledge imperfection, and to go on striving upwards.

It is, quite literally, breast beating. Strike the left side of the chest with the right fist on "*chatanu* - we have sinned", and again on "*pashanu* - we have transgressed". Few Jews do this however, except on *Yom Kippur*.

On fast days the full litany of *selichot* are recited here - that is to say, on *Behab*, the 10th of *Tevet*, *Gedaliah*, the 17th of *Tammuz*...the full collection of *selichot* take up fully fifty pages in the *siddur* - worthy of an exegesis of their own. But not here. I'm sorry.

First the confession, then the plea for forgiveness. But the plea is made in the form of a blessing, not a supplication. Receiving is implicit in the very way we ask. It is, after all, as Heinrich Heine once observed, God's job to forgive us.

"Blessed are you, O Lord, the gracious one who pardons abundantly."

As though a parent will ever not forgive a child!

What is the difference between "*chatanu* - sinned" and "*pashanu* - transgressed"? Biblical usage suggests that a *pesha* is stronger than a *chet*. A *chet* will incur a forfeit or a fine, but is expiable and may only be an error. A *pesha* has the sense of wilfulness, even of protest or rebellion against the Law and against God. That's why the words for pardon are also varied - a *selicha* for the *chet*, a *mechilah* for the *pesha*. *Selicha* is forgiveness, *mechilah* the full pardon, relative strength to relative strength. Only on *Yom Kippur* itself do we ask for and receive the highest level, beyond *selicha*, beyond *mechilah*, the full *kappara* which gives the day its name, the complete obliteration of our sins from the record books, the nulling and voiding of the entire page, so that we may start again afresh, at-one.

Three levels of sin then, as there are eight levels of charity. A pedantic religion, this Judaism.

✡

The Seventh Blessing: *Ge'ulah* - Redemption

"Re'eh ve-anyeynu ve-rivah riveynu u-ge'aleynu meherah le-ma'an shemecha, ki go'el chazak atah. Baruch atah Adonay, go'el Yisra'el."

"Behold our affliction, take up our grievance, and redeem us."

The words are from Psalm 119:153-4. What is the nature of our affliction? Boils, like Job? Ruthless, cruel enemies, such as the Amalekites whom Moses faced? Simply, as *Rashi* interpreted it (*Megillah* 17b), the trials and tribulations of our daily lives? If we're afflicted because we've sinned, then what right do we have to appeal to God to overrule His own sentence? And if we're afflicted for no reason, then there's no justice in the world, so no use anyway lodging an appeal. Or if it's men who afflict us, with no involvement of God, then what use bringing our grievance to God, who can't redeem us from what He hasn't caused?

"Behold our affliction, take up our grievance, and redeem us speedily for Your Name's sake. Blessed are You, Lord, the Redeemer of Israel."

Why speedily? Why for His name's sake? Is there a suggestion that the very reputation of the godhead may be jeopardised if a miracle isn't instantly forthcoming. This isn't a prayer, this is an act of moral blackmail!

But what actually is redemption, that much-used abstraction of the priests and theologians. A man deposits a silver candlestick with a pawnbroker, taking ten dollars against its value; and when he has the ten dollars to spare again, he goes back to the pawnbroker and redeems his silver candlesticks. Is this how God regards our lives, our souls? The answer is actually yes, though it needs some explaining.

In fact, as Roland de Vaux, one of the great modern explicators of the institutions of the ancient world, makes clear in his account of ancient Israel, the *go'el* was the defining institution of the Hebrew family. "The *go'el* was a redeemer, a protector, a defender of the interests of the individual and the group."[6] If an Israelite had to sell himself into slavery in order to repay a debt, he would be "redeemed" by one of his near relations, as the law in Leviticus 25:47-49 confirms. If an Israelite had need to sell his patrimony, the *go'el* had first option; indeed it was both his right and his duty to make the purchase, so the patrimony would remain within the clan. It was on the basis of this duty - expounded as a law in Leviticus 25:25 - that the prophet Jeremiah purchased the field belonging to his cousin Haname'el (Jeremiah 32:6ff).

Best known of all *go'el* incidents is the marriage of Ruth to Bo'az, a double *go'el* in fact. On the one hand there was the "*yabam*", the Levirate Law, which required a kinsman of Chilyon ben Elimelech to marry his widow Ruth, and father a child on her in his name. Then, in addition, Naomi had cause to sell some of her inheritance in order to release capital to live on, but the closest relative, who should have stood as *go'el*, was willing to fulfil the latter obligation, but unwilling to fulfil the former, because the child of such a union would have been able to claim the land back again. The next closest kinsman was Bo'az, and he was willing to fulfil both parts of the *go'el* obligation, and so he redeemed Ruth from childless widowhood and simultaneously redeemed Naomi from poverty. An interesting anthropological sideline to this tale - from Ruth 4:7-8 we learn that the symbolic act required to demonstrate the forgoing of the *go'el* obligation was the public removal of one sandal. It isn't stated whether this was the right or the left sandal.

One last instance of the *go'el* - the blood-vengeance. When Avner ben Ner, King Saul's cousin and the commander of his army, murdered Asahel ben Tseruyah after the skirmish at the Pool of Gibeon (2 Samuel 2), his brothers Yo-Av and Av-Yishai tracked Avner down relentlessly until they were able to take his life, eye for eye for Asah-El's. To show that it was a *go'el*, a blood-vengeance, and no other sort of killing, the dagger was plunged into Avner "below the fifth rib" - a symbol of the sacred nature of the act, for it was precisely the fifth rib that God took out of Adam in order to make Eve, and likewise the fifth rib below which the Roman soldier plunged his spear into the crucified body of Jesus.

---

[6] 'Ancient Israel, Its Life and Institutions', originally 'Les Institutions de l'Ancien Testament', les Editions du Cerf, Paris, 1960. De Vaux also led the team that worked on the Dead Sea Scrolls.

The *go'el*, then, is the godfather of the Hebrew clan, he who will redeem us from slavery, he who will ensure that our historic land remains within the tribe, he who will take vengeance on our enemies, he who will protect us…to be our *go'el*, in fact, is precisely what God offered us, as His part of the bargain, when He invited us to join with Him in covenant, and it was to God the *go'el* that we addressed the great joyful hymn "*Tsur Yisra'el*" before we began the recitation of the Eighteen Benedictions.

✡

Aneynu

"*Aneynu Adonay aneynu be-yom tsom ta'aniteynu, ki ve-tsarah gedolah anachnu. Al tephen el risheynu, ve-al taster paneycha mi-meynu, ve-al titalam mi-techinateynu. Heyeh na karov le-shavateynu, yehi na chasdecha le-nachameynu, terem nikra eleycha aneynu, ka-davar she-ne'emar, 'Ve-hayah terem yikra'u va-ani e'eneh od hem medabrim va-ani eshma.' Ki atah Adonay ha-oneh be-et tsarah, podeh u-matsil be-chol et tsarah ve-tsukah. Baruch atah Adonay ha-oneh be-et tsarah.*"

"Answer us, Lord, answer us, on this day of our fast, for we are in great distress. Do not pay attention to our wickedness, do not hide Your face from us and do not ignore our supplication. Please be near to our outcry, please let Your kindness comfort us - before we call to You, answer us, as it is said, 'And it will be that before they call, I will answer; while they yet speak, I will hear.' For you, Lord, are the one who responds in times of distress, who redeems and rescues in all times of distress and sorrow. Blessed are You, Lord, who responds in times of distress."

Added on fast days, this is a cry of distress that reflects, not the pangs of hunger, but the circumstance behind the fast. The 9th of *Av* commemorates the destruction of the Temple in Jerusalem - and not once, but twice. The first time in 586 BCE, the second in 70 CE - so tradition, which likes symmetry, tells us; though history has not yet corroborated the coincidence. The fast of the 9th of *Av* also recalls the expulsion of the Jews from Spain in 1492, which history does confirm took place on that date. The fast of the 10th of *Tevet* marks the start of the siege of Jerusalem by the Babylonians under Nebuchadrezzar, which would end with the fall of the Temple. The Fast of Esther precedes the feast of *Purim* (all Jewish festivals are ringed around with food, either its eating, or else our abstinence from eating: feasts or fasts), recalling Esther's call to fast in order to convince Ahasuerus. The fast of the 17th of *Tammuz* marks the first breach in the walls of Jerusalem in 586 BCE. The fast of *Gedaliah*, occurring on the 3rd of *Tishrey*, the day after *Rosh ha-Shana*, recalls the assassination of Nebuchadrezzar's governor in

Judea, and with it the fall of the First Commonwealth.

But there are a hundred other fasts as well, commemorating specific incidents in specific times and places. A massacre in Poland. The destruction of a synagogue in the Ukraine. Yet another expulsion, whether from France or England. The death of a great *tsaddik*. Fasts commemorated locally, rather than universally.

What a huge and terrible wail this is - and even more heart-rending in the Hebrew! What anguish! What desolation! The deep cry of a child to its parent. Desperation. Utter desperation. Why wasn't this the prayer that they prayed, when the gates of Auschwitz-Birkenau were closed behind them, when those who were selected were selected?

Or perhaps this was the prayer that they cried out - and He didn't respond?

The *Aneynu* is recited by the *chazan* in his repetition, but not by the congregation when they pray alone, in silence. Perhaps a man praying alone couldn't sustain a prayer like this, would break in saying it, without a congregation to support him. For their turn the congregation must wait till *Minchah*, afternoon prayers? Why? Not my reason, this; but from the Rabbis: because who can say that we'll be strong enough to endure the fast till evening, and thus be qualified to say the prayer?

"*Al taster paneycha mi-meynu* - do not hide Your face from us" is the obverse of the *Yevarechecha*, the Priestly Blessing, where God "turns his face to shine on us." The concept of "*histir panav*", as we have seen previously, is drawn from this. When God turns His face to shine on us, we are blessed, and only good can happen; but when He turns his face aside, we may not actually be cursed, but the possibility of woe is opened. The theological equivalent of seasonal affective disorder.

The quote in mid-prayer is from Isaiah 65:24. It's an epitome of the eighth and highest level of charity - God will answer our call even before we've uttered it.

The Eighth Blessing: *Rephu'a* - Healing

"*Repha'eynu Adonay ve-neraphey, hoshi'eynu ve-nivasheyah, ki tehilateynu atah, ve-ha'aleh rephu'a shelema le-chol makoteynu, ki el melech rophey ne'eman ve-rachaman atah. Baruch atah Adonay, rophey choley amo Yisra'el.*"

"Heal us O Lord and we shall be healed, save us and we shall be saved, for you are our praise."

The lines are from Jeremiah 17:14. They imply a measure of certainty that is so strong as to be ineffable. "Grant perfect healing to all our ailments…"

Perfect healing! Ah, if only that were truly possible…

Am I wrong to detect another pun in the writing of this prayer. It isn't after all either necessary or even logical to describe God in this context as "the king, the faithful and compassionate healer." King, yes. Compassionate healer - undoubtedly. But why faithful - I mean, why faithful in this context? The Hebrew word is spelt *Nun-Aleph-Mem-Nun*, but there's another word *Na'aman*, pronounced precisely the same, but spelt *Nun-Ayin-Mem-Nun* - the name of a commander of the Syrian army in the days of King ben-Hadad II (2 King 5), who contracted a virulent strain of leprosy that none could cure. Na'aman's wife had a Hebrew slave, who told him of the miracles of the prophet Elishah, and though the Hebrews were the enemy, Na'aman went to see Elishah, wasn't admitted, but received instruction to bathe seven times in the river Jordan, and doing so was cured. *Rephu'a shelema* indeed - perfect healing. In the realms of the miraculous, it apparently is possible.

At this point, rare indeed in Jewish prayer, the insertion of a personal request is permitted (by the Rabbis, I mean – who knows what God does or does not permit?), though not for oneself, even if it's in one's own name that it's made - a private prayer for a sick friend or relative "among the other sick of Israel". And because it's a private prayer, and because it's inserted into the *Amidah* and not part of the text, we take the advice of King David in Psalm 116:16, "I am Your servant, the son of Your handmaiden", and we pray not in the father's name but in the mother's, as it might be Yitschak ben Sarah and not Yitschak ben Avraham.

Which prayers? This is where *Rabban* Joshua's ambitions for spontaneity find form. Any prayer we may care to invent, in any language. But there are also the prescribed prayers. For example: "*Vi-yehi ratson mi-lephanecha, Adonay va-elohey avotay, she-tishlach meherah rephu'a shelemah min-ha-shamayim. Rephu'at ha-nephesh u-rephu'at ha-guph. La-choleh*…insert the name of the sick person…*be-toch she'ar choley Yisra'el.*"

"May it be Your will, Lord our God and God of our fathers, to send speedily from heaven a full recovery, a healing of the soul and of the body, to the sick…among all the other sick of Israel."

✡

The Ninth Blessing: *Birkat ha-Shanim* - The Blessing of the Years

"Barech aleynu Adonay eloheynu et ha-shanah ha-zot ve-et kol miney tevu'atah le-tovah ve-ten berachah [ve-ten tal u-matar livracha] al peney ha-adamah, ve-sabeynu mi-tuvecha, u-varech shenateynu ka-shanim ha-tovot. Baruch atah Adonay mevarech ha-shanim."

Two variants, depending on the time of year. From the 3rd day of *Pesach* until the 7th of *Cheshvan*, the opening phrase "Bless on our behalf O Lord our God, this year and its harvest for the best" is followed by "and give a blessing on the face of the earth" (the sun god of *Yevarechecha* again); but from the 8th of *Cheshvan* until the onset of *Pesach*, as the prayers for rain are introduced into the opening of the *Amidah*, so too we say here "and give dew and rain for a blessing on the face of the earth"; continuing in both variations with "and satisfy us from Your bounty, and bless our year like the best years. Blessed are You, O Lord, who blesses the years."

Outside Israel, where rain in early autumn is essential, the 7th of *Cheshvan* date may be delayed. Pragmatism. Always pragmatism to balance the pedantry.

The rain, of course, was everything, back then. Life and death, reward and punishment. In the closing paragraph of the *Shema* it has been stated unequivocally: keep the commandments and I will send the rain, break them and I will withhold it. This is the nature of the covenant.

✡

The Tenth Blessing: *Kivutz Gliyot* - The Ingathering of the Exiles

"Teka be-shophar gadol le-cheruteynu, ve-sa nes le-kabets galuyoteynu, ve-kabtseynu yachad mey-arba kanphot ha-arets. Baruch atah Adonay, mekabets nidchey amo Yisra'el."

"Sound the great *shofar* for our freedom, raise the banner to gather our exiles, and gather us together from the four corners of the earth. Blessed are You, O Lord, who gathers in the dispersed of His people Israel."

One of several prayers whose meaning has been changed by the founding of the modern State of Israel. For two millennia it represented the most earnest of all our cries of hope-in-desperation, a dream locked in the prison of the future, openable only by the coming of the Messiah. Sung originally by Isaiah (11:12), it belonged in the realm of prophecy: "And it shall come to pass in that day…He shall set up a banner for the nations, He shall assemble the outcasts of Israel, and gather together the dispossessed of Judah from the four corners of the earth."

And then it happened. Without requiring a Messiah, unless you regard Herzl or Ben Gurion. The banner was set up, blue and white stripes with a Star of David in its midriff. The outcasts assembled at every port and displaced persons' camp. The dispersed were gathered in - those, anyway, who were able to, those who weren't refused, those who didn't prefer the Diaspora, just as so many in Ezra's time had preferred to remain in Babylon.

Now, today, to recite these lines is either an anachronism or an ecstasy. An ecstasy for those who sing the words in Israel – though also an absurdity, to ask for what you have already received. An anachronism for those who do not wish the prayer to be answered; and to recite an anachronism with *kavanah* but without sincerity is the worst form of hypocrisy: a sin.

"Sound the great *shofar* for our freedom, raise the banner to gather our exiles, and gather us together from the four corners of the earth. Blessed are You, O Lord, who gathers in the dispersed of his people Israel."

Only, as two-thirds of world Jewry insist, not in my case, thank you very much.

✡

The Eleventh Blessing: *Din* - Justice

"Hashivah shophtim ke-va-rishonah, ve-yo'atseynu ke-va-tehilah, ve-haser mimeynu yagon va-anachah, u-meloch aleynu atah Adonay levadcha be-chesed u-ve-rachamim, ve-tsadkeynu ba-mishpat. Baruch atah Adonay, melech ohev tsedakah u-mishpat."

The great beauty of the Messiah - the idea of the Messiah - lies precisely in the fact that we know that he will never come, thank God. Human perfection, after all, is a truly desolating possibility, because to perfect something is, by definition, to bring it to an end. So we can place in him the full piety of our aspirations, knowing they'll never have to be fulfilled. The idealism of the Messiah is the idealism of permanent postponement. Mañana, as they say in Spanish. Like the figures in those paintings by the Douanier Rousseau, in which time appears to have been suspended, the lion will never lie down with the lamb, the outcasts will never be fully gathered in, the Shrine of Omar will never give way to the Restored

Temple, the sacrifices at the altar will never be reinstituted, the walls of Jerusalem will remain unbuilt, and we will never have to replace our pious dreams and hypocritic hopes with the reality of fulfilment. To wait for the Messiah is to abrogate all human responsibility in the living now. And as Hillel rightly pondered, "if not now, when…"

But the idealism remains valid. And the striving even more so. We set out to climb to the summit of the mountain, but the mountain is summitless, and still we go on hammering in our pegs. The idealism of the Messiah is the idealism of the Immaculate Failure.

And still we go on waiting, praying for what we don't really want. "Restore our Judges as in ancient times…" - what, government by Deborah and Gideon in place of the democracy of the *Knesset*? No, thank you. "…and our counsellors as at the outset" (the phrases are from Isaiah 1:26). The Rabbis teach that the Messiah will re-establish the *Sanhedrin* as a prologue to redemption, but the Rabbis also teach that the Messiah will only come when all the world has returned to faith and obedience - so redemption is also a prologue to redemption. This is a most convenient paradox. The Messiah will only come when men have created the right conditions for His coming. The Messiah will only come when He's already here. The Messiah will only come when He's no longer needed.

"Remove from us all sorrow and sighing, and reign over us - You, Lord, alone - with kindness and compassion, and justify us through judgement. Blessed are You, O Lord and king, who loves righteousness and judgement."

But who doesn't always dispense it - viz Abraham at Gomorrah, or Job, or Jonah.

The notion of justifying the judgement lies at the core of the mourning rituals, and especially of the mourner's *Kaddish*. I have spoken about this in relation to the Rabbis' *Kaddish*, and will have more to say at the appropriate moment.

During the Ten Days of Awe, say "O Lord the King of Judgement" in the closing blessing, in place of the simple "O Lord and King". About this notion I have nothing to say, except to note that if God is our King, and not simply our God, then our covenant makes us His servants, not His stewards; His vassals, not His holy people.

✡

The Twelfth Blessing: *Ve-la-malshinim* - Against Heretics

"Ve-la-malshinim al tehi tikvah, ve-chol ha-rishah ke-rega toved, ve-chol oyevecha meherah yikareytu, ve-ha-zedim meherah te'aker u-teshaber u-temager ve-tachniya bimheyrah ve-yameynu. Baruch atah Adonay, shover oyevim u-machniya zedim."

I quote the Art Scroll commentary on this blessing:

"Chronologically, this is the 19th blessing of *Shemoneh Esreh*; it was instituted in Yavneh, during the tenure of Rabban Gamliel II as *Nasi* of Israel, some time after the destruction of the 2nd Temple. The blessing was composed in response to the threats of such heretical Jewish sects as the Sadducees, Boethusians, Essenes and early Christians…"

Am I reading that correctly? The Sadducees an "heretical sect"! The scions of Tsadok the Priest, the first High Priest of the First Temple, who sustained the Temple cult for a thousand years and saw it end in fire and destruction under Titus and Vespasian! In this manner do revolutions take place - quietly and surreptitiously, by a word here, a paragraph there, slipped unnoticed into an obscure commentary on the texts - when thousand-year traditions are declared heresies by the rulers of the new order. The High Priest is defunct, Long Live the Chief Rabbi! No wonder Akiva refused to recite the blessing. Though this wasn't his only reason.

"And for slanderers let there be no hope, and may all wickedness perish in an instant, and may all Your enemies be cut down speedily. May You speedily uproot, smash, cast down and humble the wanton sinner - speedily, in our days. Blessed are You, Lord, who breaks His enemies and humbles wanton sinners."

The very tone of the blessing is hideously inappropriate. Harsh, bitter, callous, uncompassionate, it's a blessing over hatred, and quite incongruous to make apotheosis of such hatred, such total unforgivingness, by making of it an attribute of God. It's a blessing I have never uttered, will never utter. Rather I would have us say, in the humanitarian tone which better characterises Judaism:

"Let there be hope, even for the slanderers; let there be space and time for the wicked to understand their wickedness, and repent of it, and expiate it; let all Your enemies be offered the hand of friendship, but cut them down speedily if they insist on war. May You teach tolerance, understanding and compassion, and bring the sinners back to righteousness – myself amongst them. Blessed are You, O Lord, whose goodness encompasses everyone."

But this is not, alas, the prayer that's prayed. Instead the exaltation of hatred encourages and permits hatred. And in so doing ignores the first principles of Jewish Law: remember you were slaves in Egypt; love your neighbour as yourself, *ka ger ha ezrach*. Yea, even the Sadducees, even Reform and Reconstructionist Jews, even those who have married out or protest against hypocrisy, even those who are myrtles among reeds. And yes, even the Palestinians.

There is, besides, an immense irony here, as the next verse makes clear. For the word Sadducees, in Hebrew, is *Tsadokim*, from the root *Tsadak* meaning Righteousness or Justice. The etymology itself declares the Sadducees to have been righteous men, not heretics.

Art Scroll's commentary is based on *Berachot* 28b. However *Yerushalmi Berachot* 2:4 includes this blessing as one of Ezra's original verses, some six hundred years earlier, with a simple variation of the opening phrase. In the Ezra version it read "*al ha-minim*", again a curse upon heretics, the heretics in question being, at that time, the Aramaic-speaking Samaritans who had set up their rival "Judaism" on Mounts Ebal and Gerizim, the twin peaks of Shechem, today's Nablus. Only later, when the Samaritans had disappeared into the oblivion of history, was the verse re-predicated as a curse against the Sadducees and others, and this something in the manner of the Council of Ephesus three hundred years later, when the Christian church fathers sought to establish a universal orthodoxy for their new religion, and did so in the traditional manner of despots and fundamentalists - by anathematising all who disagreed with them. The "heretics" and "heterodox" of Gamliel's time were those who resisted the new-claimed authority of the Rabbis, or who wished to develop the religion somewhat differently in the wake of the destruction of the Temple (and it should never be forgotten that the new religion of Christianity grew up in Israel, rooted in mainstream Judaism, at exactly the same moment as the "new" religion of *Talmudic* Judaism - why, both even quote the same Scriptures, the same Rabbis, as their justifying sources). The Sadducees continued to insist upon the predominance of *Torah* over *Talmud*, Priest over Rabbi, even in the wake of the destruction of the Temple. The Boethusians weren't so different from the Sadducees in their religious outlook, though they weren't aristocrats as were the Sadducees; but they also carried the stigma of having supported the Herodians rather than the Hasmoneans - an unforgivable sin - and were regarded by the Pharisees as cynics and materialists. The early Christians were without exception Messianic Jews who believed with complete faith that the End of Days had come. As to the Essenes, they practiced a form of Judaism which nobody could regard as normative, isolating themselves away in monastic communities, adopting ideas out of

Zoroastrianism, practising such strange rites as baptism. But it was the Pharisaic Rabbis who emerged victorious, at least for now, at least amongst Jewry. So the heretics had to be denounced. So "*ve la-malshinim*" became the norm. It isn't a terribly laudable moment in the development of our liturgy.

✡

The Thirteenth Blessing: *Al ha-Tsaddikim* - For the Righteous

Whereas, by contrast, the virtues of the godly Pharisees are to be extolled, revered, and set upon a pedestal as a role-model. The four categories of the righteous, who constitute the leadership of Israel, are all Pharisaic. The *tsaddikim*, not to be confused with the *Tsadokim* though the root-word is identical; these are the thirty-six just men upon whom the harmony of the Universe depends, and whose own righteousness is defined by their strict observance of the commandments in accordance with *Talmudic* interpretation. The devout, the *hasidim* or pious ones who dedicate their lives to prayer and study. The *zekenim*, the elders, who were once the elders of the twelve tribes, but now replaced by the elders of the Great Assembly, Rabbis on the thrones of Sheikhs. And last the *sopherim*, the scholars, who write the *Torah* scrolls and study it, until they too have obtained *smicha*. As the Sadducees were anathematised in the previous blessing, so in this verse are the Pharisees glorified, and their *coup d'état* enshrined in Law. He who recites the prayer perforce endorses the *coup d'état*, recognises, despite the aspirations expressed in the fourteenth and fifteenth blessings, that the era of the Temple and the Priests is past and will never be restored, despite the prayers to God to do so. (And he who does not say the prayer perforce does not endorse the *coup d'état*, but that isn't the same as overturning it: there is no prayer for overturning it: there is no overturning it.)

Interesting to note the inclusion of the "*gerey ha-tsedek* - the righteous converts". Until Rabbinic times there was neither conversion nor any necessity for conversion. Neither Bilhah nor Zilpah, Jacob's wives, nor Asnat, Joseph's wife, converted, yet their sons founded tribes whose status in the Israelite confederacy was never questioned: indeed Ephraim and Menasheh's grandfather was the High Priest of Akhenaten in the sun-city of On. Ruth, the grandmother of King David and progenitress of the Messiah, did no more than state, "Where you go I will go, your God will be my God, your people my people", and was accepted. But the Rabbis required more than this. Commitment, conviction, avowal weren't enough. The Rabbis required submission to their authority. So began the process of selective inclusion and exclusion which has blighted Judaism to this day.

And once again, what harshness in the language - I see that I shall have to write the words down after all.

"Al ha-tsaddikim ve-al ha-chasidim ve-al zikney amcha beyt Yisra'el, ve-al pleytat sophreyhem, ve-al gerey ha-tsedek ve-aleynu, yehemu rachameycha Adonay eloheynu, ve-ten sachar tov le-chol ha-bot'chim be-shimcha be-emet, ve-sim chelkeynu imahem le-olam, ve-lo nevosh, ki vecha batachnu. Baruch atah Adonay mishan u-mivtach la-tsaddikim."

"On the righteous, on the devout, on the elders of Your people the family of Israel, on the remnant of their scholars, on the righteous converts and on ourselves…"

After enunciating who the righteous are (any choice is inherently a rejection of the alternatives; by the same principle a list of the righteous is implicitly a list by default of the unrighteous), the blessing is, "May Your compassion be aroused, O Lord our God, and may You give goodly reward to all who sincerely believe in Your name…"

What, do all the others insincerely believe? Are they unrighteous because insincere, or vice-versa? Not only are they unrighteous, they're also contemptible. This is the language of the Yezhov Terror and the Salem witch-trials.

"Put our lot with them [the righteous] forever, and we will not feel ashamed…"

Whereas they, the unrighteous, should feel ashamed. This is preposterous!

"For we trust in You. Blessed are You, O Lord, Mainstay and Assurance of the Righteous."

Such grandiloquence! Such self-glorification! God, it would seem, has been expropriated by the Rabbis. Those who do not bow down to their authority are denied God's light. One reads this, listening over one's shoulder for the imminent arrival of some Jewish Inquisition.

I regard it as one of the grave errors of Judaism that, in allowing the Rabbis to claim the inheritance of *smicha* from Moses (*Pirkei Avot* 1:1), we have lost any distinction between the legislature and the judiciary. This is the distinction, as all political philosophers agree, that keeps democracy safe against the tyranny of totalitarianism.

✡

The Fourteenth Blessing: *Binyan Yerushalayim* - the Building of Jerusalem

"*Ve-li-Yerushalayim ircha be-rachamim tashuv, ve-tishkon betochah ka-asher dibarta, u-veneh otah be-karov be-yameynu binyan olam, ve-chiseh David meherah le-tochah tachin. Baruch atah Adonay, boneh Yerushalayim.*"

"And to Jerusalem, Your city, may You return in compassion, and may You rest within it, as You have spoken. May You rebuild it soon, in our days, as an eternal structure, and may You speedily re-establish the Throne of David within it. Blessed are You, Lord, the Builder of Jerusalem."

Yerushalmi Yoma 7:1 notes that "*ve-li-Yerushalayim*" used to end, in Temple times, with the words "who dwells in Jerusalem", from which we can surely deduce that other parts of the paragraph must also have been different, for there would have been no sense in a prayer for the rebuilding of a city that still stood in all its golden glory; "who dwells" became "who builds" only after the destruction. And needs to become "who dwells" again, now that we have re-established the capital of Judaism in the holy city.

The prayer refers to the annihilation of the city by General Titus, eye-witnessed in Josephus's account:

"Soldiers were piling fire against the gates. The silver melted and ran, quickly exposing the woodwork to the flames, which were carried from there in a solid wall and fastened onto the colonnades. When the Jews saw the ring of fire they lost all power of mind and body; such was their consternation that not a finger was raised to keep out or quench the flames; they stood looking on in utter helplessness…All that day and the following night the flames were in possession; the colonnades could not be fired all at once but only bit by bit."

Thus Josephus' description of the burning of the Temple ("The Jewish War" 6:230). It wasn't Titus' wish, however - or so his long-time friend and now dependent Josephus would maintain.

"The next day Titus ordered a section of his army to put out the fire and to make a road close to the gates for the easier ascent of the legions. Then he summoned a council of war…some insisted that they should enforce the law of war, that there would be continual revolts while the Temple remained as a rallying-point for Jews all over the world. Others argued that if the Jews evacuated it and no armed man was allowed on it, it should be spared, but that if they climbed on it for military purposes it should be burnt down, for then it would be a fortress not a sanctuary, and no impiety would fall upon the Romans but on those who forced their hands. Titus replied that even if the Jews did climb on it for military purposes he would not make war on inanimate objects instead of men, and under no circumstances would he burn down a work of art; it was the Romans who would lose thereby, just as their empire would gain an ornament if it was preserved."

Titus retired to Antonia after another skirmish at the East Gate, and while he was resting in his tent a runner brought the news that the Temple had again been set on fire. "He leapt up as he was and ran to the Sanctuary to put out the blaze…Caesar shouted and waved to the combatants to put out the fire, but his shouts went unheard as their ears were deafened by a greater din, and his hand-signals went unheeded amidst the distractions of battle and bloodshed. As the legions charged in, neither persuasion nor threat could check their impetuosity; passion alone was in command…As they neared the Sanctuary they pretended not even to hear Caesar's commands and urged the men in front to throw in more firebrands. The partisans were no longer in a position to help; everywhere was slaughter and flight. Most of the victims were peaceful citizens, weak and unarmed, butchered wherever they were caught. Round the Altar the heap of corpses grew higher and higher, while down the Sanctuary steps poured a river of blood and the bodies of those killed at the top slithered to the bottom. The soldiers were like men possessed and there was no holding them, nor was there any arguing with the fire. Caesar therefore led his staff inside the building and viewed the Holy Place of the Sanctuary with its furnishings, which went far beyond the accounts circulating in foreign countries, and fully justified their splendid reputation..."

The Temple, stripped of all its spiritual dimensions, reduced only to a place of sacrifice. A *kurban*, a burnt offering, at that.

"The flames were not yet effecting an entry from any direction but were feeding on the chambers built round the Sanctuary; so realising that there was still time to save the glorious edifice, Titus dashed out and by personal efforts strove to persuade his men to put out the fire…Then, from within, a flame suddenly shot up, Caesar and his staff withdrew, and those outside were free to start what fires they liked. Thus the Sanctuary in defiance of Caesar's wishes was set on fire."

The date of the fire was the 9th *Av*, "the very month and day," Josephus continues, "which centuries before had seen the Sanctuary burnt by the Babylonians." And then, because sometimes statistics can be terribly poignant, "from its first foundation by King Solomon to its present destruction, which occurred in the second year of Vespasian's reign, was a period of 1,130 years, 7 months, 15 days; from its rebuilding in the second year of King Cyrus, for which Haggai was responsible, to its capture under

Vespasian was 639 years, 45 days."

As in so very much else, including quite probably this eye-witness description and the role of Caesar in the holocaust, Josephus was simply wrong. Cyrus came to the throne in 559, so if the Temple was rebuilt in his second year, as Ezra 6 affirms, that would make 628. The first figure should be 1,041 years, not 1,130. The reference to Haggai is also poignant. Haggai, with his fellow-prophet Zechariah, was crucial in getting the Second Temple finished, but in his prophetic book he also foresaw its destruction, "and the horses and riders shall go down, every one by the sword of his fellow." (2:22)

The burning of the Temple wasn't the end of Jerusalem however. It would take several weeks before the whole city fell, and several months before the decision was reached to torch the city, to obliterate it for all time and to build upon its ruins a new city, a Roman city, *Aeolia Capitolina*. But when the final destruction came it truly was final. Those who were of any use were taken as slaves to Rome where, *inter alia*, they would build the Coliseum. As to the Jewish God, His abstract parts were rescued by Yochanan ben Zakkai and taken to Yavneh to be preserved and hopefully revived. His physical parts, or those anyway that had survived the pyre of the Altar, became the property of Rome. The Emperor Vespasian, Titus' father, "made up his mind to build a Temple of Peace. This was completed with remarkable speed and surpassed all human imagination. Not only did he have unlimited wealth at his disposal; he also adorned it with paintings and statues by the greatest of the old masters. In fact, in that Temple were collected and deposited all those works that men had hitherto travelled over the whole world to see, longing to set eyes on them even when scattered in different lands. There too he laid up the golden vessels from the Temple of the Jews, for he prided himself on them; but their Law and the crimson curtains of the Inner Sanctuary he ordered to be deposited in the Palace for safe-keeping." (Josephus, *ibid*, 7:162)

We have to wonder how those crimson curtains survived what has just been described as a total conflagration. Probably some Roman soldiers looted them.

There's huge irony in this too. David's motivation in purchasing the threshing-floor of Ornah was precisely the same as Vespasian's - a man of war wishing to clean his hands through the dedication of a Temple of Peace. David gave his the same name - *Yerushalayim* means City of Peace. And the description of the international marvel - was this not precisely what was always said of Solomon's achievement, when he completed his father's work?

✡

The prayer recalls the destruction, but what the prayer calls for is reconstruction, and once again we're in the realms of insincerity. Since 1948, especially since 1967, Jerusalem has indeed been rebuilt, in all possible glory and under the strictest architectural controls and regulations. Nothing may go up that isn't clad in Jerusalem stone, the stone of the Temple - not stone from the actual Temple obviously, but that same soft, yellow limestone filled with light that Solomon quarried from the darkness underneath Jerusalem to complete his father's vision.

But as for the "*binyan olam*" - meaning the Temple - and the "throne of David". No sign of them as yet, nor any likelihood that a contemporary Haggai or Zechariah could exert sufficient moral pressure. Do we even want to build it, to restore it, to go backwards? I think not. And if not, then why pray for it? Like "*kivutz gliyot*", the prayer for the ingathering of the exiles, is there not something deeply lacking in sincerity, something deeply insulting to the divinity, to petition Him for something that we truly do not want?

I jest not when I ask if rebuilding is what Jews really want. There are strong political arguments against it of course, though like all political arguments these could be got around if the politicians saw self-interest in doing so. There's what I call the Mount Herzl option - the development of a modern Temple site which wouldn't necessarily return to the Mosaic but would make sense of Judaism in the twenty-first century, and give it back its centrifugal point: on Mount Herzl, because there's space, because that's where Theodor Herzl, the founder of modern political Zionism, is buried, and that too is where the Holocaust Memorial *Yad va-Shem* is situated, the catalytic incident that enabled modern Israel to become founded.

This would be *a* Temple, but it wouldn't be *the* Temple, which could only be rebuilt on its original site, and cannot be, because the holiest of Moslem shrines, not the Shrine of Omar but the *El-Axar* mosque, occupy the site. And there are other factors mitigating against reconstruction. The Temple cannot be rebuilt in our days because:

* the genealogical purity of the *Cohanim* cannot be verified
* the precise site of the Altar cannot be located
* the fabrics and dyes for the priestly garments are unavailable
* the method for making the breastplate is lost

But these aren't really arguments, they're merely prevarications and procrastinations. The genealogical purity of the *Cohanim* could perfectly well be verified by DNA; some tests have actually been carried out, and most Ashkenazi *Cohanim* turn out not to be genuine descendants, unlike the Lemba tribe in southern Zimbabwe, almost all of whom unquestionably are. The precise location of the Altar is irrelevant, since Mosaic Law doesn't stipulate its exact position; and anyway the archaeologists know almost to the millimetre where it was probably located. A new method for making the breastplate could perfectly well be modelled on the original. And as to the fabrics and dyes for the priestly garments being unavailable; this is true; but nothing in *Torah* requires specific materials, only specific colours, and these can be manufactured, even using natural products; and besides they were unavailable when Moses gave instructions for them, so use different fabrics, different dyes. Jewish law states clearly that a new place of worship can define its own customs and its own practices, so why not the Third Temple too? With or without sacrifices.

No, the truth is that the Rabbis don't want the rebuilt Temple, and not because the world wouldn't tolerate the sacrificial rites, but mostly because it would signify the fulfilment of the historic task of Yochanan ben Zakkai, the sunset of the era of the substitute; the end, not of the role of the Rabbis, who will always be needed, but of their rule. It would signify, that is, the democratisation of Judaism, the separation, at last, of the legislature from the judiciary, and no one who has that much power will ever volunteer to give it up. When Yochanan ben Zakkai established *Talmudic* Judaism, he did so, as I have repeated *ad nauseam* in this essay, quite specifically as a "substitute" for the lost Temple. If the star player is fit again, what need for the substitute? The Rabbis tells us that the Temple will only be built when the Messiah comes, but the truth is, and for the same reasons, the Rabbis don't really want the Messiah either.

✡

The Fifteenth Blessing: *Malchut Beit David* - The Kingdom of the House of David

"*Et tsemach David avdecha meherah tatsmi'ach, ve-karno tarum bi-yeshu'atecha, ki li-shu'atcha kivinu kol ha-yom. Baruch atah Adonay, matsmi'ach keren yeshu'ah.*"

"May you speedily cause the offspring of Your servant David to flourish, and enhance his pride through Your salvation, for we hope for Your salvation all day long. Blessed are You, Lord, who causes the pride of salvation to flourish."

The prophet Zechariah (6:12) spoke of "*Tsemach David*", the flourishing or sprouting of a plant from the root of David "who shall grow up out of his place, and he shall build the Temple of the Lord". (If my theories about David as a local variant of the ever-dying ever-reborn beloved son are correct, then this makes a fascinating allusion to his status as a vegetation god.) What Zechariah is alluding to, and probably intentionally, is Isaiah's prophecy of the "scion of the rod of Jesse". But the prophetic statement was always meant politically, not spiritually, a Hebrew Jacobitism, an attempt to restore a dynasty to its rightful throne. It meant an actual man, whose genealogy was provable, and not a mere sign, a mysticism, an emanation of the heavens.

So the previous blessing also makes clear, but here it's the metaphorical heir of David that's intended, the one substituted in hopelessness as exile grew more long and deep. This is no longer the earthly "anointed king", equivalent of the "crowned monarch", but a bringer of redemption and salvation at some future date. Messianism thus becomes a philosophy of desperation, of reality-evasion, precisely because it has given up false hope for today, inaction now, in favour of an unrealisable dream of tomorrow. The failure is no longer immaculate. "We hope for Your salvation all day long." Yes, but we hope against hope, because we don't expect to receive it. At least, not until the Messiah comes.

"Enhance his pride through Your salvation" does not, at first reading, appear to mean anything. The Hebrew gives "*ve-karno tarum bi-yeshu'atecha*" - a phrase that drives me back to my etymological dictionaries, largely because I'm sure I know the meanings of "*keren*", and pride isn't one of them. "*Keren* - a horn, as of an ox, a goat or a ram. A musical instrument made from animal horn." Yes, this is what I already knew. "*Karnayim ha-mizbeyach* - the horns of the altar." Literal horns, on Canaanite altars; but the Israelite ones appear to have been simply raised corners, rectangled off - it was these horns that a refugee would clutch to claim asylum. "*Karan* - to shine or radiate" - an expression used only once in Scripture, in the Book of Exodus, as a descriptor of the face of Moses after he had encountered God; presumably a poetic figure of speech, to convey the glow, the radiance, the aureole of sanctity that was glowing from his face. It was from this usage that later Hebrew adapted "*karnayim*" to mean lightning flashes (c.f. Habbakuk 3:4); from here too that mediaeval Christian art sourced its endless portraits of Moses as a horned devil. Then is its use here also perhaps intended metaphorically?

Jeremiah 48:25 uses "*keren*" metaphorically - "the horn of Moab is broken" - to signify strength or power, deriving the image from the beast which grew the horn. And in the Psalms: our prayer speaks of David after all, so where better to seek this particular trope? Psalm 75:11 has "All the horns of the wicked will I cut off, but the horns of the righteous shall be exalted." (In mediaeval England, to say that a man had horns was to declare him a cuckold; whence the puerile gesture still in vogue today, of placing the thumbs against the forehead, and twirling the fingers.) Psalm 89:18 has "For Thou art the glory of their strength, and in Your favour shall our horn be exalted." Psalm 92:11 has "But my horn shall You exalt like the horn of the unicorn." There are many, many more occurrences, and in every one the same intent - not pride, not honour, which is the Revised Singer's translation, but power, strength, and of the political variety. But before we can correct the translation, and with the translation catch up the original intention, there's one more fact to add.

Originally the blessing for Jerusalem and this one for David were a single blessing. It was only when "*al ha-minim*" was suspended, leaving the *Shemoneh Esreh* a verse short, that this was split into the two that we still have today; and it remained split when "*ve la-malshinim*" was instituted. But read it again as one prayer, and it's quite clearly a call, not for mystic salvation in some implausible future, but for the rebuilding of Jerusalem and the restoration of the Davidic dynasty – now.

"May You speedily cause the offspring of Your servant David to flourish, and increase his strength through Your salvation, for we hope for Your salvation all day long. Blessed are You, Lord, who causes the strength of salvation to flourish."

This, I believe, a more honest translation.

A political, then, not a spiritual prayer. Then perhaps my earlier remark, that "he who doesn't say the prayer perforce doesn't endorse the *coup d'état*, but that isn't the same as overturning it: there is no prayer for overturning it: there is no overturning it", isn't so certain after all. Perhaps this is that prayer.

✡

The Sixteenth Blessing: *Kabbalat Tefillah* - The Acceptance of Prayer

"*Shema koleynu Adonay eloheynu, chus ve-rachem aleynu, ve-kabel be-rachamim u-ve-ratson et tefillateynu, ki el shomeya tefillot ve-tachanunim atah, u-mi-lephaneycha makheynu reykam, al teshiveynu, ki atah shomeya tefillat amcha Yisra'el be-rachamim. Baruch atah Adonay, shomeya tefillah.*"

"Hear our voice, O Lord our God, pity and be compassionate to us and accept, with favour and compassion, this our prayer, for You are a God who listens to prayers and pays heed to supplications. O our king, do not turn us away from You empty-handed, but hear the prayer of Your people Israel with compassion. Blessed are You, Lord, who pays heed to prayer."

That we don't really expect either of the two immediately previous prayers to be fulfilled is confirmed by the terms of this blessing over prayer itself. Why else would we beg God "not to turn us away empty-handed" if we didn't anticipate precisely that? Desperation has taken root, and starved hope of nitrogen. The political hope of *Binyan Yerushalayim* and *Malchut Beit David* proved vain and became transformed into the spiritual, the mystical, the eschatological hope of the Messiah. Vain this hope also: a fantasy rather. And so we cry out, negative, doom-laden, dejected, Job-like, hopeless, "Hear our voice, O Lord our God" - as if shouting back against the angels as they open the *Shema*, the "Hear O Israel" - "pity, and be compassionate to us, and accept with favour and compassion this our prayer, for You are a God who listens to prayers and pays heed to supplications."

But why should He hear such a prayer with pity and compassion? I imagine, rather, that such a prayer would make God angry. "Why are you waiting for an imaginary Messiah? Have I not said that He will only come when you have created the right conditions? Then act now, create those conditions. Have I not, at the Creation, given you dominion over the earth, told you to subdue it and conquer it and have dominion over it? Why are you praying to be given what you already have? Did Joshua seize and build the land, or pray for it - Joshua whose own name means 'salvation'? You have the land, the city, the government, the law - why are you sitting in sackcloth and ashes bemoaning the natural death of the castor oil plant that can no longer give you succour, rejecting what you have already in order to ask to be given it again, and differently? Act now. Finish the building of Jerusalem. Erect the Temple if indeed you want a Temple. Put horns on the four corners of the Knesset. Make Israel a light unto the nations. No pity. No compassion. Get out of your self-inflicted darkness. Repair the world yourselves. Live."

Shema Koleynu has a second level though, a second purpose; and isn't merely a sequitur of the Davidic blessings. Here too may be inserted a personal petition, for livelihood or for forgiveness - inserted after "empty-handed" during the silent *Amidah*. The form of such a petition is irrelevant; indeed the Rabbis encourage personalisation, and "*ya'arot dvash*" affirms that the feelings and devotion of the petitioner are decisive. A poem then, a scream, a blank stare into the silence, or the recitation of the given words. There is no "I" in prayer, but the "I" is doubled in petition.

For those who lack the skills of extemporisation, there are given words, and they are truly wonderful - one of the great poetic figures of speech in the Talmud. "It is you, O Lord our God, who nourishes, sustains and supports all life - *mi karney re-eymim ad beytsey chinim* - from the horns of the wild ox to the eggs of lice."

So too are the terms of the petition, for it's a hard thing for any man to have to beg, to ask for alms or charity, and for a Jew it's prohibited to grovel. And yet a man may have to ask.

"Provide me with my allotment of bread, and bring food for me and for my family, before I have need of it."

Asking only for the minimum, the fundaments. Asking not after the event, when it would be charity, but beforehand, when it's prevention. Asking when there is no need, but in recognition that there might be need. Asking that it be given "in contentment but not in pain, in a permissible but not a forbidden manner, in honour but not in disgrace". In dignity, in other words. In dignity. And because it's a *mitzvah*. Twice a *mitzvah*, in fact: to give and to receive "for life and for peace, from the flow of blessing and success and from the flow of the heavenly spring" - not asking God to add to the sum of the Universe for the petitioner's sake, but merely to redirect the stream, to redistribute a portion of existing bounty. And why? Because a hungry or a desolate or a destitute or an anguished man cannot properly fulfil the commandments; so it's for God's sake, not for ours, at last. What logic! What reasoning! How irrefutable! "So that I will be able to do Your will and engage in Your *Torah* and fulfil Your commandments." In this prayer, it seems to me, lies proof absolute, that an American Jew cannot also be a Republican, nor an English Jew a Conservative. Not with sincerity to both causes.

Why petition God for daily bread, when men are capable of distributing alms. Because to require charity is inherently undignified, however carefully the giver gives. Because a man sinks lower in indignity when he asks his fellow men. Because God is exalted even higher when it's He who gives. Because beyond destitution there is still worse destitution. So "make me not needful of people's largesse, and may there be fulfilled in me the verse that states (Psalm 145:16), 'You open Your hand and satisfy the desires of every living thing', and also the verse that states (Psalm 55:23), 'Cast your burden upon the Lord and He will support you.'" Lord, give me what I need Yourself, so I do not have to ask my fellow-man, give me the basic rudiments of life, so that I never fall into a state of needing charity. It's only, after all, what God already promised us, in the terms of the Covenant, in the words of the *Shema*. In this prayer, it seems to me, lies proof absolute, that an American Jew cannot also be a Democrat, nor an English Jew a Labourite. Not with sincerity to both causes.

Yet what if our destitution is a consequence of sin, a punishment? Accompanying the petition for livelihood is a petition for forgiveness: "Please O Lord, if I have erred, if I have been iniquitous, if I have wilfully sinned before You, from the day I first existed on this earth until this very day, please Lord act for the sake of Your great name and grant me atonement for my iniquities, my errors and my wilful sins through which I have erred, been iniquitous and wilfully sinned before You, from my youth until this day. And make whole all the names that I have blemished in Your great name."

What, all the sins, from birth until today. All the sins, in one fell sweep of forgiveness. That would be a God of a most almighty magnanimity who could agree to that. The God of Nineveh indeed.

A version of *Shema Koleynu* was recited by the High Priest in the Temple. Although it's nowhere specified in the *Talmud*, it's safe to assume that the prayers would have accompanied the peace offerings and the sin offerings.

The Seventeenth Blessing: *Avodah* - Temple Service

"Retseh Adonay eloheynu be-amcha Yisra'el u-vi-tefillatam, ve-hashev et ha-avodah li-devir beytecha, ve-ishey Yisra'el u-tefillatam be-ahavah tekabel be-ratson, u-tehi le-ratson tamid avodat Yisra'el amecha. Ve-techezeynah ayneynu be-shuvecha le-Tsi'on be-rachamim. Baruch atah Adonay ha-machazir shechinato le-Tsi'on."

The final section of the *Amidah*. We have blessed, prayed, petitioned, nagged, *schmoozed* and even *kvetched*. God is still listening - unlike many in the congregation who can't sustain their concentration quite this far. But God is still listening, and we are grateful to Him for hearing us out, even if it isn't His intention to respond, in word or deed.

And why should He? This isn't even the proper forum for addressing him, nor the proper mode, nor the proper language. And so we ask again, "Look favourably, Lord our God, on us Your people Israel and their prayer, and restore the service to the Holy of Holies of Your Temple", there to "accept with love and favour the fire-offerings of Israel, so the service of Your people Israel may always be favourable to You."

And still, again, why should He - if we don't really mean it?

"May our eyes behold Your return to Zion in compassion. Blessed are You, O Lord, who restores His presence to Zion."

Yes, in 1948. In 1967. Now. Today.

Retseh is modelled on the prayers that took place at the end of the sacrifices. "*Baruch atah Adonay she-ot'cha levadcha be-yira na'avod* - blessed are You, Lord, for You alone do we worship in awe" was the original form of words, and it's still used, on one occasion only, in the festival *Musaph* following the priestly blessing.

Between the fire-offerings and the return to Zion, the *Ya'aleh* is added, on New Moons and the intermediate days of festivals, a great paean of remembrance whose source is Numbers 10:10. "In the day of your gladness and in your solemn days, and in the beginnings of your months, you shall blow the trumpets over your burnt offerings and over the sacrifices for your peace offerings, that they may be to you for a memorial before your God."

We pray that the Temple Service be remembered, by remembering the commandment to remember to pray the Temple Service. What a mass of tautology and irony. And yes, but what a memorial!

"May there rise, come, reach, be noted, be favoured, be heard, be considered and be remembered, the remembrance and consideration of ourselves, of the Messiah son of David Your servant, of Jerusalem the city of Your holiness, of Your entire people the family of Israel - before You, for deliverance, for goodness, for kindness, for grace, for compassion, for life and for peace."

A prayer for everything and everyone, in short. How marvellous!

"Remember us this day, O Lord our God, for goodness, consider us on it for blessing, help us on it for life, and in the matter of salvation and compassion, show pity, be gracious and compassionate with us, and help us, for our eyes are turned to You…" the closing phrase is from Nehemiah 9:31…"because You are God, the gracious and compassionate king."

The trumpets referred to are not the *shofar*, the ram's horn, but an early brass instrument, a kind of primitive trumpet, known as the *chatsotsrah*.

The final verse, "*ve-techezeyna*" was added after the destruction of the Temple as a prayer for re-establishment.

The Eighteenth Blessing: *Hoda'ah* - Thanksgiving

"*Modim anachnu lach she-atah hu Adonay eloheynu ve-elohey avoteynu le-olam va'ed.*

Tsur chayeynu, magen yisheynu, atah hu le-dor va-dor. Nodeh lecha u-nesaper tehilatecha al chayeynu ha-mesurim be-yadecha, ve-al nishmoteynu he-pekudot lach, ve-al nisecha she-be-chol yom imanu, ve-al niphlotecha ve-tovotecha she-be-chol et, erev va-voker ve-tsaharayim. Ha-tov ki lo chalu rachamecha, ve-ha-merachem ki lo tamu chasadecha, me-olam kivinu lach."

"We gratefully thank You, for it is You who are the Lord, our God and the God of our forefathers for all eternity; Rock of our lives, Shield of our salvation are You from generation to generation. We shall thank You and make an inventory of Your praises, for our lives which are committed to Your power, and for our souls which are entrusted to You; for Your miracles that are with us every day, and for Your wonders and favours in every season - every evening, morning and afternoon. You are named the Beneficent One, for Your compassion is never exhausted, and the Compassionate One, for Your kindness never ends - we have put our hope in You for ever."

I find myself wondering if error hasn't again crept in - or were the *Talmudic* Rabbis who composed this prayer blissfully unaware that in "*le-dor ve-dor, nodeh lecha u-nesaper tehilatecha*" they had made an anagram of Psalm 79:13, changing its meaning in the process, and doing so by the simple insertion of a comma and the omission of "*le'olam*"? In the original, "*le-dor ve-dor*" sat between "*nodeh lecha*" and "*u-nesaper tehilatecha*", and not before it, as now. I'm sure they were perfectly aware - for three lines later, defining the Compassionate One, they've made a similar anagram of Lamentations 3:22.

"*Hoda'ah*" mirrors the *Todah* section of the Temple Service that preceded *Pesukei d'Zimrah*. It's a prayer with two versions, recited contrapuntally. The first (transliterated above) is spoken by the congregation during the silent *Amidah*, and then repeated by the *chazan* during *chazarat ha-shats*. The second, transliterated below, is known as the "*Modim d'Rabbanan*", the "Rabbis' Thanksgiving"; it has no part at all in the individual *Amidah*, but is spoken in an undertone while the *chazan* repeats the first *Modim*.

"*Modim anachnu lach, she-atah hu Adonay eloheynu ve-elohey avoteynu, elohey chol bassar, yotsreynu, yotser be-reyshit. Berachot ve-hoda'ot le-shimcha ha-gadol ve-ha-kadosh, al she-hecheyitanu ve-kiyamtanu. Ken techayeynu u-tekaymeynu, ve-te'esoph galuyoteynu le-chatsrot kadshecha, lishmor chukeycha ve-la-asot retsonecha, u-le-avdecha be-levav shalem, al she-anachnu modim lach. Baruch el ha-hoda'ot.*"

"We gratefully thank you, for it is You who are the Lord, our God and God of our forefathers, the God of all flesh, our Maker, the Maker of the Universe. Blessings and thanks are due to Your great and holy name, for

You have given us life and sustained us. So may You continue to give us life and to sustain us, and gather our exiles to the courtyards of Your sanctuary, to observe Your decrees, to do Your will and to serve You wholeheartedly. We thank You for inspiring us to thank You. Blessed is the God of thanksgivings."

Both prayers recall the Covenantal relationship between Man and God, akin to the feudal relationship between a vassal or villein and his liege lord. So we bow at the opening words. So our declaration of thanks becomes a declaration of submissiveness, of acceptance, of resignation.

The second prayer is known as the "*Modim d'Rabbanan*" or "Thanksgiving of the Rabbis", because it combines several prayers by several *Talmudic* Rabbis (*Sotah* 40a); the title is in Aramaic although the prayer itself is in Hebrew. It's not only we poor ignoramuses who must submit to the divine authority, but the Rabbis too, for all that authority has been invested in them in the form of *smicha*. Yet why do we say the *Modim* on their behalf? It's almost as if we are submitting ourselves to their authority through the prayer, since we have already accepted divine authority in the silent first rendition.

But there's another explanation. *Modim* means "to thank", but it also means "to acknowledge", which alters the sense monumentally. To understand the significance of thanksgiving it should be sufficient to look at the words of Psalm 92:2, a Psalm written specifically for the Sabbath day. "It is a good thing to give thanks to the Lord, and to sing praises to His name, O most high one. To show Your lovingkindness in the morning and Your continuing trust in us at night." I'm struck that, once again, the method of praise and thanksgiving advocated in the Psalm isn't the mere recitation of the Psalm, nor the act of solemn prayer inside a house of worship, but "Upon an instrument of ten strings and upon the psaltery, upon the harp with a solemn sound. For You, Lord, have made me glad through Your work, and I will triumph in the works of Your hands."

Sing, sing, dance and make music. Celebration, not solemnity. Noise, not mournful silence and the baritone susurration of muttered private prayer. Even if we can't restore the cult of sacrifice, please o please can we restore the concert of chant and celebration, as they've done in the Reform synagogues.

✡

As so often, certain occasions require special expressions of gratitude. So on *Chanukah* and *Purim* we insert a brief retelling of the historic episodes to accompany thanks for the miracles by which the Almighty delivered us from devastation. The *Chanukah* text includes an allusion to Jeremiah 51:36: "You took up their grievance, judged their claim and avenged their wrong", and a slightly more abstruse allusion to 1 Samuel 19:5 in "for Your people Israel You worked a great victory." The *Purim* text quotes directly from Esther 3:13.

✡

"*Ve-al kulam yitbarach ve-yitromam shimcha malkeynu tamid le-olam va'ed. Ve-chol ha-chayim yoducha (selah), vi-yehalelu et shimcha be-emet, ha-el yishu'ateynu ve-ezrateynu (selah). Baruch atah Adonay, ha-tov shimcha u-lecha no'eh le-hodot.*"

The Thanksgiving concludes with a final blessing, accompanied again by a bowing of the knees. The phrase isn't from the Psalms, though it uses the metric formulation of the Psalms, and the notation "*selah*" to mark a bar or line-ending:

Everything that lives gives You thanks (*selah*)
They will praise Your name sincerely
O God of our salvation and our help (*selah*)
Blessed are You, O Lord Beneficent
To You it behoves us to give thanks

✡

Abudarham

So much laboriously dry scholarship, and suddenly a moment of real excitement - childish excitement, like seeing a favourite film star on the far side of the street. The commentary in the Art Scroll makes passing reference, the mere mentioning of a name, and in parenthesis at that, to Abudarham - to his statement on the double *Modim* that it's acceptable to petition God through an emissary, but that one must deliver one's own gratitude. There is only one significant Abudarham in Jewish history - and yes, I know that virtually nobody in all the world has ever heard of him. But I've heard of him. I've more than heard of him. I spent five years researching and writing an encyclopaedic novel about the relations between the Christians, Jews and Moslems in the Middle Ages, and my central Jewish character, Yakov fils Isaac l'Eveque, is in very large part modelled on Abudarham. And here he is, in real life - or most obscure footnote actually. But right here, and on my side of the street.

Who was he, do I hear you ask? David ben Joseph Abudarham, to render his full name, came from Seville in what was then still Moorish southern Spain (there was actually a previous David ben Joseph Abudarham, insignificant in all regards save only that he was head of the Jewish community in Toledo). In 1340 he wrote a book entitled, simply but logically, "*Sepher Abudarham*", and it was this very book that I am writing now (how nice to have a precedent that helps to justify this book). His *apologia* explains that he'd undertaken it because "the customs connected with prayer have become varied from one country to another, and most of the people do not understand the words of the prayers, nor do they know the correct ritual procedures and the reasons for them." He did, precisely as I have done - he went back to the scriptures, to the *Talmud*, to the *Responsa* of the *ga'onim*, and to the later commentators. He was particularly indebted in his researches to the "*Manhig*" of Abraham ben Natan ha-Yarchi of Lunel, the "*Minhagot*" of Asher ben Saul, the legal *dicta* of Asher ben Yechiel and particularly the "*Turim*" of Jacob ben Asher - some think he may even have been a student of ben Asher. He travelled, extensively, across the Jewish world - a book of this sort is really no different from any other form of travel writing, except that the voyage isn't through a land but through another book. His "*Sepher*" is multitudinous with source material gleaned from Spanish, Provencal, French and Ashkenazi origins, much of which survives only in Abudarham's quoted fragments. He leaned heavily on Sa'adiah's prayer book, as I have leaned heavily on the Art Scroll. He commented in great detail and with many personal asides and meditations on each of the prayers in turn, and traced the different customs in the different communities. He went further too. He included a full commentary on the Passover *Haggadah* (as I have done, elsewhere, on the liturgy for *Yom Kippur*), explored the mathematics of calendar intercalation (a huge issue at the time in the Christian world), made observations about the weekly *Torah* readings and their accompanying *Haphtarot*, even drew up fragments of astronomical tables.

In fact, Abudarham planned but never finished a similar prayer by prayer analysis of the *machzor* for *Yom Kippur*. Though it was written in 1340, the "*Sepher Abudarham*" remained unpublished until the Lisbon edition of 1490. Lord, who has made our destinies so very similar, allow my book to see the light of day more quickly than did that of my more illustrious predecessor.

✡

Birchat ha-Cohanim - The Priestly Blessing

A prayer that isn't recited now, except in Israel, in some Sephardic synagogues, and always on Sabbaths and festivals. Yet it appears in the liturgy for *Shacharit* because God commanded Aaron thus to bless the children of Israel, and the text (Numbers 6:22-27) doesn't specify when.

The ceremony of the blessing of the priests is as ancient as the Temple of Solomon itself. I've already described it earlier in this book, when the *Yevarechecha* was first referred to in the early section of the liturgy known as *Berachot ha-Torah*, the *Torah* Blessings.

The text runs:

Yevarechecha Adonay ve-yishmerecha (ken yehi ratson)
Ya'er Adonay panav eleycha vi-chunecha (ken yehi ratson)
Yisa Adonay panav eleycha ve-yasem lecha shalom (ken yehi ratson)

May the Lord bless you and keep you
(if it be Your will)
May He turn his face to shine on you and be gracious to you
(if it be Your will)
May He turn his face to you and bring you peace
(if it be Your will)

As I've commented before, it's this blessing more than any other that confirms that the Jewish God was once a sun-god, and from this blessing we learn that, if God's face is turned away (*histir panav*), a space of darkness is permitted in which the evil inclination may hold sway.

(It may seem a silly, even a glib and fatuous question, but how do they explain the existence of good and evil in Finland or Alaska? And if a Jew in Rekjavik begins his fast on rising, how does he know to end it if no sunset comes? By the moon, of course. By the moon.)

✡

The full priestly blessing, such as the one offered on *Yom Kippur*, includes an extended congregational supplication, backed in harmony by the *Cohanim* chanting melodically, between each of the three phrases, but where it's said at all in *Shacharit* it will simply be a matter of the *chazan* announcing the prayer with "*Eloheynu…ka-amar*" - "Our God and God of our forefather, bless us with the three-verse blessing in the *Torah* that was written by the hand of Moses Your servant, as it is written…", and then calling each phrase slowly and almost silently, word by word, for the *Cohanim* to echo and the congregation to punctuate with "*ken yehi ratson* - if it be Your will"; and then a final blessing by the reader after the singing of "*sim shalom tovah*".

If *Shacharit* is *davened* in a house of mourning, the Priestly Blessing is omitted. Likewise, if no *Cohanim* are present. But if it is included, and there's only one *Cohen*, the plural *Cohanim* is still employed.

The dispute over whether or not the priests should cover their faces, or the congregation, or whether or not to turn the back, is actually irrelevant, because it isn't the face but the hands that are significant in all of this. Even the *Cohanim* themselves may not look at their own or at each other's hands. As in the ritual bath, their hands are raised to form the letter *sheen* (ש), the initial letter of *El Shaddai*, Abraham's God. The fourth and fifth fingers are clenched together, as are the second and third, with the two pairs held as far apart as possible, and the thumb pressed outwards (it is a matter of much interest, amongst Jews, this capacity to stretch the fingers in this way; a genetic capacity, apparently, which those who can regard as proof and disproof of Judaic longevity and therefore authenticity; those who cannot do it, disagree). The arms are stretched above the head, with the fingers extended, something in the manner of *tsitsit*, as signifiers of the blessing.

✡

Shalom - Peace

"*Sim shalom tovah u-veracha, chen, ve-chesed ve-rachamim, aleynu ve-al kol Yisra'el amecha. Baracheynu avinu, kulano ke-echad be-or paneycha, ki ve-or paneycha natata lanu Adonay eloheynu Torat chayim, ve-ahavat chesed, u-tsedakah, u-veracha, ve-rachamim, ve-chayim, ve-shalom. Ve-tov be-eyneycha le-varech at amcha Yisra'el be-chol et u-ve-chol sha'ah bi-shelomecha. Baruch atah Adonay, ha-mevarech et amo Yisra'el ba-shalom.*"

"Establish peace, goodness, blessing, graciousness, kindness and compassion upon us and upon all Your people Israel. Bless us, Our Father, all of us as one, with the light of Your countenance, for with the light of Your countenance You gave us, Lord our God, the *Torah* of life and a love of kindness, righteousness, blessing, compassion, life and peace. And may it be good in Your eyes to bless Your people Israel, in every season and in every hour with Your peace. Blessed are You, Lord, who blesses His people Israel with peace."

Peace isn't really an accurate translation, though it's the common understanding of the word. "*Shalem*" means "whole", in the way that a fully joined up circle makes a whole but is also the symbol for its opposite: zero; and clearly a state of wholeness in the world is one where peace reigns. *Shalom* is completion, and thus it's the prayer which brings the *Amidah* to its perfect close. *Shalom* is perfection, and it's this state of universal peace which the Messiah will bring, as in the peroration of the *Kaddish*, which will shortly also form the peroration of "*Elohay Netsor Leshoni*": "*Oseh shalom bimromav, hu ya'aseh shalom, aleynu ve-al-kol Yisrael, ve-imru amen* - may He who makes peace in the heights, may He also make peace upon us and upon all Israel, and let us say *amen.*"

"*Sim shalom tovah*" is an adjunct to the *Yevarechecha*, expanding and expounding on the themes of peace, goodness, blessing, kindness, graciousness and compassion, to all of which the *Yevarechecha* refers, and which "*Sim shalom tovah*" tells us are given precisely by God turning His face to shine on us, as the *Yevarechecha* requested. It's also a complement to the *Yevarechecha*, in that the first is God's blessing given through the *Cohanim*, the second a direct petition from the individual - the former comes down from heaven, the latter goes up to heaven. This is what makes the double-prayer so special, for it's like the ladder which Jacob dreamed at Bethel, the one on which the angels travelled back and forth from earth to heaven, in that it makes a bridge.

The *Cohanim* exit from the *duchen* after "*Sim shalom tovah*", going out of the synagogue to put back their shoes. They should return to their seats only after the next *Kaddish.*

On the Ten Days of Awe the closing *barucha* of "*Sim shalom tovah*" is replaced by a prayer for inscription in the Book of Life. If the Priestly Blessing isn't given, "*Sim shalom tovah*" is omitted. By whatever route, the *chazan's* repetition of the *Amidah* closes here (omitting "*Elohey netsor leshoni*" and "*Yehi ratson*", both of which belong to the individual's recitation only), though many congregations like to add a private, supplementary prayer, "*Yehiyu le-ratson* - may the expressions of my mouth and the meditations of my hearts find favour with You O Lord, my rock and my redeemer." Famous lines, from Psalm 19:15.

Mystical Judaism encourages the one who prays to recite a verse of *Torah* before "*Yehiyu le-ratson*", one which symbolises one's own name. Either the verse should contain your name - for me the choice is almost too vast, but for many people there's only a single reference - or else begin and end with the first and last letters of your name. Some enterprising person might be interested in making a database of all the possibilities.

Elohay Netsor Leshoni

"*Elohay netsor leshoni*" and "*Yehi ratson*" complete the individual's recitation of the *Amidah*, but are not included in the *chazan's* recapitulation. "*Elohay netsor leshoni*" was written by Mar ben Rabina, a well-to-do if rather austere Babylonian *amora* of the 4th century CE whom mediaeval Jewry thought of somewhat as a saint, though contemporary psychoanalysis might well regard him as a pathological depressive. Many tales are told of him, and though it would be nice to think they were apocryphal, the evidence is compelling for their authenticity. At his wedding, in place of the normal celebratory songs and dances, Mar invited his Rabbinical instructor Rav Hamnuna Zata to sing the doleful lamentation, "Alas for us that we are to die", a paleocrystic equivalent of Leonard Cohen singing "The Future" - spiritually uplifting to those whose spirits are attuned that way, entirely suicidal to everybody else. If this wasn't lugubrious enough, at his son's wedding two decades later, Mar became so furious at the sight of so much merrymaking that he deliberately broke a precious cup, startling the gathered partymakers into asceticising their frivolities. It may well be that the custom of breaking a glass at a wedding ceremony, a custom that has many imaginative explanations but none that are accepted (mostly because the actual source is the Canaanite tradition of the groom stamping on a ripe pomegranate to splatter its seeds, a superstitious salutation to the fertility goddess), it may well be that Mar ben Rabina's action was in fact the source, or at least the source of the use of glass. Had he known it, I imagine that the *Ba'al Shem Tov* would have cursed him roundly for his excessive and his morbid joylessness. But the *Besht's* curse would have been entirely unavailing, for Mar ben Rabina, sourcing his words in Psalm 34:14 and finding them immortalised in *Berachot* 17a, had written a prayer that was an amulet against all cursing:

"My God, keep my tongue from speaking evil and my lips from cunning. To those who curse me, let my soul be silent - yea, let my soul be as the dust to all. Open my heart to Your *Torah*, and let my soul pursue Your commandments. As for those who plot evil against me, speedily nullify their counsel and disrupt their design. Act for Your name's sake; act for Your right hand's sake; act for Your sanctity's sake; act for Your *Torah's* sake. That Your beloved ones may be given rest, let Your right hand save, and respond to me."

Who were these enemies who were plotting against him? *Berachot* 54a records a number of escapes from peril, but doesn't specify whether his enemies were fellow Jews, or Babylonians. Given his maudlin nature and the scale of his misanthropy, it's hard to imagine anybody not becoming his enemy. He stated publicly (*Av. Zar* 2b-3a records it) that even those non-Jews who kept the Noachide laws would still not merit a reward in heaven, which appears to disagree with the view repeatedly expressed by the

Almighty. *Sanhedrin* 105a notes his attack on the prophet Balaam, the arch-prophet of the gentile world, for bestiality, and adds that he advocated the expounding of the biblical passages that bore his name in order to ruin his reputation.

The opening phrase of "*Elohay netsor leshoni*", the one taken from Psalm 34:14, counterpoints the phrase that preceded the opening of the *Amidah* - "*Adonay sephatay tiphtach u-phi yagid tehilatecha* - Lord open my lips that my mouth may declare Your praise" - making still another bookend. Something in the tone and manner of the *Ne'ilah* service at *Yom Kippur*, it presents its petition with increasing fervour, an almost despairing last gasp, calling on God to answer the prayers in the *Amidah*, challenging Him not on human but on His own moral terms. Do this because You are God, because this is Your continuing role in the mime-play of Creation, because this is your justification on the 8th day. Perhaps this was the source of Heinrich Heine's cynical: "God will always forgive; it's His job."

Judaism is a broad synagogue, capable of embracing many views and many characters; at a moral level it spans the humanism of the *Akeda* and the miraculousness of the Sea of Reeds; in human terms there are no greater extremes than Israel ben Eliezer, the *Ba'al Shem Tov*, the epitome of joy and celebration, and Mar ben Rabina, the archetype of the ascetic.

The references to the "right hand" which hint at residual Tammuz-worship and are much *op cit* in Christianity, are from Psalms 60:7 and 108:2.

To close "*Elohey netsor leshoni*", though Rabina did not specify it - or, more exactly, to close the individual's silent recitation of the *Amidah* with due formality, *Oseh Shalom* is now recited. Bow and take three steps back. Bow left on "*oseh*", bow right on "*hu ya'aseh*", bow forward on "*ve-al kol*".

Yehi ratson mi-lephanecha

"*Yehi ratson mi-lephanecha*" comes in part from *Pirkei Avot*, the Ethics of the Fathers (5:23), a collection of Rabbinic wisdom studied regularly on the six *Shabbat* afternoons between *Pesach* and *Shavu'ot*, and partly from the prophet Malachi, who lived in Jerusalem in the 5th century BCE after Zerubabel had rebuilt the Temple but before Nehemiah had carried out his reforms. Thus, yet again, bookends are formed, the two ends of the Temple period, both cited in petition for its reconstruction.

As "*Yehi ratson*" is integral to the *Amidah*, but "*Elohay netsor leshoni*" is not, many argue for a reversal of the order of their recitation. Since "*Yehiu le-ratson*" is intended to close the *Amidah*, many argue for its repetition after whichever of the other two is recited last. I love this sort of semantic pedantry. It's what prevents opinion from becoming fixed as dogma, keeps tradition fluid, adds a dialectical element that promotes dynamism and allows both refutation and innovation. Nothing is certain, not even the validity of doubt.

✡

Havineynu

Inevitably there are those who are too stressed, too sick, or in some other way unable to recite the whole *Amidah* three times daily. For such people the Rabbis have developed a condensed version, in which the thirteen middle blessings are reduced to one, the opening three and the closing three remaining intact. This version is called "*Havineynu*".

"*Havineynu Adonay eloheynu la-da'at derachecha, u-mol et levaveynu le-yiratecha, ve-tislach lanu liheyot ge'ulim. Ve-rachakeynu mi-machov ve-dashneynu binot artsecha, u-nephutsoteynu mey-arba tekabets, ve-ha-to'im al dat'cha yishapeytu, ve-al ha-resha'im taniph yadecha, ve-yismechu tsaddikim be-vinyan irecha u-ve-tikon heychalecha, u-ve-tsemichat keren le-David avdecha u-va-arichat ner le-ven yishai meshichecha. Terem nikra atah ta'aneh. Baruch atah Adonay, shomeya tefillah.*"

"O Lord our God, grant us understanding to know Your ways, purify our hearts to revere You, and forgive us so that we may be redeemed. Remove us from pain, and satisfy us with the goodness of the earth. Gather our scattered people from the four corners of the world, judge those who transgress Your will, lift up Your hand against the wicked, then shall the righteous rejoice with the rebuilding of Your city and the re-establishment of Your sanctuary, with the flourishing of the might of David Your servant, and the establishing of the glory of the son of Jesse, Your Messiah. Even before we call, answer us. Blessed are You, Lord, who pays heed to prayer."

Some of the *Talmudic* sages wanted *Havineynu* to be fixed as the standard form for any who can't manage the full *Shemoneh Esreh*. Maimonides supported this. But *Havineynu* cannot be said during *Ma'ariv* of *shabbat* or festivals, because the fourth blessing is integral to *Havdalah*, the concluding blessings at the end of *shabbat*, nor between *Shemini Atseret* and *Pesach*, when the ninth blessing is integral to the prayers for rain; which leaves half a year of weekdays - barely enough to justify its usage.

And if even *Havineynu* isn't possible - if one is in danger, or at the front line, or on the Jonaic sea - the Rabbis prescribe this blessing, recitable sitting, standing, or even lying down if needs must.

"*Tsarchey amcha Yisra'el merubim ve-datam ketsarah. Yehi ratson mi-lephanecha Adonay eloheynu ve-elohey avoteynu she-titen le-chol echad ve-echad kedey pharnasato u-le-chol geviyah u-geviyah dey machsorah.*"

"The needs of Your people are many and they are unable to express their wants. May it be Your will, O Lord our God and God of our fathers, to give each and every one his daily sustenance and to everyone whatever he lacks."

This, surely, is the root of Jesus' revision. This, surely, is the *Ba'al Shem Tov's* prayer, the one of legend, the special prayer that his disciples didn't know, the one that he would pray when he went into the forest alone to ask God to intercede on behalf of his stricken people.

Chapter Eleven: *Tachanun* - Mercy

Vidu'i - Confession

The *Vidu'i* is the prologue to *Tachanun*, so it isn't recited if *Tachanun* isn't recited. It's a personal testament, but written in the plural, because every penitent confesses to the community, within the community, and as part of the community - local and universal. Normally it's recited standing, albeit slightly bowed to show contrition; but surely this must be an error; if the *Vidu'i* is a prologue to *Tachanun*, then should it not be recited in the same posture as *Tachanun*, seated, with the head reclining on one arm - the leaning position which we're told to reverse at *Pesach*, and consequently, here, the right arm?

The full *Vidu'i* is found in the service for *Yom Kippur* - elsewhere too, but that is where it finds its most profound significance. One cannot receive absolution from sin until one has first admitted to sin. In other words, it's an act of self-nemesis, a voluntary humbling, an assault on arrogance – and a far more appropriate assault than the one in "*Yehi ratson*" that accompanies the morning blessings - a recognition of the limits of our own humanity: what the Greeks called *anagnorisis*.

The *Zohar*, the *Kabbalistic* "Book of Splendour" which is a compendium of Jewish mysticism, teaches that God created the world by naming it, and that the words of the naming obviously required letters, so the letters of the *aleph-bet* must have been present at the Creation (unless God named the world into existence in a language other than Biblical Hebrew!). To recite the letters, then, in the manner of the *Vidu'i*, is to take part in the repairing of Creation, for the alphabetical acrostic returns the cosmos to its proper order. *Tikkun* - restoration - is thereby connected with *Techinah* - a word meaning both the prayer for mercy and the mercy itself - the sort of *gematria* that mysticism most enjoys.

And which also leads on to another famous *Midrash*, one whose source I have been unable to trace. But no matter. My gratitude to Rabbi Alan Burns, for recounting this and many other anecdotes on his regular visits to Polack's:

Rabbi Akiva overheard a man in synagogue reciting not the prayers but the *aleph-bet*, over and over again.

"I don't know the prayers," the man explained. "But I do know the letters of the *aleph-bet*. And since all the letters of the *aleph-bet* are needed to make the words of the prayers, all I need to do is say the letters and God can rearrange them into the proper words Himself."

Prayer, then - a simple anagram. Can we, in this way, make prayers even out of words that are not directed towards God?

"Eloheynu ve-elohey avoteynu, tavo lephanecha tefillateynu, ve-al titalammi-techinateynu, she-eyn anu azey phanim u-keshey oreph, lomar lephaneycha Adonay eloheynu ve-elohey avoteynu, tsaddikim anachnu ve-lo chatanu, aval anachnu va-avoteynu chatanu."

"Our God and God of our forefathers, may our prayer come before You and do not ignore our supplication, for we are not so brazen and obstinate as to say before You, Lord our God and God of our forefathers, that we are righteous and have not sinned - no indeed, we and our forefathers admit to being sinners."

First, a call to God to hear our confession, based on three verses from the Psalms - 88:3, 55:2 and 106:6. Then the catalogue of confession, an alphabetical acrostic in which each letter of the alphabet is represented once, except for the *omega*, the final letter, *Tav*, which is repeated three times; and the whole rendition accompanied word for word by the striking of the chest above the heart with the right fist; but gently, because this is penitence, not percussion.

"Ashamnu, bagadnu, gazalnu, dibarnu dophi. He'evinu, ve-hirshanu, zadnu, chamasnu, taphalnu sheker. Ya'atsnu ra, kizavnu, latsnu, maradnu, ni'atsnu, sararnu, avinu, pashanu, tsaradnu, kishinu oreph. Ra'ashnu, shichatnu, ti'avnu, ta'inu, titanu."

The catalogue is impressive by any standards, an inventory of sins so reprehensible no single individual could possibly have committed all of them and still expect divine forgiveness. It consists of guilt, treason, robbery, slander, incitement to wrongdoing, premeditated wickedness, extortion, false accusation, the giving of evil counsel, deceit, scorn, rebellion, provocation, indifference, sexual perversion, wantonness, persecution, obstinacy, cruelty, corruption, the commission of abominations, and general straying - a list whose hierarchy might be interesting to ponder were this not an alphabetical acrostic. Fascinating that the last of all should implicate God too; more than implicate Him, it's a positive accusation, a passing of the buck of blame. "You have let us go astray." I reject this absolutely. I reject it because it's an attempt to abrogate responsibility, and as such undermines the purpose and the sincerity of the confession (a version of the Nuremburg Nazis' "I was only obeying orders" - only in this case the orders came from fate and destiny and heaven). But also because the phrase is unnecessary, prolix. This isn't about blame, this is about the moral and psychological process of confessing, which is an act of the most intense purgation. Blame is a different kind of sullying, and the objective here is cleanliness.

And besides, the ensuing verse repairs this, albeit contradictively. The reacceptance of blame on the one hand, the certainty of God's sincerity on the other.

What of course is terribly problematic about this list, is that it mirrors precisely the inventory of accusations made against Jewry by mediaeval Christians and contemporary anti-Semites. And here we are admitting they're right.

"*Sarnu mi-mitzvotecha u-mi-mishpatecha ha-tovim, ve-lo shavah lanu. Ve-atah tsaddik al kol ha-ba aleynu, ki emet asita va-anachnu hirshanu.*"

"It is we who have turned away from Your commandments and from Your good laws - but to no avail. But You are justified in all that has befallen us, for You have acted with sincerity while we are the ones who did wrong."

Once again, the justification of the judgement. God is right, even when He appears to be wrong. How can this be? Read the closing chapters of the Book of Job.

✡

El Erech Apayim

And indeed, that last verse contains phrases from Job (33:27) as well as Nehemiah (9:33). "*El erech apayim*", which follows, contains a phrase from Exodus 34:5, which is continued (34:6/7) in the closing verse, along with 34:9 and a phrase from Psalm 86:5.

He who prays alone should stop where "*Sarnu*" stops. But when the community prays together, "*El erech apayim* - the Thirteen Attributes of Mercy" are added. One strange law supplemental here - when "*El erech apayim*" is said without a *minyan*, we're told, it should be *leyned*, not sung. And this is strange because we've also just been told that it never should be said without a *minyan*.

"O God You are slow to anger. You are called the Master of Mercy, and

You have taught us the way of repentance. May You remember this day and every day the greatness of Your mercy and Your kindness to the offspring of Your beloved ones. Turn to us in mercy for You are the Master of Mercy. With supplication and prayer we approach Your presence in the manner that You made known to the humble one [Moses] in ancient times. Turn back from Your fierce anger as it is written in Your *Torah*, 'In the shadow of Your wings may we find shelter and lodging as on the day the Lord descended on a cloud [to appear to Moses on Mt Sinai].

"Overlook our sin and erase our guilt as on the day You stood there with Moses. Give heed to our cry and hearken to our declaration as on the day when he called out with the name Lord, and there it was said…" the *chazan* and the congregation recite the final phrases together, and loudly...

"*Adonay, Adonay, el rachum ve-chanun, erech apayim, ve-rav chesed ve-emet, notser chesed la-alaphim, noseh avon va-phesha ve-chatah ve-nakeh. Ve-salachta la-avoneynu u-le-chatateynu u-nechaltanu. Selach lanu avinu ki chatanu, mechal lanu malkeynu ki pashanu, ki atah Adonay tov ve-salach, ve-rav chesed le-chol koreycha.*"

"Lord, Lord, God of Compassion of Grace, slow to anger and abundant in kindness and truth, preserver of kindness for thousands of generations, forgiver of iniquity, wilful sin and error, He who cleanses. May You forgive our iniquities and our errors and make us Your heritage. Forgive us, O our father, for we have erred, pardon us, our king, for we have wilfully sinned, for You Lord are good and forgiving and abundantly kind to all who call upon You."

The Thirteen Attributes are not spelled out in muster, but are easily deducible: slow to anger; the master of mercy; teacher of the way of repentance; bestower of kindness; compassionate; gracious; abundant in kindness and truth; preserver of kindness for thousands of generations; forgiver of iniquity; forgiver of wilful sin; forgiver of error; He who cleanses. Some might argue that this is really only really seven or eight, the remainder being repetitions. But this is another of those occasions where the English lacks the range of meanings that the different Hebrew words contain. And besides, Thirteen Attributes makes such a lovely symmetry with the Thirteen Principles of Faith of Maimonides and the Thirteen Principles of Rabbi Yishmael.

"*Adonay, Adonay, el rachum ve-chanun*" is another of those moments of sublime intensity that one looks forward to in synagogue with special affection and expectation - like waiting for the singing of "Jerusalem" on the last night of the Proms, or the moment in Beethoven's 9th when the entire chorus bursts into the "Ode to Joy". Aside from here, in *Tachanun*, it's introduced, on festivals, to the prayers that accompany the opening of the Ark, unless the festival occurs on *shabbat*, when to everybody's disappointment it's omitted.

How to paraphrase in mere prose the drama of the spiritual experience? Envisage the entire congregation standing, facing the Ark, wrapped in their prayer shawls like swaddling clothes. Bo'az and Yachin, the two congregants called to open the Ark, stand pillar-like one on either side of the closed doors and curtain of the Ark. Facing the Ark, the *chazan* leads the "*Ayn kamocha*", the customary outset of this ceremony, followed by "*Av ha-rachamim*". Then Bo'az pulls the cord to open the curtain, and Yachin the handle of the doors, to reveal several *Torah* scrolls, resting in the Ark, wrapped in velvet of deepest blue or purple, clad in silver breast-plate and crowned with jangling bells the size of snapdragons and the shape of pomegranates. The *chazan* chants "*Va-yehi binso'a*", like "*Ayn kamocha*" a lively tune and populist melody, an easy-sing-along. This is what happens every Saturday, but on festivals, at this point, it changes - both mood and ritual. Where the *chazan* and the second *oleh* would normally go now to take out the two scrolls for the reading of the Law, instead there's a pause of the most powerful solemnity.

"*Adonay, Adonay, el rachum ve-chanun, erech apayim, ve-rav chesed ve-emet, notser chesed la-alaphim, noseh avon va-phesha ve-chatah ve-nakeh.*"

Only this, not the full verse that's said in *Tachanun*. Sung out rapturously, a call as invocatory as the sounding of the *shofar*. Each word stretched out, like a piece of cat gut on an ancient lyre, stretched as though to test its capacity for tension, stretched to the very limits of its tautness, so that if you held the note a millisecond longer it would break the fragile ambience of spiritual concentration which, still held, it locks in balance. "*A-do-nay, a-do-nay, el ra-chum ve-cha-a-nun*" - this first part so unutterably slow it's almost painful, but the pain is exquisite; the tune entirely on one note, except for the slight rise to the "*ra*" on "*rachum*", an even slighter rise to the "*cha*" on "*chanun*" - "*e-rech a-pay-im, ve-rav chesed ve-em-et*" - and again the slow monotone, *maximo adagio*, sustained, drawn out, the merest slant upward at the end of each syllable of the first three words, sloping through "*ve-rav chesed*", only to fall again on "*ve-emet*" - "*notser chesed la-alaphim*" - climbing semitone by semitone as if along the breves of Jacob's Ladder; then, sustaining the upper octave, and in trumpeting rhythm, and quicker now, *adagio* become *andante*, working towards *crescendo* – "*nos-eh a-von, va-phesha, ve-chatah ve-nakeh*" - and end, please end, only it doesn't end, the last note doesn't return to where music is expected to return, to conclusion, to completion, to the rounding off of tonic dominant and sub-dominant; it hangs, pendulous as the pomegranate bells on the *Torah* scrolls themselves, an agony of waiting.

But resolved, by singing the entire phrase again. And then a third time.

We could, would willingly, sing it a fourth and fifth and sixth time too, because the mantra has absorbed us, enraptured us, even the state of animated suspension in which it leaves us at the end. But three times is all, and exactly like "*Avinu malkeynu*" it's we who are left unfinished, stranded like Moses on the summit of Mount Nebo, stranded on the sub-dominant. Glorious moment. The transfiguration of liturgy into *aria*.

But only on festivals. Alas, in normal daily prayers the phrase is simply spoken.

✡

Avinu Malkeynu - Our father, Our king

By the third repetition, "*Adonay el rachum*" almost became that rare event in Jewish liturgy - a mantra. "*Avinu malkeynu*", recited only on fast days and during the Ten Days of Awe that conjoin *Rosh ha-Shanah* with *Yom Kippur*, is precisely that. Its methodology is constant, rhythmic, chanted repetition, set on a rising-falling beat of almost hypnotic, and always rhapsodic power. It's a song that has to be driven, the way an unwilling horse has to be driven, with continuous nagging of the whip.

"*Avinu malkey-ey-ey-nu*" - stress on the middle syllable of "*avinu*", and on the second syllable of "*malkey*", the elongations of the second word stretching it out like worn elastic till the saving "*nu*" revives it. And that is only the first phrasing of the word, for the first line. The second phrasing is identical. The third omits the elongation, as does the fourth, and then, at last, the purpose of the line is reached and stated. There are more than forty of these lines, more than fifty in the Sephardic version - a variable number in either case because different occasions add or omit particular phrases - and the length of the main phrase determines whether one can manage all four repetitions of the eponym, or reduce to fewer. So endless repetition is tempered by constant variations, often extemporised, in much the way that Bach and Wagner (yes, I dare to name him in a Jewish text) develop music by the tiniest shifts and variations of otherwise identical rhythms and harmonies. So whoever leads the prayer service is also included in the piece's composition, setting the pace and flow *rubato*, requiring the congregation's close attentiveness in order not to breach the harmony. Each line is demanding, by the very nature of the stresses and the elongations and the repetition. Each subsequent line is more demanding still, for the same reason as the previous, but also because one more stone has been added to the basket, and the hill we're climbing is extremely steep. In the *Ne'ilah* service on *Yom Kippur*, when it's virtually the culminative act of twenty-five hours of unbroken prayer, study and fasting, the hill can easily become a mountain - but a holy mountain, a Sinai. So we remain steadfast, and keep on climbing. The joy of coming out into the clouds of lower heaven is nowhere in Judaism better or more deeply expressed than in the ecstatic coda, which switches to an entirely different tempo, rhythm, melody and tone, and remains for me the most potent religious and spiritual moment in the Jewish calendar. Yet even that last line ultimately disappoints - deliberately disappoints, in the way that freedom always proves to be a terrible anti-climax - for it ends, once again, on the hanging sub-dominant and never returns to the tonic chord. You are left feeling, Sisyphus-like, that you want, that you're ready, to begin the whole ascent again. But it isn't required.

The origins of "*Avinu malkeynu*" are related in the *Talmud* (*Ta'anit* 25b). There was a drought in Roman Palestine in the early decades of the 2nd century CE. The sages called for a national day of fasting and prayer, in order to petition God to send the rain, but no rain fell. Then Rabbi Akiva offered up five supplications in the form of "*Avinu malkeynu*", and behold the heavens opened. In the years that followed, in times of national need, more lines were added.

Question: why do we not continue to recite "*Avinu malkeynu*" in times of distress, and especially on *Shemini Atseret*, the festival that brings the eight days of *Sukkot* to an end, specifically with the introduction of the prayers for rain? I have no answer to this question.

The text is far too long and various to give in full. But a sample of the lines reveals the range and the variety of purposes in Jewish prayer. The range of moods as well. Because we pray to God when we're in distress, but also in our times of joy; we ask for favours but we also remind God of the favours He owes us; we pray to humble ourselves but also to make protest; we pray because we're alone and in order to celebrate being part of a community, local and ephemeral, but also eternal across space and time; we pray to remember and we pray lest we forget, which isn't quite the same thing; we pray as a form of studying, and we pray because we have studied; we pray for what we do not have but also to give thanks for what we have received…

Our father, our king, we have sinned before You
Our father, our king, we have no king but You
Our father, our king, wipe out all our enemies
Our father, our king, send complete recovery to the sick
Our father, our king, fill our storehouses with abundance

Our father, our king, remember that we are but dust
Our father, our king, act for the sake of the martyrs
Our father, our king, treat us with charity and kindness

✡

Tachanun

Tachanun means "supplication", though it's now used erroneously to mean a "petition" or even an "intercession", because these are its method and its aspiration. The longer form of *Tachanun*, beginning "*ve-hu rachum*", is recited only on Mondays and Thursdays, the same days, the Biblical market days, on which the *Torah* is also read; the shorter form begins with *Nephilat Apayim* – "the putting down of the head".

✡

Ve-hu rachum

"He, the Merciful One, is forgiving of iniquity and does not destroy, frequently withdrawing His anger, not arousing His entire rage. You, Lord, do not withhold Your mercy from us; may Your kindness and Your truth always protect us. Save us, Lord our God, and gather us from among the nations, to give thanks to Your holy name and to glory in Your praise. If You preserve iniquities, O God my Lord, who could survive? For with You is forgiveness, that You may be feared. Do not treat us according to our sins, do not repay us according to our iniquities. Though our iniquities testify against us, O Lord, act for Your name's sake. Remember Your mercies, Lord, and Your kindnesses, for they are from the beginning of the world. May the Lord answer us on the day of distress, may the name of Jacob's God make us impregnable. Save, Lord - the King will answer us on the day we call. Our father, our King, be gracious with us and answer us though we have no worthy deeds, treat us with charity for Your name's sake. Our Master, our God, hear the sound of our supplications, recall for us the covenant of our forefathers and save us for Your name's sake."

The humanism of this is extraordinary. As if we were saying: Don't treat us as we deserve to be treated, but as you know You should be treating us. Don't make an example of us as sinners; make Yourself an example of goodness.

It's almost as if we're still seeking to propitiate in the most ancient manner: the rendering up of sacrifices on a burning altar; the act of self-prostration before the icon of the Altar. At one level, the highest expression of the goal of synagogue prayer: the replacement of the vanished Temple. At another level, the lowest form of grovelling, a return to the practises that preceded Temple sacrifice. Judaism is compounded of such paradoxes. They too are part of the dialectic that gives it its dynamism.

The text is yet another preface in a book of prefaces, yet another scriptural anthology in what is ultimately an anthology of anthologies compounded of itself.

"He the merciful..."	Psalm 78:38
"Do not withhold..."	Psalm 40:12
"Save us..."	Psalm 106:47
"If You..."	Psalm 130:3-4
"Do not treat..."	Psalm 103:10
"Though our iniquities..."	Jeremiah 14:7
"Remember..."	Psalm 25:6
"May The Lord answer..."	Psalm 20:2
"Save, Lord..."	Psalm 20:10

Nothing written, nothing added, but an embroidered tapestry of scriptural quotations - as though prayer were itself a form of *Midrash*, a religious equivalent of literary criticism, a means of drawing precise themes and specific topics from the universal whole - calling on God to hear our prayer with mercy and compassion.

There is, as so often in Jewish prayer, just the tiniest hint of bullying, of arm-twisting - "*Le-ma'an shemecha* - do this for Your name's sake." If Israel is perceived to suffer, to be refused forgiveness, to be denied its favours, what damage might this inflict upon the reputation of the Almighty, among Jews certainly, but worse, among the *Goyim* too (c.f. Exodus 32:12 and Numbers 14:16). For the Jews to acknowledge that their God is superior to any other God, and therefore to continue worshipping Him and Him alone, occasional proof is still required.

Ah but the relationship between the Jew and his God is subtle and complex! The exertion of pressure sounds rather like the tactics of the pubescent child, who's just beginning to work out the rudiments of adult psychology, and to turn it to advantage. The equally tiny hints of sycophancy, of special pleading, are entirely adult, and entirely naughty - "Do not treat us according to our sins, do not repay us according to our iniquities." Are we asking God to turn a blind eye, to let us off - to break His own laws? And would we not be the very first to cry out against injustice if God were to do what we are asking now? Such are the contradictions inherent, not in the religion, but in the relationship.

✡

Ve-atah Adonay eloheynu

The last five verses of the sixteen-verse prayer recited by Daniel (9:4-19), to petition God when the Babylonian exile seemed to have no end in sight.

"In the first year of the reign of Darius, the son of Ahasuerus, over the seed of the Medes, king of the realm of Chaldea, in the first year of his reign I, Daniel, considered in the books the number of the years whereof the word of the Lord came to Jeremiah the Prophet, that he would accomplish seventy years in the desolations of Jerusalem. And I set my face to the Lord God, to seek by prayer and supplication, with fasting and sackcloth and ashes. And I prayed to the Lord my God and made my confession, and said, 'O Lord, the great and dreadful God, keeping the covenant and showing mercy to them that love Him and keep His commandments, we have sinned, we have committed iniquity, we have done wickedly, we have rebelled, even by departing from Your precepts and from Your judgements. We have not hearkened to Your servants the Prophets, who spoke in Your name to our kings, our princes and our fathers, and to all the people of the land. O Lord, righteousness belongs to You, but unto us confusion of faces, as at this day; by the men of Judah, and to the inhabitants of Jerusalem, and unto all Israel, those that are near and those that are far off, through all the countries to which You have driven them, because of their trespass that they have trespassed against You. O Lord, to us belongs confusion of face, to our kings, to our princes, and to our fathers, because we have sinned against You. To the Lord our God belong mercies and forgivenesses, though we have rebelled against Him. We have not obeyed the voice of the Lord our God, to walk in His laws, which He set before us by His servants the Prophets. Yea, all Israel has transgressed Your law, even by departing, that they might not obey Your voice; therefore the curse is poured upon us, and the oath that is written in the law Moses the servant of God, because we have sinned against Him. And He has confirmed His words, which He spoke against us, and against our judges who judged us, by bringing upon us a great evil, for under the whole heaven has not been done as has been done at Jerusalem. As it is written in the law of Moses, all this evil is come upon us, yet we did not make our prayer before the Lord our God, that we might turn from our iniquities, and understand Your truth? Therefore has the Lord watched upon the evil, and brought it upon us, for the Lord our God is righteous in all His works which He does, for we did not obey His voice. And now, O Lord our God, who has brought Your people out of the land of Egypt with a mighty hand, and has gained renown, as at this day; we have sinned, we have done wickedly. O Lord, according to all Your righteousness, I beseech You, let Your anger and Your fury be turned away from Your city Jerusalem, Your holy mountain; because for our sins and for the iniquities of our fathers, Jerusalem and Your people are become a reproach to all that are about us. Now therefore, O Our God, hear the prayer of Your servant, and his supplications, and cause Your face to shine upon Your sanctuary which is desolate, for Your name's sake."

I've quoted the whole text, though only the closing verses from "And now, O Lord Our God, who has brought" are in the prayer. It makes an interesting contrast with "*Ve-hu rachum*". There's no bullying or special pleading now, no asking God to turn a blind eye or to break His own commandments. This is pure confessional, admission of heinous sin and request for forgiveness - national sin not individual, the sin of turning away from God, of disregarding the Covenant. Is Daniel creating the lines of his confession, or is he quoting them - "*chatanu, ve-avinu, ve-hirshanu, u-maradnu*" in verse 5, and its partial echo, "*chatanu, rashanu*" in verse 15, take us back to that alphabetical acrostic in the *Vidu'i* in which we listed all our sins. The question isn't insignificant, for it's a key to the dating of the text.

The opening phrase claims that the story was set in the first year of the reign of Darius, the son of Ahasuerus (Artaxerxes in the Persian). This would be Darius II, whom the Persians called Ochus and the Greeks Nothos or "bastard", marking the fact that he was the illegitimate son of Artaxerxes. A cautionary tale indeed, the life of Ochus. Manipulated and bullied by his half-sister Parysatis, he seized the throne in 424 BCE from his half-brother Sogdianus, who had himself stolen it from the rightful heir of Artaxerxes, Xerxes II. Ochus' reign was of truly Macbethian proportions, for which Parysatis probably deserves at least an equal amount of the blame, and very little out-damned-spotting by all contemporary accounts.

This sets the prayers of Daniel in 423 BCE, in other words at precisely the epoch when Ezra was re-establishing the Jewish occupation of Israel and the Temple was being rebuilt. Those historical circumstances are entirely at odds with what Daniel has to say about Jerusalem; and the words he uses are at least three centuries ahead of time.

In fact, as I pointed out earlier, Daniel wasn't a factual account at all, but an allegory, a fiction, and it was written at the time of the Maccabean revolt against the Seleucid Greeks, in 167 BCE. When the author of Daniel speaks of "departing from Your precepts and from Your judgements", he really means the Hellenised Jews of his own epoch. When he speaks of "those that are near and those that are far off, through all the countries to which You have driven them" he's referring to a diaspora which simply didn't exist in Ezra's time. And when he speaks of "a great evil, for under the whole heaven has not been done as has been done at Jerusalem", it's the desecration of the Temple that he means - the Greeks deliberately sacrificed pigs on the Altar, to render it unusable by Jews; the action which led to the rebellion by Mattathias Hasmonean, and the rise of the hundred-and-fifty year dynasty of Judah Maccabee.

In Paris, during the Nazi occupation, Jean-Paul Sartre wrote a version of the Greek myth of Orestes and Electra, entitling it "Les Mouches - The Flies". It told of the heroic struggle by the eponymous heroes to liberate their country from the demoniacal tyrants Aegisthus and Clytemnestra, the eponymous flies representing the Erinyes or Furies, symbols of the evil that escaped from Pandora's Box. For the play to be performed in Paris, it required a licence from the occupying authorities; extraordinarily one was granted, for after all a play set amongst the ancient Greeks was surely harmless, and the philistines who ran the Reich simply lacked the wherewithal to recognise the real object of the allegory? I like to imagine that the author of Daniel had much the same ploy in mind when he wrote his allegory; and I hope a similar success.

Chateh

Verses 15-17 of the Daniel fragment are in "*Ve-atah Adonay*" above; the last two follow now, accompanied by references to Isaiah (64:7), Joel (2:17) and Psalm 103:13.

"Incline your ear, my God, and listen, open Your eyes and see our desolation and that of the city upon which Your name is proclaimed; for not because of our righteousness do we cast down our supplications before You, rather because of Your abundant compassion. O my Lord, heed us. O my Lord forgive us. O my Lord be attentive to us and act, do not delay. For Your sake, my God, for Your name is proclaimed upon Your city and upon Your people.

"Our Father, the merciful father - show us an omen for good and gather in our dispersed from the four corners of the world. Let all the nations recognise and realise that You are the Lord our God. And now, Lord, You are our father; we are the clay and You are our moulder, and Your handiwork are we all.

"Save us for Your name's sake, our rock, our king and our Redeemer. Pity Your people, Lord, let not Your heritage be an object of scorn, for nations to dominate. Why should they say amongst the nations, 'Where is their God?' We know that we have sinned and there is no one to stand up for us - let Your great name stand up for us in time of distress. We know that there are no worthy deeds in us - treat us with charity for Your name's sake.

As a father has mercy on his children, so may You have mercy on us, O Lord, and save us for Your name's sake. Have compassion on Your people, have mercy on Your heritage; have pity, we beg You, according to Your abundant mercy. Be gracious with us and answer us, for Yours, Lord who performs wonders eternally, Yours is the righteousness."

There's a strong sense in this of an on-going competition amongst the world's divinities, in which the cheerleaders of *Yahweh* are urging Him on to ever greater deeds and still more miraculous miracles, so as to prove that He is the quickest, the strongest, the most merciful, the wisest, better than any other god.

But I deplore the self-deprecation - "there are no worthy deeds in us; treat us with charity". I deplore this descent to grovelling and sycophancy - "have pity, we beg You". I deplore this return again to special pleading and to bullying - "for Your name's sake". I deplore the reduction of worship to a heavyweight contest over fifteen rounds between *Yahweh* and Ba'al and Zeus.

"Heed us, heed us, heed us." The petition becomes an act of demonstration. In the streets of Jerusalem, during the 1980s, the ultra-pious carried placards, and intoned through megaphones, "*Mashiach Achshav* - Messiah Now!" Perhaps they'd misunderstood that it's the quality of their actions and not that of their protests that will hasten His arrival. Or perhaps they simply weren't shouting it loud enough, or often enough.

✡

Habet-na

But the prayer goes on, without restraint. A child who nags his parent quite this unrelentingly will gain either reluctant accession or terminal rejection. Still we must try. Seven trumpets of rams' horns. And try again. Heed us, Lord our God. And try again. And fail again. And try yet again. And fail better.

"Look, we beg You, and have mercy on Your people speedily for Your name's sake. In Your abundant mercy, Lord, our God, pity, have mercy on us, save the sheep of Your pasture. Do not let Your anger dominate us, for on You do our eyes depend. Save us for Your name's sake, have mercy on us for the sake of Your covenant. Look and answer us in time of distress, for salvation is Yours, Lord. Upon You is our hope, O God, of forgiveness. Please forgive now, O good and forgiving God, for You are God, the gracious and compassionate king."

The closing phrase is from Nehemiah 9:31.

So many different modes of the relationship between Man and God. In these prayers it's Beckettian man at his most grovelling, and the Covenant appears to be little more than a contract between the vassal and his feudal lord, subject to *droit de seigneur* in every facet of the subordinate partner's life. How very different from the relations between Abraham and God at Gomorrah, between David and God when the Ark was brought from Gibeon. Now a father, now a brother, now a wise and trusted friend. Just as there are very different strains in Judaism itself (belief in the world to come opposing belief that everything is simply dust and ash; belief that Man has free will and responsibility for the earth opposing subordination to the totality of Law and the predetermined will of God; belief in "*ha-yom, ha-yom, ha-yom*", living for today, opposing the belief in the End of Days when the Messiah will bring comfort) so there are very different modes in our relationship with God. It isn't possible to hold all Jewish beliefs without collapsing into contradiction and hypocrisy; or else schizophrenia. It isn't possible to keep all of the commandments all of the time. Ultimately we are all myrtles among reeds.

Ana

"Please, O gracious and compassionate king, remember and look to the Covenant between the parts. May there appear before You the binding of the only son - for Israel's sake, Our father our king - be gracious with us and answer us, for Your great name has been proclaimed upon us. O maker of miracles at all times, treat us according to Your kindness. Gracious and Compassionate one, look and answer us in time of distress, for Yours, Lord, is the salvation. Our father, our king, our protector, do not treat us according to the evil of our deeds. Recall Your mercies, Lord, and Your kindnesses, according to Your abundant goodness save us and have pity on us, we beg you, for we have no God other than You, our Rock. Do not forsake us, Lord our God; be not distant from us, for our souls are diminished by sword and captivity, pestilence and plague, and every distress and woe. Rescue us, for we place all our hope in You. Do not humiliate us, Lord our God. Illuminate Your countenance within us, recall for us the covenant of our forefathers, and save us for Your name's sake. Observe our troubles and hear the voice of our prayers, for You hear the prayers of every mouth."

Save us, Lord, not because we deserve it - our sins are many and we acknowledge all of them - but because the evil that has befallen us is greater than our sins. A prayer that clearly wasn't written in a time of peace and tranquillity, but which belongs, as do so many, to an epoch of brutal anti-Semitism. Which epoch? It doesn't matter; the point here isn't the date or the details but the contrast between the prayer and the person who prays. Because we recite it in a time of peace and tranquillity - not in Israel perhaps, but in the suburbs of Melbourne or Milan - oblivious to the context of the writing, the hyperbole of the prayer in our own mouths. "We deserve to be punished, Lord - but surely not like this?" How can we justify reciting this, when mercifully it isn't true? "Save us, Lord, because what is happening here is disproportionate." A terrible cry of anguish – but not ours, though we spokesperson it. Should we not at least provide it with an explicatory preface?

Ana pleads, where nagging, bullying and demanding have proved no use. We have to ask, after so many paragraphs of this - what is it that drives a man, a nation, to such depths of despondency that he'll fall down on his knees, calling on God in this protracted and self-demeaning manner? National catastrophe - no less. These are the prayers of Job, after he's buried his children. These are the prayers of Jeremiah, witnessing the destruction of the Temple. These are the prayers of Hugo Gryn (*zichrono livro'ach* - may his memory be a blessing), after he'd been selected to be Isaac, but his father and his brother to be rams. These are the prayers of Yosl Rakover[7], and the poems of Bernhard Aaronsohn[8], scratched on the barrack wall at Auschwitz-Birkenau:

> What is happening here is the Will of God
> We are its Executors
> You are its Inheritors

These are the prayers of men for whom the only alternative is not to curse God and die - because they've already cursed God, and it didn't work, they didn't die, He punished them instead like Sisyphus, by compelling them to go on living in the torment of their fates. These are the prayers of men for whom the only alternative would be surrender.

And when we pray these prayers, in the economic prosperity of Moor Allerton, in the comfort of Teaneck, in the safety of Tel Aviv, in the arrogance of the West Bank, it isn't we who are in despair, not we who are begging, but binding ourselves to them through repetition of their prayers. "Please O Gracious and compassionate king, let it never be forgotten that

[7] "Yosl Rakover Talks to God" by Zvi Kolitz.
[8] From my novel "The Flaming Sword".

our ancestors were slaves in Egypt, exiles in Babylon, threatened with genocide by Haman, enslaved by Rome, murdered raped pillaged and persecuted in a thousand Christian pogroms, locked up in Auschwitz to be burned. Lord, we who do not need to grovel, we who deplore the act of grovelling, we whose turn may well yet be to come, bind us with our predecessors, who were not so fortunate, and teach us to say these prayers without deploring them, so that we will know how to say them properly if the time should come."

Ana contains a reference - "Do not forsake us" - from Psalm 38:22.

✡

El Rachum

"O compassionate and gracious God, have mercy on us and on all Your works, for there is none like You. Please, Lord our God, forgive our wilful sins. Our father our king, our rock and our redeemer, living and enduring God, who is mighty in strength, generous and good to all his works; for You are the Lord our God. O God who is slow to anger and full of mercy, treat us according to Your abundant mercy and save us for Your name's sake. Hear our prayer, our king, and rescue us from our foes; hear our prayer, our king, and rescue us from every distress and woe. You are our father, our king and Your name is proclaimed upon us - do not set us aside. Do not abandon us, our father; do not cast us away, our Creator; do not forget us, our Moulder. For You are God, the gracious and compassionate King."

This is becoming tormentuous - as it's supposed to. Again and again, the same phrases, *repetitio ad nauseam*, endless as torture, endless as nightly interrogation, unsleeping as a *refusenik* in his cell or a zealot on Mount Masada. Is there no end to it? No, there is no end to it. That's the whole point. That's why we go on praying. Because at the very bottom of this pit, beyond the suffering inflicted by human beings, beyond the suffering inflicted by Life, beyond the suffering inflicted by God, beyond the darkness and the nothingness, beyond the very bottom of the bottom of the infinity of eternality of nothingness itself, beyond the unimaginable beyondness of beyondity and nihil deepening into uncreation precreation and the impossibility of anything ever being made again, there remain two forms of torment still worse than all of this combined. The loss of faith in Self. The loss of faith in God.

Thus Spake Zarathustra.

"*El rachum*" includes references to Jeremiah 14:9 and Nehemiah 9:31. Banal as it is to add these footnotes, they too are an important aspect of this meditation: because everything returns to its source, whether in the divine or in the text. Nor are they really any different from anything else I have described. What in the world is more banal than evil?

✡

Ayn Kamocha

"There is none like You, gracious and compassionate, Lord our God. There is none like You, God who is slow to anger and is abundant in kindness and in truth. Save us with Your abundant mercy, from storm and anger save us. Remember Your servants Abraham, Isaac and Jacob, pay no attention to our stubbornness, our wickedness, our sinfulness. Turn back from Your flaring anger and relent from the evil meant for Your people…"

"The evil *meant* for Your people." Does it really, truthfully say that? Meant! This is shocking, bewildering, astounding. The conviction that evil doesn't happen because men will it, and execute it; that evil happens because God wills it. Not even that He simply allows it – the divine complacency of *histir panav*, where God fails to turn His countenance to shine on us, or actively determines not to turn His face to shine on us, and in the gloom, the dusky twilight where no shadows are cast, in the hours of darkness when trolls and furies, vampires and *lilim*, goblins and all the other fantasy messengers of the Adversary are free to roam, then evil may take place. No, not even that. Far worse. "The evil *meant* for Your people." Not our fault at all, not even in our remit to prevent, or expiate, but some judicial act of God's against our grandparents, or even our great-grandparents.

This paragraph runs counter to every other paragraph of *Tachanun* and *Vidu'i*, and yet it also expresses the Unity of the Jewish God better than any other, by candidly accepting that all things are God, because God created everything. Elsewhere, in the acknowledgement of sin both personal and universal, we accept tort: that whatever happens to humanity is ultimately humanity's own fault. But not here. Here we touch something much deeper in the human psyche, or at least the Jewish psyche, that nagging *angst*, that the Holocaust (to use one obvious example) was somehow our own fault, that we deserved it, that it came upon us like a penalty clause in a breached contract (Leviticus 26:16ff is the text in question), that it was an aspect of the sub-text of the Covenant (verse 24 especially), that it was in the small print (oy! verse 33! and 36! and 38! we can't say we weren't warned), that God only offered us the covenant, not the extended warranty (verse 38:

"And ye shall perish among the nations, and the land of your enemies shall eat you up.")

And so we ask God, not simply to spare us from the evils men may perpetrate, but from the evils God may perpetrate as well. Save us from Yourself. Allow Your *yetser ha-tov* to overcome Your *yetser ha-ra*. And what a role-model if He can do it!

"...Remove from us the scourge of death for You are compassionate, for such is Your manner; doing undeserved kindness in every generation. Have pity upon Your people, Lord; rescue us from Your wrath; remove from us the scourge of plague and harsh decree, for You are the Guardian of Israel. Yours, my Lord, is the righteousness and ours is the shamefacedness. What complaint can we make? What can we say? What can we declare? What justification can we offer? Let us examine our words and analyse them - and return to You, for Your right hand is extended to accept the penitent. Please, Lord, save us now; please, Lord, bring success now. Please, Lord, answer us on this day that we call. For You, Lord, we have waited; for You, Lord we have hoped; for You Lord, we long. Do not be silent while letting us suffer, for the nations have declared, 'Their hope is lost.' Let every knee and every erect being bow to you alone."

Mashiach achshav! *Mashiach achshav*! Messiah - now! Messiah - now!

"Remove us from the scourge of death" defines the ultimate human difficulty with God. We yearn for life to be sacred, and attribute actual sanctity to God, because He, after all, created life; but we also know that life is not sacred, that God will kill each one of us eventually – the 6-week foetus in the womb, the mother in childbirth, the father on the battlefield, the grandfather by heart attack, the grandmother in a road accident rushing him to hospital...by whatever means, accidental, medical, even homicidal or suicidal, every one of us is doomed to die. How do we rationalise such a paradox: that God the Creator is also the sustainer of life, *but only up until a certain point*? How? By inventing the delusion of an after-life, and a resurrection? By doing so, even in conflict with the *Torah*'s certainty that there is only "ashes to ashes and dust to dust", that "*Adonay natan, Adonay lakach* – God gives, God takes away"?

This is not the "*Ayn kamochа*" that introduces the reading of the Law, but another anthology of scriptural references, on this occasion with the threads distinctly visible.

"Remember Your servants.." Deuteronomy 9:27

"Turn back..."	Exodus 32:12
"Yours is the righteousness..."	Daniel 9:7
"Let us examine..."	Lamentations 3:40
"Save, now..."	Psalm 118:25
"Save us on the day..."	c.f. Psalm 20:10

✡

Ha-poteyach yad

"You who open Your hand for repentance, to welcome rebels and sinners, our soul is confounded by the abundance of our depression - forget us not eternally. Arise and save us for we take refuge in You. Our father, our king, if we lack righteousness and good deeds, recall for us the covenant of our forefathers and our daily testimonies that 'the Lord is the One and Only'. Look upon our affliction, for many are our sufferings and the distresses of our hearts. Have pity on us, Lord, in the land of our captivity, and do not pour Your wrath upon us - for we are Your people, the members of Your covenant. O God, look upon the impoverishment of our honour among the nations and how they abhor us like menstrual impurity. How long will Your strength be in bondage and Your splendour in the enemy's power. Arouse Your strength and Your zeal against Your enemies. Let them be shamed and broken of their strength, and may our travails not seem petty to You. May Your mercies meet us swiftly in our time of distress, and if not for our sake, then act for Your own sake and do not destroy our remnant's remembrance. Be gracious to the nation that ascribes Oneness to Your name twice daily, constantly and with love saying, 'Hear O Israel, the Lord our God, the Lord is One.'"

That phrase "*ad matay uzecha ba-shevi, ve-tiphartecha be-yad tsar* - how long will Your strength be in bondage and Your splendour in the enemy's power", works on me like a *petite madeleine.* "*Uzecha*" is strength in the way we've already witnessed it, the concept of temporal rather than spiritual power - the dynasty of David in Jerusalem. "Your splendour in the power of the enemy." Which enemy? Rome probably, given the period of history when *Tachanun* was written. But the memory triggered in me is Edom, Yehudah ha-Levi's poetic synonym, and not for the Imperial Rome which conquered and destroyed Jerusalem, but for the Catholic Rome which now held it in thrall.

> My heart is in the East
> and I in the depths of the West
> My food has no taste

How can it be sweet?
How can I fulfil my pledges and my vows
When Zion is in the power of Edom
and I in the fetters of Arabia?
It will be nothing to me to leave all the goodness of Spain
So rich will it be to see the dust of the ruined sanctuary

Yehudah ha-Levi was the vertex of Hebrew poetry in the golden age of Jewish history in north Africa and Spain when Jew and Moslem lived and flourished side by side, when Maimonides studied at the feet of Averroes, when the two cultures picked over the rediscovered skeleton of ancient Greece, and made the dry bones live again. Ha-Levi was born in Tudela, in that part of middle Spain where Islam and Catholicism locked horns, somewhere around 1075. As a young man seeking knowledge he moved to the centre of Jewish artistic and intellectual life in Granada (*Garnata al-Yachud* – Granada of the Jews, to give it its proper name: the Christians called it Elvira), where he was befriended by its central figure, the poet Moses ibn-Ezra. When Granada was destroyed in 1090 he travelled, first to Lucena, then briefly to Seville, before trying to settle in Toledo. That sojourn too ended in calamity, when the Jewish community was driven out in 1109. Ha-Levi went next to Cordoba, but like Theodor Herzl almost a millennium later, he'd come to the realisation that the future for the Jewish people lay either in extermination or a return to Zion - a belief expressed poetically and philosophically in "*Ha-Kuzari*", his most famous work.

Whether he ever got to Zion himself isn't recorded. We know that his friends and family resisted his travel plans, and at the very least managed to delay them. We know that he paid visits to both Alexandria and Cairo. Most probably he died in Egypt, en route to Zion, in 1141, but an apocryphal legend - the deaths of all poets should be recorded in apocryphal legends such as this one - has him succeeding at last, after many trials and tribulations, in reaching the very gates of Jerusalem, where he was cut down by the scimitar of a Moslem brigand.

And as to the *petite madeleine*? In my middle twenties I wrote a pair of novels, focussed on the life of Bernhard Aaronsohn, later the Israeli artist Ari Ben Aaron. The second novel, "A Little Oil & Root", found Bernhard in his Israeli incarnation, bringing refugees from war-torn Europe, fighting in the *Haganah* in the War of Independence, a pioneering *kibbutznik* on the Lebanese border, the father of a martyr of the *Yom Kippur* War, finally a disenchanted old man, dying of disillusion in an Israel that had let him down. Through him, the tale of the Land of the Broken Promise, the failed fulfilment of Ha-Levi's dream. The first novel, "The Flaming Sword", recounted Bernhard's childhood, from his growing up in Nazi Germany, through his years in England when he was sent away for his own safety, to the novel's core, his participation in the Black Resistance, that futile band of abject heroes who, with pen-knives and paraffin-bottles, tried single-handedly to defend the bridge of Jewish civilisation against that most barbarian of all barbarians, the *Ubermensch.* To the section of the novel which told of Bernhard's time in England I gave the title, borrowed from ha-Levi's poem quoted above: "In the Power of Edom."

Petites madeleines, for those who have never tried them, are soft and sweet and utterly ruined if you dip them in a cup of tea; Marcel Proust made much of them as a trigger for recovering memories, in his great novel "*A la Recherche du Temps Perdu.*"

The phrase which gives rise to all this circumlocution - "*ve-tiphartecha be-yad tsar*" - is a reference to Psalm 78:61. The concluding phrase of "*Ha-poteyach yad*" is from Deuteronomy 6:4.

What follows "*ad matay uzecha*" is disturbing. "Arouse Your strength and Your zeal against Your enemies. Let them be shamed and broken of their strength, and may our travails not seem petty to You. May Your mercies meet us swiftly..." To ask God to shame our enemies and to break their strength is to ask Him to be unmerciful *to them*, even though the doing of it may be merciful *to us*. So the miracle of the Red Sea was also the drowning of the army of Pharaoh. So the return to Zion is the displacement of the Palestinians. So omelettes require broken egg shells. So every human and divine act infers, implies its opposite – and sometimes rather more than inference and implication.

So much for the preface.

✡

Nephilat Apayim - Putting Down The Head

"*Va-yomer David.*" It's at this point that *Tachanun* properly begins, seated, with the head bowed. To explain this, a historical digression is required.

Who wrote the prayers in *Tachanun*? The "*Kol Bo*", an anonymous collection of *Responsa*, mostly plagiarised from Maimonides at the end of the 13th century, tells that three Rabbis, Shmuel, Binyamin and Yoseph, were set adrift in rudderless boats by the Romans, after the destruction of the Temple in Jerusalem. They came ashore on an island where the local ruler persecuted them. Each of the three composed a personal plea to God, petitioning His help in their plight. Which clearly God heard. Because the ruler died, and his successor treated the three Rabbis well. In gratitude to

God, they wrote down their prayers, made copies of them, and distributed them to Jewish communities everywhere, believing they had efficacious properties that could be repeated universally, as if through the contagion of a healing virus (this is the point at which prayer becomes indistinguishable from superstition). The prayers in question became the text of *Tachanun*.

The tale is self-evidently apocryphal. In fact *Tachanun* was already a part of Temple worship long before the Roman era, providing a space for private worship after the morning *Tamid* sacrifice and the Priestly Blessing. Private worship! Now there's a concept not generally considered in Judaism (*Rabban* Gamliel would have rejected it entirely), where prayer is of necessity a communal activity, and where even the individual's recitation of the *Amidah* is regulated and communalised - we pray alone together, but we never pray together alone, and though we may pray entirely alone, we still say only those prayers which all the world are saying simultaneously; so that we aren't really alone, even when we're physically on our own. But in Temple times, apparently, there was still space for individuation. As soon as the Divine Name was uttered by the Priest, the worshippers, who had been standing until now, would fall flat on their faces, and in that position would utter *Tachanun* - a far cry from the comfortable pillow of today.

When the Temple fell, *Tachanun* entered the synagogue liturgy, where it became transformed from private meditation into public worship. To compensate, private meditation could be fulfilled through the *Vidu'i* and the *Selichot*, the confession and the prayers for forgiveness. But these prayers are personal, not individual; that's to say they are formulated liturgy which the individual recites privately within the forum of the community, whereas the beauty of Temple *Tachanun* lay in its granting to the individual the right and the space to formulate the expressions of his own heart and soul, in his own words. Temple *Tachanun* encouraged poetry, synagogue *Tachanun* only encourages piety. Individuality, of course, is the counterweight of totalitarianism.

Tachanun changed almost as soon as it entered the synagogue. We know from *Talmudic* sources that such distinguished *Rabbanim* as Eleazar ben Hyrcanus, Abbaye, Rava and especially Rav refused to prostrate themselves, and not because their contemporary colleagues had declared prostration to be illegal outside the Temple precincts, but because they considered it demeaning to such distinguished personages as themselves. So the first answer to my earlier question about the *Mah Tovu* (why do we state that we will prostrate ourselves, but never in fact do so) lies not in *Midrash* but in arrogance!

As with most custom and practice in Judaism, tradition evolved so slowly as to be deniable as transformation. The mere slippage of a *dageesh*. The records of the Babylonian *ga'onim* show that *Tachanun* was still encouraged as late as the 12th century, but somewhere between then and the compilation of the "*Shulchan Aruch*" - paradoxically this was the era of *piyyut*, the greatest creational phase of Jewish poetry since Solomonic times - it lost its status and its stature. Joseph Caro's "Prepared Table", the "*Shulchan Aruch*", reduced *Tachanun* merely to an optional custom, provided it with a fixed, immutable form of words, and retained the individuation of original *Tachanun* only in the fact that it isn't led by the *chazan*. But what a terrible loss to Judaism! What a terrible indictment! In the beginning was the Word, and the Word was with God, and the Word shall remain with God until the end, except for those synonyms of the Word which the Rabbis have expropriated, because it's no longer passed on to ordinary men. Speaking as a poet, I beg to protest.

The story of the rather differently dissenting Rabbis isn't really sufficient to explain the ending of the custom of prostration; nor is the prohibition against it outside the Temple precincts - for there's evidence of prostration continuing well into the era of the *ga'onim*. Then what did happen to "*nephilat apayim*", the practice of falling on one's face; and when? I've already asked this question earlier, in relation to "*Mah Tovu*", but here it's a matter not of interest so much as of fundamental principles. In Numbers 16:22, after Korach's rebellion, when Moses and Aaron wished to make special petition to God in a moment of national urgency, "they fell upon their faces and said…" The Hebrew here is "*va-yiplu al-peneyhem*", the same phrase as that of *Tachanun*, albeit in a different conjugation. Again, in Joshua 7:6, when Israel was being pursued by the men of Ai and rout seemed certain, Joshua petitioned God for aid in crisis, "and Joshua rent his clothes and fell to the earth upon his face before the Ark of the Lord until the evening…" Once more it's the same phrase: "*va-yipol al-panav.*"

At what point did we claim back our humility and make of it an arrogance? As late as Maimonides' time the custom of prostration was still in force in some North African communities - hardly a problem given the nature of Moslem prayer. But it was clearly dying out. Was it a reaction against the modes of Islam, in the same manner as the *Hasidim* of Poland in the 18th century, who adopted the strange mode of dress they still wear today (a funereal pastiche of the costume of the Polish aristocracy), precisely in order to appear different from the non-Jews?

To prostrate oneself is to declare complete abjection, an act of the highest, as well as the lowest surrender. To stand before God, as in the *Shemoneh Esreh*, is to make a declaration of virtual equality. But to sit? In the presence of God? While asking a favour? This is the announcement of a whole new covenant arrangement, less a prayer-service than a tea-ceremony with chocolate biscuits. Only kings sit down with kings, in such a casual manner, leaning on one elbow. Are we at prayer with God, or playing chess? At the moment that we rose from our prostrations, we proclaimed the literal ascent of Man. What then did we proclaim when we adopted the sitting position?

What took over in Maimonides' time wasn't simply the custom of sitting to pray, but the habit of leaning on one arm. The custom wasn't new - it had simply failed to catch on before. The "*Bava Metziah*" ("middle gate" in Aramaic), a tractate of the *Mishnah* which deals with such abstruse and esoteric matters as lost property, the four types of caretakers, embezzlement and fraud, usury, and the rights of chattels and hired labourers, advocates the recitation of *Tachanun* in the sitting position (we can presume the influence of the Roman couch in this), but with the head resting on one arm "submissively". I can easily imagine the Princesse de Guermantes favouring such a posture as one which conferred social dignity while allowing an immense show of piety that might very well not be insincere. What I cannot imagine, in my own professional capacity, is how to distinguish "submissively" from "gone to sleep" when praying head-on-arm in a synagogue for teenagers.

But which arm (now we really are getting down to the nub and gristle of *Talmudic* dialectics)? The left arm is regarded as the weaker one (in the sense of *gauche* rather than *sinister*), and since *Tachanun* is a petition rendered in times of weakness, it was considered by the Sages to be the most appropriate side on which to lean. However, during *Shacharit*, the left arm is strengthened by the donning of *tefillin*, and so we lean on the right arm in the morning, but on the left if *Tachanun* is recited during *Minchah*, the afternoon prayers.

Throughout my childhood I was puzzled by a certain line in the Passover *Haggadah*. It was a line I knew particularly well, because it was one of the four questions of the "*Mah Nishtana*", and if there's one piece of liturgy that every Jewish child knows by heart it's the "*Mah Nishtana*" (it's the moment, uniquely, when the child, and specifically the youngest child, assumes predominance over all the grown-ups; a moment waited for all year, but over sadly in a flash).

"Why is this night different from all other nights?"

In fact there's only this one question, but four instances are cited, supplementary and subsidiary to the main question. The fourth states:

"On every other night we may eat either sitting or leaning, but on this night we all lean."

In my family there was never any choice between sitting and leaning.

English manners were at odds with Rabbinical injunctions, and English manners always won. Elbows, like milk bottles, were objects that simply didn't show themselves at table. And so the invitation to lean during the Passover meal, to lean as an act of rebellion-through-piety, was irresistible. But which way? To the left, or to the right? Since *Tachanun* isn't recited on a *yom tov*, the laws of *Tachanun* don't apply. So on the weak arm, or on the strong arm? The Rabbis don't say. But I will say. When God led us out of Egypt, out of the house of slavery, he did so with a "*yad chazak*", a "strong arm". Since Passover commemorates and celebrates this exodus from Egypt, should we not also lean upon our "*yad chazak*"?

Why is *Tachanun* omitted on a *yom tov*? For that matter, why is it omitted if a boy is present in *shul* in the week of his *Bar Mitzvah* and his first laying of *tefillin* (nor is *Kaddish* said by mourners in such a circumstance)? For the latter question, it's because the boy's special merits in that week accrue to the whole community (including the community of the recent dead), which make of it a *yom tov*, and the joy of a *yom tov* should never be spoiled or undermined by grief or supplication. The same is true of a bridegroom in the week of his marriage. Nor is *Tachanun* recited in a House of Mourning (this isn't an issue of morbidity, but of respect), nor if the *mohel* or *sandek* about to perform a *Brit Milah* - a circumcision - are present. Nor on any festive occasion. Neither joy may be lowered by supplication, nor grief ridden roughshod by it.

The month of *Nisan* is completely exempted from the recitation of *Tachanun*, and this is why. On each of the first twelve days of *Nisan* a tribal prince was inaugurated in the Mosaic desert, and gave a sacrifice of thanksgiving - each an identical offering, so there could be no rivalry amongst the tribes; these therefore are *yom tayvim*. Then there's the day before *Pesach*, when the search for *chamets*, unleavened bread, takes precedence and declares the *chag*; then there's the Fast of the First-Born on the eve of *Pesach* itself; followed by the eight days of the *matzot* and the *isru chag*, the day that follows the pilgrim festival and which retains a certain measure of its holiness because the pilgrims will be returning to their homes in a state of grace. And allowing for at least one *shabbat* in the remaining period (*Pesach* ends on the 22nd, the month on the 30th), virtually nothing remains of the month. Since the Rabbis have democratically decreed that a majority must always impose its spirit on the remainder - an edict which seems to be applied more conspicuously to dates than to people - *Nisan* is outvoted and even disenfranchised in the matter of private meditation.

Perhaps the boy who is *Bar Mitzvah* will not continue to lay *tefillin*. Perhaps he'll grow up a heretic, an idolator, a *mumar*, an apostate: a myrtle among reeds. Perhaps he'll be one of those who bring shame and consternation upon Israel (bringing consternation, especially to grandparents, is generally the worst crime in Judaism). And what about the bridegroom? Perhaps he'll beat his wife, take mistresses, issue a divorce but not a *get*, leave his wife chained and abandoned, *agunah*? How can we be sure that merit will indeed accrue?

So it's asked in many communities. And in those communities it's the custom to say *Tachanun*, and *Kaddish*, even on those occasions when the *Bar Mitzvah* and the *chatan* are present. This is Judaism at its most pessimistically realistic.

End of historical digression. Having recited the prefatory prayers, if it's a Monday or a Thursday, or beginning with "*Nephilat apayim*" on other days, sit down, press the head against the right arm (we're davening *Shacharit*, remember), and recite, privately, but with fervour, the lines from 2 Samuel 24:14:

"And David said to Gad, 'I am completely devastated. Let us give ourselves into God's hands, for He is abundant in His mercy; but let me not fall into human hands.'"

Wise man! But one so very broken. In one of the most obscure texts in the entire *Tanach*, David has just been chastised by the prophet Gad for the sin of conducting a census. We're not told explicitly what is the nature of the sin, but it isn't difficult to work it out. Exodus 30:12 is explicit on the law of the census: "When you make a census of the children of Israel, every man who is counted shall give a ransom for his soul to the Lord. This they shall give, every one who passes among them to be counted, half a *shekel* after the *shekel* of the Sanctuary - equivalent to twenty *agorot* - as an offering to the Lord." This is the "*kapper*", the origin of *Yom Kippur*, a fine levied against any man who takes human life in a manner that can't be construed as murder (for example, a farmer whose bull gores a man to death, or an employer whose worker falls from a roof - manslaughter, in modern parlance). This applied especially to the military muster, for any soldier was liable to kill in war, and the *kapper* redeemed his soul *pre facto*.

In 2 Samuel 24, King David gave orders for a census, and though it isn't stated, and though his nephew Yo-Av's reasons for declaring it abominable seem not to be explained by this, scholars have long assumed that, because he was unwilling to provoke rebellion through the imposition of a new tax, he didn't require the *kapper*. Through the prophet Gad, God proclaimed his fury and gave David a choice of punishments, all in the form of national calamity and national atonement ("*kappara*"): seven years of famine, three months of military losses, or a three-day epidemic of fatal proportions. David chose the latter, for the reason that God would have to inflict His punishment directly, and would be unable to do so, because His Mercy and

His Compassion would prevent Him. And so it proved - God halted the punishment after just a day and a half.

None of this is explicitly contained is the prayer we recite - nonetheless it's there in the source and context - only the statement of distress and the hope that we will fall neither into the hands of God nor those of men. Any one of us can share this hope, though we may disagree as to which of the two might be the worse. But, more prosaically, we continue:

"O Compassionate and Gracious One" - you would think we were addressing *Allah*; and of course, in a very real sense, we are - "I have sinned before You. Lord who is full of mercy, have mercy on me and accept my supplications."

"I". The unprecedented "I". Through the whole preface to the *Tachanun* we spoke in the first person plural, acknowledging our status as mere stars, mere *nebulae*, in a vast Milky Way, a Jacob's Ladder of galaxies and constellations. But now we are the axis of an egocentric universe. No longer "our sin" but "my sin". A man, alone, existential, speaking directly, personally, to his own understanding of the deity. No intermediary Rabbi, channelling the terms of reference. Direct apprehension, Man to God as in a whirlwind or a burning bush or a still, small voice. Yes, this is the moment for which I come to synagogue.

Only the "I" turns straight back into the King - David, not *Adon Olam*. This isn't entirely devoid of satisfaction for me, though I imagine it's somewhat less so for those who bear a different name. But only somewhat. If to say "I" is to say "David", then it's also to say "*Mashiach*", the First, though not the Last. I mean, the *Alpha*, if not yet the *Omega*.

The Psalm in question is 6:2-11: "*Adonay al-be'aphcha*".

✡

Adonay al-be'aphcha

"Lord, do not rebuke me in Your anger, nor chastise me in Your rage. Favour me, Lord, for I am feeble; heal me, Lord, for my bones shudder. My soul is utterly confounded, and You, Lord, how long? Desist, Lord, release my soul, save me as befits Your kindness. For there is no mention of You in death; in the underworld who will thank You? I am wearied by my sighing, every night I drench my bed with my tears. I soak my couch. My eye is dimmed because of anger, aged by my tormentors. Depart from me, all evil-doers, for the Lord has heard the sound of my weeping. The Lord has heard my plea, the Lord will accept my prayer. Let all my foes be shamed and utterly confounded. They will regret and be instantly ashamed."

✡

Adonay Elohey Yisra'el

On Mondays and Thursdays, as we've already seen, additional prayers are recited before and during *Tachanun*. So, after Psalm 6, and before "*Shomer Yisrael*", more prayers are added, each with the same refrain to punctuate them:

"Lord God of Israel, turn back from Your flaring anger, and relent from the evil meant for Your people." (Exodus 32:12)

The word "evil" stands out once again. No question of the meaning of the word; the Hebrew gives "*ra'ah*", which is indeed the standard word for "evil". But this is "evil" coming, once again, directly from God, confirming yet again the Unity: if the Lord our God is One, how could it be otherwise? A God who contains both the *Shiva* and the *Vishnu*, the *Orhmazd* and the Adversary, the Destroyer and the Sustainer, two sides of the same, single coin. Perhaps we shouldn't be surprised to find it in a Psalm of such paganness that it even includes the concept of the Underworld, *She'ol.*

The additional prayers contain further scriptural allusions: Psalm 44:14, 44:23, Isaiah 53:7, Lamentations 5:5, Deuteronomy 7:6, Psalm 115:2, Daniel 9:19, Exodus 32:13, Jeremiah 42:2 and Psalm 79:9.

But why Mondays and Thursdays? Mondays and Thursdays (the second and fifth days of the Jewish week) are important for more than just *Tachanun* - regularly they're fast days, either to mourn the loss of the Temple or to pray for rain. *Midrash* tells us that Moses went up to Mount Sinai for the second set of tablets on the first day of the month of *Elul*, which fell on a Thursday that year, and that he came down forty days later, on the 10th of *Tishrey*, the Monday of *Yom Kippur* (*Bava Komma* 82a). Ezra instituted the meetings of the Rabbinical Courts on Mondays and Thursdays, and these, according to the *Kabbalah*, are also the days on which the Heavenly Courts are in session. Ezra also instituted the annual cycle of the reading of the *Torah*, the full weekly reading on the Sabbath, its opening read previously in every market-place of Israel, on Mondays and on Thursdays, because these were the days when the markets happened to be. Quite probably this is the real historical source of the significance of the two days, a fortuitous coincidence exalted to the status of a holy law, with all the other incidents and references pragmatically interpolated later.

As to the text of this additional section, it comes in the form of five verses and a refrain, but is regarded as coming in the form of four verses, an extra verse, and then the refrain, the extra verse being rather inconvenient and therefore described as an addition, for reasons that should quickly become clear.

Tradition ascribes this section to King Hezekiah, and claims that he wrote it during the siege of Jerusalem by Sennacherib (700 BCE). The initial letters of the four verses and the refrain are, in order, *Yud*, *Hey*, *Zayin*, *Chet* and *Kuph*, which make an anagram of Hezekiah's own name (the unhelpful fifth verse has an initial *Ayin*); the commentators note Hezekiah's modesty in disguising his name anagrammatically, but fail to offer the obvious explanation of the fifth verse (an additional ruse in the matter of self-concealment). To add mysticism to mysticism, the *Kabbalistic* work "*Or Ha-Yashar*" also points out that "*Adonay Elohey Yisrael*", the name by which God is known in the refrain, totals up numerically to 613, which is the number of the commandments given by God to Moses on Mount Sinai (except that it isn't; around 300 are given; the rest, as we have seen, are deduced).

At the conclusion of Psalm 6, we also conclude leaning, and resume our normal sedentary position. If *Tachanun* is said at home, or in any room that has no Ark or *Torah* scroll, we shouldn't lean at all, but recite the whole of *Tachanun* while sitting upright.

✡

Shomer Yisrael - Guardian of Israel

On all occasions *Tachanun* is completed by "*Shomer Yisrael*".

"O Guardian of Israel, protect the remnant of Israel, let Israel not be destroyed: those who proclaim *Shema Yisra'el* - Hear O Israel.

"O Guardian of the unique nation, protect the remnant of the unique people; let not the unique nation be destroyed: those who proclaim the Oneness of Your name, 'The Lord our God, the Lord is One'.

"O Guardian of the holy nation, protect the remnant of the holy people, let not the holy nation be destroyed: those who proclaim threefold sanctifications to the Holy One [the *Kedushah*].

"Become favourable through compassion and become appeased through supplications. Become favourable and appeased to this poor generation who has no other helper. Our father, our king, be gracious with us and answer is, though we have no worthy deeds; treat us with charity and kindnesses, and save us."

Variations on the same form of words, again and again. But, after all, we've been praying these prayers this morning for well over an hour, and in our lifetimes for many a long year, and in the history of the nation for over two thousand years - and after so many and such extensive conversations between ourselves and God, what else actually is there, new or old, for us to talk about?

✡

Va-anachnu - We know not what to do

"We know not what to do - but our eyes are upon You. Remember Your mercies, Lord, and Your kindnesses, for they are from the beginning of the world. May Your kindness be upon us, Lord, just as we awaited You. Do not recall against us the sins of the ancients; may Your mercies meet us swiftly, for we have become exceedingly impoverished. Be gracious to us, Lord, be gracious to us, for we are abundantly sated with scorn. Amid rage - remember to be merciful. For He knew our nature, He remembers that we are dust.

"Assist us, O God of our salvation" - this recited by the chazan alone - "for the sake of the glory of Your name. Rescue us and atone for our sins for Your name's sake."

"*Va-anachnu*" includes references from 2 Chronicles 20:12, Psalm 25:6, 33:22, 79:8, 123:3, Habakkuk 3:2 and Psalms 103:14 and 79:9.

✡

Because *Tachanun* contains scriptural references, but no studying of those portions of scripture; and because the end of *Tachanun* marks a division in the order of the service, for these two reasons a half-*Kaddish* rather than the full *Kaddish d'Rabbanan* is recited at the culmination, standing, to bring *Tachanun* to its formal end.

On Mondays and Thursdays, as Ezra required, the *Torah* scrolls are now opened and read. On Sundays, Tuesdays, Wednesdays and Fridays, the service proceeds directly to *Ashrey*.

✡

Chapter Twelve: *Kriyat ha-Torah* - The Reading of the Law

The "*Sepher Torah*" - the "Book of the Law", comprises five separate volumes, known by their Greek or Latin nomenclatures as Genesis (*Bereyshit*), Exodus (*Shemot*), Leviticus (*Va-Yikra*), Numbers (*Ba-Midbar*) and Deuteronomy (*Devarim*). The Hebrew names derive from the first word, or the first key word, at the opening of each of the five books. The Greek and Latin names derive from the *Septuagint*, the translation of the *Tanach* (such is the proper Hebrew name for what Christians call, deliberately insultingly, the "Old" Testament) made for the Greek-speaking Jewish community of Alexandria in the first half of the 3rd century BCE, at the time of its glorious foundation under the first two Ptolomies. The custom established by Ezra is a weekly reading cycle from the start of *Bereyshit* to the end of *Devarim*, beginning and ending at the joyous autumn festival of *Simchat Torah* on the 23rd of *Tishrey*. The Five Books are subdivided into fifty-four *sidrot* or weekly portions, also known as *parashot*, one for each week of the Jewish calendar, thereby enabling the entire *Torah* to be read within the year. (Just for the historical interest, before Ezra the *Torah* was originally divided into 154 sections, and the cycle of reading was triennial. The division into paragraphs belongs to the Christian Council of Nicaea in 325 CE, the division into chapters to Archbishop Stephen Langton, around 1248.)

On *shabbat* the full weekly *sedra* is recited; on Mondays and Thursdays only the opening section of the seven into which each weekly *sedra* is further subdivided. On *shabbat* a member of the congregation is called to make a blessing before and after each of the seven sub-*sidrot*, as well as an eighth who is called to the repetition of the closing verses - the "*maphtir*" - and who then remains to make the blessings before and after the "*haphtorah*", the accompanying reading from the Prophets, and if he is capable to chant that reading too. On Mondays and Thursdays that single opening section is split in three, to enable three members of the congregation to participate. On all occasions the first person called should always be a Cohen, the second a Levite, and after that any member of the tribes of Israel. There is no greater honour in a synagogue than to be called up to the Reading of the Law.

The practices for "*Kriyat ha-Torah* - the Reading of the Law" are more complex on *shabbat* than weekdays. I propose to confine myself here to weekday practices.

✡

El Erech Apayim

The ceremony begins with the recitation of "*El erech apayim*", a matter of some dispute among Ashkenazi Jews, those from the western lands (Germany, Bavaria, Lower Poland) disagreeing with those from the eastern *heim* (Greater Poland and Lithuania) as to the correct form of words. It's a pedantry over a handful of syllables, in which I refuse to become involved. Most prayer books now print both versions; and so mixed are the communities in the English-speaking world that many achieve the ideal compromise by saying both at once.

"O God, slow to anger and abundant in kindness and truth" (Exodus 34:5) opens both versions. "Do not chastise in Your anger" (Psalm 6:2) competes with "Do not conceal Your face from us" (Psalm 27:9). "Pity, Lord, Your people" (Joel 2:17) is shared, but one version has "and save us from any evil", while the others insists, "and rescue us from evil". Both then conclude with "we have sinned against You, Master; forgive us, we beg You, in accordance with Your abundant mercy, O God." The dispute is entirely semantic: the intention in both cases remains identical.

Va-yehi binso'a

Two congregants approach the Ark, making pillars either side: like the pillars known as Bo'az and Yachin at the entrance to the Temple Courtyard. One draws back the curtain, the other the wooden doors, revealing the *Torah* scrolls. From the *amud*, the reading desk, the *chazan* recites "*va-yehi binso'a*", which reminds us that "when the Ark would travel, Moses would say, 'Arise, Lord, let Your foes be scattered, let those who hate You flee from You.'" (Numbers 10:35). To which is added the phrase of Isaiah (2:3), "For from Zion will the *Torah* come forth, and the Word of the Lord from Jerusalem." Both of which statements merit the benediction, "Blessed is He who gave the *Torah* to His people Israel in His holiness."

Berich Shemeh

In some communities, generally the more orthodox, a *Kabbalistic* meditation, "*Berich shemeh*", is now recited silently. The text is from the *Zohar*, the "Book of Splendour", (*Vayakhel* 369a) the central text of mystical

Judaism, a book attributed to the *Talmudist* Simeon ben Yochai, but in fact written by Moses ben Shem-Tov de Léon, in Spain at the end of the 13th century. De Léon was a close friend of another revered *Kabbalist*, Abraham Abulafia - he who dared to call the Pope to account for the persecution of the Jews, and who was only saved from death by burning as a punishment for his accusation when the pontiff unexpectedly died. De Léon's post-modernist hoax was perpetrated on the assumption that the alleged "collected *Midrashim*" of an acknowledged *Talmudist* would carry more weight than any published under his own name. It has taken till the present day to find him out, and even now not all scholars are convinced.

"Blessed is the name of the Master of the Universe, blessed is Your crown and Your place. May Your favour remain with Your people Israel forever; may You display the salvation of Your right hand to Your people in Your holy Temple, to benefit us with the goodness of Your luminescence and to accept our prayers with mercy. May it be Your will that You extend our lives with goodness and that I be numbered among the righteous, that You have mercy on me and protect me, all that is mine and that is Your people Israel's. It is You who nourishes all and sustains all; You have power over everything. It is You who has power over kings, and kingship is Yours. I am a servant of the holy one, blessed be He, and I prostrate myself before Him and before the glory of His *Torah* at all times. Not in any man do I place my trust, nor on any angel do I rely - only on the God of heaven who is the God of truth, whose *Torah* is truth and whose prophets are true and who acts liberally with kindness and with truth. In Him do I trust, and to His glorious and holy name do I declare praises. May it be Your will that You open my heart to the *Torah* and that You fulfil the wishes of my heart and the heart of Your entire people Israel for good, for life and for peace. Amen."

Nothing to be gained from rehearsing yet again the same old arguments. What interests me especially about this prayer is the extent to which it - which is to say the *Kabbalah*, the world of mysticism - has transformed religion into a function, not of the spiritual or the moral but of the intellectual life. Absent the recurrent themes of mercy and compassion, which denote active relationships between one creature and another. Absent any sense of *Torah* as a covenant or a philosophy for daily life. Here we have entered an abstract world, of notions concepts and conceits, any one of which can and no doubt will be argued till the Messiah comes home. What, after all, is Truth? How are we to understand the ideas of "luminescence", of "power"? Even the double mention of "heart" in the closing phrases seems to reflect again that ancient belief that the heart was the habitat of thought: the heart and not the brain. Why, even the concept of prostration that occurs here reads more like intellectual submission than the physical act of lying on the floor upon one's face.

✡

Gadelu

After "*Berich Shemeh*" the *chazan* takes a *Torah* scroll out of the Ark, holds it against his right shoulder and, facing the congregation from the *duchen*, recites "*Gadelu*" (Psalm 34:4).

"*Gadelu l'Adonay iti, u-neromemah shemo yachdo.*"

"Declare the greatness of the Lord with me, and let us exalt his name together."

✡

Lecha Adonay

Then turn - to the right - towards the congregation, and proceed to the *bimah*, circling the synagogue, allowing time for the congregants to step forward and kiss the fringes or the outer garment of the scroll with the fringes of their *tsitsit* or the *tsitsit* or their prayer-shawls, with their prayer-book even, but never with their lips or fingers touching it directly. And while proceeding, sing in unison "*Lecha Adonay*", stirring words and melody drawn from 1 Chronicles 29:11 and Psalm 99:5 and 9.

"*Lecha Adonay ha-gedulah ve-ha-gevurah ve-ha-tipheret ve-ha-netsach ve-ha-hod, ki chol ba-shamayim u-va-arets, lecha Adonay ha-mamlachah ve-ha-mitnaseh le-chol le-rosh. Romemu Adonay eloheynu ve-hishtachavu la-hadom raglav, kadosh hu. Romemu Adonay eloheynu ve-hishtachavu le-har kadsho, ki kadosh Adonay eloheynu.*"

"Yours, Lord, is the greatness, the strength, the splendour, the triumph, and the glory; even everything in heaven and earth. Yours, Lord, is the kingdom, and the sovereignty over every source of life. Exalt the Lord our God, and bow at His footstool. He is holy. Exalt the Lord our God, and bow at His holy mountain, for the Lord our God is holy."

This is the joyful celebration of the giving of the Law which is the pinnacle and climax of all Jewish worship. But perilously close, o perilously close, to that nadir of Jewish sin, idolatry.

✡

Av ha-rachamim

The scroll is now undressed - another honour awarded to a member of the congregation. It wears a velvet cover over the parchment, with two silver crowns of *rimmonim* over the handles, and a silver breastplate pendulous from the handles, the silver *yad* - an imitation hand with pointing finger, used to follow the reading rather than have a human finger touch the delicate and holy parchment text - alongside it. Inside its coverings, the parchment is bound in a cord of velvet - secure, but soft enough to avoid damaging the precious cloth. While the scroll is being undressed and the cord binding the parchment untied, "*Av ha-rachamim*" is spoken silently.

"May the father of mercy have mercy on the nation that is borne by Him, and may He remember the covenant of the spiritually mighty. May He rescue our souls from the bad times, and upbraid the evil inclination to leave those borne by Him, graciously make us an eternal remnant, and fulfil our requests in good measure, for salvation and mercy."

"*Av ha-rachamim*" has an entirely different tone and attitude, rarely encountered in the Jewish liturgy, a politeness that's almost deferential, a form of request that isn't supplicatory, that involves no breast-beating, no sycophantic litany of His attributes. It's a most dignified prayer, almost English in its quality of reserve, one that seems to me extremely modern.

✡

Ve-tigaleh

Ever since the custom of reading the *Torah* aloud in synagogue was inaugurated, the Rabbis have insisted that, because God gave the Law to Israel through an intermediary, so too should it be given in synagogue. No one should ever stand alone at the *amud* for the reading of the Law. The preferred number is three - the *chazan*, who reads the Law, the *oleh*, who has been called to say the blessings before and afterwards, and the *gabbai*, whose many duties include following the text separately to correct any errors in the reading, calling each *oleh* according to the set formula, pronouncing the "*mi-she-berach*", the blessing on the *oleh* afterwards, marking the place in the text where the *oleh* should kiss the text with his prayer-shawl before and after the blessings, closing or covering the scrolls between sections of reading - providing, in short, the duties of a guard of honour for the *Torah*.

After "*Av ha-rachamim*" then, the *gabbai* places the undressed scroll upon the *amud* and calls the Cohen to the reading of the Law with "*ve-tigaleh*".

"And may His kingship over us be revealed and become visible soon, and may He be gracious to our remnant and the remnant of His people the family of Israel, for graciousness, kindness, mercy and favour. And let us all respond, amen. All of you ascribe greatness to our God and give honour for the *Torah.* Cohen - approach. Arise"…the Hebrew name of the *oleh* is given...*ha-Cohen.* "Blessed is He who gave the *Torah* to His people Israel in His holiness. All of you who cling to the Lord your God, you are all alive today."

If no Cohen is present, a Levite will do; if no Levite, then any *Yisra'el*, and God bless you. A person is called by their Hebrew name, with their father's Hebrew name and "*ben*" meaning "son of" - as in the patriarchal *Ya'akov ben Yitschak*, Jacob son of Isaac. Superstition over the holiness of the *Torah* scrolls is such that the law against idolatry is always close to being breached. Here, the person called presses the fringes of his prayer shawl against the first word to be read, then kisses the fringe before reciting the blessing for the reading. Alternately he may use the leather strap of his *tefillin* or the cord that binds the parchment. But never direct contact, always through the intermediary of something holier than thou.

So the ceremony of reading may begin.

Benedictions of the *Torah*

For every fragment of *Torah* that is read, the same blessing beforehand.

"*Baruchu et-Adonay ha-mevorach* - Blessed be God, the blessed one."

To which the congregation responds:

"*Baruch Adonay ha-mevorach le-olam va'ed* - Blessed be God, the blessed one, eternally."

The *oleh* repeats the congregational response and then continues:

"*Baruch atah Adonay eloheynu melech ha-olam, asher bachar banu mi-kol ha-amim ve-natan lanu et Torato. Baruch atah Adonay noten ha-Torah* - Blessed are You Lord our God, king of the Universe, who chose us from all the nations and gave us His *Torah*. Blessed are You, Lord, giver of the *Torah.*"

Individualism surfaces once more. If the *oleh* has recently survived a dangerous experience, he may offer a personal thanksgiving at this moment, according, of course, to a fixed formula. If the *oleh* has a son whose *Bar*

Mitzvah falls that week, there's a special prayer which thanks God for releasing him from the burden of bearing his son's punishments, as a Jewish father must until his son reaches the age of maturity at thirteen. If the *oleh* is related to a person who is sick, special petitions for their recovery may be inserted. And if it's the *oleh*'s *yahrzeit*, the anniversary of the death of a close relative, the *gabbai* on his behalf will recite the prayer for the deceased, "*El maleh rachamim*". If not the Cohen or the Levi, the Israel will always be one of these, if there is one such in the synagogue that day.

The Thanksgiving blessing - recited by one who has survived a dangerous experience - properly belongs in the Temple Service, for it was the custom in Temple times to bring a Thanksgiving sacrifice after surviving any life-threatening experience. Now a blessing is recited instead, if possible within three days of the event. Which events count? The answer is derived from Psalm 107 - completion of a sea journey, completion of a hazardous land journey, recovery from major illness, release from captivity.

The *Bar Mitzvah* blessing derives from the *Midrash Rabbah* to Genesis 25:27. The Biblical text reads: "And he came near, and kissed him, and he smelled the smell of his raiment, and blessed him, and said, 'See, the smell of my son is as the smell of a field which the Lord has blessed.'"

The idea behind this is obvious and valid - as Isaac blessed his son upon reaching maturity, so should all fathers. But is there not something slightly undermining, something distinctly odd, about founding a custom in an act of treacherous deceit, given that what is recounted in this story is the stealing of his father's blessing by Jacob from his brother Esau?

Custom and practice have established precise hierarchies for the Reading of the Law. On a Monday and Thursday, as on *shabbat* afternoon, on *Chanukah* and *Purim*, no more than three call-ups. On *Rosh Chodesh* and *Chol ha-Mo'ed*, which is to say the New Moon and the intermediate days of Festivals, four. On Festivals, five. On *Yom Kippur*, six. And on the morning of *shabbat*, not less than seven, not more than ten. The exception to this is the eve of *Simchat Torah*, where the service is deliberately prolonged, and if necessary the whole *sedra* re-read and re-read over and over, in order to call up every male present in the *shul*.

As to who should be called, if there are more seeking an *aliyah* than can be called without breaching what is called "*tircha d'tsibbura* - the patience of the congregation", here, in its hierarchy, is the official list:

* a bridegroom on the day of his wedding
* a bridegroom on the Sabbath before his wedding (the "*aufruf*" in

Yiddish)

* a *Bar Mitzvah*
* a father celebrating the birth of a child
* a bridegroom on the Sabbath after his wedding
* a *yahrzeit* for a parent falling on that Sabbath
* a *yahrzeit* due the following week
* one who has recovered from illness
* one embarking on, or returning from, a journey overseas
* a visitor to the synagogue

Precedent appropriate to the occasion, which is joyful, because any event connected to the *Torah* is always joyful.

It's also customary not to call members of the same family consecutively.

Reading the Law

The person called isn't expected to read the portion of the Law which he has blessed; though of course he may, and a *Bar Mitzvah* should if he is capable. The role is the pronouncing of the blessing, the holding of the handles of the *Torah* scrolls and the pointing to the text with the silver *yad*, as an aide to the *chazan*. Why? Because many Jews don't read Hebrew at all, not even the simple book version, where a system of simplifying vowels has been added to a language whose 22-letter alphabet is entirely consonantal. Because many of those Jews who can read Hebrew don't know the complex rubric of cantillation, which like the vowels isn't marked on the *Torah* scroll. Imagine, not simply reciting Shakespeare, but singing Shakespeare to a complex melody for which no annotation is provided; and not simply singing it, but doing so from a text devoid of vowels:

T b r nt t b tht s th qstn whthr ts nblr n th mnd t sffr th slngs nd rrws f trgs frtn r t tk p rms gnst s f trbls

But to hold the handles of the scrolls, to kiss at the right place, to say the blessings fore and aft, and to follow with your eyes and inner ear - this is tantamount to reading. The *chazan* reads on your behalf, and it's regarded less as surrogational than ventriloquial.

Call - bless - read - bless again. After the reading the *oleh* recites a second blessing.

"*Baruch atah Adonay eloheynu melech ha-olam, asher natan lanu Torat emet, ve-chayey olam nata betocheynu. Baruch atah Adonay noten ha-Torah* - Blessed are You, Lord our God, king of the Universe, who gave us the *Torah* of truth and implanted eternal life within us. Blessed are You, Lord, the giver of the *Torah*."

Blessings in Judaism go in both directions. The *oleh* blesses God, for giving him and us the *Torah*. But it's a great honour and privilege and duty to be called to the reading of the Law, and this too merits a benediction. So, while the next *oleh* approaches the *amud*, the *gabbai* blesses his prelector.

"*Mi she-berach avoteynu Avraham, Yitschak ve-Ya'akov, hu yevarech et...asher alah la-Torah. Ha-kadosh baruch hu yevarech oto ve-et mishpachto ve-yishlach berachah ve-hatslachah be-chol ma'aseh yadav, ve-nomar amen* - May He who blessed our forefathers Abraham, Isaac and Jacob, may He bless...who has been called to the reading of the *Torah*. May the holy one, blessed be He, bless him and his family, and bestow blessings and success on all the works of his hands, and let us say *amen*."

Then the next *oleh*, and the next, until the full number has been called and the correct portion fully read. But this is far from the closure of the ceremony. Whenever scripture is read, it's followed by a half-*Kaddish*. The scroll is left on the *amud*, but covered up, while the congregation stands to "magnify and exalt" the name of God in a version of the half-*Kaddish* which in this circumstance is always sung. Then two more members of the congregation are called, the first the "*Hagbahah*", who will hold up the open *Torah* to the full view of the congregation, turn a full circle showing it, and then sit for the scroll to be re-dressed. While he turns the congregation stands, many of them holding out a crooked finger or their *tsitsit* towards the scroll in a gesture of affection and obeisance (as if to kiss it, but without kissing it), and sing:

"*Ve-zot ha-Torah asher sam Moshe liphney beney Yisra'el, al pi Adonay be-yad Moshe* - This is the *Torah* that Moses placed before the children of Israel, upon the command of God, through the hand of Moses." (Deuteronomy 4:44 and Numbers 9:23)

In some congregations the verse "*ayts chayim hi le-machazikim bo*" is added, a meditative compilation from Proverbs 3:18, 3:17, 3:16 (why the reverse order is unclear) and Isaiah 42:21.

"It [the *Torah*] is a tree of life for those who grasp it, and its supporters are praiseworthy. Its ways are ways of pleasantness and all its paths are peace. Lengthy days are at its right; at its left are wealth and honour. The Lord desired, for the sake of Israel's righteousness, that the *Torah* be made great and glorious."

✡

Yehi ratson

The second of the two additional *olim* is for "*Gelilah*", the re-dressing of the scroll in readiness for its return to the Ark - the same person who undressed called again to clad the scroll anew. While he dresses it, the *gabbai* recites "*Yehi Ratson*", a set of four petitions, and the "*Acheynu*", which the congregation recite first and the *gabbai* endorses. These are omitted when *Tachanun* is not recited.

"*Yehi Ratson*" derives from Rav Amram ben Sheshna, the *Ga'on* of Sira near Babylon in the 9th century, whose "*Machzor de-Rav Amram*", a series of epistolary *Responsa*, is widely regarded as the first prayer book - or at the least the first *siddur*, an organised structure for the annual cycle of prayer.

"May it be the will of our father who is in heaven to establish the house of our lives and to settle His presence within us, speedily in our days - and let us say *amen.* May it be the will of our father who is in heaven to have mercy upon us and upon our remnant, and to keep destruction and plague away from us and from all His people of the family of Israel - and let us say *amen.* May it be the will of our father who is in heaven to preserve among us the sages of Israel, them, their wives, their sons, their daughters, their disciples and the students of their disciples in all their dwelling places - and let us say amen. "May it be the will of our father who is in heaven that we may hear and be informed of good tidings, salvations, and consolations, and that our dispersed be gathered from the four corners of the earth - and let us say *amen.*"

And the closing "*Acheynu*":
"Our brothers, the entire family of Israel, who are delivered into distress and captivity, whether they are on sea or dry land - may The Omnipresent One have mercy on them and remove them from distress to relief, from darkness to light, from subjugation to redemption, now, speedily, and soon - and let us say *amen.*"

Whatever mysticisms, whatever miracles, whatever rituals, whatever poetries - in the end it comes back, over and again, to this fundamental humanism: I equals we. We is never the ephemeral us who are gathered here, but always the perennial human being, everywhere and at all times. For it isn't only God who is eternal and universal. What applies to God applies also to Man - we too are One.

✡

Yehallelu

"*Yehi Ratson*" and *gelilah* finished, the *oleh* of *hagbahah* gives the scroll back to the *chazan*, who recites "*Yehallelu* - let them praise the Name of the Lord for His name alone will have been exalted" - while the Ark is being re-opened. The congregation respond, singing "*Hodu al erets*" (Psalm 148:13-14).

"*Hodu al erets ve-shamayim, va-yarem keren le-amo, tehilah le-chol chasidav livney Yisra'el am kerovo, hallelu-Yah.*"

"His glory is above earth and heaven. And He will have exalted the pride of His people, causing praise for all his devout ones, for the children of Israel, His intimate nation. *Hallelu-Yah.*"

And then, while the scroll is once again being processioned round the synagogue to the Ark, "*Le-David Mizmor*" (Psalm 24) - a different Psalm is sung on Saturdays.

"The earth and all its fullness, the inhabited land and those who dwell in it, belong to the Lord. For He founded it upon seas, and established it upon rivers. Who may ascend the mountain of the Lord, and who may stand in the place of His sanctity? One with clean hands and a pure heart, who has not sworn in vain by my soul and has not sworn deceitfully. He will receive a blessing from the Lord and just kindness from the God of his salvation. This is the generation of those who seek Him, those who strive for your presence - Jacob. Raise up your heads, O gates, and be uplifted, you everlasting entrances, so that the king of glory may enter. Who is this king of glory? He is the Lord, the mighty and strong, the Lord, the strong in battle."

✡

U-venucha

The procession echoes the earlier procession, complete with the kissing of the scrolls as it proceeds. While the scroll is being placed in the Ark the congregation sings "*U-venucha*" with its collation of references - Numbers 10:36, Psalm 132:8-10, proverbs 4:2, 3:18, 3:17 and Lamentations 5:21. A complement to "*Va-yehi binso'a*".

"And when it [the Ark] rested he would say, 'Return, Lord, to the myriad thousands of Israel. Arise, Lord, to Your resting place, You and the Ark of Your power. Let Your priests be clothed in righteousness, and Your devout ones will sing joyously. For the sake of David Your servant, do not turn away the face of Your anointed one. For I have given you good counsel - do not forsake my *Torah*.'"

And then the *chazan* alone: "It is a tree of life for those who grasp it, and its supporters are praiseworthy. Its ways are made of pleasantness and all its paths are peace. Bring us back to You, Lord, and we shall return. Lord, renew our days as of old."

So the doors of the Ark are closed, the curtain drawn back, and those who have stood before the Ark retire, as one does from the presence of a king, stepping backwards. The ceremony of the Reading of the Law is done. If a sermon is to be delivered, this is the place most apposite for it to be inserted.

Chapter Thirteen: Conclusions

In many communities the honour of leading the service is shared. A mourner may claim the honour, a Rabbi may deserve it, but any man who can *daven* may *daven*. Nor is there a limit to the number of prayer leaders in any given service: one for "*Mah Tovu*", another for the *Shacharit* Blessings, a third for *Pesukei d'Zimrah*, a fourth for the *Shema*, and a fifth to take us from the *Amidah* to the conclusion of the service - plus a sixth for "*Ayn Kamocha*" and a seventh to *leyn* from the *Torah*, on days when the scrolls are taken out. But the Rabbis say that the moment of taking out the scrolls, and now, after they've been put back, these are the two points most appropriate to a change of *chazan*.

Ashrey

Shemoneh Esreh and *Tachanun* represent the climax of spiritual elevation; the *Torah* reading brings God directly into the *shul*; *Ashrey* represents a return to the quotidian, the mundane.

I've already explained the roots of *Ashrey*, the alphabetical acrostic with its single phrase missing, at its earlier appearance in *Pesukei d'Zimrah*.

La-menatseyach

Psalm 20, addressed "*la-menatseyach* - to the conductor of the royal orchestra", now follows, except on certain festive occasions: *Rosh Chodesh*, *Erev Pesach*, *Chol ha Mo'ed* of festivals, *Tisha b'Av*, *Erev Yom Kippur*, *Purim* and *Shushan Purim*, the 14th and 15th *Adar* (*Purim Katan*), and in a house of mourning - all logical exceptions, because it's a Psalm of intense joy sung in a day of distress, an announcement of the "pangs of the Messiah", the "*chevley Mashiach*", which will precede redemption and salvation. Stark contrasts. But it's only through relativity that anything has meaning and acquires value: life in the face of death, joy against pain, love versus hatred. So the agony of childbirth equates to the orgasm which engendered it. So Israel will face its most severe trials, right there, where the Messiah is about to be anointed.

There are even those who argue that the Holocaust itself was the "pangs of the Messiah". A bitter pill to swallow if it was.

The Psalm is normally read silently, the *chazan* uttering only the last two lines, from "*chemah*" to the end.

"May the Lord answer you on the day of your distress, may the name of Jacob's God make you impregnable. May He dispatch your help from the Sanctuary, and support you from Zion. May He remember all your offerings and consider your burned sacrifices generous (*selah*). May He grant you your heart's desire and fulfil your every plan. May we sing of joy at your salvation, and raise our banner in the name of our God, may the Lord fulfil all your requests. Now I know that the Lord has saved His anointed one; He will answer him from His sacred heaven, with the omnipotent salvations of His right arm. Some with chariots, and some with horses, but we - in the name of the Lord our God, we call out. They slumped and fell, but we arose and were invigorated. Lord save us. May the king answer on the day we call."

The text is in many ways bewildering. If the "you" who is constantly referred to is simply the "*menatseyach*" of the title, then we must wonder what was his terrible distress that David himself felt impelled to write a Psalm on his behalf - or was this a bestowal of the highest form of privilege and patronage, the priest-king acting as intermediary for a single individual? And if it isn't the "*menatseyach*", then who is intended by the word "you"? The whole family of Israel? I wonder if a careful re-examination of the syntax wouldn't lead to a reappraisal of this, as a Psalm actually addressed *to* the Messiah, both the priest-king in Jerusalem and the future son of God.

U-va le-Tsi'on

In fact, once the scrolls have been returned to the Ark, the "*avodah*", the "service of worship" (the translation is tautological, but necessarily so to bring out its full meaning) is really ended. What causes it to continue isn't religion, but protocol. After any act of worship, there needs to be a Psalm of praise - so *Ashrey* follows the return of the scrolls, because the return of the scrolls is accompanied with reverential acts of kissing and bowing. But *Ashrey* is scriptural, so it requires a *Kaddish* to complete it. There may also be those who arrived late to this Gormenghastian world, and so a *Kedushah* is needed to enable them to finish their individual prayers. And custom and practice have prescribed a mourner's *Kaddish*.

But previously none of this took place. According to the authorities of the first millennium, the service did indeed end with the return of the scroll and

Ashrey. Then those who wished would leave, while the scholars stayed behind to hear a learned exposition or to take part in a study group. When scholarship was undertaken, passages were recited from the Prophets, especially those passages known as "verses of consolation", that look forward to redemption with the coming of the Messiah. "*U-va le-Tsi'on*", from Isaiah 59:20-21, is one such, and probably this is the one that's been retained because it refers both implicitly and explicitly to the *Torah* that's just been read and studied.

And yet again - so many times now we've seen this - custom and practice cannot be expunged. So "*U-va le-Tsi'on*" continues to this day, not as the culmination of a lecture, but as a reminder of a lecture which history prohibited.

"'A redeemer shall come to Zion, and to those of Jacob who repent from wilful sin'," - these are the words of the Lord. 'And as for Me, this is My covenant with them,' said the Lord. 'My spirit that is upon you and My words that I have placed in your mouth shall not be withdrawn from the mouth of your offspring, nor from the mouth of your offspring's offspring,' said the Lord, 'from this moment and forever.'"

Ominous, portentous words, from the visions of the prophet Isaiah (59:20-12), continuing the theme of the forthcoming Messiah which so dominates the latter phases of the service. The words are recited together by the entire congregation. Then the *chazan* alone states the last line, a quotation from Psalm 22:4, which leads immediately into the *Kedushah*.

✡

Kedushah d'Sidra

"You are the holy one, enthroned upon the praises of Israel. And one angel will call to another and say..."

The *Kedushah* is the key to "*U-va le-Tsi'on*", a recitation in unison of the praises sung by the angels. *Sotah* 49a (*Talmud*) states that the whole world has been in physical demise since the destruction of the Temple, but that it endures because both men and angels sing the praise of God sufficiently that He sustains it. Survival not by evolution, not even by "truth, peace and judgement" as the *Pirkei Avot* suggest - but by flattery!

"'Holy, holy holy is the Lord God of the Heavenly Host, the whole world is filled with His glory.' And they receive permission from one another and say: 'Holy is the most exalted heaven, the abode of His presence, holy on earth, the product of His strength, holy forever and ever is the Lord God of the Heavenly Host - the entire world is filled with the radiance of His glory.' And a wind lifted me, and I heard behind me the sound of a great noise: 'Blessed is the glory of the Lord from his place.' And a wind lifted me, and I heard behind me the sound of the powerful movement of those who praised, saying: 'Blessed is the honour of the Lord from the place of His abode and of His presence. The Lord shall reign for all eternity. The Lord - His kingdom is established forever and ever.'"

A thousand years later *Rashi* declared *Torah* study to be the primary focus of holiness. So, in "*U-va le-Tsi'on*", both are expressed, and as if to reinforce it the "verses of consolation" alternate between the original Hebrew and Aramaic *Targumim*, extended glosses rather than translations, made by Yonatan ben Uziel, a contemporary of Rabbi Jesus of Genasseret and one of the outstanding, if much criticised, pupils of the great Hillel (for many years the Aramaic Pentateuch was attributed to him, as well as his rendering of the Prophets; but this has now been disproven); and by Onkelos, the actual translator of the *Tanach* into Aramaic.

"*Kadosh, kadosh, kadosh...*"	Isaiah 6:3 in Hebrew
"*U-mekablin...ziv yekareh*"	*Targum* to Isaiah 6:3 in Aramaic
"*Va-tisa'eyni...mimkomo*"	Ezekiel 3:12 in Hebrew
"*U-netalatni...shechinteh*"	*Targum* to Ezekiel 3:12 in Aramaic
"*Adonay yimloch le-olam va'ed*"	Exodus 15:18 in Hebrew
"*Adonay...olmayah*"	*Targum* Onkelos to Exodus 15:18 in Aramaic

The neat trick of this synthesis of scriptural quotation with interpretative gloss is that it involves the whole congregation in a moment of *Torah* and Prophetic and *Talmudic* study, even those who have no intellectual capacity for such a task. A Jew doesn't have to be Maimonides to sing *Yigdal.* The process equalises.

Rashi

Rashi. The name crops up over and over, but I haven't paused to explain it. Rabbi Solomon ben Isaac (*Rashi* is an acrostic of his initials), was a native of Troyes, in the Champagne region of central France, and if Maimonides was the most important figure in Sephardic Jewry in the middle ages, *Rashi* was his equal amongst the Ashkenazim. For two hundred years Troyes was *the* centre of mediaeval Jewish scholarship, a significance due entirely to *Rashi* and those of his sons and grandsons who were also his principal disciples (Troyes' centrality ended, like most important incidents of Jewish history in the Diaspora, in pogrom - the blood libel was pronounced there in 1288, and within forty years its entire Jewish population had been exterminated or expelled.)

Born in the town in 1040, he grew up amongst merchants, engravers and especially bankers. Usury was anathema to Christians, but armies couldn't be fed or equipped without the loan of money, any more than castles and cathedrals could be built, and it was the Jews who were compelled to capitalise the ventures. The arrival of the first Jews in England coincided with the Norman Conquest – they were its financiers. Virtually every Norman castle and cathedral for the next three hundred years would in large part be financed by loans from Jewish bankers - with pogroms and expulsions used less from religious fervour than as a convenience to evade repayment.

Rashi studied at Mainz and Wurms, the major Rhineland centres of Ashkenazi Jewry, before returning to Troyes aged 25, where five years later he established his own Rabbinic *yeshiva* in his home-town. There, until his death in 1105, he produced a commentary on virtually the entire Babylonian *Talmud*, so close to definitive that every edition of the *Talmud* since has included both the original and the *Rashi*; like a Hoover, his name has become generic, so that now there is *Rashi* the man, and there is also the act of emulating him. After the *Talmud* he also produced an equally mega-commentary on the *Tanach* - he managed everything except the Books of Ezra, Nehemiah, Chronicles and Job - whose status is hardly less.

Rashi's style is terse and uncompromising - he seems to presume that his reader will have the same encyclopaedic knowledge that he had, and therefore requires neither footnote nor explication. His language is concise and straightforward - no flowery prose, no purple passages, no extraneously complicated convolutions or rhythmic scansions or attempted alliterations; no deployment, alongside sub-clauses, of obscure allusions (to Chushi'el ben Elchanan, say, the founder of *Talmudic* studies in late 10th century Magreb). Nor would *Rashi* have enjoyed the many careful jests in that last sentence - he conveys no sense of humour whatsoever in his writings. But honest, scrupulously honest - a man of lesser ability wouldn't have had the confidence to be so honest. To give an example: exploring the phrase "*meley'atcha ve-dimacha lo te-acher*", in Exodus 22:28 (most scholars agree that a word must be missing, and reinstate it, giving it the meaning "You shall not delay [to offer the first] of your ripe fruits and your liquors"), *Rashi*'s exegesis leaves no room for remonstration. "I do not know," he wrote, "what it means." He said precisely the same about Isaiah 13:21, "*Ve-ravtsu sham tsiy'im u-malu vateyhem ochim*" - a verse that might not be out of place in the Revelation of St John of Patmos ("Wild beasts of the desert shall lie there, and their houses shall be full of doleful creatures, and owls shall dwell there, and satyrs shall dance there.")

What *Rashi* added to *Talmudic* scholarship was the literal translation. Until then there was only *Midrash*, the process of interpreting text in order to deduce a law or a divine intention. Literality allowed the Bible to be read as history, as anecdote, even as myth, and more importantly, it allowed the authors to have meant what they wrote, rather than reconstituting everything as a kind of code (Barthes and Foucauld and the post-modern deconstructionists would have detested him). Writing about Genesis 3:8 - "And they heard the voice of the Lord God, walking in the garden in the cool of the day" - he states explicitly, "I am only concerned with the literal meaning of the scriptures, and with such *aggadot* as explain the biblical passages in a fitting manner", and he was prepared, in the manner of Akiva, to use even the cantillation as a guide to explanation. Bible Criticism, nine hundred years ahead of its time! Had it been available, I have no doubt that *Rashi*, who specialised in both linguistics and philology, would have been quite happy to use the techniques of comparative mythology and cross-cultural studies by which his Rabbinic successors of today feel so absurdly threatened. Nor was he averse to the vernacular. On more than a thousand occasions, where he could find no better way of explaining complex Hebrew or Aramaic terms, he used colloquial French or German in their stead.

In 1096 Pope Urban II launched the First Crusade, a concerted attempt to wipe out European Jewry under the pretext of a concerted attempt to wipe out Levantine Islam. Godfrey de Bouillon, the eldest son of Count Eustace II of Boulogne and of Ida, the sister of Godfrey Duke of Lorraine, commanded the onslaught, an inspiration to his fellow Frenchmen who took more seriously than any other group of would-be genocidalists the call for vengeance upon those who had supposedly betrayed and murdered Christ. The bloodshed in France, and after France on every highway to the Holy Land, was Hitlerian. In Jerusalem in 1098 Godfrey was proclaimed king - but in his great humility he refused to wear a crown, since his Saviour had only been given one of thorns, and that in mockery; he took the title "Defender of the Holy Sepulchre" instead. On August 12th, 1099, Godfrey defeated the Egyptian Sultan on the Plains of Ashkelon, bringing the First Crusade to a satisfactory end. Legend tells of a prediction, whispered throughout Europe, that Godfrey would return to his native city - Baisy in Belgian Brabant - no longer a king nor the commander of an army, but a destitute beggar, accompanied by just three horsemen, and that he would be dead within the year. Whether or not Godfrey himself heard the augury isn't recorded; only that it came to pass precisely as had been foretold; only that the author of the oracle was *Rashi*, Rabbi Solomon ben Isaac of Troyes, who pronounced it as a curse upon the man he held responsible for the deaths of so many of his friends and relatives.

✡

But like every other worshipper in synagogue, I am interrupting the prayers with my chatter. Let us resume "*U-va le-Tsi'on*".

After the calls of the angels, "*Adonay elohey Avraham*" completes the opening section of "*U-va le-Tsi'on*", yet another compilation whose principal source as ever is the Psalms. The full list is 1 Chronicles 29:18, Psalm 78:38, 86:5, 119:142, Micah 7:20, Psalm 68:20, 46:8 and 20:10.

"The Lord, God of Abraham, Isaac and Israel, our forefathers, may You preserve this forever as the realisation of the thoughts in Your people's heart, and may You direct their hearts towards You. He, the merciful one, is forgiving of iniquity and does not destroy; frequently He withdraws his anger, not arousing His entire rage. For You, my Lord, are good and forgiving, and abundantly kind to all who call upon You. Your righteousness remains righteous forever, and Your *Torah* is truth. Grant truth to Jacob, kindness to Abraham, as You swore to our forefathers from ancient times. Blessed is my Lord for every single day. He burdens us with blessings, the God of our salvation (*selah*). The Lord God of the Heavenly Host is with us, a stronghold for us is the God of Jacob (*selah*). Lord God of the Heavenly Host, praiseworthy is the man who puts his trust in You. Lord, save! May the king answer us on the day that we call."

"Grant truth to Jacob, kindness to Abraham" - why, do they not have these? Certainly honesty isn't one of the traits that most obviously characterises Jacob - twice cheating Esau, once of his birthright, once of the elder brother's blessing; deceiving his father over the blessing; perpetrating an elaborate ruse over several years by hybriding his father-in-law Laban's white sheep into his own speckled ones, and then deceiving him further by spiriting his wealth and family away at dead of night, his favourite wife concealing her father's household gods under her skirts and pleading menstruation to prevent him seeking for them. But Abraham, unkind? Because of the sending away of Hagar and Ishmael, which was certainly severe? Because of his duplicity in the matter of Avi-Melech king of Gerar, when he pretended that his wife was his sister? I can go no further than *Rashi* in his commentary, regarding the phrase as metaphorical (a curious conclusion, you might think, for a man so dedicated to the literal), meaning not Jacob and Abraham themselves, but us, their descendants.

References in this, the final prayer in the first half, include 1 Chronicles 29:18 and Psalm 78:38, 86:5, 119:142; Micah 7:20, Psalm 68:20, 46:8 84:13 and 20:10.

The second half begins with "*Baruch hu eloheynu she bera'anu lichvodo* - Blessed is He, our God, who created us for His glory", which is the normal benediction over *Torah* study; an appropriate prayer to remind us that the Reading of the Law which we've just finished wasn't for entertainment but for study. In full:

"Blessed is He, our God, who created us for His glory, separated us from those who stray, gave us the *Torah* of truth and implanted eternal life within us. May He open our hearts through His *Torah* and imbue our hearts with love and awe of Him, that we may do His will and serve Him wholeheartedly, so that we do not struggle in vain nor bring forth for futility."

"Nor bring forth for futility." It isn't the habit of the prayer book to be epigrammatic. And never quite so powerfully so as this. The phrase is in fact a reworking of Isaiah 65:23, "They shall not labour in vain, nor bring forth for futility; for they are the seed of the blessed of the Lord, and their offspring with them."

The second section ends with another version of "*Yehi ratson mi lephanecha*", one which includes references to Psalm 30:13, Jeremiah 17:7, Isaiah 26:4, Psalm 9:11 and Isaiah 42:21.

"May it be your will, Lord our God and God of our forefathers, that we observe Your decrees in this world, and merit to live and see and inherit goodness and blessing in the epoch of the Messiah and for the life of the World to Come. So that my soul might sing to You and not be stilled, Lord my God, forever will I thank You. Blessed is the man who puts his trust in the Lord, for then the Lord will be his surety. Trust in the Lord forever, for in God, the Lord, is the strength of the world. Those knowing Your name will trust in You, and You do not forsake those who seek You, Lord. The Lord desired, for the sake of Israel's righteousness, that the *Torah* be made great and glorious."

Echoes of the *Talmudic* lecture live on today, not only but especially in this section of prayer. Everything in the service has been building towards this. Confession, repentance, redemption, petition, supplication, scriptural reference, *Talmudic* study, praise, benediction, everything has pointed to this final goal, the supplanting of the Old Covenant by the New. *Torah* and Messiah, these are the real pillars of the Judaism of the synagogue. *Torah* and Messiah - in that order. But in this prayer, this act of praising and thanksgiving, the two become so interwoven, it's hard to tell them apart.

It isn't uncommon for preachers - *magiddim* - to end their discourses with the petition "*U-va le-Tsi'on go'el, ve-nomar amen* - and may the Redeemer come to Zion, and let us say *amen*". The identical phrase is used, in British synagogues, to end the "Prayer for the Royal Family", recited before returning the scroll to the Ark on Sabbath morning; a note of the divided allegiance of British Jewry, as commanded so to be by Jewish law - to render unto Caesar the tribute that's due to Caesar, in the form of honouring the host when one is the guest, paying respect to the landlord, and tithes to the liege to whom one is vassail or villeyne.

On *Rosh Chodesh*, the new Moon, this is the point at which the *tefillin* are removed. This is because, on *Rosh Chodesh*, an additional service is recited, a *Musaph*, and *tefillin* are never worn for *Musaph*. It's introduced by a half-*Kaddish*. But on regular weekdays, where there is no *Musaph*, the full *Kaddish* is recited.

✡

Kaddish Shalem - Full *Kaddish*

Also known as "*Kaddish Titkabal*" from the opening word of the extra line added into this version.

"*Titkabal tselot'hon u-va-ut'hon di chol beyt Yisra'el kadam avuhon di vishmaya ve-imru amen* - May the prayers and supplications of the entire family of Israel be accepted before their father who is in heaven. And let us all say *amen*."

✡

Aleynu

Abba Arikha, known simply as *Rav*, was the leader of the Babylonian *Amora'im* in the 3rd century of the common era. Ordained as a rabbi by Judah ha-Nasi himself (the patriarch of Judea; the redactor of the *Mishnah*; heir of Gamliel; the man without whom, really, there would have been no *Talmud*), Rav founded the academy at Sura and, with his colleague Mar Samuel, the head of the Nehardeya academy, a physician and astronomer as well as being the leading authority on Jewish civil law, laid the foundations for the Babylonian *Talmud*.

Somewhere in the 3rd century, Rav wrote a preface to the "*Malchuyot*", a series of prayers that acknowledge God as King, and which are recited during the long *Amidah* of *Rosh ha-Shana*. In that preface he declared that "it is our duty to praise the Master of all..." words which are now known as the *Aleynu*.

In the last decade of the 10th century, Hai bar Rav David *Ga'on* was head of the rabbinical academy of Pumbedita, established by Judah ben Ezekiel in 259 BCE. It had already moved once before, to Perez-Shavur, during the period of Persian rule, but the Arabs had allowed it to return. Now Hai Ga'on moved it again, establishing it in Baghdad itself, which Haroun al-Rashid had made the centre of art and science across the civilised world two centuries earlier. With his colleague Sherira ben Hanina *Ga'on* (all great rabbinic eras are marked by contrasting, synthesising, balancing partnerships), Hai Ga'on turned Pumbedita into the greatest rabbinical academy of its day.

A Rabbinic *Responsum* is attributed to Hai Ga'on which has a bearing on the *Aleynu*. This claims that the *Aleynu* was composed by Joshua ben Nun himself, Moses' successor, after he had brought the children of Israel safely across the Jordan. Did Hai Ga'on not know of Rav's preface to the "*Malchuyot*"? Improbable, given each of their involvements in the Babylonian academies. No, like the redaction of the *Torah* itself, it's a matter of retroactive validation, of adding to the *Torah* during the several phases of its composition those practices and ethics which the Rabbis wished to establish as dogma. (I recognise that what I'm saying is heretical: dogma insists that the whole *Torah* was given to Moses, in exactly the form in which we have it now, in Hebrew, at Mount Sinai; history, which is also a matter of faith, insists that the final text was not completed until the time of the Masoretes, between the 7th and the 11th centuries CE). So we can see the practices of the priesthood in the Second Temple period reflected in the Book of Leviticus. So we can see tax and slave codes for an iron-age, urban people in the laws given to a bronze-age nomadic group. So a fundamental duty described by an important but still relatively obscure Babylonian Rabbi is given immense weight of authority by ascribing it to Joshua. By seeming to take the credit away from Rav, Hai Ga'on in fact honours him still more. It's in precisely the same way that the Psalms are ascribed to David, the Proverbs and the Song of Songs to Solomon.

Hai Ga'on's view is reiterated by Ele'azar ben Yehudah of Wurms (1165-c1230), the codifier of the laws, *Kabbalist* and liturgical poet whose wife and daughters were amongst those massacred in the Holy Crusade of 1196. Ele'azar was the last of the major scholars of what was known as the "*Hasidei Ashkenaz*" movement, a social and ideological movement within Jewry whose great literature was compiled in the early years of the 13th century, but whose influence began small and became smaller. Alongside Ele'azar ben Yehudah - whose great-grandfather bore the unusual name of

Kalonymos - there were also his grandfather Samuel the Pious and his father Judah: a family dynasty with a particular line on mysticism and the esoterica, and a fundamentalist view of moral behaviour that included the most severe asceticism, mortification of the flesh as a means of repentance, and a call for martyrdom "where necessary" - a truly Catholic attitude, in its day, as any contemporary Benedictine monk could have affirmed. The movement's main contribution to posterity is the "*Sepher Hasidim* - the Book of the Pious".

Ele'azar reiterates Hai Ga'on's ascription of the *Aleynu* to Joshua, and so does the "*Kol Bo*". Ele'azar's comment comes in "*Sepher ha-Rokeyach*", a *halachic* work which sets out the principles of *Hasidism* in the Middle Ages (those who think that *Hasidism* was the 18th century invention of the *Ba'al Shem Tov* should check their references), and the "*Kol Bo*", which is a culling of many sources, probably plagiarised Ele'azar rather than attempting a scholarly exposition of its own - the "*Kol Bo*", if published today, would probably acquire an even more populist title, the "Jewish Idiot's Guide To Morals And Ethics" or some-such, rather than "*Kol Bo*" which now means "supermarket" - a demonstration anyway of its status as anthology, not dialectic.

Whether Rav or Joshua is its real author, the "*Kol Bo*" was the final stone in the pulpitisation of the *Aleynu*, its position of special honour in the synagogue of Jewish prayer, from the early 14th century onwards. From that time, every statutory service ends with the recitation of what is virtually a *credo*, and for the martyrs of France and Germany throughout the Middle Ages, it was with the *Aleynu* on their lips that they preferred to die - the *Aleynu*, rather than the *Shema*, as we would think today. By reciting the prayer three times daily, we not only state the same *credo*, but also give merit to the souls of the martyrs, and in this way the *Aleynu* also bestows a validation on the controversial "*Kaddish* of the Orphans", which follows it.

"It is our duty to praise the master of all, to ascribe greatness to the moulder of primeval creation, for He has not made us like the nations of other lands, and has not placed us like the other families of the earth; for He has not assigned our portion like theirs nor our lot like all the multitudes of them. (For they bow down to vanity and emptiness and pray to a god who cannot help them.) But we bend our knees, bow, and acknowledge our thanks before the king who reigns over kings, the Holy One blessed be He. He stretches out the heavens and establishes the foundations of the earth, the seat of His homage is in the heavens above and His powerful presence is in the loftiest heights. He is our God and there is no other. Our king is true, there is nothing beside Him, as it is written in His *Torah*, 'You are to know this day and take to your hearts that the Lord is the only God - in heaven above and in the earth below - there is no other."

Fundamental contradictions within Jewish belief once more? "He is our God and there is no other." "The Lord is the only God - in heaven above and in the earth below - there is no other." And yet the Ten Commandments state quite explicitly, "You shall have no other gods before me" - a phrase which intrinsically confirms the existence of other gods, albeit "after Him" - and throughout the scriptures we read of the existence of other gods - berated, attacked and railed against, but still existent. "*Al-panay* - before me" is a difficult term, having a sense both of physical and temporal position. But it does imply, at minimum, the existence in the Universe of other gods - and this is a problem because God who is "the master of all" and the "moulder of primeval creation" must have made those gods too, and for a purpose.

So is there one God and "no other", as the *Aleynu* states? The answer lies, not in the existential but in the essential - it isn't a matter of whether these gods exist or not, even of whether YHVH exists or not. Faith is purely a matter of acknowledgement. When we state in the *Aleynu* that He is the only God, we mean "He is the only God whom we acknowledge", and it's precisely this that makes the differentiations given by Rav in that opening paragraph. We don't insist that YHVH is the Only God - except for us. But He isn't some kind of divine unicorn, simply the first god, the acme and the apogee, the primary among many. Beyond this no explanation is feasible. This is the precise point at which reason and faith are set apart.

The *Aleynu* is recited standing - another measure of its importance in the Middle Ages was its receiving equal status in this way with *ha-Tefillah*, the *Shemoneh Esreh* itself. In many communities the first paragraph is sung to a mnemonical tune, a nursery melody that ensures the prayer is known by heart. In all communities the whole of the first paragraph should be audible on the lips of every member of the congregation. But not so the second paragraph, which may be sung or recited in the same manner as the first, or read in silence, or muttered in an undertone, or even left out altogether, as most Reform *shuls* do - there seems to be no fixed rule for this. The *chazan* recites aloud the last two lines, from "*ve-ne'emar*", invariably to the loud accompaniment of the assembly - loud and relieved, for the calling of "*ve ne'emar*" signals the beginning of the end of what has been a long and spiritually gruelling undertaking. Or so it should have been. One should emerge fulfilled but exhausted from the ceremonies of prayer, at once drained and replenished. The elation of Jacob at Penu'el, when he spent all night wrestling with the angel, and achieved his stalemate.

"Therefore we put our hope in You, Lord our God, that we may soon see

Your mighty splendour, to remove detestable idolatry from the earth, and false gods will be utterly cut off, to perfect the Universe through the Almighty's sovereignty. Then all humanity will call upon Your name, to turn all the earth's wicked toward You. All the world's inhabitants will recognise and know that to You every knee should bend, every tongue should swear. Before You, Lord our God, they will bend every knee and cast themselves down and to the glory of Your name they will render homage, and they will all accept the yoke of Your kingship that You may reign over them soon and eternally. For the kingdom is Yours and You shall reign for all eternity.

"*Ve-ne'emar*...And it is said, 'The Lord will be king over all the world - on that day the Lord will be One and His name will be One."

This is the Messianic *credo*. There are other gods, but they are false gods. Others worship them now, but eventually they will recognise their foolishness and turn to the true God. So they will vanish through lack of believers, and then indeed there will only be One God, and all the world will worship Him - and then, and only then, will the birth pangs of the Messiah turn to parturition. Triumph. Crescendo. Completion. Except that nothing ever ends. Not in the infinitude of God's realm anyway. Not in Jewish prayer.

As always, the text contains scriptural references - and it begs the question: how could Joshua have written a piece whose scriptural references post-date him by innumerable centuries? The unrecited parenthesis in the first paragraph ("*she-hem...yoshia*) is from Isaiah 45:20. "*She hu noteh shamayim...*" is from Isaiah 51:13. The verse ending "*eyn od*" is from Deuteronomy 4:39; that ending "*kol lashon*" from Isaiah 45:23. "*Le'olam va-ed*" is from Exodus 15:18 and the closing phrase is from Zechariah 14:9.

The unrecited parenthesis belongs to a tale that's well worth the telling. In the year 1400 a certain Jew, now baptised a Christian and keen to prove his fervour in his new-found faith, spread the slander that a phrase in the *Aleynu* had been written with the express intention of slurring the Christians. "For they bow to vanity and emptiness and pray to a god who cannot save them." Strangely he based his proof, not on the obvious inference of the word "*yoshia* - save" (the word that probably started the Joshua confusion in the first place), with its irrefutable scriptural connection to the Messianic covenant, but gematrically on the numerical value of the word "*yarih* - emptiness", which happens to equate to the sum of *Yeshu* – Jesus, itself a variant of *yoshia*-Joshua.

The name of the apostate has been lost, but not the ramifications of his slander. Sometimes for fear of persecution, overtly threatened, sometimes as a consequence of legislation, but always at the behest of Christianity, the verse was dropped, despite Jewish scholar after Jewish scholar seeking to refute its slanderous nature. The attempts failed, but they continued on and on, even as late as 17th century Amsterdam, when Rembrandt's friend the publisher and scholar Menasseh ben Israel - he who negotiated with Cromwell the reacceptance of Jews in England - included it in his "*Vindiciae Judaeorum*".

Given that the persecutions have now stopped, why do we not take the verse out of its brackets and re-establish it? Some have argued that we should - Rabbi Yehoshua Leib Diskin amongst them. Some have already instituted the measure, without waiting for official approval. For others it's a matter of custom and practice, which may be changed to add the new but which remain immutable in the face of the existing. For others again it's an opportunity to remember, and to commemorate, and this cannot be gainsaid. But surely it's only meaningful if the omission is a positive omission, explained and understood, and not the mere unspokenness of leaving out?

Al Tira

Another of the optional prayers, but also one of the most devastating in its poetry of eschatological apocalypse. What must they have thought who recited it - why, at any moment of our history: during the Crusades, the Cmielnicki massacres, the Holocaust itself?

"Do not fear sudden terror, or the holocaust of the wicked when it comes."

Who, then, should we fear, if not this? The word employed is "*Sho'ah*" – "*sho'at reshayim* - the holocaust of the wicked" - and it's not a 20th century invention, but a quote from that most sublimely unapocalyptic of all the scriptures, the Book of Proverbs (3:25).

"Plan a conspiracy and it will be annulled; speak your piece and it shall not stand, for God is with us."

Twenty years ago I used those words from Isaiah 8:10 in my novel about the Jewish resistance to the Holocaust - putting them into the mouth of one of the resistors, aiming them at the Nazis. What heroism! What defiance! What a dreadful contrast with those who collaborated in their own victimhood, forming the *Judenraten*, going like sheep to the slaughter. How can such a prayer as this be optional, in the light of Jewish history? It should be mandatory, twenty times a day. The phoenix-cry of the Jewish people, with the refrain "never again". More than just a prayer - a motto: "It won't happen to me."

"Even when you grow old, I shall remain unchanged; even in your ripe old age, I shall still endure. I created you and I shall bear you. I shall endure and rescue you."

Again Isaiah (46:4). Continuity. Transcendence. Something that endures beyond our human transience. Yes. The pulse that goes on beating when ours no longer beats. Yes. An eternality among the deaths. Yes. Yes. Yes. Triumph. Crescendo. Completion. Yes. Yes. Yes.

✡

Kaddish Yatom - The "Mourner's" *Kaddish*

And so we come to the most controversial moment of the entire liturgy, and the most problematic. I do not propose a full account of the controversy - readers interested in the subject should find the copy of Leon Wieseltier's "*Kaddish*" that they acquired when I recommended it earlier, and read his beautiful and scholarly meditation on the history and nature of the prayer. I shall merely *précis*.

The source of the *Kaddish* is a phrase of Ezekiel, "Thus will I magnify Myself and sanctify Myself, and I will be known in the eyes of many nations, and they shall know that I am the Lord." Magnified and sanctified. "*Yitgadal ve-yitkadash*". The *Kaddish* is a prayer, not for Man, but for God.

I've already mentioned, when we met the *Kaddish* in its other incarnations earlier in the liturgy, that there are four variant forms of the prayer. The *Kaddish d'Rabbanan* or Rabbis' *Kaddish*, recited after scriptural reading or study. The *chetsi* or half-*Kaddish* which punctuates key moments of the service. The *Kaddish Shalem* or *Titkabal*, which concludes the service prior to *Aleynu*. The *Kaddish Yatom*, which is widely known as the "Mourner's *Kaddish*", though in fact it should properly be called the "Orphan's *Kaddish*". Today the *Yatom* is said by any mourner for any close family member, though in principle it should be said only by those bereaved of a parent.

Wieseltier traces the history of the *Kaddish* as a mourning ritual, and finds a story of Rabbi Akiva from the 2nd century which appears to validate it. Only the story is told, not in the *Talmud* where Akiva's thoughts and tales are generally collected, but in the "*Machzor Vitry*", a thousand years later, the work of one of *Rashi*'s greatest disciples, Simchah ben Samuel of Vitry-le-Brule in Champagne, in north-east France. This is how Simchah recounts it:

A tale of Rabbi Akiva. He was walking in a cemetery by the side of the road, and encountered there a naked man, black as coal, carrying a large burden of wood on his head. He seemed to be alive and was running under the load like a horse. Rabbi Akiva ordered him to stop.

"How comes it that a man does such hard work?" he asked. "If you're a servant and your master is doing this to you, then I will redeem you from him. If you're poor and people are avoiding you, then I'll give you money."

"Please, sir," the man replied. "Don't detain me, because my superiors will be angry."

"Who are you," Rabbi Akiva asked, "and what have you done?"

The man said, "This man whom you're addressing is a dead man. Every day they send me out to chop wood."

"My son, what was your work in the world from which you came?"

"I was a tax collector, and I would favour the rich and kill the poor."

"Have your superiors told you nothing about how you might relieve your condition?"

"Please, sir, do not detain me, for you'll irritate my tormentors. For such a man as I, there can be no relief. Though I did hear them say something - but no, it's impossible. They said that if this poor man had a son, and his son were to stand before the congregation and recite the prayer '*Baruch Adonay ha-mevorach* - bless the Lord who is blessed', and if the congregation were to answer '*amen*', and the son were also to say '*Yehey shemeh rabah mevorach* - may His great name be blessed', they would release him from his punishment. But this man never had a son. He left his wife pregnant and he didn't know whether the child was a boy or a girl. And if she gave birth to a boy, who would teach the boy *Torah*? For this man didn't have a friend in the world."

Immediately Rabbi Akiva took upon himself the task of discovering whether this man had fathered a son, so that he might teach the son *Torah* and install him at the head of the congregation to lead the prayers.

"What's your name?" he asked.

"Akiva," the man answered.

"And the name of your town?"

"Lodkiya."

Rabbi Akiva was deeply troubled by all this and went to make his enquiries. When he came to that town, he asked about the man he'd met, and the townspeople replied, "May his bones be ground to dust!" He asked about the man's wife, and he was told, "May her memory be erased from the world!" He asked about the man's son and he was told, "He's a heathen

- we didn't even bother to circumcise him!" Rabbi Akiva promptly circumcised him and sat him down before a book. But the boy refused to receive *Torah.* Rabbi Akiva fasted for forty days. A heavenly voice was heard to say, "For this you mortify yourself?" "But Lord of the Universe," Rabbi Akiva replied, "it's for you that I'm preparing him." Suddenly the Holy One, blessed be He, opened the boy's heart. Rabbi Akiva taught him *Torah*, and "Hear O Israel", and the benediction after meals. He presented the boy to the congregation and the boy recited the prayer "*Baruch Adonay ha-mevorach* - bless the Lord who is blessed", and they answered "*Yehey shemeh rabah mevorach* - may his great name be blessed".

At that very moment the man was released from his punishment. The man came immediately to Rabbi Akiva in a dream, and said, "May it be the will of the Lord that your soul find delight in the Garden of Eden, for you have saved me from the sentence of Gehenna."

Rabbi Akiva declared, "Your name, O Lord, endures forever, and the memory of You through all the generations."

For this reason it became customary that the evening prayers on the night after the Sabbath are led by a man who doesn't have a father or a mother, so that he can say *Kaddish* and "*Baruch Adonay ha-mevorach* - bless the Lord who is blessed" and the congregation may answer "*Yehey shemeh rabah mevorach* - May His great name be blessed".

Sisyphus, redeemed by the *Kaddish*; and by an act of humanism, of philanthropy, which exalts civilised behaviour far beyond Law or custom or tradition! But it's a tale founded in unrealities of almost mythological proportions - a parable rather than an anecdote. And we're left wondering, was the man Rabbi Akiva himself, redeeming his own soul through charity? Or a dream of his own father? Or a *doppelganger*, a coincidence, a literary jest? We ought to be in the territory of Rabbi Nachman of Breslau, the mentor and precursor of Franz Kafka, whose unfinished tales are amongst the most enigmatic in all literature. Or did Nachman learn his techniques from Akiva?

It wasn't until the 11th or 12th century that the *Kaddish* became properly established as an accepted, let alone a central feature of the liturgy, and even then amidst continuing controversy. Who should say it - a person for their own grief, or a person who is not bereaved on behalf of one who is? An issue of pastoral care rather than ethic or precedence or protocol. When should it be said, and where, and how often - the Akiva parable, after all, only denotes the evening prayers on the night after *Shabbat*? Should all mourners in a community recite it together, or one of them on behalf of all the others? Mediaeval Rabbis drew up lists of pedantic complexity outlining the hierarchy of precedence. But every community differed, even though every Rabbi quoted the same source - that apocryphal tale of Akiva - to justify his own different *Responsum.* In the end the Mourner's *Kaddish* came into being as the final act of every prayer service, recited simultaneously by all the mourners who so wished, each at his own pace, each in his own dialect, regardless of the cacophony. It can be the most anarchic, and is always the most intensely individualistic moment, and the only one in which the reverential silence of the whole community can be absolutely guaranteed, granting space without equivocation unto grief. The mourner's *Kaddish* is the one Jewish prayer that was granted, not by God, nor Prophet, not by *mitzvah*, nor *chok*, nor *halachah*, not by *amora*, *tanna*, rabbi nor *ga'on*, but by popular demand.

To say *Kaddish* is to fulfil the most fundamental precept of prayer and to provide an answer to what appears to be a paradox. The paradox first. Jewish faith accredits God with absolute wisdom, absolute knowledge, and absolute justice. He knows our destinies, His decision as to what those destinies will be is founded on an understanding far deeper than we can hope to match (see again the final chapters of the Book of Job for details), and behind His decision lies His ineffable justice. If this is so, and if our faith is "perfect", then what on earth are we doing, petitioning Him to change our destinies, pleading with Him to reconsider his decisions about our fates, presenting Him with sycophantic supplications in hope to influence His wisdom and to make Him rethink His truths? Prayer, in these terms, is at best naïve, at worst futile; and beyond that, frankly, insulting. Or is prayer also something different, something more? *Kaddish* provides the answer, and it's known as "the justification of the judgement". "*Baruch atah Adonay eloheynu melech ha-olam, dayan ha-emet - blessed are you O Lord our God*" - the final words may be translated one of two ways, but I prefer to assume the double-meaning is intentional, and to give both – "the true Judge and the Judge of truth." So does a person say, immediately upon hearing of the death of a close relative. The justification of the judgement. God has decreed that a life shall end. "*Yitgadal ve-yitkadash shemey raboh.* Let Your great name be magnified and sanctified." We accept the verdict. But to accept a verdict doesn't mean we have to like the verdict, or approve it. Our right to challenge God, our need to challenge God, is as much a statement of faith as it is of doubt. In Islam, prayer is entirely an act of submission, of the human to the divine. In Judaism, the act of prayer is an act of sanctification, of the human in the realm of the divine.

✡

The Jewish Rites of Mourning

The Jewish rites of mourning, of which the Mourner's *Kaddish* forms a central focus, are extremely detailed and complex, but precisely because of so elaborate a structure, they enable both the bereaved and the community to deal with death in a logical and a coherent and a time-phased manner. The rites of mourning are intended for the living, not the dead.

Judaism is realistic about death, even despite the superstitious and the eschatological mysticism that have crept in about after-lives and resurrections of the dead. Yes "all Israel have a portion in the world to come" (*Mishnah Sanhedrin* 11:1, *Pirkei Avot* 1:1), but that's in a mystical future, post-Armageddon, post-Messiah. In Psalm 115:17 a more realistic truth is uttered, that "the dead cannot praise the Lord". In Genesis 3:19 "dust you are and unto dust you shall return". In Ecclesiastes 12:17, "the spirit returns to God who gave it". In *Berachot* 17a Rabbi Yochanan affirms without flinching or equivocating that "the end of Man is death". And Job, famously, not only accepts death but continues to praise - to magnify and sanctify - the almightiness of God. "*Adonay natan, adonay lakach, baruch shem Adonay* - the Lord gives, the Lord takes away, blessed be the name of the Lord."

When hearing of the death of a member of one's family, the Jewish custom is to tear an item of clothing - the left lapel is stipulated, but the act is symbolic of the ancient sackcloth and ashes, and who wears jackets with lapels now anyway? - and to recite the blessing which justifies the judgement, which approves, in other words, the decision of the Heavenly Court, that that person's time has come. "*Baruch atah Adonay eloheynu melech ha-olam, dayan ha-emet* - blessed are you O Lord our God, the true Judge and the Judge of truth."

Laws and practice take account of both the subject and the object. The dead must be treated with respect (though there are sinners of such degree that burial and mourning are prohibited). But in the usual run, the dead are wrapped in white robes after being washed - white for equality more than purity. Men may be wrapped in a prayer shawl, provided that the *tsitsit* have been cut, because the *tsitsit* represent his earthly duties which death has abrogated. The body may not be embalmed, nor displayed in an open coffin, nor cremated - which would construe a *kurban*, a burned offering - nor, officially, subjected to autopsy, unless it's required by Gentile law or might safeguard the lives of others through the detection of a contagion, infection or hereditary disease. Burial must be immediate, but not on *shabbat* or the first day of a festival. The acts of caring for the dead are the responsibility not of the family but of the "*chevra kadisha*", the communal burial society.

So much for the dead. What really matters are the living, the concern for their mental, emotional and spiritual well-being, and the "*nichum avelim*", the extension of comfort.

Grief is the most intense at the moment of learning of death, and needs to be gradually lessened as the mourner returns to and resumes the daily life. So Jewish law provides for several stages of mourning, each less exacting than the last.

At the first stage the mourner isn't even called a mourner, but "afflicted" or "miserable" - "*onan*" in Hebrew. A distinction that must once have been made in English too, between "bereft" and "bereaved". "*Onanut*" is the brief period between death and burial, during which time none of the positive commandments are performed.

(As a sidenote, our understanding of the "sin" of Onan - Genesis 38:3-10 - is modified when we remember that Onan was himself a mourner, that the meaning of his name and his status were identical; it is entirely possible he refused to complete the act of intercourse with his late brother's wife, precisely because it's forbidden to procreate during the period of mourning; it's also possible he had intercourse with her during the mourning period, but knew he shouldn't, and spilled his seed to protect himself against forensic evidence should a child result. This matters: *Onanut* has long been understand as both the sin of masturbation and of *coitus interruptus*, when in fact it is only the latter; but it has also been regarded - *Niddah* 3a - as the source of the death penalty.)

The second stage is "*shiva*", the seven days of formal mourning. *Shiva* is observed for parents, children and siblings only, in the home of the deceased if possible. In Biblical times, as evidenced for example by the death of Absalom, the mourner covered his face (2 Samuel 18:33-19:4), and rent his clothing and sat on the ground in dust and ashes (Job 1:20/21, 2:8-13); today low wooden stools or footstools or even cushions are encouraged in the Ashkenazi rites, though Sephardim continue to sit on the ground. Mourners will wear no leather, especially shoes, will not go to work or take part in pleasurable activities, including bathing if it's for comfort, the wearing of freshly laundered clothes, sexual relations, *Torah* study (except for books that deal with mourning), and men will refrain from shaving; while both sexes refrain from body ointments. The day of the burial is counted as the first day of *shiva*; on the *Shabbat* of the week of mourning, *shiva* is suspended.

The third stage is "*sheloshim*" or "thirty", the period, including the *shiva*, of

30 days from the burial to the completion of a month of mourning; but the laws apply only to the 23 days after the *shiva.* The mourner will return to work, to normal life, but will refrain from celebratory activities and will continue to leave the hair and beard uncut. At the end of the *sheloshim*, mourning for children or siblings ends completely; only for parents does it continue.

The final stage is "*avelut*", or "mourning", and it continues until twelve months – twelve Hebrew months - after the day of burial, though in fact the rites are only practised for eleven months, because the body is deemed to take a year to decompose, and at the end of that time the soul is judged; to go on praying for that soul until the last implies a fear that it may be judged as wicked, and so mourning ends a month early to avoid the imputation of wickedness.

Once the twelve months are complete, mourning should end; indeed it's forbidden to continue practices or restraints that imply a continuation of grief. The living having buried the dead, the dead should not be granted the power to bury the living also. Bereavement is best served by interring oneself in life.

But during those months there is still an abstention from partying, and there is still the *Kaddish.* A son is duty-bound to recite the *Kaddish* three times daily (even if he's only half an orphan), at each of the daily services, provided that there's a *minyan.* This is fundamental, and communities will work harder to find a *minyan* for the Mourner's *Kaddish* than for any other reason. A man may pray alone, but it's always better to pray alone within the community, and best of all to pray in harmony with a congregation. In particular the *Kaddish.* As much as the son must say his lines, so the congregation, like a Greek chorus, is duty-bound to provide the *Responsa*, "May His great name be blessed forever and ever", and the simple, cathartic conclusion: *amen.*

Just as the *Kaddish* makes no overt reference to God, so also it makes no reference to the dead or to the act of mourning. In fact, it appears not to be a mourner's prayer at all, and nothing in the text would indicate this purpose to one who came upon the prayer by chance. The *Kaddish* is a paean to the glory of Almighty God - magnified and sanctified - and a petition for redemption and salvation through God's emissary the Messiah. And of course, in one sense, this does imply the dead, for "all Israel have a portion in the world to come". The *Kaddish* is thus both the ultimate justification of the judgement, and the ultimate poem of consolation. The end of grief is eschatology.

Three interesting leniencies in Jewish law apply to mourners. Although women are absolved of time-bound commandments, of which *Kaddish* is one, and although a woman's voice should not be heard in synagogue (something Siren-like about them that drives us poor men onto the rocks of lust), a daughter may nonetheless say *Kaddish* for her parents. The triumph of compassion over bigotry.

Secondly, though a child who hasn't reached *Bar Mitzvah* isn't yet bound by the commandments, and shouldn't lead a prayer service, it's "permissible and proper" to recite the *Kaddish* - a further victory for "*rachamim*", for humanism.

Thirdly, if there is no son or daughter to recite the *Kaddish*, another person may be engaged to say it, even another member of the family, even - you. So any Jew may be engaged, as every Jew will eventually be bereaved. So to know the *Kaddish*, this alone, this before any other prayer or rite or act, before even the *aleph-bet* or kosher food or keeping *shabbat*, this knowledge of the *Kaddish* becomes another of the first principles of being Jewish.

✡

Psalm of the Day

So secure is its position today, there are innumerable instances - too many to list - where the Mourner's *Kaddish* is followed by a Psalm, in order that the Mourner's *Kaddish* may be said again. The morning service is one such case.

In Temple times, the recitation of the daily Psalm was counted amongst the duties of the Levites. Each day in the Jewish calendar is given, so to speak, a minus number, in that Day One - Sunday in the Christian calendar - isn't the first day of the week so much as the first day towards the next *shabbat*, for which every day is a preparation. Hebrew days have no names, but only these minus numbers; but each day that leads to *shabbat* also reflects the primal days that led to the original *shabbat*, days of imperfection and uncreation because the world wasn't yet fully made, but only transient and potential. So in the Temple one candle of the *Menorah* was lit each day, the symbolic permanent presence of the Founding Light of Creation (Genesis 1:3-5). So also one Psalm was read, each from a different category of the Psaltery.

✡

The First Day Towards *Shabbat*: Psalm 24, a Psalm of David. An affirmation of God the Creator and of Man's subordinate position: only he who is clean may take his share of what is God's. This is the Psalm that was sung when the scrolls were returned to the Ark.

✡

The Second Day Towards *Shabbat*: Psalm 14, a song of the sons of Korach.

"Great is the Lord and much praised, in the city of our God, on the mount of His holiness. Fairest of sites, joy of all the earth, is Mount Zion, on the northern slopes of the great king's city. In her palaces God is known as the Stronghold. For behold, the kings assembled, they came together. They saw and they were astounded, they were confounded and hastily fled. Trembling gripped them there, convulsions like a woman in the travails of labour. With an east wind You smashed the ships of Tarshish. As we heard, so we saw in the city of the Lord, God of the Heavenly Host - may God establish it until eternity (*selah*).

"We hoped, O God, for Your kindness, in the midst of Your Sanctuary. Like Your name, O God, so is Your praise - to the ends of the earth; righteousness fills Your right hand. May Mount Zion be glad, may the daughters of Judah rejoice, because of Your judgements. Walk about Zion and encircle her, count her towers.

"Mark well in your hearts her ramparts, raise up her palaces, that you may recount it to the succeeding generation, that this is God, our God, forever and ever. He will guide us like children. *Amen*."

Exodus 6:24 and Numbers 26:58 denote the *Bene Korach* as members of the tribe of Levi, and as such cousins of both Moses and Aaron. When Dotan and Aviram, the chiefs of the *Bene Re'uven*, rebelled against Moses' authority, the *Bene Korach* took the Reubenite side and were swallowed up, either by earth or fire, as punishment. But not all the *Bene Korach* can have been implicated in the rebellion, because in Davidic times they were still there, providing choristers to the Temple, and also - if the lists in Chronicles are correct - gatekeepers, guardians of the vessels and treasures, and even Temple bakers. So important did the *Bene Korach* become that *Talmudic aggadah* devotes whole pages to their eponymous ancestor, while the *Qur'an* (*Suras* 28:76-82, 29:38, 40:25) makes him one of the world's wealthiest men, Moses' brother-in-law, and the third in the evil trinity of those who wished to destroy Israel - Haman and Firawn (Pharaoh) being the other two.

As to the Psalm itself, it describes itself as a "*Shir Mizmor*", meaning a Psalm for choir and orchestra, both of which the *Bene Korach* would have provided. It's less a praise of God than an exaltation of Jerusalem, in which the earthly Zion becomes a symmetry for the heavenly Zion, reflecting the division of earth and sky made on the second day of Creation. The Jewish world isn't dualistic, but if I may coin a phrase, dichotomistic - not either/or but syllogistic, a harmony fused through the dialectic, in the synthesis of disagreement. So the firmament may be described as uniting Heaven and Earth, as well as separating them. So a wall may keep one in, another out. So an open hand held out may beg, or proffer. So the conflict between Korach and Moses - a dispute over esoterica - may be punished as a mutiny and still lead to the reformation and the strengthening of the cult. In Jewish culture the passionate disagreements have always been the most powerful dynamic. So Korach survived his own condemnation. So we remember him as both good and wicked, and praise his contributions.

✡

The Third Day Towards *Shabbat*: Psalm 82, described as "*Mizmor le-Asaph*", which almost certainly means a song, accompanied by orchestra, not written by Asaph, but written to be sung by him, so that the opening phrase serves as a dedication - a dative, not a genitive.

"God stands in the divine assembly, in the midst of judges shall He judge. Till when will you judge lawlessly and favour the presence of the wicked (*selah*).

"Judge the needy and the orphan, vindicate the poor and impoverished. Rescue the needy and the destitute, from the hand of the wicked deliver them. They do not know nor do they understand; in darkness they walk; all foundations of the earth collapse. I said, 'You are angelic, sons of the most high are you all'. But like men you shall die, and like one of the princes you shall fall.

"Arise, O God, judge the earth, for You allot the heritage among all the nations."

I have struggled whether to write "You" or "you" in the second verse – to determine, that is, whether the Psalm is complaining that God judges lawlessly, or that men do so. The Psalm speaks of justice and equality and contains a powerful hint of protest at its absence both from the Divine and from the human realms. But the protest is also a plea - do not judge them too harshly, for those who sin aren't always responsible for their actions. It seems to me this may well be the first time in history that the concept of the innocent victim - and victim not of another human being's calumny but of society's misdoings, its failure to provide work or education or moral sustenance or spiritual support - the first time such a sentiment was elaborated.

✡

The Fourth Day Towards *Shabbat*: Psalm 94:1-95:3.

"O Lord and God of vengeance - appear now! Arise, O Judge of the earth, render recompense to the haughty. How long shall the wicked, O Lord, how long shall the wicked exult? They speak freely, they utter malicious falsehood, they glorify themselves, all workers of iniquity. Your nation, Lord, they crush, and they afflict Your heritage. The widow and the stranger they slay, and the orphans they murder. And they say, 'God will not see, nor will the God of Jacob understand'. Understand, you boorish people, you fools! When will you acquire wisdom? He who implanted the ear, shall He not hear? He who fashioned the eye, shall He not see? He who chastises nations, shall He not rebuke? He who teaches man knowledge, the Lord knows the thoughts of man, that they are futile. Praiseworthy is the man whom God disciplines, and whom You teach from Your *Torah*. To give him rest from the days of evil, until a pit is dug for the wicked. For the Lord will not cast off His people, nor will He forsake His heritage. For justice shall revert to righteousness, and following it all will be of upright heart. Who will rise up for me against evildoers? Who will stand up for me against the workers of iniquity? Had the Lord not been a help to me, my soul would have dwelt in silence. If I said, 'My foot falters'; Your kindness, Lord, supported me. When my forebodings were abundant within me, Your comforts cheered my soul. Can the throne of destruction be associated with You? Those who fashion evil into a way of life, they join together against the soul of the righteous, and the blood of the innocent they condemn. Then the Lord became a stronghold for me, and my God, the rock of my refuge. He turned upon them their own violence, and with their own evil He will cut them off. The Lord our God will cut them off.

"Come, let us sing to the Lord, let us call out to the rock of our salvation. Let us greet Him with thanksgiving, and with praiseful songs let us call out to Him. For a great God is the Lord, and a great king above all heavenly powers."

Addressed "*El Nekamot Adonay* - to the Lord and God of Vengeance", this is an outburst of hatred against mankind, bitter enough for Nietzsche's Zarathustra or Scrooge in his "humbug" phase. The wicked are lashed, morally excoriated, the bones of their sins picked clean. They are described as "boors" (*bo'arim*) and "fools" (*chesilim*), as "malicious" (*yedabru atak*), and as "iniquitous" (*po'aley aven*). But God will give them their just desserts.

"Praiseworthy is the man whom God disciplines, and whom You teach from Your *Torah*." Again I have struggled with "you" or "You". The change of pronoun between 2nd and 3rd person is commonplace in the Psalms, so it could go either way. I am inclined to regard the ambiguity as deliberate: praiseworthy is God for giving us the *Torah*, to enlighten us; praiseworthy are we when we teach the *Torah*. And if this is correct, can we draw the same conclusion from the previous struggle?

✡

A pattern appears to emerge as the Psalms move through the week. Only the clean may approach the God of Justice. An account of the worst of all possible sinners. A complaint about the absence of Justice, and a vindication of the innocent sinners. A general rant against wickedness that concludes with Justice now made manifest. As we approach nearer and nearer to the Sabbath, so we approach nearer and nearer to the harmony of resolution. And so:

The Fifth Day Towards *Shabbat*: Psalm 81.

"Sing joyously to the God of our strength, call out to the God of Jacob. Raise a song and sound the drum, the sweet harp with the lyre. Blow the shofar at the moon's renewal, at the time appointed for our festive day. Because it is a decree for Israel, a judgement day for the God of Jacob. He imposed it as a testimony for Joseph when He went out over the land of Egypt - 'I understood a language I never knew. I removed his shoulder from the burden; his hands let go of the kettle. In distress you called out, and I released you. I answered you with thunder when you hid. I tested you at the Waters of Meribah' (*selah*).

"Listen, My nation, and I will attest to you. O Israel, if you would but listen to Me. There shall be no strange god within you, nor shall you bow before an alien god. I am the Lord your God, who brought you out of the land of Egypt. Open wide your mouth and I will fill it. But My people did not heed My voice and Israel did not desire Me. So I let them follow their heart's fantasies, I let them follow their own counsels. If only My people would heed Me, if Israel would only walk in My ways. In an instant I would subdue their foes, and against their tormentors I would turn My hand.' Those who hate the Lord lie to Him - so their destiny is eternal.

"But He would feed him with the cream of the wheat, and with honey from the rocks He would sate you."

Addressed "*La-Menatseyach al ha-Gittit*" and "*Le-Asaph*". "*Gittit*" presents a problem. *Rashi*, who like Maimonides is never wrong (this is a matter of faith, reverence and custom, not of empirical fact) claims the "*gittit*" was a musical instrument made at Gat. But which Gat? A "*gat*" was simply a wine-press, and the land of Israel was awash with them. An instrument, then, used at the wine-ceremonies? In which case, knowing that the Dionysus rites in neighbouring Lebanon used the lyre, was a *gittit* perhaps a small lyre? The "*menatseyach*" was the conductor of the "*gittit*" section of the orchestra. The third line of the Psalm refers to the "*toph*", "*kinnor*" and "*navel*", which scholars know for certain were, respectively, the drum, harp and twelve-stringed lyre, so clearly this was composed for string and percussion only, without either wind or horns, except in variations of the Psalm used for the New Moon, when a blast on the *shofar*, the ram's horn, may well have been included.

But more likely the reference to the *shofar* is poetic, for the verse goes on to sound the trumpet for the Judgement Day itself, the final culmination of the process of Creation, the final completion of the pattern of the seven days.

It is, in truth, a most peculiar poem. It occupies a space of history well before and well after its writing, in that it claims to be Davidic, but its subject is the life of Joseph, and its casuistry and sophistry are entirely *Talmudic*. For Man to "judge", it polemicises, he must have knowledge, including, especially, knowledge of what is right and wrong. But that knowledge is the sin of Eden, for which Man lives in a state of constant punishment. Only when Man accepts the *Torah* can he be redeemed from original sin. Only when Man accepts the *Torah* will he be able to choose good over evil.

This sounds simple enough, but it contains two overwhelming inferences. That the fruit of the tree of knowledge of good and evil *is* the *Torah*. That God - pay close attention to this line - that God *intended Adam and Eve to commit the sin.*

There is also a fascinating literary device used in this Psalm, and in several others, the counterpoint of two distinct voices, without textual narrative to say who is speaking: sometimes the Psalmist, sometimes God Himself. Nothing in the whole of literature repeats this device, until William Faulkner employed it in "As I Lay Dying"; and so trepidatious was he of its impact, he included in the textual narrative chapter headings to denote the speaker.

And in the Psalm that follows, a variation on that counterpoint - the Psalm sometimes addressed to God, sometimes descriptive of Him.

✡

The Sixth Day Towards *Shabbat*: Psalm 93. God in his full grandeur, almighty, eternal, universal, transcendent. The leitmotifs of the daily psalms are woven now into their finished tapestry. The earth and the heavens are complete. God steps back from the canvas to admire His work. On the other days when He does this, it's good. Today, the last, the sixth day of Creation, it's more than good – it's very good.

"The Lord will have reigned, He will have put on his grandeur; the Lord will have donned might and girded Himself; He even made the world firm so that it should not falter. Your throne was established from of old; eternal are You. Like rivers they raised, O Lord, like rivers they raised their voice, like rivers they shall raise their destructive power. More than the roars of many waters, mightier than the waves of the sea - You are mighty on high, Lord.

"Your testimonies are exceedingly trustworthy about Your house, the sacred dwelling. O Lord, may it be for long days."

With each of the six daily Psalms, the final paragraph is recited by the *chazan* alone.

✡

There are variations to the pattern of the Daily Psalm. On *Rosh Chodesh*, the New Moon, regardless of which day of the week it falls, Psalm 30 is recited instead in some communities, Psalm 104 in others. 30 was the Psalm written for the dedication of the royal palace of King David on Mount Zion, a great hymn of praise extolling the glories of the Almighty, and appropriate to the day for its celebration of newness and renewal. 104 recites again the catalogue of Creation, including the moon itself on the 4th day - "*asah yareyach la-mo'adim* - He made the moon for festivals" - and rejoices in the gifts of God.

And if the morning prayers are recited, not in *shul* but in a mourner's house, Psalm 49 is substituted, addressed to the conductor of the choir and orchestra of the *Bene Korach*, and containing both animadversions against the wicked and teaching in the style of Ecclesiastes, which is to say advice on how to live one's life so as to ensure receipt of one's portion in the world to come. Consolation to the mourner.

And after the recital of the Daily Psalm, the repetition of the Mourner's *Kaddish*. The need for consolation also is eternal.

✡

Second Recitation of the Mourner's *Kaddish*

So the morning service ends with the last praying of the Mourner's *Kaddish*, a petition towards the coming of the Messiah, that "He who makes peace in the heights, may He make peace on us, and upon all Israel."

But *shalom*, as I have observed previously, doesn't only mean peace. *Shalem* - present in the name Jerusalem, and in the name Solomon, who built the Temple - *shalem* means "wholeness", "harmony", "perfection". *Shalom* is a metaphor for God Himself.

May God perfect Himself.
May God perfect Mankind.
May the kingdom of earth be as the Kingdom of Heaven.
May the two realms be united
in peace
    in harmony
and in perfection

ve-imru - and let us say -
    amen.

Chapter Fourteen: After *Shacharit*

For most Jews, the Mourner's *Kaddish* is where the morning service ends (for most religious Jews; the majority of the Jewish people don't attend a synagogue at all, not even on Sabbaths and High Holy Days; or only those). For the most fastidious, there's still more - a number of readings which the *Kabbalists* suggest should be studied now.

✡

Shesh Zechirot - Six Remembrances

1. The Exodus from Egypt (Deuteronomy 16:3)

"*Le-ma'an tizkor et yom tsetcha mey-erets Mitsrayim kol yemey chayeycha* - that you may remember the day of your departure from Egypt all the days of your life."

The phrase is regarded as sufficient on its own, unrequiring of the full text - because of all texts, this is the one we are expected to know without needing it written down, because it's the duty of every father to teach it to his children, to read it with his children at the *Pesach seder*, the Passover meal. And besides, the telling of the story isn't the point. The point is the act of remembering, of commemorating.

On the day of departure from Egypt, God did to the Egyptians what he forbade Abraham to do - the killing of the first-born. Divine justice operates by different criteria from human justice.

On the day of the departure from Egypt, God instituted the Law of the Red Cross, to protect the innocent from the hand of the Angel of Death. But at the Sea of Reeds God also acknowledged the fault implicit in such a miracle, enabling humanism yet again to trump the supernatural.

On the day of the departure from Egypt, there was no time to gather up the leaven for the making of tomorrow's bread, and so we ate *matzah (*this isn't actually correct, as I will explain shortly, but it has become the tradition). So much for Man being unable to live by bread alone. Here Man lives, triumphs, rejoices, and by *matzah*, which isn't even bread.

On the day of the departure from Egypt, the children of Israel left slavery for liberty. And for Sinai, for the *Torah*, for the Land of Israel, for their own posterity. This is the seminal, the defining experience.

We remember, because what Moses instructed the children of Israel in the wilderness also applies to us today. How, when we were not there, when we only know of the experience at second-hand, through *haggadah*? Surely only first-hand experience is valid? That, after all, is about to be the lesson of the second of the Six Remembrances - isn't it?

✡

2. The Giving of the *Torah* at Sinai (Deuteronomy 4:9-10)

"*Rak hishamer lecha u-shemor naphshecha me'od, pen tishkach et ha-devarim asher ra'u eyneycha, u-phen yasuru mi-levavecha kol yemey chayeycha, ve-hodatam le-vaneycha ve-li-veney vaneycha, yom asher amadeta liphney Adonay eloheycha be-chorev.*"

"Only beware and guard yourself carefully, lest you forget the things your eyes have seen, and lest they stray from your heart all the days of your life. You are to make them known to your children, and to your children's children - the day you stood before the Lord your God at Horeb."

Do not forget what you have seen - judgement is formed and nourished, not by what is read, taught, imposed by doctrine, but through personal experience. The Justice of the *Torah*, its fundamental humanism, depends entirely on the experience of Egypt - having lived as victims of oppression, slavery, injustice, inhumanity, exploitation, there are only two prophylactics: to take the opportunity to do the same to someone else, and heal your wounds through vengeance: or to make a set of laws that prevent any future repetition, that ensure that no one else is ever afflicted as you were afflicted, and so heal your wounds through transcendence. So do not forget. Do not even misremember. Do not allow others to forget or misremember. And teach your children, so the next generation neither forgets nor misremembers. So, at Passover, we continue to tell the tale of Egypt. So, three thousand years from now, when all the world in its perennial pursuit of the comfortable has managed at last to forgive and to forget the Nazi Holocaust, the Jews will continue to recall it, to be discomfited by it; the Jews will be different from all the other nations of the world, the Jews will forgive - but still remember.

But the previous question still hangs in the air unanswered. Isn't only first-hand experience valid? This is the greatest miracle of all Jewish miracles, and it's Man-made, not God-given - the great psychological transformation and transfiguration, perpetrated in the act of remembering. "*Avadim hayinu be-Mitsrayim* - we were slaves in Egypt." By telling, vividly, repeatedly, by making the act of remembering conjunctive with the act of living, the event is rendered personal. Every Jew that ever lived was there in Egypt, when the wounds and traumas were inflicted. Every Jew that ever lived was there at Sinai, when the healing laws were given. Every Jew that ever lived and read the books and saw the films of Auschwitz-Birkenau lived through sufficient of the real Auschwitz-Birkenau to know he had been selected for an experience beyond the normal human realm, and couldn't believe that he survived it. Every Jew bears the scars of every other Jew. To be unable to understand this miraculous stigmata is to be unable to understand Judaism, or Jewish history, or Jewish prayer. Let alone the bee-hive community of Jewish humanism.

✡

3. The Attack by Amalek (Deuteronomy 25:17-19)

But there is another side, the side of the Inclination towards Evil, the dark side of the moon-goddess, the obverse of humanism, and this too is ever-present in the Jewish consciousness.

"*Zachor asher asah Amalek, ba-derech be-tsetchem mi-Mitsrayim, asher karcha ba-derech, va-yezanev becha kol ha-necheshalim achareycha, ve-atah ayeph ve-yageya, ve-lo yare elohim. Ve-hayah be-haniyach Adonay eloheycha lecha mi-kol oyevecha mi-saviv, ba-arets asher Adonay eloheycha noten lecha nahalah le-rishtah, timcheh et zecher Amalek mi-tachat ha-shamayim, lo tishkach.*"

"Remember what Amalek did to you on the way, as you departed from Egypt; how he encountered you on the way and cut down the weaklings trailing behind you, while you were faint and exhausted, and he did not fear God. It shall be that, when the Lord your God gives you respite from all the enemies who surround you, in the land which the Lord your God has given you as a bequest, that you will erase the memory of Amalek from beneath the heavens. Do not forget."

"Justice, not vengeance" we learned above. Yet here we find the opposite. Amidst the humanism, this *go'el*, this blood-feud with its perpetration of the most appalling vengeance: precisely the sort of vengeance we've just renounced. And with the same secondary injunction: "Do not forget". This is not justice, this is an eternal *fatwa*. When the prophet Samuel sent King Saul to fulfil the *go'el*, and Saul exterminated the whole tribe of Amalek but kept alive its king Agag, and his sheep and cattle too, Samuel stripped Saul of the kingship and personally fulfilled the *cherem*. Because God demands sacrifices.

I find this story almost too painful to read, and took several months trying to make sense of it, religiously and psychologically, when I fleshed out the skeleton in my novel "City of Peace". It's a most terrible calumny, an atrocity of inhuman proportions, a war-crime really - and yet divinely sanctioned. Nay, divinely required. But how can the God of Justice also be the God of Vengeance, which is the ultimate injustice? It's the apology at the Sea of Reeds again, the apology of the rainbow after the flood, the apology by reinstatement and due compensation that was made to Job. (It's the evidence that God's almightiness is also, paradoxically, a definition of His imperfection, and a reminder that these two are not the same). It's the Biblical Dir Yassin and Sabra and Shatilla - as important didactically to every generation since as were the incidents of Egypt. I'm drawn back to the journals of Rabbi Solomon Klinitsky, the inspirational grandfather of the Canadian poet Leonard Cohen:

"Soldiers in close formation. Paratroops in a white Tel Aviv street. Who dares disdain an answer to the ovens? Any answer."

Is that why the Rabbis of the *Talmud* enjoined us to this particular remembrance? Were they, too, horrified by the *go'el* against Amalek, and wished to add a cautionary *addendum* to the lexicon of proper Jewish *minhag* - civilised behaviour? Do we remember, not in order to act (as in the previous remembrances), but precisely in order *not* to act? Are we reminded, not lest we forget, but lest we perpetrate? O I hope so, I hope so, I hope so. If it came to my turn, I too would find it impossible to take off the head of Agag – though this, of course, is what the victors did at Nuremberg. I too would be manacled by the creed of Simon Wiesenthal, greatest of all Nazi-hunters, who called his autobiography, immensely "deliberate in judgement" as the "*Pirkei Avot*" counsels, "Justice not Vengeance".

"I did not like to see the young men stunted in the Polish ghetto," wrote Solomon Klinitsky upon a visit to the State of Israel. "Their curved backs were not beautiful. Forgive me, it gives me no pleasure to see them in uniform. I do not thrill to the sight of Jewish battalions. But there is only one choice between ghettos and battalions, between whips and the weakest patriotic arrogance…"[9]

He doesn't say what that single choice is. But then, he doesn't really need to. It's self-apparent.

✡

4. The Golden Calf (Deuteronomy 9:7)

"*Zechor, al tishkach, et asher hiktsaphta et Adonay eloheycha ba-midbar* - remember, do not forget, how you angered the Lord your God in the wilderness."

---

[9] Quoted from "The Spice-Box of Earth" by Leonard Cohen.

The sin of disobedience - so we're encouraged to understand the story. While Moses was high up in the clouds of Horeb, the children of Israel persuaded Aaron to refashion their combined jewellery collections into a Golden Calf, so they could worship it instead. When Moses returned he was so infuriated by the sight of their idolatry that he dropped the Tablets of the Law, then punished the people by melting down their calf and, strangest of all eucharists, making them drink the yellow liquid. The sin of disobedience - and the accompanying injunction against idol-worship.

Ever since I first heard this tale as a child it has left me itching with doubts; research as an adult has enabled me to scratch the skin, but eczema is eczema and the itching doesn't go away; *au contraire*, scratching makes the itching worse. We know the tale as history, seen from the past; but just for a moment, try to see it as though it were a present event. Moses is a prince of Egypt, brought up by the Pharaoh's daughter; he even bears an Egyptian name, Moshe or Mousa, a name known from many Pharaohs including the most famous of them all, the one he served, Ra-Mousa, or Rameses. The legends of his birth reflect those of the Egyptian saviour-god Osher, whom we know as Osiris, and whose name appears as Asher in the list of Hebrew tribes. His brother bears the name Haroun - *Aharon* in Hebrew, Aaron in English - which identifies him with Hor, Greek Horus, Osiris' father and the god whom Osiris will eventually supplant. When the Amalekites attacked the stragglers of Israel, the two men who held up Moses' arms to ensure the presence of God in the battle and thereby victory, were Aaron and Chor, the same Chor who would be left in charge of the camp when Moses went to receive the Law - Chor whose name is connected etymologically to Chorev – Horeb - the very mountain of his command.

When Moses first asks Pharaoh to let his people go, it isn't an exodus that he's planning, not a wilderness journey to the Hebrew Promised Land, but simply a three-day excursion into the desert so the people might celebrate the rites of spring, and (Exodus 5:1-3) the festival of unleavened bread (yes, the *matzah* was a part of the planned celebration, not an accidental consequence of fleeing). The locus of this pilgrimage is the principal mount in the Sinai range, Mount Chorev, the "white mountain", sacred to Horus. How was Horus represented by the Egyptians? As a Golden Calf. If Moses was angry with the people, it wasn't because they were worshipping idols, nor because they were worshipping a golden calf *per se* - Moses lived under the aegis of Osher, not of Hor, whose symbol was the falcon; his grievance was his own apparent overthrow, symbolised by the nature of the worship.

There are other patches of psoriatic skin. These Hebrews, fleeing across the desert, were slaves, had been slaves for the best part of three hundred years. Where, pray, do slaves acquire jewellery? Sufficient jewellery to manufacture a Golden Calf? And as to God's anger - "let Me alone that My wrath may wax hot against them and that I may consume them" he tells Moses (Exodus 32:10) upon sending him back down the mountain to sort out the dissidence. That I may consume them? What, another Sea of Reeds for which to apologise afterwards, another act of divine destruction by the all-merciful all-compassionate all-forgiving one? Another divine tantrum? Another *go'el*, like that against Amalek? Moses, exactly like Abraham before the Cities of the Plain, Moses challenges God. "Why does Your wrath wax hot against Your people, which You have brought out of the land of Egypt with such great power and with a mighty hand? Why should the Egyptians speak and say, 'To make mischief with them did He bring them out, to slay them in the mountains, and to consume them from the face of the earth'? Turn from Your fierce wrath, and repent of this evil against Your people."

Repent! A man who dares instruct a divinity to repent!

"And the Lord repented of the evil which He thought to do against His people."

And the Lord *repented* of the *evil* which He thought to do against His people! These are dramatic, potent, totem words, *repented*, and *evil*. These are words which raise a man of true humanity higher even than a moody, challengeable god.

Then what is it that we're enjoined here to remember, when we're told to remember how we angered the Lord our God in the wilderness? Our disobedience, or His penitence? Or perhaps, despite the clear instructions of the prayer book, the entitling of this section as "Remembrance of the Golden Calf", perhaps the Rabbis have misunderstood the reference to God's anger in Deuteronomy 9:7. Because there is another, altogether different incident.

In Numbers 11:1 "the people complained, and it displeased the Lord; and when He heard it, His anger was kindled; and the fire of the Lord burnt amongst them, and consumed those that were in the outermost parts of the camp." What did they complain about? The lack of meat, their boredom with eating manna, a drab incondiment that "tasted like coriander seed but had the colour of bdellium"; a desire for "Egyptian fish, for cucumbers, for melons, leeks, onions and garlic" - the garlic especially; manna without a sprig of finely chopped and lightly fried garlic is simply unimaginable. Then "the people cried to Moses, and when Moses prayed to the Lord, the fire was quenched." What did Moses pray? "Turn from Your fierce wrath, and repent of this evil against Your people" - as he had previously? No, he joined in the complaint.

"Why have You afflicted Your servant? Why have I not found favour in Your sight, that You lay this burden of all this people on me? Did I conceive all this people? Did I beget them, that You should say to me,

'Carry them in your bosom, as a nurse carries a suckling child, carry them to the land which you promised their fathers?' Where am I supposed to find enough meat to feed this people…" He whinges on for several verses yet, the primordial kvetch… "I can't bear this people on my own, they're too heavy for me…And if You deal thus with me, better You kill me. If I have found favour in Your sight, kill me with Your own hand rather than let me see such wretchedness."

When the people complained, God got so angry He started to make human *kurbanim*, burnt offerings, in the outermost camp - till Moses stopped him. But when Moses joins in the complaint, God doesn't even bother to get angry - He quite simply gives in.

"Gather seventy of the elders of Israel…bring them to the Tent of Meeting…I will come down and talk with you all there…I will take the spirit that is on you and share it amongst them…sanctify yourselves against the morrow and you will eat meat, for you have wept in the ears of the Lord…you shall eat not one day, not two days nor five days, not ten days nor twenty days, but a whole month, until it comes out of your nostrils and is loathsome to you..." Oh, I like that part, the infantile tantrum which is the divine sulk, seen before and to be seen again so often. But what a marvellously complex picture! What splendid literature! The multi-faceted personality, the fragmented psyche - why this portrait of God is positively post-Freudian! And still - why are we poring over this for learning's sake? What is it that we're meant to understand?

Throughout these tales, I find myself, again and again - but try not to because I know it's a blasphemy - I find myself *desperately disappointed* by this God of ours. What kind of a God is He, who can drew Leviathan out with a hook, and then say sorry because the hook hurt the poor sea monster's lip? What kind of a God is He, who can order the extermination of Amalek even while He's preparing the ordinances of the *Torah*? What kind of a God is He, who sends avalanches and earthquakes and volcanoes to wipe out His creation because He's no longer convinced that it's even good, let alone very good - and then *repents* of the *evil* He has done? A God who sulks and has temper-tantrums. A God who takes the slap on the wrist unflinchingly from His own creation, who gives in to Moses as he gave in to Abraham? A God who apologises for the "collateral damage" caused by His own miracles? A God who sees the people cry for boredom with the divinely-provided manna, and instead of chastising them with harsher commandments and hair-shirts and months of ceremonial prayer and penitence, Marie Antoinette-like calls out "Let them eat roast desert quail", with *sauce de l'aile* and onions *sautés*, and a cucumber mint to dip the *matzah* in no doubt, and melon for dessert. Just like they used to eat in Egypt. No. No. No. This isn't what we expect of our divinities!

But God created Man in His own image. So we have no choice but to expect. To accept God's contrariness, even His hypocrisy, is to accept our own. To understand God is to understand ourselves. This is why we read this fragment. This is why we stay behind, when prayer is done, to study.

✡

5. The Remembrance of Miriam (Deuteronomy 24:9)

"*Zachor et asher asah Adonay eloheycha le-Miryam, ba-derech be-tsetchem mi-Mitsrayim* - remember what the Lord your God did to Miriam, on the way, when you were departing from Egypt."

I like the technique of telling us to remember, but not actually telling us what to remember. So, unless you happen to be a scholar who knows each and every detail…this isn't, after all, one of the once upon a time tales told to children like the Exodus and the Golden Calf...you're compelled to go and look it up. And when you look it up, you find that you've found nothing, because the phrase in Deuteronomy 24:9 is a reference to elsewhere in the *Torah*, but the text refrains from saying where. The compulsion towards scholarship, coerced upon the unscholarly by their own need to know! The apotheosis of curiosity.

The reference, it transpires, is to Numbers 12:10. Miriam and Aaron raised a controversy over Moses' marriage to an Ethiopian woman - the text gives "*ha-ishah ha-Kushit*" which presents a problem, because both Ethiopia and Midian are separately referred to as Kush. If Midian is intended - and most Jewish commentators claim it is - then this must surely have been Tsipporah, the daughter of Jethro the Priest of Midian, whom Moses married when he fled Egypt after killing an overseer who was brutalising a Hebrew slave - but why on earth would Miriam and Aaron be making a fuss about that marriage now, well over a decade later? Unless he'd taken a second wife, also from Midian. And if it was an Ethiopian woman whom he'd married only now, was their complaint because she was black, because he was already married, because to marry her he had first had to set Tsipporah aside, or because he was practising the theoretically permitted but actually rarely practised right of male polygamy? The text simply doesn't say - anything at all.

In fact the controversy seems to be about power, not marriage - "Has the Lord indeed spoken only with Moses? Has he not spoken also with us?" complain the siblings, and God overhears, summons the three of them to the Tent of Meeting, asserts Moses' priority against their claims to equality, "and when the cloud was removed from over the Tent, behold Miriam was leprous, as white as snow; and Aaron looked upon Miriam, and behold she was leprous."

Nasty, itchy stuff, leprosy - Biblical leprosy of this sort probably wasn't leprosy at all, but psoriasis or eczema, and its white-as-snowness is particularly interesting, because Jewish tradition regards Chor as Miriam's husband, and as I noted previously Chor means white as Chorev means "the white mountain"; this whiteness thus takes us yet again to the mythology of the moon-goddess, enabling Miriam to play the role of Isis where Moses is Osher and Aaron Hor. But in the story that is given, rather than the mythology from which it was sourced, Miriam was excluded from the camp for seven days, for fear it might be contagious; and Moses prayed that her sins not be punished in this way; and whether because of her isolation, his prayers, or some other medicine, her skin complaint cleared up.

Strange story. Has something been redacted out by the Masoretes, the Rabbis of the early middle ages who compiled the final version of the *Tanach*? And what, pray, are we meant to learn from remembering this?

I confess to mild sarcasm in the preceding paragraphs; but I'm truly perplexed by all of this. I go back to the commentaries, hoping for illumination, and I discover this:

"Miriam criticised her brother Moses, on the grounds that he didn't live with his wife."

No - unless this is corroborating the possibility that he'd moved in with another woman, whether bigamously or without formally divorcing Tsipporah first. But it's nowhere stated in the text. No reason at all is given for the controversy. This is Rabbinic speculation - the need to find an explanation where none exists rather than admit ignorance. And anyway, the very next paragraph of the commentary shows this not to be its intention; it isn't philanderousness nor abuse of the *droit de seigneur* but its very opposite, asceticism, which the commentator is presuming.

"She failed to consider that a man of Moses' humility and unselfishness would not have done so unless he had been commanded always to hold himself in readiness for prophecy, a condition that required abstinence."

This is acceptable as exegesis - verse 3 makes specific reference to Moses' meekness, while verse 6 has God speaking of Moses' prophetic role - but still it doesn't tell us what or why we should remember. And the meekness is somewhat questionable anyway, given the nature of Moses' confrontation of God's injustice in the remembrance that preceded this one - "a man who dares instruct a divinity to repent" I called him then.

"Miriam was punished with *tsara'at*, a disease similar to leprosy, and was healed because of Moses' prayers. This teaches us never to slander another person."

Tsara'at is indeed a disease similar to leprosy - its specifics and the laws relating to its treatment can be found in Leviticus 13:47-59 and 14:34-37. But here I am, staying on after a long morning's *davening*, hoping to learn something deep and significant and profound from the Rabbi's *shi'ur* and the texts set by the sages for enlightenment through study, and all I'm to be given is a badly redacted text, enigmatised by obscurities, misinterpreted, offering nothing more educational that "this teaches us never to slander another person" when actually no slander has provably taken place? It isn't enough. It isn't enough.

✡

6. The *Sabbath* (Exodus 20:8)

"*Zachor et yom shabbat le-kadsho* - remember the Sabbath day and keep it holy."

Whereas this, this on its own, without requiring commentary let alone dispute, this is self-evident, this is more than enough.

✡

Chamishey ha-Parashot - The Five Readings

1. The Thirteen Principles of Faith

I've already discussed these at some length, when we encountered the *Yigdal* at the very beginning of the service, and shan't repeat myself.

The reading of the Thirteen Principles is normally concluded with "*Li-shu'atcha kiviti Adonay. Kiviti Adonay li-shu'atcha. Adonay li-shu'atcha kiviti*", an anagrammatic prayer based on Genesis 49:18 - "I long for your salvation Lord"; and with a second, similarly anagrammatic prayer, whose origins I cannot find and which, for some reason, the Art Scroll fails to translate (I suspect because its editors don't understand the phrase either; but I've just learned, through the "Six Remembrances", to avoid making such slanderous assertions.) "*Le-purkanacha sabrit Adonay. Sabrit Adonay le-purkancha. Adonay le-purkancha sabrit.*" I'm not sure why the Art Scroll's editors found this is a problem. "*Purkanchah*" is from the root "*perek*", which is generally used to mean "breaking" or "cutting off", but which Psalm 136:24 uses to mean "redemption", the meaning I'm inferring here. "*Sabrit*" is from the root "*siber* - to hope". The threefold text then makes perfect sense, as well as perfect symmetry, as "Lord I hope for your redemption."

✡

2. The Ten Commandments (Exodus 20:1-14)

"I am the Lord your God, who delivered you from the land of Egypt, from the house of slavery. You shall have no other Gods before Me. You shall not make for yourselves graven images nor any facsimile of anything that is in the heavens above nor on the earth below, nor that is in the waters beneath the earth. You shall not prostrate yourself before them, nor worship them; for I am the Lord your God - a jealous, who visits the sins of the fathers upon the children, even until the third and fourth generations of those who hate Me, and showing mercy unto thousands of those who love Me and keep My commandments. You shall not blaspheme the name of the Lord your God, for the Lord will not him blameless who takes His name in vain.

"Remember the Sabbath day and keep it holy. Six days you shall labour and do all your work, but the seventh day is the rest day of the Lord your God; on it you shall not do any form of work, nor your son, nor your daughter, nor your manservant, nor your maidservant, nor your cattle, nor the stranger who is within your gates; for in six days the Lord made heaven and earth, the sea, and all that is in them, and He rested on the seventh day; for this reason the Lord blessed the Sabbath and declared it holy.

"Honour your father and your mother, that your days may be long upon the land which the Lord your God has given you.

"You shall not commit murder. You shall not commit adultery. You shall not steal. You shall not bear false witness against your fellow man. You shall not covet your neighbour's house, nor his wife, nor his manservant, nor his maidservant, nor his ox, nor his ass, nor anything that belongs to him."

Maimonides be damned - these are the Ten Principles of Jewish Faith, and no need for any others!

✡

3. The Chapter of Repentance (Deuteronomy 30:1-10)

"It will be that, when all these things come upon you, the blessing and the curse that I have placed before you; and you will take it to your heart among all the nations to which the Lord your God has cast you. Then you will return to the Lord your God, and heed His voice according to everything that I command you today; you and your children, with all your heart and with all your soul. Then the Lord will bring you back from your captivity and have mercy upon you, and He will again gather you in from among the people where the Lord your God has scattered you. If your dispersed will be at the ends of heaven, from there the Lord your God will gather you in and from there He will take you. The Lord your God will bring you to the land that your forefathers inherited and you will possess it; and He will benefit you and increase you beyond your forefathers. The Lord your God will circumcise your hearts and the hearts of your offspring, to love the Lord your God, with all your heart and with all your soul, that you may live. The Lord your God will place all these curses on your enemies and upon those who hate you and have persecuted you. But you shall repent and listen to the voice of the Lord, and perform all His commandments in which I instruct you this day. The Lord your God will give you prosperity for all time, in all your handiwork, in the fruit of your womb, in the fruit of your livestock, and the fruit of your land; for the Lord will return to rejoice over you for all time as He had rejoiced over your forefathers. When you heed the voice of the Lord your God, to observe His commandments and His decrees that are written in this book of the *Torah*; when you will return to the Lord your God, with all your heart and all your soul."

Another of those anachronistic texts of Deuteronomy which lead the scholars to date it anything up to a millennium after Moses. It speaks, not of the first Diaspora that began in 586 BCE, not even of the end of that Diaspora, but of a second Diaspora, and of its ending, "and He will again gather you in from among the people where the Lord your God has scattered you". It's this text - not alone, but more than any other - which "justifies the judgement" of the United Nations, which also granted the Land of Israel to the Family of Jacob by covenant, in its case on May 14th 1948.

The theme of reward and punishment occurs again, and again I'm struck by the sense of Judaism as a kind of spiritual protection racket, in which God controls the numbers and takes His ten per cent, and provided that we stay in line doles out the favours when we need them. "You wanna de rain to make-a your crops grow? Den you's a-betta keep all My commandments or you's a-gonna wake up one morning wid a famine on your land and serious infertility, you *capiche* what I'm meaning?" This is less God than Godfather, and only one of several versions of the deity we have encountered. I suspect it's also the one that drives most people both into and away from their religion.

What is meant by "circumcising your hearts"? The Hebrew says "*mol Adonay eloheycha et levavecha*", which unquestionably does mean "circumcise your hearts", but metaphorically of course. It's the symbol underlying the circumcision, not the physical act, which provides the explanation too. The customary nomenclature for the rite is "*Brit Milah* - the Covenant of the Word", the removal of the foreskin being little different from the notarising of a legal document, a visible sign of authorised consent; though it's also an act of sacrifice, a giving-up of something particularly precious, so that the act of circumcision must also be seen as making the sexual organ holy: a fertility tribute to the mother-goddess if ever there was one. To "circumcise the heart" then is to make an emotional and intellectual commitment to the covenant which the clipping of the foreskin had already denoted physically.

Understanding this may also help us better understand Moses' statement, in Exodus 6, that he was a man of "uncircumcised lips" – a phrase I discussed earlier, with reference to the calling of the Prophet Isaiah.

The reading is usually concluded with a supplication:

"*Yehi ratson mi-lephanecha*...May it be Your will, my God and the God of my forefathers, that You dig a tunnel beneath Your throne of glory to bring back in complete repentance all the evildoers of Your people the House of Israel. And among them bring me back in complete repentance before You, for Your right hand is outstretched to accept penitents and You desire repentance. Amen."

A tunnel! A direct passage by which those condemned to purgatory can make their ways back to the land of the living, like Orpheus and Persephone and Dante Alighieri. A place from which to rise from the dead, and thence to ascend, to sit - the supplication uses the precise phrase - on the "right hand" of God. The Hebrew is "*she-tachtor chatirah*", a noun and a verb both formed from the same root, "*chatar*", "to break through", or "to dig". Actually the tunnel isn't strictly correct (I've borrowed the Art Scroll translation). Ezekiel 8:8, 12:5 and 12:7, following the transitive verb with an accusative noun, uses it to mean "breaking through a wall", in the specific sense of a thief breaking into a house. Job 24:16 has the same usage. But where the tunnel is deduced is Amos 9:2 "though they dig down into the Underworld, My hand will lift them out of there; though they climb up to heaven, from there will I bring them down." The Hebrew here gives "*im yachteru vi-She'ol*", which treats the Underworld as Hades, the place you would reach if you dug a tunnel downwards through the mud and rocks - the fiery hinterland of planet earth.

But the tunnel in the supplication goes down into *She'ol* from the Throne of Glory, which we would normally read as heaven in the skies. What if the Sanctuary itself were meant, the Palace of Yahweh on the summit of Mount

Moriah? We know from the conquest of Yevus by King David that a deep tunnel ran through the hill of Ophel to what are called the Cotton Caves in the Valley of Hinnom - it was through that tunnel that Yo'av led his men in secret to take the town. The Pool of Gihon in Jerusalem was regarded as the navel of the cosmos, one of the four source rivers of Eden. The Valley of Hinnom - *Gey Ben Hinnom* in Hebrew, Gehenna in English, and itself almost certainly a variant or corruption of Gihon, the pool in the same valley – was the place where Solomon was anointed in 1 Kings 1, though later it became the city's cemetery and refuse tip.

Dig your tunnel, Lord. Dig your tunnel deep enough into the loam and clay and golden limestone of Jerusalem, into the hell-harrowing Psalms and legends of King David, and we will discover once again - roots of Judaism in the most pagan, polytheistic cults of our ancestors the Habiru!

✡

4. The Chapter of Reverence for God (Deuteronomy 10:12-11:9)

"And now, Israel, what does the Lord your God require of you? Only to revere the Lord your God, to go in all His ways and to love Him, and to serve the Lord your God with all your heart and all your soul. To observe the commandments of the Lord and His decrees in which I have instructed you this day, for your benefit. Behold, to the Lord your God belong the skies and the most exalted heaven, the earth and all that is in it. Yet the Lord delighted only in your forefathers to love them, and He chose their offspring after them - you - from among all peoples this day. Cut away the barrier of your heart, and be stubborn no longer. For the Lord your God, He is the God of all powers and the Master of all Masters, the great, mighty and awesome God who will favour no one and will accept no bribery, who carries out justice for the orphan and the widow, and who loves the stranger to provide him with food and clothing. You are to love the stranger, for you were strangers in the land of Egypt. Revere the Lord your God, serve Him, cling to Him, and swear by His name. He is your praise and He is your God, who did with you all these great and fearsome things that your eyes have beheld. With seventy people your forefathers descended to Egypt, and now the Lord your God has made you as abundant as the stars of heaven. You shall love the Lord your God, you shall observe His charge, His decrees, His ordinances, and His commandments all the days. It is your duty to know this day - for I speak not with your children who did not know and who did not see the chastisement of the Lord your God, His greatness, His strong hand and His outstretched arm, His signs and His deeds that He performed in Egypt, to Pharaoh, the king of Egypt and to his entire land. And what He did to the army of Egypt, to its horses and its chariots; who made the water of the Sea of Reeds inundate them, when they chased after you; and the Lord destroyed them, to this very day. And what He did for you in the wilderness, until you arrived at this place; and what he did to Dotan and Aviram, the sons of Eli'av ben Reuben, when the earth opened its mouth wide and swallowed their households, their tents, and all the resources that sustained them, among all Israel. For your own eyes have seen all this great work that He has accomplished. You are to observe the entire commandment in which I have instructed you this day, so that you can be strong, and come to possess the land, to which you cross over, to inherit it. And so that you can prolong your days upon the land that the Lord swore to your forefathers to give to them and to their offspring, a land flowing with milk and honey."

Charges, decrees, ordinances, and commandments. In Hebrew "*mishmarto, ve-chukotav, u-mishpato u-mitzvotav.*"

Mishmeret is the performance of an office or function, the doing of a particular job or task; in its root form it's a guard or watchman, both in the military sense of patrolling a city wall or prison, and in the priestly sense of studying the heavens for the movements of the stars and planets, the indications of the new moon or the start of the Sabbath. In Temple times each of the tribes sent *mishmarot* to serve in the sanctuary rotationally, to aid the *Cohanim* in carrying out the sacrifices, in looking after the Temple site, providing both the choir and orchestra. Today we would think of the *mishmarot* more as those who serve the synagogue and the community - the President and Secretary and Treasurer of the *shul*, the *chazan* and the *gabbai*, the *mohel* who performs the circumcisions, the *shochet* who slaughters meat in the approved manner.

Chok originally applied only to time-bound laws, those which defined the appointed seasons and the festivals, particularly the Sabbath; but in *Talmudic* usage it came to mean any established or definite regulation, most particularly the laws of nature and those laws in the *Torah* which were explicitly decreed by God - as opposed to those, the majority, which were deduced.

A *mishpat* is a sentence handed down in a court of law, in this sense a Rabbinic court. The *mishpatim* refer, not to the *Torah* but to the *Talmud*, not to Divine Law but to human interpretation, not to original decree but to case-law that establishes a precedent.

But none of the above are meaningful without the *mitzvot*, the commandments themselves, given by God through the *Torah*. *Mitzvot* are neither laws nor rules nor regulations nor decrees nor judgements nor precedents - they are precepts. If there is one value that separates Jews from every other people and religion, it lies here; where the rest of the world demands the privilege of a "Charter of Human Rights", the *Torah* imposes on the Jews a "Charter of Human Responsibilities".

This reading which is not a prayer nonetheless concludes with a supplication:
"*Yehi ratson mi-liphanecha*...may it be Your will, Lord my God and the God of my forefathers, that you implant Your reverence and Your love in my heart and in the hearts of all Israel Your people, to revere Your great, mighty and awesome name with all our heart and with all our soul, a reverence for the exaltation of the Infinite One, blessed and exalted be Your name, for You are great and Your name is awesome. *Amen* (*selah*)."

✡

5. The Chapter of Manna (Exodus 16:4-36)

Talmud Yerushalmi states that whoever recites this passage on a daily basis can be assured that he too will receive his daily portion of sustaining food. Nevertheless, and not for lack of faith - God forbid! – it's considered more worthy to recite the passage after first making this supplication:

"*Yehi ratson mi-lephanecha*...May it be Your will, Lord our God and God of our forefathers, that You prepare a livelihood for Your entire people, the House of Israel - and my livelihood and the livelihood of the members of my household - with ease and not with pain, with honour and not with disgrace, in a permissible and not in a forbidden manner, so that we will be able to perform Your service and study Your *Torah* - as You nourished our forefathers in the wilderness, in a desolate and an arid land."

The arm-twisting works both ways! God godfathers us - keep My commandments or else! But we employ the same tactics against him too. "For your name's sake"! Or here, "if you want us to be students of your *Torah*, give us jobs and decent salaries, or we'll be unable to, and..." the inference is loud and very clear - "it will be Your fault." As parents with their children, children with their parents, so Man with God and God with Man. Today's atheists, and Israel's *yeshiva buchers*, place the same burden of responsibility upon their secular governments instead.

I shan't write out the entire "Chapter of Manna", only because it's too long. It's found in Exodus 16:4-36 and it complements that incident which made God angry that I've already spoken about - the incident that I believe was intended in the fourth of the Six Remembrances. Two verses before the reading, "the whole congregation of the children of Israel murmured against Moses and Aaron in the wilderness...would to God we had died by the hand of the Lord in the Land of Egypt when we sat by the fleshpots and ate bread till we were full; for you have brought us out into the wilderness, to kill this whole assembly with hunger." God's response on this occasion isn't anger but compassion.

"Behold, I will cause bread to rain down on you from heaven, so the people can go out and gather every day the needs of that day" - there is of course the conventional rider -"so that I can test whether they will walk according to My teaching or not" - and the necessary double-portion on the sixth day, so no one need break the holiness of the Sabbath by collecting food.

Interesting that when Moses reports this to the people he adds that "the Lord has heard the complaints that you bring against Him; for what are we? Not against us are you raising your complaints, but against the Lord."

But after this extraordinary abrogation of authority, the text becomes confusing. "In the afternoon you will eat meat and in the morning you will be sated with bread, and you will realise that I am the Lord your God." Having stated that He would "cause bread to rain down on you from heaven", what He actually sends isn't bread at all, but quails in the afternoon, and in the morning dew which, upon evaporating, left behind "something thin, as thin as frost upon the ground…and Moses said 'This is the bread that God has given you to eat." No description is given beyond this, but from that incident in Numbers 11 we know that it "tasted like coriander seed but had the colour of bdellium", and from this text that, if it were left until the following morning "it bred worms and became putrid". It's called manna, which means "a portion", because each person was entitled to one per day. "The children of Israel ate the manna for forty years until they arrived at a populated land."

As with each of these readings, I find myself perplexed as to what the moral or didactic purpose is. A note of gratitude for what God provides? If so, it's entirely undermined by the whingeing and the moaning in Numbers 11, where it's precisely the ingratitude of His people that's so vividly described. Is reading, then, an opportunity to make amends? I think it must be, and it makes me doubly sure the Rabbis have misunderstood the allusion in Deuteronomy 9:7.

Four Prayers

The first for livelihood, which is strange, since we've already made such a prayer, in the prefatory supplication to the Chapter of Manna. Then two "Departure Prayers", followed by Psalm 67. Finally a prayer "Upon

Leaving The Synagogue" and a special "Prayer for a Person about to Engage in Commerce".

✡

The order of unwinding the *tefillin* (which may begin at any time after "*u-va le-Tsi'on*"). The head *tefillin* first. The hand-*tefillin* second. The body from the synagogue last of all, but slowly, slowly, because a man should be in no hurry to depart his God and resume the impious hypocrisies of the outer, daily world.

Chapter Fifteen: *Hallel*

In a book which is attempting to unravel the daily prayers, you might well ask why am I slipping down the side-road of *Hallel*, the series of Psalms from 113 to 118, which aren't recited in the daily prayers at all, except on festivals, and even then not at all on *Rosh ha-Shana*, *Yom Kippur* or *Purim*, and only in part (Psalms 115:1-11 and 116:1-11 are omitted) on Passover and at the New Moon. The answer is that I don't have an answer, only a compelling side-road. Those wearing *tefillin* should remove them first.

Two traditions regarding the *Hallel*. According to the first, the six Psalms were sung by pilgrims as they climbed the hill-roads to Jerusalem to make the *chag*, the thrice-yearly pilgrimage on *Pesach*, *Shavu'ot* and *Sukkot*. According to the second, the six Psalms were sung by the Priests as they ascended the ramp to the *duchen*, the platform in front of the Ark. The probability is that both traditions are rooted in fact.

Whereas the third tradition is almost certainly false. According to this tradition, recorded talmudically in *Pesachim* 117a, *Hallel* was known long before King David wrote it down. It was sung, in fact, at the Reed Sea, at the culmination of the Joshuaic conquest, and by Deborah and Barak after defeating Sisera; and after David wrote it down, by Hezekiah after the retreat of Sennacherib, by the three who Nebuchadnezzar put into the furnace, and by Mordechai and Esther after the demise of Haman. What all these incidents share is the threat of national disaster and its overcoming, for which a series of songs of praise would indeed have been befitting. It's this common factor which leads to the singing of *Hallel*, in Israel today, on *Yom Atsama'ut*, Independence Day, and on *Yom Yerushalayim*, the anniversary of the liberation of Old Jerusalem in 1967.

Five key incidents are commemorated in the Hallel Psalms: the Exodus from Egypt, the miracle of the Sea of Reeds, the giving of the *Torah*, the future resurrection of the dead, the coming of the Messiah. I do like the idea of a song that's capable of recording the future.

"Baruch atah Adonay eloheynu melech ha-olam, asher kidshanu be-mitzvotav, ve-tsivanu likro et ha-Hallel"

"Blessed are you, Lord our God, King of the Universe, who sanctified us with His commandments, and commanded us to read the *Hallel*."

The singing of *Hallel* is prefaced by a prayer-blessing for the singing of

Hallel, and concludes with a *Kaddish* because all reading and studying of scripture must be concluded with a *Kaddish.* During *Chanukah* only the half-*Kaddish* is recited, but on all other occasions it's the full *Rabbanan.*

✡

Psalm 113

"*Hallelu-Yah*! Give praise you servants of the Lord; praise the name of the Lord. Blessed be the name of the Lord, from this time and forever. From the rising of the sun to its going down, the Lord's name be praised. High above all nations is the Lord, above the heavens is His glory. Who is like the Lord our God who is enthroned on high, yet deigns to look upon the heaven and the earth?

"He raises the needy from the dust, from the trash heaps He lifts the destitute, to seat them with nobles, with the nobles of His people. He transforms the barren wife into a glad mother of children. *Hallelu-Yah.*"

The first paragraph recited by the whole congregation, the second only by the *chazan.*

We have encountered the prayer already. Its second verse, "Blessed be the name of His glorious kingdom for all eternity. Blessed be the name of the Lord from this time and forever" forms part of the *Yitbarach* meditation; and is reflected in the line attributed to the angels and muttered in an undertone as an appendix to the *Shema*: "*Baruch shem kavod malchuto le-olam va-ed*".

My contention, oft-repeated in this book, is that the original Hebrews worshipped a male sky-god known to us by the Tetragrammaton YHVH, and his female consort, the fertility goddess, who is represented in the three lunar phases as Asherah, the new moon (nymph), Yah, the full moon (mother) and Lilith (Hecate, the aged crone), the waning moon; and that Pharisaic Judaism, developing as a patriarchal religion, subordinated the fertility goddess, in part absorbing her by attempting to masculinise her, in part transforming her through the concept of *Shechinah*, the feminine principle or the female side of God.

Others will no doubt argue the validity of this theory, but I would contend that the *Hallel* Psalms in particular reveal the goddess. Not exclusively, by any means - the doxology, the songs of praise, are addressed to both partners in the celestial and earthly marriage. "From the rising of the sun to its going-down" is self-evidently the masculine divinity of the *Yevarechecha*, as is His enthronement on high, looking down on the heaven and the earth - a sky-god who made himself manifest in the avatar of the sun. But it's Yah who is praised first and last, masculinised here, but clearly she who "transforms the barren wife into a glad mother of children."

✡

Psalm 114

"When Israel came out of Egypt, when the family of Jacob left behind the people of a foreign tongue, then Judah became his sanctuary, Israel his dominions. The sea saw and fled, the Jordan turned backwards. The mountains skipped like rams, the hills like young lambs.

"What ails you, O sea, that you flee? O Jordan, that you turn backward? O mountains, that you skip like rams? O hills, like young lambs? Before the Lord's presence did I, the earth, tremble; before the presence of the God of Jacob, who turns the rock into a pond of water, the flint into a flowing fountain."

We are in the realms of the miraculous again, memories of past miracles at the time of the Exodus. The fleeing sea was the turning-back of the Sea of Reeds, but the turning Jordan belongs to a much later episode, the crossing of the Jordan after the conquest of Jericho, when the priests carried the Ark of the Covenant on huge rocks laid out as a footbridge - rocks that would then be used to form the twelve-dolmen henge at Gil-Gal (Joshua 3:9-17) which was anachronistically already there when Jacob dreamed the ladder of the angels (Genesis 28:10ff). The gambolling of the hills and mountains appears to be poetic hyperbole rather than scriptural allusion. The turning of the rock into a pond of water was a miracle with a touch of hubris; for doing it once without permission, at Meribah, Moses was denied the right to take his people into the Promised Land.

Tradition maintains that Judah was singled out to be the royal tribe, first because Judah was the brother who took Joseph's side and saved him from the conspiracy to murder him, secondly here, at the Exodus, when Nachshon ben Aminadav of the tribe of Judah was the first to wade into the retreating waters of the Sea of Reeds. But the reference to Judah isn't to his seniority among the tribes; rather it's to his geographical hosting of the Temple. Clearly the Psalm belongs to late First Temple times, considerably post David and Solomon. It's evident from the language of the great Prophets in which the Psalm is written. But more palpably from the historic division, Judah versus Israel. In the first centuries after the Conquest, during the period of the Judges, there was no meaningful tribal confederacy - that was one of the achievements of King David, and even he only partially achieved it. The northern tribes (Asher, Dan, Naphtali, Zevulun, Yissachar, Menasheh, Gad and Ephraim) were known collectively as Ephraim, not Israel, while in the south Simeon had already disappeared among the Bedou and the Amalekites, Reuben had been absorbed into Edom and Moab, leaving only the tiny territory of Benjamin, and Judah. If David had written the Psalm, he wouldn't have made reference to the Sanctuary, because as yet there was none; and he would have referred to Ephraim, not Israel. Only after the civil war following the death of Solomon did the name Israel take root.

✡

Psalm 115

"Not for our sake, not for our sake but for Your name's sake, give glory, for Your kindness and Your truth. Why should the nations say, 'Where is their God now?' Our God is in the heavens; whatever He pleases, He does. Their idols are silver and gold, the handiwork of man. They have a mouth, they cannot speak; they have eyes but cannot see. They have ears but cannot hear; they have a nose but cannot smell. Their hands cannot feel; their feet cannot walk; they cannot utter a sound from their throat. Those who make them, whoever trusts in them, should become like them.

"O Israel, trust in the Lord, their help and their shield is He. House of Aaron, trust in the Lord, their help and their shield is He. You who fear the Lord, trust in the Lord, their help and their shield is He."

Was there ever written a more sneering mockery? This is the ultimate onslaught against idol-worship, outrivaled by the abstract deity of the Hebrews. This is what so shocked Titus when he went into the burning Temple in order to rescue for Rome what gold and silver he could find; in the Roman custom, he wanted to steal the idols and icons, because to conquer the symbols of a nation's religion is to strangle its life-blood. But in the *Devir*, the Sanctuary, there were no idols or icons, not of gold and not of clay. In the First Temple he would have found two *cherubim* with vast wings; but in the Second Temple the God of the Hebrews was an emptiness, a void, an absence, a space unfilled - or, rather, He had become an abstraction of the human mind; a metaphor. Grown out of the compost of the goddess of mother-earth, nurtured out of the radiance of the sun and the promise of rain by the god of the sky - but transcended beyond idolatry, elevated to the metaphysical. You cannot take a metaphor prisoner. You cannot destroy what is ultimately a state of mind. Whereas the straw men of the pagans, their stone *teraphim* and their carved *asherim* - mere sculptures and totem-poles.

A pattern emerges, then. In the first Psalm, praise for the ancient forms of the deity - sun, sky, earth, moon. In the second, praise for the miraculous, the God of the Sea of Reeds. In the third, praise for the transcendental. We are not simply praising God; we are praising the evolution of God, His growth into the One we know now. And in the next Psalm, praise for the Creator God who makes, steps back from His Creation, and allows it to live its own life, without further interference.

Psalm 115 is read in two parts, verses 1-11 above, and now the remainder, verses 12-18. Once again I have split the paragraphs to denote which part the congregation, which part the *chazan* alone.

"The Lord who has remembered us will bless - He will bless the House of Israel, He will bless the House of Aaron, He will bless those who fear the Lord, the small as well as the great. May the Lord increase you, you and your children. You are the blessed of the Lord, maker of heaven and earth.

"As for the heavens - the heavens are the Lord's, but the earth He has given to Mankind. Neither the dead can praise God, nor any who descend into silence. But we will bless God from this time and forever, *Hallelu-Yah*."

The distinction between the House of Israel and that of Aaron is less complex than that between Judah and Israel. The latter is our ethnic denotion, the former our religious. In Judaism, we all fall into one of three camps - or two, technically, but one is itself divided. Aaron and Moses were of the tribe of Levi, and in the distribution of the land after the conquest Levi alone received no portion, except for three "refuge-cities" in every tribe, because the tribe had been dedicated to the service of the Ark. The descendants of Aaron, the elder brother, are the Cohanim; the descendants of Moses, the younger brother but still the House of Aaron, fulfil all other duties of the tribe, still called to this day the levitical duties. And as to the rest of us – we're all plainly and simply Israel.

"Neither the dead can praise God, nor any who descend into silence." Hmmm! "*Dumah*" is the Hebrew word, and it gives us the English word "dumb". Genesis 25:14 and Isaiah 21:11 both encounter a clan of the Bene Yishmael, living on the borders of the Nefud desert, who called themselves Dumah - but this isn't they, unless again a metaphor is intended. *Dumah* was Hades, the underworld, in other parts of Hebrew literature - those of the Davidic period - known as *She'ol*. But *Talmudic* Judaism rejects the concept of an underworld; hence the common translation of *Dumah* as silence; though the context here restores it without leaving space for noisy argument.

✡

Psalm 116

"I love Him, for the Lord hears my voice, my supplications. Because He has inclined his ear to me, so in my days shall I call to Him. The pains of death encircled me, the confines of the grave have found me, trouble and sorrow I would find. Then I would invoke the name of the Lord, 'Please Lord, save my soul.' Gracious is the Lord and righteous; our God is merciful. The Lord protects the simple. I was brought low, but He saved me. Return my soul to your rest, for the Lord has been kind to you. For You have delivered my soul from death, my eyes from tears, my feet from stumbling.

"I shall walk before the Lord in the lands of the living. I have kept faith, even though I say, 'I suffer exceedingly.' It was in haste that I complained, 'All mankind is deceitful.'"

We've met the sun and sky god, the moon and earth goddess, and now, hinted at at the end of Psalm 115, fully described here in Psalm 116, now we meet the third part of the trinity of the ancient world, the god of the underworld himself. Why are they called the Psalms of David, when it's patently obvious that David had no hand in writing them, if indeed there ever was a historical personage who bore that name? The answer, I think, lies as ever in the meaning of the name. *David* means "beloved", and was a diminutive form of *Yedid-Yah*, "Beloved of Yah", which was also the name given to Solomon before he adopted *Shlomo* as his king-name. But "The Beloved" was also the epithet by which Adonis was known across the whole Levant[10], when he wasn't simply called *Adon* - the Lord, *Adon* being the Levantine pronunciation without its Greek nominative ending - in Hebrew *Adonay*. Was a Psalm of David then a Psalm addressed to "the Lord"? Adonis' Egyptian counterpart, Osiris, and his Babylonian counterpart, Tammuz, both served as Lord of the Underworld. The town of Bethlehem Ephratah where David was born should be pronounced *Beit-Lechem Ephratah* – "the House of the Corn-God of the Euphrates": Tammuz. It makes much more sense of the notion that the Messiah will be a direct descendant of David if this reading should prove to be correct.

Again we sing the Psalm in two parts, verses 1-11 above, verses 12-19 now.

[10] Christian mythology keeps it too: "This is my beloved son in whom I am well pleased" (Matthew 3:17)

"How can I repay the Lord for all His kindness to me? I will raise the cup of salvation and invoke the name of the Lord. I will pay my vows to the Lord in the presence, now, of His entire people. The death of the devout is difficult in the eyes of the Lord. Please Lord, for I am your servant, I am your servant, the son of your handmaid, release my bonds.

"To You I will sacrifice thanksgiving offerings, and I will invoke the name of the Lord. I will pay my vows to the Lord in the presence, now, of His entire people. In the courtyards of the House of the Lord, in your midst O Jerusalem. *Hallelu-Yah.*"

The last line once again self-confirming that this was written later than the time of David - the courtyards of the House of the Lord were the sacrificial space in Solomon's Temple.

Psalm 117

Recited first by the congregation, then repeated by the *chazan.*

"*Hallelu et Adonay kol goyim, shabechu-hu kol ha-umim. Ki gavar aleynu chasdo, ve-emet Adonay le-olam. Hallelu-Yah* - Praise the Lord all nations, praise Him every people. For His kindness has overwhelmed us, and the truth of the Lord is eternal. *Hallelu-Yah.*"

Psalm 118

The culmination of *Hallel* is one of the most structurally complex of all the Psalms. It's written in five parts, three of them choral and responsive, the fourth recitative but without the *chazan*'s completion, the fifth a concluding benediction. It also uses - almost like an act of showing off - many of the favourite technical tricks of Hebrew poetry - parallelism, the echo line, the dirge metre.

The first part is responsive, the *chazan* delivering the line, the congregation the refrain.

"*Hodu l'Adonay ki tov - ki le'olam chasdo.*
Yomar na Yisra'el - ki le'olam chasdo.
Yomru na beyt Aharon - ki le'olam chasdo.
Yomru na yirey Adonay - ki le'olam chasdo."

"Give thanks to the Lord for He is good - His mercy is eternal.
Let Israel say that His mercy is eternal.
Let the House of Aaron say that His mercy is eternal.
Let those who fear the Lord say that His mercy is eternal."

After which the Psalm continues in more familiar manner.

"In my distress I called upon Yah, and She answered me with magnanimity. The Lord is with me, I have no fear, how can any man affect me? The Lord is with me through my helpers, therefore I can face my foes. It is better to take refuge in the Lord than to rely on Man. It is better to take refuge in the Lord than to rely on noblemen. All the nations surround me; in the name of the Lord I cut them down. They encircle me like bees, but they are extinguished as a fire does thorns; in the name of the Lord I cut them down. You pushed me hard that I might fall, but the Lord assisted me. Yah is my might and my praise, and will be my salvation. The sound of rejoicing and salvation is in the tents of the righteous. The Lord's right hand does valiantly. The Lord's right hand is raised triumphantly. The Lord's right hand does valiantly. I shall not die. But I shall live and relate the deeds of Yah. Yah has chastened me exceedingly, but she did not let me die.

"Open for me the gates of righteousness, and I will enter them and thank God. This is the gate of the Lord, the righteous shall enter through it."

There will be critics of this translation, I know. Most translations offer "the Lord" for "YHVH" and "God" for "Yah". I am happy with the former. In refusing to translate Yah as God, in preferring simply to leave the name in its original wherever it occurs in the text, I have altered the English "he" to "she" - but nowhere in the original Hebrew is there any gender indication where Yah is used; indeed, the text seems to have been constructed precisely to avoid gendering.

We tend, in worship, to say the words, to sing the melodies, without thinking what it is that we're saying. This Psalm more than almost any other requires thought, for it is, to say the least, a curiosity. At the end of Psalm 115 we appeared to descend into the underworld; in Psalm 116 we sang out of desperation, out of the darkness of the underworld, asking God to revive us, offering all manner of thanksgivings if He did so. I have the strong sense of an epic being enacted, the descent of David, the Beloved, into the Underworld, his harrowing of hell, his eventual return to sit at the right hand of the Almighty. The story of the boy David in the first book of Samuel is an account of the relentless pursuit of the Beloved (David) by the King of the Underworld (*Sha'ul* – Saul, but the same root also gives *She'ol* -

Hell). I believe that the "I" of these Psalms is not I, the one who sings Hallel, but "I, David", singing like Orpheus in the pit of despond; or more precisely, "I, Tammuz", being sung to by the wailing women at the north gate of the Temple (Ezekiel 8:3). And if I am correct, then "*ozray* – helpers" should be translated as "priests", or even "priestesses" instead.

Where lies the proof of this - if anywhere? In the otherwise meaningless line, a *mishmash* of mixed metaphors, "they encircle me like bees, but they are extinguished as a fire does thorns; in the name of the Lord I cut them off." Make sense of it if you can - but I'm afraid you can't, not as it's rendered here. Bees do not encircle, they attack in swarms. You can't extinguish bees in the sense of putting out a fire. And fires don't extinguish thorns - *au contraire*, they kindle them, if the thorns are dry, or might be extinguished by them, if the thorns happened to be wet enough. No, once again we must go back to etymology.

"*Kol goyim sevavuni, be-shem Adonay ki amilam. Sabuni gam sevavuni, be-shem Adonay ki amilam. Sabuni chi-devorim do'achu ke-eysh kotsim, be-shem Adonay ki amilam.*"

The confusion lies first in the similarity in Hebrew between "*sevavuni* - to encircle", and "*sabuni*" - the second *vet* missing; or not missing, because it was never there in the first place. The English translations uniformly render both as "encircle", as if they were the same word. But while "*sevavuni*" does indeed mean "encircle", from the root "*savav*", the root of "*sabuni*" is "*sava*", which properly means "to absorb", and is invariably used to mean the absorption of intoxicating substances (Deuteronomy 21:20, Proverbs 23:20, Isaiah 56:12 et al).

Confusion then exacerbates confusion; having made one deduction, the others follow logically, but if the first deduction is incorrect, then false syllogisms are all that remain. The "*devorim*", for example, aren't really bees at all. A single bee is a "*devorah*", but the feminine plural should give "*devorot*". "*Devorim*" on the other hand are plagues, the masculine plural of "*dever*". But I wonder if a linguistic pun isn't being played here, linking the two meanings.

"*Do'achu*" is here in the passive, *pu'al*, form, and not the active, *pa'al* - yet another simple grammatical error of the translators. "*Do'achu*" is also attached to the two words that precede it, not the two that follow it, by the normal metric rule of the Psalms, in which lines are made up in 3 + 2 and never in 2 + 3. What is extinguished is the plague, not the fire. It's the thorns which put out the fire, not the fire the thorns. Though in fact they're not thorns at all, unless by another pun equivalent to the "*devorim-devorot*". That's to say, "*kotsim*" are indeed thorns, but the word here isn't the noun "*kotsim*" but the third person plural of the verb "*lakuts*", "to make weary", or "to cut off".

"*Amilam*" is the most complicated. The *aleph* prefix indicates the first person singular of the future tense; the final *mem* suffix is an accusative pronoun, "them". The middle, *mem-lamed*, has been foreshortened by the suffix, the third letter of the root absent. Normally we would assume a *heh*, because *heh* is a weak letter and regularly dropped; only there is no verb based on the root *mem-lamed-heh*, but only the noun "*milah*", meaning "a word". If on the other hand the missing letter was an *aleph*, the only other possibility, then we have the transitive verb "to fill", which, whenever it's followed by an accusative, as it is here, means specifically "to fill a cup for drinking" (c.f. Isaiah 65:11 et al). The cup that's filled in the name of Yahweh is, of course, the same one that was mentioned in the second half of Psalm 116 - "I will raise the cup of salvation and invoke the name of the Lord" - the *kiddush becher*, in whose name a blessing is then made. This at least makes sense.

And finally, the use of the word "*Goyim*", which means nations, but which is always pejorative. Given the sneering attack on idol worship in Psalm 115, and the call to follow YHVH in Psalm 117, it seems to be only proper to translate "*Goyim*" here as "heathens" rather than "nations".

So what we end up with isn't a meaningless account of encircling bees and fires that douse instead of kindling. What we end up with is - and I've extended the translation to try to give the full meaning of what is surely just a figure of speech - the victory of Yah and YHVH over the pagan idols:

"All the heathens surround me, because I have made a blessing in the name of the Lord. When they surround me, they try to intoxicate me (with their beliefs and practices), but I fill their cups with the strong liquor of the Lord. If they swarm around me like a burned-out plague (of bees?), trying to intoxicate me, I will cut off the source of their fire, I will fill their cups in the name of the Lord."

The third section echoes rather than parallels the first, each of the following lines being said twice.

"*Odecha ki anisani va-tehi li lishu'a*
Even ma'asu ha-bonim hayetah le-rosh pinah
Me-et Adonay hayitah zot hi niphlat be-eyneynu
Zeh ha-yom asah Adonay nagilah ve-nismechah vo."

"I thank You, for You have answered and become my salvation.
The stone the builders despised has become my cornerstone.
This emanated from the Lord, it is wondrous in our eyes.
This is the day the Lord has made, let us rejoice and be glad on it."

The fourth section echoes the first and parallels the third. It too is antiphonal, each verse recited twice.

"*Ana Adonay hoshi'a na - ana Adonay hoshi'a na*
Ana Adonay hatslicha na - ana Adonay hatslicha na."

"Please Lord save now - Please Lord save now.
Please Lord bring success now - Please Lord bring success now.

The final section provides the closing benediction. Again each line is sung twice, but congregationally this time, rather than antiphonally.

"*Baruch ha-ba be-shem Adonay, be-rachnuchem mi-beyt Adonay. El Adonay va-ya'er lanu, isru chag ba-avotim, ad karnot ha-mizbeyach. Eli atah ve-odecha, elohay aromemecha. Hodu l'Adonay ki tov, ki le'olam chasdo.*"

"Blessed is he who comes in the name of the Lord; we bless You from the House of the Lord. The Lord is God; He put the lights in the heavens for us. Bind the festival offering with cords at all four corners of the Altar. You are my God and I will thank You; my God and I will exalt You. Give thanks to the Lord, for He is good; His kindness endures forever."

Assailed by false gods and men who would evangelise their worship, driven into the underworld of desolation and self-doubt - driven, metaphorically, into the forty-day wilderness and sorely tempted - the Beloved has endured, and returned – this the real source of the "*aliyah*", the "going up". The Temple is established, God is in His heavens, and all is now well with the world. The cycle of *Hallel* is complete.

✡

Yehallelucha

A completion that is now doubly acknowledged, through the *Kaddish* that follows, but first through the "*Yehallelucha*".

"All Your works shall praise You, Lord our God. And Your devout ones, the righteous who do Your will, and Your entire people, the House of Israel, with glad song will thank, bless, praise, glorify, exalt, extol, sanctify and proclaim the sovereignty of Your name.

"For to You it is fitting to give thanks, and unto Your name it is proper to sing praises, for from this world to the world to come You are God. Blessed are You, Lord, the King who is lauded with praises."

And end with *Kaddish*.

✡

EPILOGUE

I spent, in the end, fourteen and a half years at Polack's, and during that time had numerous opportunities to join students at their home synagogues, mostly in the UK, but also in Italy, Germany, Russia and France. Because of our position within the Bristol Jewish community, I spent many hours in prayer services at both the orthodox and the Liberal & Progressive synagogues. But strangely, though I had students, family and friends within the Reform movement, I had not attended a service in a Reform temple since childhood, and knew what I knew about it only through research. But in the spring of 2004 I was appointed Director of Education – a title that included both academic Head of School and administrative Chief Executive - of the Leo Baeck Day School in Toronto, where I would spend the next four years; and after that as Director of Education at a Reform Temple in Miami, Florida, where I looked after its Nursery, its day school, its religious school, its summer camp and some of its adult education. I was also invited to join the Board of PARDES, the Reform day schools network across north America, and became its President in 2009. So people who know me today, who read this book, are likely to think of me as a Reform Jew, and may even be surprised at both the orthodoxy, and the secularity, of this account. The truth remains, as I stated at the opening of this book, I am neither a Reform nor a Conservative nor an orthodox Jew. I am what is now being called "post-denominational", and for a while was called "pluralist", a term dropped because frankly none of us can find an adequate explanation of its intent. I am, it might perhaps be better to say, an ambivalent Jew. An agnostic is a person who admits they do not know what they do and do not believe; I know exactly what I do and do not believe, but I remain in the same state of uncertainty, and suspect that this will increase rather than decrease the more I go on questioning and learning. I see this as a positive, not a negative.

My first adult visit to a Reform synagogue was for a cousin's *Bar Mitzvah*, in London in 2004, shortly before I left for Canada. So many things were so very different from my experiences of the previous decade and a half, that it took my memory by surprise and very nearly sent me home to rewrite this book. The *chazan* facing the congregation, as though he were an emissary from God (or a Cohen in the Temple), rather than facing the Ark with the assembled worshippers, their *shaliach tsibbur*, their emissary to God. The female voices mixed with the male in the choir - something expunged from Judaism for centuries, a recollection of Miriam and Deborah and Hannah. The use of musical accompaniment (including electric instruments, on the Sabbath!), overruling the *Talmudic* injunction against musical accompaniment as a sign of perpetual mourning for the Temple - a technical breach of *halachah,* as I have noted earlier in this book, to go on mourning in this way once the year of mourning was complete. The men and women sitting together, some of the women clad in prayer shawls and wearing skull caps. All of this was strange, but still - explainable, justifiable within the traditions; *halachically* legitimate even if it defied every orthodox custom and tradition; in some instances more correct than orthodox traditions.

Reform presents a modernising challenge to orthodoxy, and yet, at times, I found myself as much in disagreement or bewilderment in this synagogue as I did within the orthodox. The abbreviation of the *Amidah* to a form that would have satisfied neither Gamliel nor Akiva nor any of the other protagonists in that original debate. How justify this then? The *Shema* recited standing. The complete absence of a *Musaph*. The Ark facing west. So many differences, some pleasing, some shocking, some simply confusing. Where I'd spent many months inside this book, asking the question "why?", I now found myself inside a different set of practices, asking the equally necessary question "why not?"

The use of English, for example. Not extensively – I'd been led to expect much more - but often enough. The "*Orach Chayim*", one of the four sections of Joseph Caro's codification of the Laws, the "*Shulchan Aruch*" (101:4; 62:2), as well as Chafetz Chayim's later commentary on Caro, confirm the *halachic* ruling that one may pray in any language that one understands, even in synagogue, but that the community should pray collectively in Hebrew. I have to confess that I always prefer to pray in Hebrew, for the simple reason that, like opera, I'm able to switch off my understanding of the words, their meaning, and concentrate purely on their poetry, their musicality. To understand with the conscious mind is to render prayer intellectual, and the spiritual collapses under the weight of nonsense contained in so much of the meaning. To pray without understanding is to allow symbol to trump significance, and the music washes through you, till the soul is purged.

I asked the Rabbi afterwards about some of my concerns, and he made various attempts at explanation, none of which convinced me. But then he handed me a copy of the Rabbi's prayer book - the congregational copy was a mere digest - and there, in the frontispiece, was the name of Rabbi Hugo Gryn. I asked no further questions. If this set of customs and practices was good enough for Hugo, then frankly it was good enough for me. As with *Rashi* and Maimonides, one doesn't squabble over the pedantics of *halachah* with a *tsaddik* - a saint.

The Rabbi's justification for standing for the *Shema* was simply that this is now the accepted custom in many synagogues, orthodox as well as Reform, even though it runs counter to the older custom of not standing. The defence, I presume, resides in *kavanah*, the intent behind prayer, a word which in English devolves both into intention and intensity. "He who prays must direct his heart to heaven" - so says the *Talmud* (*Berachot* 31a). Anything less than this is unacceptable, mere formulation of words, perfunctory and mechanical. So, earlier, in the same column of *Talmud* (5:1), we read that "one should stand for prayer only when one's state of mind is reverent". Why not, then, stand for the *Shema*? And why not go even further, as some congregations do, and sing rather than recite the *Shema*? Song is integral to the Jewish tradition, from the Psalms to the *zemirot* to the *piyyut* of the Middle Ages. Rabbi Judah ben Samuel of Speyer (in those days they called it Regensburg), known as Shmuel *he-Chasid*, wrote in the latter years of the 12th century, with a psychological insight worthy of Piaget, that the use of melody to enhance prayer is also the finest deepener of *kavanah*. In the beginning, it seems, wasn't simply the Word, but the Trope, the *Nusach*, and the Cantillation. In the beginning was the Word - sung.

During the years since I left Polack's, and have lived in Canada and the United States, I have attended services of the Reconstructionist and the Renewalist movement, independent *minyanim* in people's homes, cross-denominational services at educational conferences, and even cross-faith services with Moslem or Christian worshipers. I have witnessed yoga as an aspect of prayer, and could see little difference in its methodology or purpose than the act of *shockeling*. I have seen 13-year-old girls at their *Benot Mitzvah* lead the entire Friday evening and *shabbat* morning services as skilfully as any *chazan* or Rabbi, and highly trained and experienced *chazanim* and *rabbonim* who had no notion how to bring a community to God. I have led hundreds of services myself, sometimes a capello in the orthodox manner, sometimes with solo guitar, sometimes as a member of a jazz-rock band delivering Friday Night Live to dancing seniors or Hip-Hop T'filah to teenage campers. Out of all this one certainty, and one alone, has sustained itself unchallenged: not God, about whom my doubts remain as deep as ever; not *halachah*, whatever that may be. One certainty, which I hope the discussion in this book has clarified, if not confirmed. That there is no correct way of being Jewish. That the term orthodoxy is a falsehood, because our entire religion is based on supposition that we cannot prove, our laws mostly the result of a system of deduction that wasn't even agreed unanimously by the committee that invented it, and whose deductions may therefore be false. Many times along the years, as Head of School, I have said to prospective parents, and prospective students, that I couldn't care less how you define yourself as a Jew, and how you choose to make that definition meaningful in your life; just so long as you take being Jewish seriously. To those who will, inevitably, criticise much of the commentary in this book, I would say the same thing. Be the Jew you are, and don't criticise others for being the Jew they are. Let God be the judge, whatever you mean by God.

What is recorded, described, analysed and subjected to highly personal commentary in these pages is not, of course, the whole of Jewish prayer. Far from it. We've entered the synagogue on the first morning of the week, and we've prayed from dawn until the sun is fully risen. There are still the afternoon and evening services, this day and every day, the special services for Friday night and Saturday, those for the New Moon, those for each of the Biblical festivals, the Rabbinic festivals, the modern festivals; there are still the weddings and *B'nei Mitzvah*, the births and deaths, the tombstone settings and the memorial services, and every other occasion on which a blessing or a petition or a song of praise is needed, whether by Man or by God. Someone else, perhaps, will write the books of those prayer services. If you have liked or at least found interesting, what you have read here, a sister-volume entitled "Day of Atonement" will take you on a similar journey through the prayers and rituals of Yom Kippur.

Max Jacob, a character in a set of novels that I wrote in my mid-twenties, was once asked if he was a practising Jew, and replied that every Jew was a practising Jew, it was just that some Jews practised more than others, and some had higher hopes or lower hopes of one day getting the darned thing right. Elsewhere I gave him this phrase, slightly more poetic, in response to a question about why Jews prayed the same service over and over again, unchanging, unvaried:

"It's rather like taking on a score as a musician," he answered. "We rehearse the morning service daily, like a concert pianist not yet ready to perform."

On which I note that the second star has just appeared in the sky, while a text-message reminds me I am delivering the *D'var Torah* this evening, not at a local synagogue but to a seminar group of students of comparative mythology at the university. No need for a *cipah* or a *tallit* there. A copy of Joseph Campbell's "Hero With A Thousand Faces" and Raphael Patai's "Hebrew Myths" will suffice.

David Prashker
Miami 2013

ABOUT THE AUTHOR

David Prashker was born in London in 1955 and has lived in France, Israel, Canada and the United States, where he is currently based. Director of Jewish educational and cultural institutions for 25 years, he is the author of thirty books, including contemporary and historical novels, short stories, poetry, songs, plays and scholarly works. You can follow his blog at apps.theargamanpress.com/Blog/ or find him at his website Davidprashker.com. For more information about his books, go to theargamanpress.com.

www.ingramcontent.com/pod-product-compliance
Lightning Source LLC
LaVergne TN
LVHW020528100826
845148LV00010B/1382

* 9 7 8 0 6 1 5 9 1 7 6 6 5 *